5th Workshop on Cognitive Aspects of the Lexicon 2016 (CogALex V)

Held at COLING 2016

Osaka, Japan
12 December 2016

ISBN: 978-1-5108-3333-3

Preface

Whenever we read a book, write a letter or perform a (web or dictionary) search, we always use lexical items (words or more complex constructions), the expressive shorthand versions of more or less abstract thoughts. Yet, lexemes are not only expressive means, i.e. vehicles transporting thoughts, they are also means to conceive them. They are mediators between language and thought, allowing us to move quickly from one idea to another, summarizing, expanding or specifying possibly underspecified thoughts. Of course, lexemes can do a lot more, allowing us to organize, memorize and access knowledge, and even reveal hidden meanings via information contained in the target or its surrounding words (subliminal communication). No doubt the lexicon is a key component of language.

Lexical items are generally viewed as *objects*, yet when it comes to speaking, reading or writing, they are *processes*, that is, they carry meaning which they convey via an abstract (part of speech) and concrete form (phonemes, graphemes). Obviously, in order to access a lexeme (at least) its form must be stored. This is done *holistically* in the case of external resources (paper or electronic dictionary), which represent word forms as single tokens, and *distributed* in the case of the human brain, which decomposes the form into syllables and phonemes. While knowing the form is important, its storage is by no means sufficient. We may still fail to access it when needed. More importantly, when consulting a dictionary (off-line processing) other types of knowledge are used, most prominently meta-knowledge and cognitive states. *Meta-knowledge* is revealed by the fact that search is generally initiated via a close neighbor of the target lexeme, to be continued then via one of the links connecting the source and the target (synonym, hypernym, etc.). *Cognitive states* are revealed by the information given at the onset of the search. They express the information available at that very moment. As psychologists have shown, authors always know something concerning the eluding word. Alas, what information is available when being in this state varies from person to person and from moment to moment. It is unpredictable knowledge. Hence the importance of building a resource flexible enough to accommodate any of them, allowing the user to start from anywhere and to access the target via many diverse routes.

Ironically, although – once expressed – many of these observations sound obvious, most of them have been overlooked by the various communities dealing with the lexicon, its acquisition, usage or modeling (e.g. lexicographers and computational linguists). Nevertheless one must admit that things have actually changed quite a bit, and some of these changes are so deep, fast and wide-ranging that it is sometimes hard to keep track of them, and be aware of the new problems and possibilities. As this evolution is in full swing, and in order to contribute to its dynamism, we organize CogALex (Cognitive Aspects of the Lexicon), whose mission is to build a bridge between the different communities. More precisely, our goal is to provide a forum for computational lexicographers, researchers in NLP, psychologists and users of lexical resources to share their knowledge and needs concerning the construction, organization and use of a lexicon by people (lexical access) and machines (NLP, IR, data mining).

History, topics of interest and focus of the current workshop

Starting at Coling 2004 (Geneva) with the workshop *Enhancing and Using Electronic Dictionaries*, there have been four follow-up events so far (CogALex I–IV), each co-located with Coling (Manchester, UK, 2008; Beijing, China, 2010; Mumbai, India, 2012, and finally, Dublin, UK, 2014). Encouraged by the enthusiasm and interest expressed by the participants of these CogALex events, we decided to organize another edition of the workshop. Like in the past, we invited researchers to address various unsolved problems. This time we put stronger emphasis though on *relations* (lexical/conceptual) and on *distributional semantics*, to explore their relevance with respect to a cognitive model of the lexicon.

The interest in distributional approaches has grown considerably over the last few years, both in computational linguistics and cognitive sciences. An additional boost has come from the recent popularity of deep learning and neural embeddings. While all these approaches seem to have great potential, their added value in addressing cognitive and semantic aspects of the lexicon still needs to be demonstrated.

We were also interested in the organization of the mental lexicon and its potential to enhance lexical resources. Given recent advances in the neurosciences, it appears timely to seek inspiration from studies concerning the human brain. There is also a lot to be learned from other fields using graphs and networks, even if their object of study is something else than language, for example biology, economy or society.

As two years ago we proposed a shared task, or rather a "friendly competition". The goal of this year's edition was the automatic identification of semantic relations from corpus data (see below for details). Also, like in the past, we were interested in the enhancement of lexical resources and electronic dictionaries, so we invited contributions from researchers involved in the building of such tools. The idea is to discuss modifications of existing resources by taking the users' needs and knowledge states into account. Given the diversity of our goals we solicited papers including, but not limited to the following topics, each of which can be considered from various viewpoints: *linguistics* (theoretical or practical), *neuro-* or *psycholinguistics* (tip-of-the-tongue problem, associations), *network related sciences* (sociology, economy, biology), *mathematics* (vector-based approaches, graph theory, small-world problem), etc.

Organization, i.e. structure of the lexicon

- Micro- and macrostructure of the lexicon;
- Indexical categories (taxonomies, thesaurus-like topical structures, etc.);
- Distribution of information and relations between words.

The meaning of words and techniques for revealing it

- Lexical representation (holistic, decomposed);
- Meaning representation (concept based, primitives);
- Distributional semantics (count models, neural embeddings, etc.).

Analysis of the input given by a dictionary user

- What information do language producers provide when looking for a word (terms, relations)?
- What kind of relational information do they give: typed or untyped relations?
- Which relations are typically used?

Methods for crafting dictionaries or additional functions like indexes

- Manual, automatic or collaborative building of dictionaries (crowd-sourcing, serious games, etc.);
- (Semi-)automatic induction of the link type (e.g. synonym, hypernym, association, etc.);
- Extraction of associations from corpora to build semantic networks supporting navigation.

Dictionary access (navigation and search strategies)

- Search based on sound (rhymes), meaning or functionally related words (associations);
- Determination of appropriate search space based on user's knowledge, etc.;
- Identification of typical word access strategies (navigational patterns) used by people.

Shared task on the corpus-based identification of semantic relations

The shared task was organized by Stefan Evert, Alessandro Lenci and Enrico Santus, with the precious help of Anna Gladkova. Its goal was the automatic identification of semantic relations from corpus data, which has great potential: it promises an efficient and scalable solution to NLP tasks, while (possibly) providing a cognitively plausible model for human acquisition and usage of such relations.

Semantic relations play a central role in human lexical retrieval (navigation) and the organization of words in the lexicon, the resource within which search takes place. Hence learning about them may shed some light on the mental lexicon and the knowledge people have when searching for a word. Discovering whether words are semantically related and how so (which kind of relation holds between them?) is also an important task in natural language processing (NLP) by and large, with a wide range of applications, such as automatic thesaurus creation, natural language generation (automatic creation of outlines), ontology learning, paraphrase generation, etc.

The aim of this "friendly competition" was not so much to find the team with the best-performing system, as to test different distributional models and other corpus-based approaches on a challenging semantic task, in order to gain a better understanding of their respective strengths and weaknesses.

The task was split into two subtasks:

1. Given a pair of words (e.g. *dog – fruit*), decide whether they are semantically related or not.

2. For each word pair (e.g. *cat – animal*), decide which of the following semantic relations holds between them: synonymy, antonymy, hypernymy, meronymy, or none (random combination).

The organizers provided a data set based on WordNet and ConceptNet, which was then cleaned by native speakers in a CrowdFlower task. The remaining word pairs were split into a training set and test set, and evaluation was carried out in terms of precision, recall and their harmonic mean (F_1). In subtask 2, the overall score was determined as the weighted average over all four semantic relations.

Outcome of the call and a word of thanks

We received 30 submissions, of which seven were accepted as full papers with oral presentation, eight as poster presentations, and seven as shared task papers.

We would like to take this opportunity to express our sincerest thanks to all the members of the Programme Committee. Their expertise was invaluable to ensure a good selection of papers despite the tight schedule. Their reviews were helpful not only for us to make the decisions, but also for the authors, helping them to improve their work.

Last, but not least, we would like to thank Chris Biemann for having accepted to be our invited speaker. His talk – *Vectors or Graphs? On Differences of Representations for Distributional Semantic Models* – fits perfectly well in this workshop.

We hope that the work presented here will inspire you, generate fruitful discussions, and possibly lead to new ideas, insights and collaborations.

The CogALex-V Organizers
Michael Zock, Alessandro Lenci, Stefan Evert

Organisers

Michael Zock (LIF, CNRS, Aix-Marseille University, Marseille, France)

Alessandro Lenci (Computational Linguistics Laboratory, University of Pisa, Pisa, Italy)

Stefan Evert (Friedrich-Alexander-Universität Erlangen-Nürnberg, Germany)

Programme Committee

Biemann, Chris (Universität Hamburg, Germany)
Babych, Bogdan (University of Leeds, UK)
Brysbaert, Marc (Experimental Psychology, Ghent University, Belgium)
Cristea, Dan ("Al. I. Cuza" University, Iasi, Romania)
De Deyne, Simon (University of Adelaide, Australia)
de Melo, Gerard (IIIS, Tsinghua University, Beijing, China)
Evert, Stefan (FAU Erlangen-Nürnberg, Germany)
Ferret, Olivier (CEA LIST, France)
Fontenelle, Thierry (CDT, Luxemburg)
Grefenstette, Gregory (Inria, Paris, France)
Hirst, Graeme (University of Toronto, Canada)
Hovy, Eduard (CMU, Pittsburgh, USA)
Hsieh, Shu-Kai (National Taiwan University, Taipei, Taiwan)
Lafourcade, Matthieu (LIRMM, Université de Montepellier, France)
Lapalme, Guy (RALI, University of Montreal, Canada)
Lebani, Gianluca (University of Pisa, Italy)
Lenci, Alessandro (University of Pisa, Italy)
L'Homme, Marie Claude (University of Montreal, Canada)
Mititelu, Verginica (RACAI, Bucharest, Romania)
Paradis, Carita (Centre for Languages and Literature Lund University, Sweden)
Pihlevar, Taher (University of Cambridge, UK)
Pirrelli, Vito (ILC, Pisa, Italy)
Polguère, Alain (ATILF-CNRS, Nancy, France)
Purver, Matthew (King's College, London, UK)
Ramisch, Carlos (AMU, Marseille, France)
Rayson, Paul (UCREL, University of Lancaster, UK
Rosso, Paol (NLEL, Universitat Politècnica de València, Spain)
Sahlgren, Magnus (Gavagai Inc. & SICS, Sweden)
Schulte im Walde, Sabine (University of Stuttgart, Germany)
Schwab, Didier (LIG, Grenoble, France)
Sharoff, Serge (University of Leeds, UK)
Stella, Massimo (Institute for Complex Systems Simulation, University of Southhampton, UK)
Tokunaga, Takenobu (TITECH, Tokyo, Japan)
Tufiş, Dan (RACAI, Bucharest, Romania)
Zarcone, Alessandra (Saarland University, Saarbrücken, Germany)
Zock, Michael (LIF-CNRS, Marseille, France)

Table of Contents

Workshop Program

Vectors or Graphs?
On Differences of Representations for Distributional Semantic Models

Chris Biemann
Language Technology Group
Computer Science Dept.
University of Hamburg, Germany
`biemann@uni-hamburg.de`

Abstract

Distributional Semantic Models (DSMs) have recently received increased attention, together with the rise of neural architectures for scalable training of dense vector embeddings. While some of the literature even includes terms like 'vectors' and 'dimensionality' in the definition of DSMs, there are some good reasons why we should consider alternative formulations of distributional models. As an instance, I present a scalable graph-based solution to distributional semantics. The model belongs to the family of 'count-based' DSMs, keeps its representation sparse and explicit, and thus fully interpretable. I will highlight some important differences between sparse graph-based and dense vector approaches to DSMs: while dense vector-based models are computationally easier to handle and provide a nice uniform representation that can be compared and combined in many ways, they lack interpretability, provenance and robustness. On the other hand, graph-based sparse models have a more straightforward interpretation, handle sense distinctions more naturally and can straightforwardly be linked to knowledge bases, while lacking the ability to compare arbitrary lexical units and a compositionality operation. Since both representations have their merits, I opt for exploring their combination in the outlook.

1 Introduction

Rooted in Structural Linguistics (de Saussure, 1966; Harris, 1951), *Distributional Semantic Models* (DSMs, see e.g. (Baroni and Lenci, 2010)) characterize the meaning of lexical units by the contexts they appear in, cf. (Wittgenstein, 1963; Firth, 1957). Using the duality of form and contexts, forms can be compared along their contexts (Miller and Charles, 1991), giving rise to the field of Statistical Semantics. A data-driven, unsupervised approach to representing word meaning is attractive as there is no need for laborious creation of lexical resources. Further, these approaches naturally adapt to the domain or even language at hand. Desirable, in general, is a model that provides a firm basis for a wider range of (semantic) tasks, as opposed to specialised solutions on a per-task basis.

While most approaches to distributional semantics rely on dense vector representations, the reasons for this seem rather technical than well-justified. To de-bias the discussion, I propose a competitive graph-based formulation. Since all representations have advantages and disadvantages, I will discuss some ways of how to fruitfully combine graphs and vectors in the future.

1.1 Vectors – a solution to Plato's Problem?

Vector space models have a long tradition in Information Retrieval (Salton et al., 1975), and heavily influence the way we think about representing documents and terms today. The core idea is to represent each document with a bag-of-words vector of $|V|$ dimensions with vocabulary V, counting how often

Proceedings of the Workshop on Cognitive Aspects of the Lexicon,
pages 1–7, Osaka, Japan, December 11-17 2016.

each word appears in the respective document. Queries, which are in fact very short documents, can be matched to documents by appropriately comparing their vectors. Since V is large, the representation is sparse – most entries in the vectors are zero. Note, however, that zeros are not stored in today's indexing approaches. When Deerwester et al. (1990) introduced Latent Semantic Analysis (LSA), its major feature was to reduce the dimensionality of vectors, utilising the entirety of all documents for characterising words by the documents they appear in, and vice versa. Dimensionality reduction approaches like Singular Value Decomposition (SVD) and Principal Component Analysis (PCA) map distributionally similar words (occurring in similar contexts) to similar lower-dimensional vectors, where the dimensionality typically ranges from 200 to 10'000. Such a representation is dense: there are virtually no zero entries in these vectors. A range of more recent models, such as Latent Dirichlet Allocation (LDA), are characterised in the same way – variants are distinguished by the notion of context (document vs. window-based vs. structured by grammatical dependencies) and the mechanism for dimensionality reduction. With the advent of neural embeddings such as word2vec (Mikolov et al., 2013), a series of works showed modest but significant advances in semantic tasks over previous approaches. Levy and Goldberg (2014b), however, showed that there is no substantial representational advance in neural embeddings, as they approximate matrix factorisation, as used in LSA. The advantage of word2vec is rather its efficient and scalable implementation that enables the processing of larger text collections. Improvements on task performance can mostly be attributed to better tuning of hyperparameters[1] – which however overfits the DSM to a task at hand, and defies the premise of unsupervised systems of not needing (hyper)supervision.

But there is a problem with all of these approaches: the *fallacy of dimensionality*[2], following from a simplification that we should not apply without being aware of its consequences: there is no 'appropriate number' of dimensions in natural language, because natural language follows a scale-free distribution on all levels (e.g. (Zipf, 1949; Steyvers and Tenenbaum, 2005; Mukherjee et al., 2008), inter al.). Thus, a representation with a fixed number of dimensions introduces a granularity – 'major' dimensions encode the most important distinctions while 'minor' distinctions in the data cannot be modelled if the granularity is too coarse. This is why the recommended number of dimensions depends on the task, the dataset's size and even the domain. In principle, there are two conclusions from studies that vary the number of dimensions to optimise some sort of a score: (a) in one type of study, there is a sweet spot in the number of dimensions, typically between 50 and 2000. This means that the dimension is indeed task-dependent, (b) the 'optimal' number of dimensions is the highest number tested, indicating that it probably would have been better to keep a sparse representation. Interestingly, the most frequent reason researchers state, if asked why they did not use a sparse representation, is a technical one: many machine learning and statistical libraries do not natively operate on sparse representations, thus run out of memory when trying to represent all those zeros.

2   Graph-based Sparse Representations

Since I am proposing to de-bias the discussion on DSMs from the domination of vectors towards a more balanced view, I am exemplifying a graph-based DSM in this section. The JoBimText (Biemann and Riedl, 2013) framework is a scalable graph-based DSM implementation, developed in cooperation with IBM Research (Gliozzo et al., 2013). It is defined rather straightforwardly: lexical items $j \in J$ are represented by their p most salient contexts B_j, where saliency is measured by frequency or a statistical measure that prefers frequent co-occurrence, such as LMI (Evert, 2004) or LL (Dunning, 1993). Similarity of lexical items is defined as the overlap count of their respective contexts: $sim(j_k, j_l) = |(x|x \in B_{j_k} \& x \in B_{j_l})|$. We call the graph of all lexical items with edges weighted by this similarity a distributional thesaurus (DT). Despite its simplicity, or maybe because of that, this DSM compares favourably to other DSMs (Riedl, 2016), including Lin's thesaurus (Lin, 1998), Curran's measure (Curran, 2004), and word embeddings (Mikolov et al., 2013; Levy and Goldberg, 2014a) on word similarity tasks, especially for large data. It was further successfully used for word expansion in word sense disambiguation (Miller et al., 2012), as a

---

[1] "If you want to get good results, you should tune your hyperparameters. And if you want to make good science, don't forget to tune your baselines' hyperparameters too!" - Omer Levy, pers. communication

[2] not to be confused with the curse of dimensionality, which refers to adverse phenomena when representing problems in too high-dimensional spaces

entry	similar terms	hypernyms	context
mouse:NN:0	rat:NN:**0**, rodent:NN:**0**, monkey:NN:**0**, ...	animal:NN:**0**, species:NN:**1**, ...	rat::NN:conj_and, white-footed:JJ:amod, ...
mouse:NN:1	keyboard:NN:**1**, computer:NN:**0**, printer:NN:**0** ...	device:NN:**1**, equipment:NN:**3**, ...	click:NN:-prep_of, click:NN:-nn, ...
keyboard:NN:0	piano:NN:**1**, synthesizer:NN:**2**, organ:NN:**0** ...	instrument:NN:**2**, device:NN:**3**, ...	play:VB:-dobj, electric:JJ:amod, ..
keyboard:NN:1	keypad:NN:**0**, mouse:NN:**1**, screen:NN:**1** ...	device:NN:**1**, technology:NN:**0** ...	computer:NN:nn, qwerty:JJ:amod ...

Table 1: Examples of PCZ entries for "mouse:NN" and "keyboard:NN" based on dependency contexts (cf. (Erk and Padó, 2008)) from a newspaper corpus. Trailing numbers indicate sense identifiers. Similarity and context scores are not shown for brevity.

feature for lexical substitution (Szarvas et al., 2013), for multiword identification (Riedl and Biemann, 2015), decompounding (Riedl and Biemann, 2016) and for resolving bridging mentions in co-reference (Feuerbach et al., 2015).

The key to a scalable implementation is rooted in the pruning parameter p (typically p=1000), which has two functions: it reduces noise in the representations by only keeping the most salient contexts, and it limits the size of the representation, which is a list of key-value-pairs of fixed length (as opposed to a vector of fixed length). In other words: While there is a maximum size of the representation, as given by p, it is not the case that the information is compressed in a vector of fixed dimensionality, since 'dimensions', if one wants to call them such, are different for each represented item.

Of course, it would be possible to represent item-contexts or the distributional thesaurus in sparse matrices of very high dimensionality, but this view would not take the inherent sparseness into account and might obscure possible optimizations.

Using the JoBimText DSM as a core, we extend this model in several ways. First, we perform word sense induction (WSI) on the ego-networks of lexical items in the DT (Biemann, 2006), utilising the property of many graph clustering algorithms that do not require the number of clusters as input (like e.g. k-Means). Further, we add taxonomic links (hypernyms) from Hearst-pattern-like extractions (Hearst, 1992). WSI allows us to disambiguate the model, which results in what we call a Proto-conceptualization (PCZ) (Faralli et al., 2016), see Table 1. The PCZ consists of entries that correspond to word senses, a list of similar senses, a list of hypernyms and a list of contexts that are salient for the sense. Note that it is straightforward to add these and other typed, weighted relationships in a graph-based framework, cf. (Hovy, 2010). Furthermore, it is straightforward to link this kind of structure to existing structured resources, such as lexical-semantic networks and ontologies, see (Pavel and Euzenat, 2013; Faralli et al., 2016).

While it is possible to represent the similarity graph of terms or concepts of a graph-based DSM with real-valued matrices, it is not straightforward to convert it into a metric space since the overlap similarity measure is not a distance measure. For example[3], we find the most similar word to "anaconda" to be "python" in the snake sense with a similarity score of 36 and "snake" with a similarity score of 31. However, "python" snake's list of most similar terms starts with "snake, serpent, rattlesnake, cobra...", with "anaconda" appearing at rank 26.

3 Comparison of Graph-based and Vector-based DSMs

Above, I already hinted at fundamental differences between vector-based (VDSMs) and graph-based (GDSMs) distributional semantic models. In this section, these differences and their consequences are described in more detail. Most differences are rooted in the fact that VDSMs encode lexical items in a metric space, where a point in the n-dimensional space corresponds to the coordinates given by the n-dimensional vector. This is not the case for GDSMs for lack of fixed dimensionality. In all of the aspects discussed below, there exist solutions for both representations, but in many cases, one of the representations is more suitable than the other.

Word Similarity In word relatedness or similarity evaluations, where the global similarity ranking of word pairs should be predicted by the DSM, VDSMs excel since the graph-based model does not relate lexical items that are dissimilar at all, therefore not being able to discern a difference in degree of

---

[3] using the Google Books Syntactic Dependencies model on www.jobimtext.org/jobimviz-web-demo/

relatedness e.g. between rooster:voyage and asylum:fruit (from RG65; (Rubenstein and Goodenough, 1965)). On the other hand, the ability of the GDSM only return a set of minimally similar items has been experimentally shown to be advantageous when using DSM similarity for lexical expansion (cf. (Miller et al., 2012)).

Similarity Computation and Semantic Neighbourhood Similarity computation in the metric space of the VDSM is computationally expensive and needs engineering solutions like K-d-trees (Bentley, 1990) or approximation (Sugawara et al., 2016) to make it feasible to return the top-n-similar list of items, which is a frequently used function in statistical semantics. In GDSMs, on the other hand, similarity is directly read off the representation. Pre-computation of all similarities in VDSMs is possible, but does not scale well, cf. (Panchenko et al., 2016).

Word Sense Representations Another consequence of the metric space is that neighbourhoods of lexical items are populated with similar lexical items across all frequency bands. This leads to the following situation when trying to induce word senses: Suppose we hypothesise for a lexical item like "bank" that it has more than one sense and we want to cluster the neighbourhood to get two sense representations. As for most ambiguous words, the sense distribution is biased: in our hypothetical collection, the monetary sense of bank is much better represented than the river bank sense. In this situation, the vector for "bank" is surrounded by other money-bank-terms (such as names of banks). The larger the underlying corpus, the higher is the amount of these terms, most of them rare (see e.g. (Pelevina et al., 2016)). We either do not find river-bank terms in the neighbourhood or we have to extend the neighbourhood until we pull in a lot of unrelated words into our subspace we use for clustering. This might be a reason why in word sense induction, graph-based algorithms are very popular while there are only few approaches that determine the number of sense embeddings per item automatically (as e.g. (Neelakantan et al., 2014)).

Word analogy and other arithmetics Word analogy tasks are a classic use-case for word embeddings, and there are further works, which learn vector operations that represent semantic relations. While many of these approaches in fact learn prototypical heads of the respective relation (Levy et al., 2015), word analogy and relational arithmetics are much less straightforward in GDSMs.

Compositionality This is another task where the VDSM representation is more suited than GDSMs. While in general, a scalable computation in GDSMs allows to compute representation and similarities for frequent multi-word units (Riedl and Biemann, 2015), the computation of compositional vectors from single vectors in VDSMs is more attractive since it generalises to unseen combinations, even phrases and sentences (Bentivogli et al., 2016).

Interpretability and Robustness of Representation The lack of interpretability of vectors and their dimensions is one of the strongest points of critique on dense vectors: while sometimes, post-hoc explanations for some of the dimensions are found, it holds in general that most or nearly all latent dimensions have no direct interpretation, and running the same model on a somewhat different collection would yield entirely different dimensions and embeddings. This is where sparse models shine, as their representations are readable. For example, it is possible to query the GDSM described above *why* anaconda and python are similar (because they coil up, are snakes, swallow, digest, gorge, tighten, and co-occur in conjunctions with other snakes, easily readable off the shared context representation) – and the same 'reasons' for similarity will be found in other corpora as well, assuming they contain a sufficient amount of snakes.

Learnability and Cognitive Plausibility A cognitively plausible model should be able to learn continuously and iteratively from an input stream of language. This point is not well-addressed by both representations. While it is agreed upon that human brains operate on distributed neural representations, this is where the commonalities between humans and static, per-task neural architectures already end. One major divergence lies in the epochal training, which humans do not need, especially when extending their vocabulary. Dense vector representations are either produced by a single operation that requires the entire corpus and vocabulary to be known beforehand (e.g. LSA) or by sampling methods that are obtained by several iterations over the input data, which also require a fixed vocabulary. Count-based sparse methods do not suffer from the fixed vocabulary restriction; however, it is also implausible that the sparse full co-occurrence counts are stored, and most of the current implementations are technically implemented in batch mode, not providing the possibility to update the model through processing further material.

For restrictions of space, this list of differences ends here. There are different criteria and use-cases for DSMs, and there are solutions or at least circumventions for most of the critical points I have risen. However, what should become clear is, that there is a substantial difference and some representations are in fact more adequate than others, depending on the scenario or task.

4   Conclusions and Outlook

Where do we go from here? If this position paper has convinced you as a reader to re-visit the assumption that DSMs *must* be represented in vector spaces, then I have already reached my goal. Now that we hopefully agree that there is value in both vector-based and graph-based representations, the next natural question is how to combine them to get the best of both worlds. Ideally, depending on the tsk, problem, and engineering constraints, it would be desirable to switch between both representations, or to inform one another at construction time.

A starting point to a combination might be to break down methods that use DSMs into their parts and to gauge which representation is more suitable. For example, take word sense induction and disambiguation: As mentioned above, it might be advantageous to cluster graphs instead of vectors because there are straightforward methods that do not require the number of clusters to be set beforehand (which is a 'big no-no' in WSI) and because vector space neighbourhoods of words with biased sense distributions might be overpopulated by the dominant sense. However, for disambiguation, it might be an advantage to use dense representations since they are less sparse and thus allow a higher recall in sense assignment in context. Or, for another example, imagine that we would like our systems not only to recognise word analogies, but also to explain why the system perceives an analogy. While we can use dense vector spaces to generate/recognise the analogy, we can search for commonalities and differences in the sparse context representation to yield a plausible and readable explanation.

Finally, what will be really needed in the future in order to support adaptive, interactive, iterative and contextualised applications also on the level of language processing are semantic models with a robust representation and are enhanced and improved in the moment new text is processed by the application.

Acknowledgments

Numerous people were involved in the conception of this position paper, which provides the basis for an invited talk at CogALex 2016. Especially, I would like to thank Martin Riedl, Alexander Panchenko, Alfio Gliozzo, Markus J. Hofmann, Michael Zock and many anonymous reviewers from various venues for endless discussions.

References

Marco Baroni and Alessandro Lenci. 2010. Distributional memory: A general framework for corpus-based semantics. *Comput. Linguist.*, 36(4):673–721, December.

Luisa Bentivogli, Raffaella Bernardi, Marco Marelli, Stefano Menini, Marco Baroni, and Roberto Zamparelli. 2016. Sick through the semeval glasses: Lessons learned from the evaluation of compositional distributional semantic models on full sentences through semantic relatedness and textual entailment. *Journal of Language Resources and Evaluation*, 50(1):95–124.

Jon L. Bentley. 1990. K-d trees for semidynamic point sets. In *Proceedings of the Sixth Annual Symposium on Computational Geometry*, SCG '90, pages 187–197, New York, NY, USA. ACM.

Chris Biemann and Martin Riedl. 2013. Text: Now in 2D! A Framework for Lexical Expansion with Contextual Similarity. *Journal of Language Modelling*, 1(1):55–95.

Chris Biemann. 2006. Chinese whispers: An efficient graph clustering algorithm and its application to natural language processing problems. In *Proceedings of the First Workshop on Graph Based Methods for Natural Language Processing*, TextGraphs-1, pages 73–80, New York City, NY, USA.

James R. Curran. 2004. *From distributional to semantic similarity*. Phd thesis, University of Edinburgh. College of Science and Engineering. School of Informatics.

Ferdinand de Saussure. 1966. *Course in General Linguistics*. New York: McGraw-Hill.

Scott Deerwester, Susan T. Dumais, George W. Furnas, Thomas K. Landauer, and Richard Harshman. 1990. Indexing by Latent Semantic Analysis. *Journal of the American Society for Information Science*, 41(6):391–407, January.

Ted E. Dunning. 1993. Accurate Methods for the Statistics of Surprise and Coincidence. *Computational Linguistics*, 19(1):61–74.

Katrin Erk and Sebastian Padó. 2008. A structured vector space model for word meaning in context. In *Proceedings of the Conference on Empirical Methods in Natural Language Processing*, EMNLP '08, pages 897–906, Stroudsburg, PA, USA. Association for Computational Linguistics.

Stefan Evert. 2004. *The Statistics of Word Co-occurrences: Word Pairs and Collocations*. Ph.D. thesis, University of Stuttgart.

Stefano Faralli, Alexander Panchenko, Chris Biemann, and Simone Paolo Ponzetto. 2016. Linked disambiguated distributional semantic networks. In *Proceedings of the The Semantic Web - ISWC 2016 - 15th International Semantic Web Conference, Part II*, pages 56–64, Kobe, Japan.

Tim Feuerbach, Martin Riedl, and Chris Biemann. 2015. Distributional semantics for resolving bridging mentions. In *Proceedings of the International Conference Recent Advances in Natural Language Processing*, pages 192–199, Hissar, Bulgaria.

John R. Firth. 1957. *A Synopsis of Linguistic Theory, 1933-1955*. Blackwell, Oxford.

Alfio Gliozzo, Chris Biemann, Martin Riedl, Bonaventura Coppola, Michael R. Glass, and Matthew Hatem. 2013. Jobimtext visualizer: A graph-based approach to contextualizing distributional similarity. In *Proceedings of the First Workshop on Graph Based Methods for Natural Language Processing, TextGraphs-8*, pages 884–890.

Zellig S. Harris. 1951. *Methods in Structural Linguistics*. University of Chicago Press, Chicago.

Marti A. Hearst. 1992. Automatic acquisition of hyponyms from large text corpora. In *Proc. COLING*, pages 539–545.

Eduard Hovy. 2010. Distributional semantics and the lexicon (invited talk). In *Proceedings of the 2nd Workshop on Cognitive Aspects of the Lexicon*, page 1, Beijing, China.

Omer Levy and Yoav Goldberg. 2014a. Dependency-based word embeddings. In *Proceedings of the 52nd Annual Meeting of the Association for Computational Linguistics (Volume 2: Short Papers)*, pages 302–308, Baltimore, MD, USA.

Omer Levy and Yoav Goldberg. 2014b. Neural word embedding as implicit matrix factorization. In *Advances in Neural Information Processing Systems 27*, pages 2177–2185.

Omer Levy, Steffen Remus, Chris Biemann, and Ido Dagan. 2015. Do supervised distributional methods really learn lexical inference relations? In *Proceedings of the 2015 Conference of the North American Chapter of the Association for Computational Linguistics: Human Language Technologies*, pages 970–976, Denver, CO, USA.

Dekang Lin. 1998. Automatic Retrieval and Clustering of Similar Words. In *Proceedings of the 36th Annual Meeting of the Association for Computational Linguistics and 17th International Conference on Computational Linguistics, Volume 2*, pages 768–774, Montreal, QC, Canada.

Tomas Mikolov, Ilya Sutskever, Kai Chen, Gregory S. Corrado, and Jeffrey Dean. 2013. Distributed representations of words and phrases and their compositionality. In *Proc. NIPS*, pages 3111–3119.

George A. Miller and Walter G. Charles. 1991. Contextual Correlates of Semantic Similarity. *Language and Cognitive Processes*, 6(1):1–28.

Tristan Miller, Chris Biemann, Torsten Zesch, and Iryna Gurevych. 2012. Using distributional similarity for lexical expansion in knowledge-based word sense disambiguation. In *Proc. COLING-2012*, pages 1781–1796, Mumbai, India.

Animesh Mukherjee, Monojit Choudhury, Anupam Basu, and Niloy Ganguly. 2008. Modeling the structure and dynamics of the consonant inventories: a complex network approach. In *Proceedings of the 22nd International Conference on Computational Linguistics - Volume 1*, COLING '08, pages 601–608, Manchester, United Kingdom.

Arvind Neelakantan, Jeevan Shankar, Alexandre Passos, and Andrew McCallum. 2014. Efficient non-parametric estimation of multiple embeddings per word in vector space. In *Proceedings of the 2014 Conference on Empirical Methods in Natural Language Processing (EMNLP)*, pages 1059–1069, Doha, Qatar.

Alexander Panchenko, Dmitry Ustalov, Nikolay Arefyev, Denis Paperno, Natalia Konstantinova, Natalia Loukachevitch, and Chris Biemann. 2016. Human and machine judgements about russian semantic relatedness. In *Proceedings of the 5th Conference on Analysis of Images, Social Networks and Texts (AIST'2016)*, Communications in Computer and Information Science (CCIS), pages 174–183. Springler-Verlag.

Shvaiko Pavel and Jerome Euzenat. 2013. Ontology matching: State of the art and future challenges. *IEEE Transaction on Knowledge and Data Engineering*, 25(1):158–176.

Maria Pelevina, Nikolay Arefiev, Chris Biemann, and Alexander Panchenko. 2016. Making sense of word embeddings. In *Proceedings of the 1st Workshop on Representation Learning for NLP*, pages 174–183, Berlin, Germany.

Martin Riedl and Chris Biemann. 2015. A single word is not enough: Ranking multiword expressions using distributional semantics. In *Proc. EMNLP*, pages 2430–2440, Lisbon, Portugal.

Martin Riedl and Chris Biemann. 2016. Unsupervised compound splitting with distributional semantics rivals supervised methods. In *Proceedings of the 2016 Conference of the North American Chapter of the Association for Computational Linguistics: Human Language Technologies*, pages 617–622, San Diego, California.

Martin Riedl. 2016. *Unsupervised Methods for Learning and Using Semantics of Natural Language*. Phd thesis, TU Darmstadt, Comp. Sci. Dept.

Herbert Rubenstein and John B. Goodenough. 1965. Contextual correlates of synonymy. *Communications of the ACM*, 8(10):627–633.

Gerard Salton, A. Wong, and C. S. Yang. 1975. A vector space model for automatic indexing. *Communications of the ACM*, 18(11):613–620.

Mark Steyvers and Joshua B. Tenenbaum. 2005. The Large-Scale Structure of Semantic Networks: Statistical Analyses and a Model of Semantic Growth. *Cognitive Science*, 29(1):41–78.

Kohei Sugawara, Hayato Kobayashi, and Masajiro Iwasaki. 2016. On approximately searching for similar word embeddings. In *Proceedings of the 54th Annual Meeting of the Association for Computational Linguistics (Volume 1: Long Papers)*, pages 2265–2275, Berlin, Germany, August. Association for Computational Linguistics.

György Szarvas, Chris Biemann, and Iryna Gurevych. 2013. Supervised all-words lexical substitution using delexicalized features. In *Proceedings of the 2013 Conference of the North American Chapter of the Association for Computational Linguistics: Human Language Technologies*, pages 1131–1141, Atlanta, GA, USA.

Ludwig Wittgenstein. 1963. *Tractatus logico-philosophicus. Logisch-philosophische Abhandlung*. Suhrkamp, Frankfurt am Main.

George K. Zipf. 1949. *Human Behavior and the Principle of Least-Effort*. Addison-Wesley, Cambridge, MA.

"Beware the Jabberwock, dear reader!"
Testing the distributional reality of construction semantics

Gianluca E. Lebani and **Alessandro Lenci**
Computational Linguistics Laboratory
Department of Philology, Literature, and Linguistics
University of Pisa, Italy
`gianluca.lebani@for.unipi.it, alessandro.lenci@unipi.it`

Abstract

Notwithstanding the success of the notion of construction, the computational tradition still lacks a way to represent the semantic content of these linguistic entities. Here we present a simple corpus-based model implementing the idea that the meaning of a syntactic construction is intimately related to the semantics of its typical verbs. It is a two-step process, that starts by identifying the typical verbs occurring with a given syntactic construction and building their distributional vectors. We then calculated the weighted centroid of these vectors in order to derive the distributional signature of a construction. In order to assess the goodness of our approach, we replicated the priming effect described by Johnson and Golberg (2013) as a function of the semantic distance between a construction and its prototypical verbs. Additional support for our view comes from a regression analysis showing that our distributional information can be used to model behavioral data collected with a crowdsourced elicitation experiment.

1 Introduction

In its traditional use, that can be traced back at least to the medieval Modistae school of grammarians (Goldberg and Casenhiser, 2006), the linguistic notion of *Construction* (Cxn) can be characterized as the association between a form and a (semantic or pragmatic) function. As a theoretical tool, linguists used to resort to this notion in order to refer to quirky phenomena considered to be marginally relevant for the description of the core properties of language, for instance idiomatic expressions. The prototypical instantiation of this view is the generative approach (Chomsky, 2000).

The 1980s witnessed the emerging of a new linguistic paradigm that puts the notion of Cxn at the heart of the study of language, which subsequently led to the evolution of a wide range of Constructionist approaches (Hoffmann and Trousdale, 2013). Works belonging to this literature see Cxns as linguistic patterns whose form or function cannot be predicted from their components or from other Cxns. Their realization spans in size and complexity from fixed idiomatic sequences of words (e.g., *a home from home*), to unusual semi-productive patterns (e.g. the Covariational-Conditional Cxn "The Xer the Yer": *The more I talk, the more I turn into a vegetable*), to common productive argument structures (e.g. the Ditransitive Cxn "Subj V Obj$_1$ Obj$_2$": *She gave him a kiss*).

One major breaking point between the Constructionist approaches and former formal linguistic tradition pertains to the pivotal role played by the main verb in the interpretation of the sentence. Traditionally, indeed, sentences composed by nonsensical words, such as the example of Vogon poetry in sentence (1), are expected to be completely meaningless, due to the idea that meaning comes from lexical items alone.

(1)   As plurdled gabbleblotchits on a lurgid bee.

Another consequence of the idea that meaning comes solely from lexical items is re assumption that the structural and semantic properties of a sentence are determined by the syntactic and semantic properties projected from the main verb. According to this view, the syntactic configurations in the sentences in (2) are projections of the main verb *to slice*:

Proceedings of the Workshop on Cognitive Aspects of the Lexicon,
pages 8–18, Osaka, Japan, December 11-17 2016.

(2)   a.   He sliced the bread.
        b.   Pat sliced the carrots into the salad.
        c.   Pat sliced Chris a piece of pie.
        d.   Pat sliced the box open.   (examples from Goldberg (2006))

This view has been criticized in the Constructionist tradition, following theoretical considerations as well as psycholinguistics arguments (Goldberg, 1995; Goldberg, 2006). From the theoretical side, for instance, it has been pointed out that, if argument structure is projected solely by the meaning of the verb, than it is necessary to stipulate a different meaning for each occurrence of a given verb in various argument structures. As for the sentences in (2), this view would lead to postulate special senses of this verb roughly meaning (2a) *to cut something with a sharp instrument*; (2b) *to cut something with a sharp instrument so as to move it*; (2c) *to cut something for someone else with a sharp instrument*; (2d) *to cut something with a sharp instrument so as to change its state*. In a Constructionist perspective, the verb "to slice" is always used with the intuitive meaning of *to cut with a sharp instrument*, the additional meaning coming from the construction in which it occurs, whose semantics can be paraphrased as (2a) *something acting on something else*; (2b) *something causing something else to move*; (2c) *someone intending to cause someone to receive something*; (2d) *someone causing something to change state* (Goldberg, 1995).

Psycholinguistic evidence, on the other side, mostly originates from research on language comprehension and language acquisition. As for the former, studies like Bencini and Goldberg (2000), Kaschak and Glenberg (2000), Kako (2006), Goldwater and Markman (2009) and Johnson and Goldberg (2013) support the idea that the construction of a sentence (rather than the verb only) plays a role in its interpretation. In a sorting experiment, Bencini and Goldberg (2000) showed that, when asked to sort sentences on the basis of their overall meaning, subjects were as likely to rely on the verb as on the construction. Kaschak and Glenberg (2000) and Goldwater and Markman (2009) tapped into the semantic content of different syntactic frames by using novel denominal verbs in a comprehension task. Likewise, Kako (2006) investigated the meaning of six syntactic frames by collecting linguistic judgments over phrases whose content words were replaced by nonsense words (a.k.a. "Jabberwocky"sentences like *The grack mecked the zarg*). While all these works exploited off-line tasks or explicit judgments, Johnson and Goldberg (2013) demonstrated that the constructional meaning is accessed quickly by asking their participants to perform a speeded lexical decision task on a target verb, after being exposed to Jabberwocky prime sentences. From an acquisition perspective, studies supporting the so-called 'Syntactic Bootstrapping" hypothesis show that speakers use their knowledge about the meaning of syntactic pattern in order to infer the semantics of a novel verb (Landau and Gleitman, 1985; Gleitman and Gillette, 1995; Gillette et al., 1999), thus endorsing the idea that argument structures have an abstract semantics that dynamically interacts with the semantics of the main verb.

The fact that Cxns have independent semantic content raises the question of how their meaning is acquired. Goldberg (2006) has argued that the learning of the semantic content of argument Cxn heavily relies on the meaning of high frequency verbs used with them. For instance, the most frequent verb occurring in an intransitive motion Cxn in a corpus of children's early speech is *to go*, which roughly corresponds to the meaning of this Cxn. The same goes for the ditransitive and the caused-motion Cxns and their most frequent verbs, i.e. *to give* and *to put*, respectively (Goldberg, 1999). The skewed distribution of verbs and Cxns, with a small number of "general purpose" verbs accounting for most of Cxn tokens, is therefore argued to play a key role in the acquisition of construction meaning. Among the others, Kidd et al. (2010) showed that 4- to 6-years old children were better able to recall finite sentential complement Cxn instances when these contained high frequency verbs, as opposed to when they contained low frequency verbs. Experimenting with artificial languages, Casenhiser and Goldberg (2005) not only showed that 5- to 7-year-old children are able to associate an abstract meaning to a phrasal form, but also that this process is facilitated when a verb occurs in a Cxn with a disproportionately high frequency. Barak et al. (2013) provide further support by exploiting a probabilistic computational model to investigate the acquisition of the English sentential complement Cxns. The obtained results suggest that the learning of an argument Cxn is influenced by a series of distributional properties of the input, among which verb frequency, co-occurrence frequency of a verb with the Cxn, and the frequency of each semantic verb class with the Cxn.

In this paper, we bring support to such hypothesis with a simple corpus-based method apt to infer the semantic content of a syntactic Cxn. Our proposal transposes into distributional terms the idea that the meaning of a Cxn is related to that of the verbs that most frequently appear in it. While traditionally the meaning of a Cxn has always been described in intuitive terms (see Table 1), our representation allows for the measurement of the semantic similiarity between a Cxn and other Cxns and/or lexical elements.

In the next section we will present a distributional semantic model to represent the semantic content of syntactic Cxn. We validate this model on two test beds. In the first experiment, described in section 3, we test the ability of our approach to model the Cxn-verb priming effect reported by Johnson and Goldberg (2013). Section 4 reports a second study in which we investigated whether our distributional model is able to account for behavioral data concerning the intimate semantic link between a Cxn and its prototypical verbs. Final remarks and possible improvements are reported in section 5.

2 The distributional signature of a syntactic construction

Distributional Semantic Models (Sahlgren, 2006; Lenci, 2008; Turney and Pantel, 2010, DSMs) are unsupervised corpus-based models of semantic representation realizing the so-called "Distributional Hypothesis" (Harris, 1954; Miller and Charles, 1991), that takes the similarity of the contexts in which two linguistic expressions occur as a proxy to their similarity in meaning. DSMs are typically built by searching all the occurrences of a target expression in a corpus, identifying its contexts of occurrence and representing the target-by-contexts frequencies as a matrix. Contexts can be words, syntactic relations, lexicalized patterns, documents and so on, while the vectors composing the final matrix are assumed to be the distributional representation of the semantics of the target elements. Distributional vectors can be used to evaluate the semantic distance between lexical elements by means of geometric methods (Bullinaria and Levy, 2007; Bullinaria and Levy, 2012; Lapesa and Evert, 2014) or manipulated to represent more complex linguistic entities (Baroni, 2013).

Our model implements the idea that the meaning of a syntactic Cxn is intimately related to the semantics of its typical verbs. It is a two step process, that starts by identifying the typical verbs that occur in our target syntactic Cxn and building their distributional $\vec{v}$ vectors. We calculated the weighted centroid of these verb vectors in order to build a $\overrightarrow{\text{CXN}}$ vector encoding the distributional properties of Cxn. The notion of centroid is the generalization of the notion of mean to multidimensional spaces. In a DSM it can be intuitively pictured as the prototype of a set of lexical elements, that is as a representation of the characteristics that are common to the verbs associated with our target Cxn. A positive by-product of a centroid-based representation is that it allows to soften the influence of the idiosyncratic or non-relevant properties of the verbs, as well as the influence of the noise produced by verb polysemy. Given the role of the skewed verb-Cxn frequency distribution, we weighted the salience of each verb in the calculation of the centroid on the basis of its co-occurrence frequency with the target Cxn. Coherently, then, we calculated our weighted centroids as:

$$\overrightarrow{\text{CXN}} = \frac{1}{|V|} \sum_{v \in V} f_{rel}(v, \text{CXN}) \cdot \vec{v} \tag{1}$$

where CXN is our target construction, V the set of its top-associated verbs v and $f_{rel}(v, \text{CXN})$ the relative frequency of occurrence of a verb in a construction. For instance, given a Ditransitive target Cxn, whose associated verbs are *to give* ($f_{rel} = 0.75$) and *to hand* ($f_{rel} = 0.25$), its distributional signature would be estimated as:

$$\overrightarrow{\text{DITRANSITIVE}} = \frac{0.75 \cdot \overrightarrow{give} + 0.25 \cdot \overrightarrow{hand}}{2} \tag{2}$$

Our proposal shares a "family resemblance" with the "collostructional analysis" techniques that have been extensively exploited to study the relationship between a verb and the constructions encoding argument structures, tense/aspect, mood and modality, both from a theoretical as well as from a psycholinguistic perspective (Stefanowitsch, 2013). The aim of our proposal is, however, radically different: while the collostructional paradigm has been developed to model the strength of association between a Cxn and the grammatical structures it occurs in, our primary intent is to derive the meaning of argument Cxns from the distributional semantic representations of the verbs co-occurring with them.

2.1 Implementing the model

We tested the psycholinguistic plausibility of our model by simulating the behavioral data reported by Johnson and Goldberg (2013), further reviewed in the first part of section 3. The requirement for our model is to account for the association between a Cxn and a target verb as a function of their geometric distance in the distributional semantic space. Given the exploratory nature of the work presented in these pages, we did not tune all the possible settings and hyperparameters of our DSM. Rather, whenever possible we relied on what is the common practice in the literature or on our experience.

To implement our proposal we need two kinds of information: the distributional signature of a set of verbs and their relative frequency with a set of syntactic Cxns. We extracted the latter from VALEX (Korhonen et al., 2006), an automatically built subcategorization lexicon that encodes information for 6,397 English verbs. From this list we selected, for each of the four Cxns used by Johnson and Goldberg (2013) reported in Table 1, the set of 75 top associated verbs.

To model the distributional behavior of our verbs we built a syntax-based DSM (Grefenstette, 1994; Lin, 1998; Padó and Lapata, 2007; Baroni and Lenci, 2010), that is a space in which the linguistic expressions are characterized on the basis of the parsed text dependency paths in which they occur. For instance, given the sentence *The cat ate my homework*, in a syntax-based model the distributional entry for the verb $\overrightarrow{eat}$ is represented with the `dependency:filler` patterns `subj:cat`, `obj:homework`. We extracted the raw co-occurrence statistics from the extended arcs of the American English section of the Google Books Syntactic Ngrams corpus (Goldberg and Orwant, 2013), a 146.2B tokens corpus built from 1.4M books. Verbs failing to reach the minimal threshold of 500 occurrences were discarded.

The raw co-occurrence matrix has been weighted with *Positive Local Mutual Information* (Evert, 2008, PLMI) to calculate the strength of association between a verb and a syntactic pattern. PLMI is defined as the log ratio between the joint probability of a target v and a context c and their marginal probabilities, multiplied by their joint frequency, setting to zero all the negative results:

$$PLMI(c, v) = max\left(0, f(c, v) \cdot \log_2 \frac{p(c, v)}{p(c) \cdot p(v)}\right) \qquad (3)$$

PLMI corresponds to the Positive Pointwise Mutual Information score (Church and Hanks, 1991) between the verb and the context, weighted by their joint frequency, and differs from PPMI in avoiding the bias towards low-frequency events. To ignore unwanted variance and to reduce the processing cost we adopted the context selection strategy proposed by Polajnar and Clark (2014) and limited the distributional characterization of each verb to its 240 top-associated contexts. In the final step we fed equation 1 with all the previously collected statistics on each group of 75 top-associated verbs, thus obtaining the distributional signature of our target Cxns that will be tested in the remaining of the paper.

3 Jabberwocky sentences prime associated verbs

The starting point of the reflections by Johnson and Goldberg (2013, henceforth JG) is the psycholinguistic literature showing that speakers associate semantic knowledge to argument structures, independently of the linguistic properties of the verb governing it. Moving further, these authors tested the possibility that this knowledge is used automatically, that is quickly and instinctively, in sentence comprehension.

To this end, they submitted 40 speakers with a lexical decision task in which they were required to read a Jabberwocky sentence (i.e,. a sentence whose content words have been replace by meaningless strings) and then to judge as quickly as possible if a target verb was a real lexical element or a non-word. Table 1 reports the four syntactic constructions investigated by JG, along with an informal representation of their meaning and the Jabberwocky sentence.

Half of the target words seen by each participant were non-words, while the other half were the target verbs reported in Table 2, that were further classified into three classes: "High Frequency associate"

Construction	Structure	Meaning	Jabberwocky Prime
Ditransitive	Subj V Obj$_1$ Obj$_2$	X CAUSES Y TO RECEIVE Z	*he daxed the norp*
Resultative	Subj V Obj Pred	X CAUSES Y TO BECOME Z	*she jorped it miggy*
Caused-motion	Subj V Obj Obl$_{path}$	X CAUSES Y TO MOVE Z	*he lorked it on the molp*
Removal	Subj V Obj Obl$_{source}$	X CAUSES Y TO MOVE FROM Z	*she vakoed it from her*

Table 1: JG's experimental constructions. Adapted from Johnson and Goldberg (2013, Tables 1,3).

Construction	High Frequency associate	Low Frequency associate	Semantically Related nonassociate
Ditransitive	*Gave*	*Handed*	*Transferred*
Resultative	*Made*	*Turned*	*Transformed*
Caused-motion	*Put*	*Placed*	*Decorated*
Removal construction	*Took*	*Removed*	*Ousted*

Table 2: JG's experimental target verbs. Adapted from Johnson and Goldberg (2013, Table 4).

(HF), i.e. a verb that most frequently occurs in a given Cxn; "Low Frequency associates" (LF), i.e. a verb that frequently occurs in a given Cxn, albeit significantly less than the relevant HF; "Semantically Related nonassociate" (SR), i.e. a verb whose meaning is related to the semantics of the Cxn, but that does not occurs in it. Frequencies were estimated from the 400M words COCA corpus (Davies, 2009). Each target verb could be presented either in a congruent context, i.e. after a Jabberwocky sentence instantiating the Cxn to which it is associated with (e.g., *Gave* preceded by a Ditransitive prime), or in an incongruent condition (e.g., *Gave* preceded by a Removal prime). In order to simplify the experimental design, the congruency-incongruency conditions were obtained by opposing either the Ditransitive and the Removal Cxns, or the Caused-motion and the Resultative Cxns.

The extent of priming was computed for each target verb as the difference between the reaction times in the congruent condition and the reaction time after the incongruent sentence. JG report a main effect of congruency, according to which each verb was recognized faster after a related Cxn. HF and LF associates were recognized faster in a congruent condition, both by-subject and by-item. SR verbs, on the other side, were recognized faster only in a by-subject analysis, a fact that can be attributed to the well-known weakness of semantic priming with respect to associative priming. Finally, the priming effect was recorded for all classes of verbs but those associated with the Resultative Cxn, a null effect that the authors ascribed to the plausibility of a metaphorical Caused-motion interpretation of these verbs (*$^{??}$She made/turned/transformed into the room*).

All in all, by recording a priming effect of the Jabberwocky sentences instantiating the Cxns in Table 1 over their associated verbs, JG showed not only that argument structures have an inherent abstract meaning independently of their main verb semantics, but also that this knowledge is accessed quickly and implicitly in the process of sentence comprehension.

3.1 Modeling the priming effect

The effect reported by JG not only is a viable testing ground for our model. Replicating the same results with distributional semantic methods allows us to draw conclusions concerning the psycholinguistic plausibility of distributional representations, at the same time supporting the hypothesis that construction meaning is the result of a usage-based process of abstraction from the meaning of co-occurring verbs.

In our DSM, verb and Cxn vectors lie in the same distributional space, that is, they are described by means of the same contexts. This allows us to model the "semantic congruency" of a verb and a Cxn as a measure of the geometric distance between the $\overrightarrow{\text{CXN}}$ and the $\overrightarrow{verb}$ vectors. Following a common practice in the literature, we opted to calculate vectors similarity by measuring the cosine of the angle between

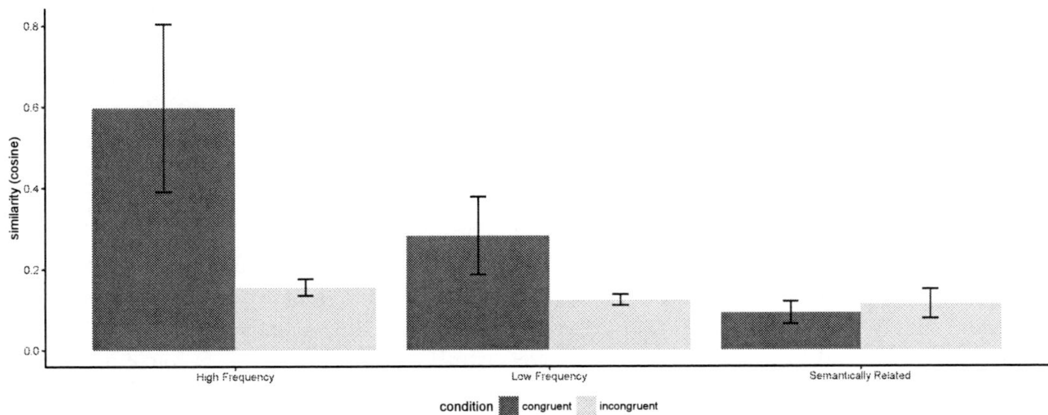

Figure 1: Mean cosine similarity scores as a function of frequency class (High Frequency, Low Frequency and Semantically Related) and experimental condition (congruent vs. incongruent). Vertical capped lines atop bars indicate standard error of the mean.

them (Bullinaria and Levy, 2007; Lapesa and Evert, 2014).

JG see their priming effect as a proof of the fact that the constructions presented in Jabberwocky sentences have a meaning strongly associated with the one of the congruent target verbs. Accordingly, we expect higher similarity scores between the $\overrightarrow{\text{CXN}}$ and the congruent $\overrightarrow{verb}$ vectors, as opposed to the similarity scores between the $\overrightarrow{\text{CXN}}$ and the incongruent $\overrightarrow{verb}$ vectors. A major difference between JG's analysis and ours, however, concerns the number of oppositions in the incongruent condition. While in JG each Cxn the congruency-incongruency conditions were obtained by opposing either the Ditransitive and the Removal Cxns, or the Caused-motion and the Resultative Cxns, we opted for a one-vs-all design, in which an incongruent condition is simply a Cxn-verb pairing inconsistent with the pattern in Table 2. We adopted this solution mainly in order to collect more data points for our analysis.

Coherently with JG, moreover, we expect an effect of the frequency class. That is, we expect higher similarity scores between the $\overrightarrow{\text{CXN}}$ and its High Frequency $\overrightarrow{verb}$ vectors, as opposed to the similarity scores between the $\overrightarrow{\text{CXN}}$ and the Semantically Related $\overrightarrow{verb}$ vectors, with the case of the Low Frequency $\overrightarrow{verb}$ vectors falling somehow in the middle.

3.2 Results and discussion

A two-ways ANOVA was conducted to compare the effect of the condition (congruent vs. incongruent) and of the frequency class (HF, LF and SN) on the similarity between each verb and the centroid of its class. Following JG, we expected weaker effects due to the relatively low number of items.

We found a significant main effect both for condition $F(1, 42) = 15.91$, $p < .001$, and frequency class $F(2, 42) = 4.86$, $p < .05$. Overall, our verbs are more similar to their congruent construction ($m = 0.32$, $sd = 0.32$) than to their incongruent construction ($m = 0.13$, $sd = 0.09$). Post-hoc analysis using Tukey Honest Significant Differences indicated a significant overall difference only between HF ($m = 0.27$, $sd = 0.27$) and SN ($m = 0.11$, $sd = 0.11$) cosines ($p < .05$), but no significant difference involving the LF verbs ($m = 0.16$, $sd = 0.12$).

A significant interaction between the two conditions has been found as well $F(2, 42) = 7.79$, $p < .01$ (see Figure 1). Post-hoc analysis using Tukey Honest Significant Differences indicated a significant difference between congruent ($m = 0.6$, $sd = 0.41$) and incongruent ($m = 0.155$, $sd = 0.07$) condition for HF verbs ($p < .001$), between HF verbs and SN ($m = 0.09$, $sd = 0.06$) verbs in their congruent conditions ($p < .001$), and between HF and LF ($m = 0.28$, $sd = 0.19$) verbs in their congruent conditions ($p < .05$), but no other meaningful contrast reaches statistical significance.

A one-way ANOVA was conducted to compare the effect of the Cxn type on the cosine similarity between each verb and the centroid of its Cxn. We were interested in assessing whether there was a significant difference in how similar each Cxn vector is to its 75 most associated verbs, i.e. in how dense is the semantic space around each Cxn vector. The answer was affirmative: we found a significant main effect of the Cxn on the cosine similarity for all the four conditions $F(3, 277) = 0.0012, p < .01$. Post-hoc analysis using the Bonferroni correction for multiple comparisons indicated a significant ($p < .01$) difference in the densities of the removal ($m = 0.19$, $sd = 0.12$) and of the resultative constructions ($m = 0.11$, $sd = 0.13$), a significant ($p < .05$) difference in the difference in the densities of the removal and of the ditransitive constructions ($m = 0.13$, $sd = 0.12$), and a marginally significant ($p < .1$) difference in the densities of the removal and of the caused motion constructions ($m = 0.14$, $sd = 0.12$). No significant difference in densities has been found for all the other comparisons. This is coherent with the null effect on Resultative Cxn that puzzled JG. But while these ascribed it to a design flaw, i.e. to the fact that Resultative verbs could have a metaphorical Caused-motion interpretation, our results suggests a different interpretation. The fact that in our design we implemented all the possible pairwise oppositions, indeed, suggests that the null effect on the Resultative Cxn is due to the low density of this group of vectors. This is in turn related to the fact that the verbs co-ccurring with the Resultative construction are less semantically homogenous. An in-depth study of the reasons behind the higher distance between the prototypical Resultative verbs and the Cxn is left for further investigation.

All in all, we found a pattern that mirrors the priming effect reported by JG. In our DSM, the congruency condition, that in JG leads to faster reaction times, is associated with significantly higher similarity scores. Apart from being a further confirmation of the link between the meaning of a Cxn and that of its typical verbs, these results confirm the psycholinguistic plausibility of our centroid-based approach.

4 Isn't frequency enough? Analyzing crowdsourced production data

Works investigating the acquisition of Cxns usually stress the role played by the top-frequent verbs. Psycholinguistic findings (Casenhiser and Goldberg, 2005; Kidd et al., 2010) as well as computational simulations (Barak et al., 2013) stress the importance of many frequency-related characteristics, such as the marginal frequency for the verb and the relative frequencies of the verb and of the verb semantic class. Up to this point, one may wonder if the semantic resemblance between a Cxn and its most-associated verbs may be explained simply as a function of frequency, rather than the distributional similarity between verb and Cxn vectors. We tested this hypothesis by collecting linguistic production data from native speakers and assessing whether the inclusion of semantic similarity in a frequency-based model would result in a significant increase in fit.

4.1 Data collection

Behavioral data were collected from English speakers by crowdsourcing our task through the Crowdflower marketplace. 40 Crowdflower certified "highest quality" contributors from the U.K., the U.S.A. or Canada were recruited. Each participant was allowed to complete only a hit (i.e., a "Human Intelligent Task"). In each hit the workers were required to generate, for each of the Jabberwocky prime tested by JG (see Table 1), five verbs that could replace the nonsense main verb of the sentence. They received the following instructions:

> *"In this task you will see English sentences containing invented words: e.g. He TREBBED the stig.*
> *Imagine that these sentences were created by a machine that replaced real English words with invented ones.*
> *The capitalized word is a verb. Your task is to guess this verb.*
> *TASK: For each test sentence, write 5 English verbs that could replace the capitalized word."*

Workers were also required to complete, for each Jabberwocky sentence, a language comprehension question of the form "is ghase an English word?". Participants failing to provide 5 descriptions for all the Cxns were not allowed to complete the hit, while participants that did not answer correctly to all the

Model 1	Model 2	Δ AIC	Δ BIC	RSS	F
intercept only	frequency	-7.19	-4.9	216.1	9.53 **
frequency	frequency + similarity	-4.34	-2.05	134	6.35 *
frequency + similarity	frequency * similarity	-9.8	-7.51	220.3	12.1 ***

Table 3: Results of the production frequency models comparisons. AIC: Akaike Information Criterion; BIC: Bayesian Information Criterion; RSS: reduction of residual sum of squares; F: F-test statistics and significance values (* = $p < .05$; ** = $p < .01$; *** = $p < .001$).

	Estimate	SE	t
(intercept)	7.06	5.85	1.21
frequency	-0.73	0.99	-0.74
similarity	-64.44	21.39	-3.01 **
frequency:similarity	10.97	3.15	3.48 ***

Table 4: Parameters included in the final model and relevant statistics (** = $p < .01$; *** = $p < .001$).

test questions were rejected. On the average, workers needed approximately 6 minutes ($m = 364.075$", $sd = 256.23$") to complete a valid hit. The data collection process took approximately 18 hours.

The workers accepted by the system submitted a total of 800 Cxn-verb pairings, that were subsequently manually filtered and formatted. This processing phase lead to the removal of the verbs submitted by one scammer and to the identification of 376 unique Cxn-verb pairings.

4.2 Modeling production frequency

We ran a linear regression analysis on the crowdflower-collected data with production frequency as dependent variable and the joint frequency $f(verb, \text{CXN})$ estimated from VALEX and the verb-Cxn cosine similarity calculated with our model as predictors. We were interested in assessing whether the frequency of production of a verb-Cxn in our crowdsourced data could be modeled on the basis of its relative frequency alone or whether the semantic similarity between the Cxn and the verb plays a role as well.

In a preprocessing phase we removed from the crowd-sourced data all those data points corresponding to verb-Cxn pairings that occurred in VALEX less than 100 times. This reduced our dataset to 73 Cxn-verb pairings. Moreover, the raw frequency extracted from VALEX were log-transformed to approximate a normal distribution. Collinearity in the data matrix was evaluated by calculating the Variance Inflation Factors ($VIF = 1.27$) and the Condition Number ($\kappa = 20.76$). While a $VIF < 5$ value is undoubtedly reassuring, the κ value may be cause for concerns, even if it well below the critical threshold of 30 that is commonly taken as an indication of the risk of high collinearity (Cohen et al., 2003; Baayen, 2008).

We defined the simplest model as the one in which the only predictor is the log-transformed joint frequency estimated from the corpus. As shown by Table 3, this model looks significantly better that the intercept-only model. We then enriched this model by adding the cosine similarity between each verb and the construction centroid, obtaining significant improvement in the goodness-of-fit. Finally, we added the interaction between corpus frequency and cosine similarity, thus obtaining our best fitting model ($F(3, 69) = 10.45, p < .001, R^2 = 0.312, R^2_{adj} = 0.282$). The low R^2 values were not unexpected due to the fact that crucial sources of variance has not been controlled or taken into consideration for the present study, such as the socio-cultural background of the speakers, the different varieties of the English language they were proficient in, the time spent in completing the micro-task and so forth. In this model the significant predictors are the semantic similarity and its interaction with the joint frequency, as reported in the Table 4.

Figure 2 shows the partial effects of the corpus frequency at different levels of semantic similarity (top row) and those of the semantic similarity at different levels of corpus frequency (bottom row). At

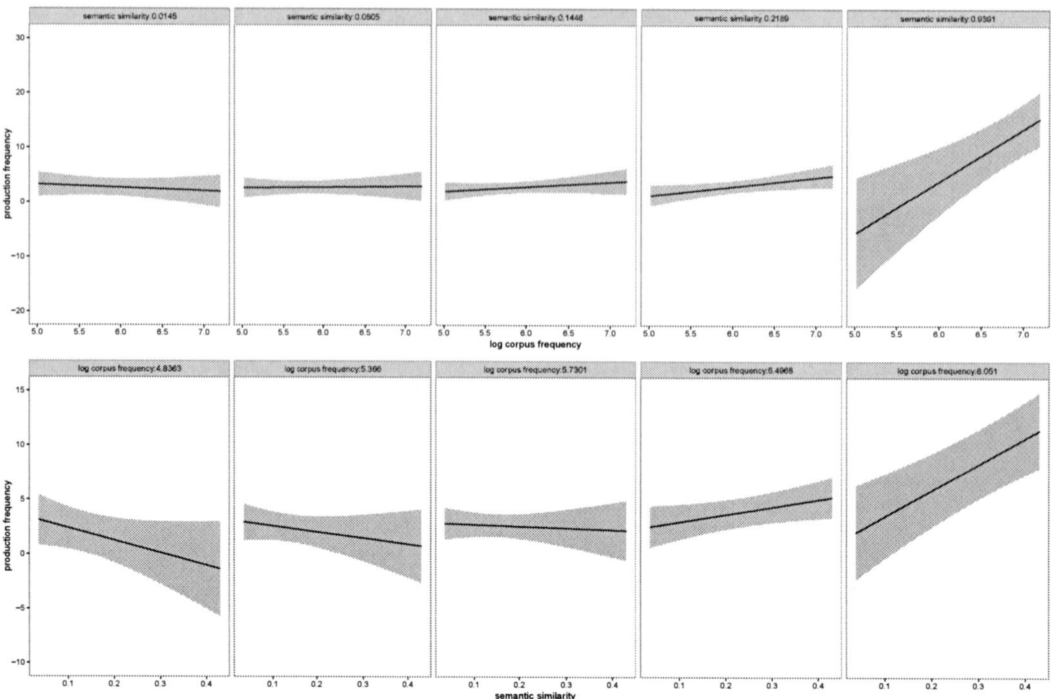

Figure 2: Effect displays for the interaction of (log transformed) corpus frequency and semantic similarity. A 95% confidence interval is drawn around the estimated effects.

high levels of similarity and frequency the interaction between these two variables is synergistic, i.e. their joint effect is superior than the sum of their effects in isolation, while becoming antagonistic at low levels of similarity and/or frequency.

All in all, we interpret these results as proving that the distributional information encoded in the distributional semantic representation of Cxns we have tested in this paper is able to model the linguistic behavior of adult native speaker over and above the variance that can be explained by the joint frequency of the single verbs in a given Cxn. The analysis of its possible theoretical implications are outside the scope of this paper, but we take this result as an additional confirmation of the goodness of our proposal.

5 Conclusion

We proposed a simple unsupervised corpus-based model that represents the meaning of a syntactic construction as the weighted centroid of the vectors encoding the distributional behavior of its prototypical verbs. Given the exploratory nature of this work, we did not explore the full parameter space of our model, an issue that follow-up studies could investigate, e.g. by comparing the alternative DSM implementations ability to model the priming effect magnitude (Ettinger and Linzen, 2016).

Our model and experimental results show that distributional semantics is able to provide a usage-based representation of the semantic content of argument constructions, which is consistent with the available evidence concerning the psycholinguistic reality of construction semantics (Bencini and Goldberg, 2000; Kaschak and Glenberg, 2000; Kako, 2006; Goldwater and Markman, 2009; Johnson and Goldberg, 2013) and how this knowledge is acquired (Goldberg, 1999; Casenhiser and Goldberg, 2005; Kidd et al., 2010). At the same time, the increment in descriptive and explanatory power obtained by moving from a simple frequency-based measurement to a more complex frequency-based approach like ours shows the importance of developing a more articulate account of the relationship between a syntactic construction and its prototypical verbs.

References

R. Harald Baayen. 2008. *Analyzing linguistic data. A Practical Introduction to Statistics Using R.* Cambridge University Press, Cambridge, UK.

Libby Barak, Afsaneh Fazly, and Suzanne Stevenson. 2013. Modeling the Emergence of an Exemplar Verb in Construction Learning. In *Proceedings of the 35th Annual Meeting of the Cognitive Science Society (CogSci 2013)*, pages 1815–1820.

Marco Baroni and Alessandro Lenci. 2010. Distributional Memory: A General Framework for Corpus-based Semantics. *Computational Linguistics*, 36(4):673–721.

Marco Baroni. 2013. Composition in Distributional Semantics. *Language and Linguistics Compass*, 7(10):511–522.

Giulia M. L. Bencini and Adele E. Goldberg. 2000. The Contribution of Argument Structure Constructions to Sentence Meaning. *Journal of Memory and Language*, 43(4):640–651.

John A. Bullinaria and Joseph P. Levy. 2007. Extracting semantic representations from word co-occurrence statistics: a computational study. *Behavior Research Methods*, 39(3):510–526, aug.

John A. Bullinaria and Joseph P. Levy. 2012. Extracting semantic representations from word co-occurrence statistics: stop-lists, stemming, and SVD. *Behavior Research Methods*, 44(3):890–907, sep.

Devin Casenhiser and Adele E. Goldberg. 2005. Fast mapping between a phrasal form and meaning. *Developmental Science*, 8(6):500–508.

Noam Chomsky. 2000. *New Horizons in the Study of Language and Mind.* Cambridge University Press, Cambridge, UK.

Kenneth W. Church and Patrick Hanks. 1991. Word Association Norms, Mutual Information, and Lexicography. *Computational Linguistics*, 16(1):22–29.

Jacob Cohen, Patricia Cohen, Stephen G. West, and Leona S. Aiken. 2003. *Applied Multiple Regression/correlation Analysis for the Behavioral Science.* Lawrence Erlbaum Associates, Mahwah, NJ, 3rd edition.

Mark Davies. 2009. The 385+ million word Corpus of Contemporary American English (1990-2008+): Design, architecture, and linguistic insights. *International Journal of Corpus Linguistics*, 14(2):159–190.

Allyson Ettinger and Tal Linzen. 2016. Evaluating vector space models using human semantic priming results. In *Proceedings of the 1st Workshop on Evaluating Vector Space Representations for NLP*, pages 72–77.

Stefan Evert. 2008. Corpora and collocations. In Anke Lüdeling and Merja Kytö, editors, *Corpus Linguistics. An International Handbook*, volume 2, pages 1212–1248. Mouton de Gruyter, Berlin, GE.

Jane Gillette, Henry Gleitman, Lila R. Gleitman, and Anne Lederer. 1999. Human simulations of vocabulary learning. *Cognition*, 73(2):135–76, dec.

Lila R. Gleitman and Gillette. 1995. The Role of Syntax in Verb Learning. In William C. Ritchie and Tej K. Bhatia, editors, *Handbook of Child Language Acquisition*, pages 279–295. Academic Press, Lndon, UK.

Adele E. Goldberg and Devin Casenhiser. 2006. English Constructions. In Bas Aarts and April McMahon, editors, *The Handbook of English Linguistics*, pages 343–355. Wiley-Blackwell, Malden, MA.

Yoav Goldberg and Jon Orwant. 2013. A Dataset of Syntactic-Ngrams over Time from a Very Large Corpus of English Books. In *Second Joint Conference on Lexical and Computational Semantics (*SEM)*, pages 241–247.

Adele E. Goldberg. 1995. *Constructions. A construction Grammar Approach to Argument Structure.* The University of Chicago Press, Chicago, IL and London, UK.

Adele E. Goldberg. 1999. The Emergence of the Semantics of Argument Structure Constructions. In B. MacWhinney, editor, *The Emergence of Language*, pages 197–212. Lawrence Erlbaum Associates, Mahwah, NJ.

Adele E. Goldberg. 2006. *Constructions at work. The nature of generalization in language.* Oxford University Press, Oxford, UK.

Micah B. Goldwater and Arthur B. Markman. 2009. Constructional Sources of Implicit Agents in Sentence Comprehension. *Cognitive Linguistics*, 20(4):675–702.

Gregory Grefenstette. 1994. *Explorations in Automatic Thesaurus Discovery*. Kluwer Academic Publishers.

Zellig S. Harris. 1954. Distributional structure. *Word*, 10:146–162.

Thomas Hoffmann and Graeme Trousdale, editors. 2013. *The Oxford Handbook of Construction Grammar*. Oxford University Press, Oxford, UK.

Matt A. Johnson and Adele E. Goldberg. 2013. Evidence for automatic accessing of constructional meaning: Jabberwocky sentences prime associated verbs. *Language and Cognitive Processes*, 28(10):1439–1452.

Edward Kako. 2006. The semantics of syntactic structures. *Language and Cognitive Processes*, 21(5):562–575.

Michael P. Kaschak and Arthur M. Glenberg. 2000. Constructing Meaning: The Role of Affordances and Grammatical Constructions in Sentence Comprehension. *Journal of Memory and Language*, 43(3):508–529.

Evan Kidd, Elena V.M. Lieven, and Michael Tomasello. 2010. Lexical frequency and exemplar-based learning effects in language acquisition: evidence from sentential complements. *Language Sciences*, 32(1):132–142.

Anna Korhonen, Yuval Krymolowski, and Ted Briscoe. 2006. A Large Subcategorization Lexicon for Natural Language Processing Applications. In *Proceedings of the 5th Edition of the Language, Resources and Evaluation Conference (LREC 2006)*, pages 1015–1020.

Barbara Landau and Lila R. Gleitman. 1985. *Language and Experience: Evidence from the Blind Child*. Harvard University Press, Cambridge, MA.

Gabriella Lapesa and Stefan Evert. 2014. A Large Scale Evaluation of Distributional Semantic Models: Parameters, Interactions and Model Selection. *Transactions of the Association for Computational Linguistics*, 2:531–545.

Alessandro Lenci. 2008. Distributional semantics in linguistic and cognitive research. A foreword. *Italian Journal of Linguistics*, 20(1):1–30.

Dekang Lin. 1998. Automatic Retrieval and Clustering of Similar Words. In *Proceedings of the 36th Annual Meeting of the Association for Computational Linguistics and 17th International Conference on Computational Linguistics (COLING - ACL 1998)*, pages 768–774.

George A. Miller and Walter G. Charles. 1991. Contextual correlates of semantic similarity. *Language and Cognitive Processes*, 6(1):1–28.

Sebastian Padó and Mirella Lapata. 2007. Dependency-Based Construction of Semantic Space Models. *Computational Linguistics*, 33(2):161–199.

Tamara Polajnar and Stephen Clark. 2014. Improving Distributional Semantic Vectors through Context Selection and Normalisation. In *Proceedings of the 14th Conference of the European Chapter of the Association for Computational Linguistics (ACL 2014)*, pages 230–238.

Magnus Sahlgren. 2006. *The word-space model: Using distributional analysis to represent syntagmatic and paradigmatic relations between words in highdimensional vector spaces*. Phd thesis, Stockholm University.

Anatol Stefanowitsch. 2013. Collostructional Analysis. In Thomas Hoffmann and Graeme Trousdale, editors, *The Oxford Handbook of Construction Grammar*, pages 290–306. Oxford University Press, Oxford, UK.

Peter D. Turney and Patrick Pantel. 2010. From Frequency to Meaning: Vector Space Models of Semantics. *Journal of Artificial Intelligence Research*, 37:141–188.

Regular polysemy: from sense vectors to sense patterns

Anastasiya Lopukhina
Neurolinguistics Laboratory,
National Research University
Higher School of Economics (HSE);
Russian Language Institute RAS
alopukhina@hse.ru

Konstantin Lopukhin
Scrapinghub
kostia.lopuhin@gmail.com

Abstract

Regular polysemy was extensively investigated in lexical semantics, but this phenomenon has been very little studied in distributional semantics. We propose a model for regular polysemy detection that is based on sense vectors and allows to work directly with senses in semantic vector space. Our method is able to detect polysemous words that have the same regular sense alternation as in a given example (a word with two automatically induced senses that represent one polysemy pattern, such as ANIMAL / FOOD). The method works equally well for nouns, verbs and adjectives and achieves an average recall of 0.55 and an average precision of 0.59 for ten different polysemy patterns.

1 Introduction

Polysemy is widely spread in natural language. Many studies in linguistics show evidence that certain word classes share polysemy patterns, which means that there are regularities in the way polysemous words vary in their meaning (Shmelyov, 1966; Lakoff and Johnson, 1980; Apresjan, 1995; Pustejovsky, 1995; Paducheva, 1998). These regularities can be explained by analogical processes like semantic shifts (*lamb* can denote either ANIMAL or FOOD), metonymy (*church* can denote either ORGANIZATION or LOCATION) and metaphor (e.g. *dirty* in contexts such as *dirty shoes* and *dirty words*). Because of its significance, regular polysemy has been extensively investigated in lexical semantics (Apresjan, 1971, 1995; Nunberg and Zaenen, 1992; Nunberg, 1995; Uryson, 2003; Zaliznyak, 2006). However, this phenomenon has been little studied in computational semantics and even less in distributional semantics. Several studies that aimed to model regular polysemy in semantic vector space were focused on word vectors. Del Tredici and Bel (2015) proposed a method, based on word embeddings and regular semantic alternations, that allows detecting polysemous nouns among all nouns and representing them in a way that accounts for asymmetry in sense predominance. Di Pietro (2013) detected sense alternations by performing word sense disambiguation using vectors of words that denoted sense domains, such as ANIMAL or FOOD. Boleda and colleagues (2012b) compare word vectors for polysemous nouns with average vectors of monosemous words in predefined sense domains. Their study relied on the CoreLex meta sense inventory that was built using WordNet. Thus, the aforementioned methods all use semantic word vectors to detect sense alternations.

For the task of regular polysemy detection, we use sense vectors and not word vectors. We believe that this is a more natural approach to the problem, because it allows us to study regular sense alternations as they are: we deal directly with senses and their location in semantic vector space. Our approach has two major advantages: first, we believe that it is less affected by sense skewness than methods based on word vectors, because vectors of different senses are distinct, even if senses have very different frequencies, while in case of word vectors, a much more frequent sense will determine the word vector, as noted by Del Tredici and Bel (2015). Second, theoretically our approach is not limited by regular alternation between just two senses, as in previous studies (Boleda et al., 2012a, 2012b; Vieu et al., 2015), but can be naturally extended to three or more senses.

Proceedings of the Workshop on Cognitive Aspects of the Lexicon,
pages 19–23, Osaka, Japan, December 11-17 2016.

The sense vectors we use in our study are built automatically on a big corpus. The technique of automatic word sense induction (WSI) allows us to represent senses as clusters of semantically similar instances. Usually, the technique does not use any external resources such as dictionaries, thesauri or sense-tagged data. WSI was successfully applied to the lexicographical task of novel sense detection, i.e. identifying words which have taken on new senses over time (Lau et al., 2012). Besides, WSI provides data for the study of diachronic variation in word senses (Bamman and Crane, 2011). Although Boleda and colleagues (2012b, p. 153) noted that automatic word sense induction could lead to more flexible and realistic models of regular polysemy, to the best of our knowledge, the WSI technique was not used in any previous research of this type.

In this study, we propose a model for regular polysemy detection that is based on sense vectors and allows us to work directly with senses in semantic vector space. We performed an experiment on Russian nouns, verbs and adjectives and subsequently discuss the limitations of our method.

2   Method

The core of our method can be described as follows: in semantic vector space we take two senses of a word (s_a and s_b; with predefined regular alternations such as ANIMAL / FOOD) and search for similar pairs (s_i, s_j) of another word, where s_a is close to s_i and s_b is close to s_j. This approach is very similar to how regular polysemy is defined in (Apresjan, 1995, p. 189). To be more precise, given word w and its senses s_a and s_b, and another candidate pair of senses (s_i, s_j) for word w_k, we define their pattern similarity measure $PatternSim$ as:

$$PatternSim((w, s_a, s_b), (w_k, s_i, s_j)) = \min(sim((w, s_a), (w_k, s_i)), sim((w, s_b), (w_k, s_j))) \quad (1)$$

where sim is a cosine similarity measure between sense vectors, and (w, s) is a sense vector. Using this similarity measure between pairs of senses, we take the top N_{lim} of all possible candidate pairs having similarity above threshold δ, where N_{lim} and δ are hyperparameters of the method.

Sense vectors are produced by the adaptive Skip-gram model AdaGram, which is a non-parametric extension of Skip-gram word2vec model to word senses. It automatically learns the required number of representations for all words at a desired semantic resolution (Bartunov et al., 2015). It is able to learn a dense vector embedding for each sense of a word, where the number of senses is determined using a constructive definition of the Dirichlet process via the stick-breaking representation. AdaGram has an efficient online learning algorithm and was evaluated on word sense induction tasks of SemEval-2007 and 2010 (Bartunov et al., 2015, pp. 8-9). Hyperparameter α controls granularity of produced senses, and other hyperparameters, such as vector dimension and window size, have the same role as in word2vec algorithm. Sense vectors produced by AdaGram can be represented as words that are nearest neighbors (e.g. *Monty, Perl, Molurus* for different senses of the word *python*) or by context words with the highest PMI.

In (Lopukhina and Lopukhin, 2016) a qualitative and quantitative evaluation of several WSI methods, including AdaGram, was performed on 15 Russian nouns. Other methods included LDA, context clustering, clustering of word2vec neighbors. For the quantitative evaluation, the authors measured similarity of suggested clustering to the existing dictionary senses with Adjusted Rand Index (ARI) and V-measure scores. For the qualitative evaluation, they assessed the interpretability of the derived senses, the number of duplicate senses, the number of mixed senses and derivation of rare senses. Trained on a 2 billion word Russian corpus with $\alpha = 0.15$, AdaGram discovered the largest number of senses, and was a close second in both ARI and V-measure. Compared to context clustering, which was first in the quantitative evaluation, AdaGram is much more efficient and was able to discover even rare senses.

3   Experiment

We aimed to study how well the proposed technique detects polysemous words that have the same regular sense alternation as in a given example. An example is a word with two automatically induced senses that represent one polysemy pattern (such as ANIMAL / FOOD). We manually selected ten polysemy patterns: four for nouns, three for verbs and three for adjectives, nine of them from the most famous and reliable description of regular polysemy for Russian, *Lexical Semantics* by Jury Apresjan (1995), in which he thoroughly classifies and illustrates more than 80 productive and non-productive regular polysemy types for the aforementioned parts of speech. We also took one polysemy pattern for verbs from an ongoing work led by Valentina Apresjan (2016). Besides, we checked that word senses, which were part of the polysemy pattern in question, were presented in the corpus and were thus detected by the AdaGram model (e.g. *zheleznyj* 'iron': *iron gates* is sense #3 in AdaGram / *iron will* is sense #4 in AdaGram).

Polysemy patterns for nouns:
ANIMAL / FOOD (e.g. *gus'* 'goose');
AMOUNT / CONTAINER (e.g. *butylka* 'bottle');
ACTION / RESULT (e.g. *ushyb* 'injury' / 'bruise');
MUSIC / DANCE (e.g. *val's* 'waltz ').

Polysemy patterns for verbs:
AUTONOMOUS RELOCATION / NONAUTONOMOUS RELOCATION (e.g. *jehat'* 'to move (about a car)' / 'to drive (a car)');
PRODUCE SOUND / SPEAK (e.g. *blejat'* 'to bleat');
CEASE TO EXIST / RUN OUT OF INNER RESOURCE (e.g. *tajat'* 'to melt' / 'to melt away').

Polysemy patterns for adjectives:
MADE OF SOME MATERIAL / MAKING A SIMILAR IMPRESSION (e.g. *derevjannyj* 'wooden');
SURFACE PROPERTY / HUMAN PROPERTY (e.g. *nezhnyi* 'delicate');
HAVING SOME TASTE / MAKING A SIMILAR IMPRESSION (e.g. *kislyj* 'sour').

Then, for each pattern we selected 4-7 examples that were used for evaluation. All the examples were extracted from *Lexical Semantics* (1995) or from (Apresjan, 2016). We were guided by the following principle: Words should be semantically similar, namely synonyms, antonyms or co-hyponyms. In the study by Jury Apresjan (1995), polysemy patterns such as ACTION / RESULT embrace a large number of semantically very different words from *ushyb* 'injury' / 'bruise' to *risunok* 'drawing' and *ispravleniye* 'correction'. For the purpose of the present study, we chose words from one semantic domain (e.g. *ushyb* 'injury' / 'bruise'; *ukus* 'bite' / 'wound'; *perelom* 'breaking of a bone' / 'fracture'; *porez* 'cut', words denoting different injuries and their result on/in the human body).

The experimental setup was as follows: Sense vectors were built using AdaGram with $\alpha = 0.10$, window size 5, vector dimension 300, maximum number of senses 10 and minimal token frequency 100. Corpus used for training contained about 2 billion tokens and was a combination of ruWac (a representative snapshot of the Russian Web), lib.ru (a Russian online library) and Russian Wikipedia. Corpus was lemmatized with Mystem 3, lowercased and cleared of punctuation.

4 Evaluation

In order to study how well our method is able to detect word sense alternations, we evaluated recall and precision in two separate experiments. In both cases, two words were selected from each polysemous pattern group as "anchor" words, while other words of the group were treated as "target" words. Each of the anchor words (with its two senses) was given as input to the method, thus defining a sense alternation by an example.

In the recall evaluation we checked how many of the target words were actually produced, given the anchor word. Recall was evaluated with two different limits on the number of detected words N_{lim}, 5 and 50. Note that we did not expect a high recall with $N_{lim} = 5$, as we believe that there can be other words besides target words that have the same alternation. Another reason is that there were sometimes more than 5 target words in the group, therefore it was impossible to achieve perfect recall with just $N_{lim} = 5$. Different parts of speech did not show significant variation of recall. The average recall for ten groups was **0.22** for $N_{lim} = 5$ and **0.55** for $N_{lim} = 50$.

In order to evaluate precision, we took anchor words and for each of them extracted the top five candidates ($N_{lim} = 5$) that were produced by our method. These candidates were checked by a lexicographer:

if a candidate shared the same polysemy pattern with the anchor word, it was accepted. The average precision for ten groups was **0.59**, with three groups having perfect precision. In most cases, words that were rejected were semantically similar to the anchor word, but they did not exhibit the polysemy pattern in focus. For example, wrong candidates for the word *ukus* 'bite' / 'wound' were *snake, insect* and *mosquito*, which can be subjects of the action; wrong candidates for the word *stakan* 'glass' were *tea* and *coffee*, which denote the content; and wrong candidates for the word *kislyj* 'sour' were *garlicky* and *fried*, which mean HAVING SOME TASTE, but do not exhibit the meaning MAKING SIMILAR IMPRESSION.

5 Discussion

The method for detecting words of a predefined polysemy pattern showed promising results in both precision and recall. The method allows obtaining words with the same sense alternations, given one example directly from the corpus, and works equally well for nouns, verbs and adjectives. However, the method we propose has limitations that can be explained by the nature of the method and the way distributional models are built.

One of these limitations is that some senses of words that are a part of a polysemy pattern can hardly be distinguished by means of the distributional model and are not clearly represented in a vector space model. For example, many verbs, as described in *Lexical Semantics* (1995), have a 'causation' component in one of their meanings, e. g. *lit'* 'to pour' in contexts such as *He poured the last of the water down the sink* and *The water pours from the tap*. These two senses can be distinguished syntactically or by taking word order into account, but this cannot be achieved by our proposed model. Some verbs differ in the properties of the objects they attach, e. g. *varit'* 'to cook' in contexts like *to cook potatoes* (potato changes its properties) and *to cook soup* (soup appears); this difference cannot be captured by our model. The problem of sense discrimination by context is most evident for verbs.

Another limitation is caused by the difference between the notion of "regular polysemy" in theoretical studies and in its computational implementation. Lexicologists formulate sense alternation principles in a very general sense and thus, semantically different words may have the same polysemy pattern, e.g. adjectives *gornyj* 'alpine' in contexts such as *alpine range* and *alpine ski*, *glaznoj* 'ocular' / 'eye' in contexts such as *ocular fundus* and *eye drops*, and *krysinyj* 'rat' in contexts such as *rat tail* and *rat poison* share the same pattern RELATING TO SMTH / DESIGNED FOR SMTH. Semantically different words cannot be detected with distributional models because they appear in different contexts, which means that the method we propose is limited by synonyms, antonyms and co-hyponyms.

We believe that our model for regular polysemy can also be applied to an unsupervised discovery of patterns. The $PatternSim$ measure defined above (eq. 1) can be used to cluster all pairs of a particular part of speech, hence each cluster will represent a distinct regular polysemy pattern. Another possible extension is to change $PatternSim$ in a way that will account for the direction of a vector between two senses. Given two senses s_a and s_b of word w and another pair of senses s_i and s_j of word w_k, we believe that these two pairs of senses will be more similar if vectors $s_a - s_i$ and $s_b - s_j$ have similar directions.

6 Conclusion

In this study, we describe an approach to the automatic detection of regular sense alternations from the corpus given an example. Our approach is based on sense vectors and gives the opportunity to deal with senses directly. It allows finding semantically similar words that share the same polysemy patterns. It works equally well for nouns, verbs and adjectives and achieves an average recall of 0.55 and average precision of 0.59 for ten different polysemy patterns.

Our model uses sense vectors that are produced with the AdaGram method and, being a distributional model, does not fully cover all types of regular alternations that are described in the theoretical literature; it is only applicable to sense alternations in semantically similar words.

The method we describe can be useful for theoretical studies of regular polysemy and for lexicographers. It is available online at `http://adagram.ll-cl.org/about`.

Acknowledgements

This research was supported by RSF (project no.16-18-02054: "Semantic, statistic, and psycholinguistic analysis of lexical polysemy as a component of a Russian linguistic worldview"). We thank the anonymous reviewers for their comments on the manuscript and valuable suggestions.

References

Apresjan, Jury D. 1971. Regular polysemy. *Proceedings of the Academy of Sciences of the USSR. Department of Literature and Language.* Vol. 30, Moscow. pp. 509-523.

Apresjan, Jury D. 1995. *Lexical Semantics. Selected works.* Volume I, Moscow.

Apresjan, Valentina Ju, 2016. Ischeznut' 'to disappear' and propast' 'to vanish': polysemy and semantic motivation. *Computational Linguistics and Intellectual Technologies: Proceedings of the International Conference "Dialog 2016"*, pp. 16-28, Moscow.

Bamman, David and Gregory Crane. 2011. Measuring historical word sense variation. *Proceedings of the 2011 Joint International Conference on Digital Libraries (JCDL 2011)*, pp. 1-10, Ottawa, Canada.

Bartunov, Sergey, Dmitry Kondrashkin, Anton Osokin, and Dmitry Vetrov. 2015. Breaking sticks and ambiguities with adaptive skip-gram. Accessed September 17, 2016. https://arxiv.org/abs/1502.07257.

Boleda, Gemma, Sabine Schulte im Walde, and Toni Badia. 2012a. Modeling regular polysemy: A study of the semantic classification of Catalan adjectives. *Computational Linguistics* 38:3, pp. 575-616.

Boleda, Gemma, Sebastian Padó, and Jason Utt. 2012b. Regular polysemy: a distributional model. *First Joint Conference on Lexical and Computational Semantics* (*SEM), pp. 151-160, Montral, Canada.

Del Tredici, Marco and Núria Bel. 2015. A Word-Embedding-based Sense Index for Regular Polysemy Representation. *Proceedings of NAACL-HLT*, pp. 70-78.

Di Pietro, Giulia. 2013. *Regular polysemy: A distributional semantic approach.* (2013). Master thesis, Universit`a di Pisa.

Lakoff, George and Mark Johnson. 1980. *Metaphors We Live By.* University of Chicago Press.

Lau, Jey Han, Paul Cook, Diana McCarthy, David Newman, and Timothy Baldwin. 2012. Word sense induction for novel sense detection. *In Proceedings of the 13th Conference of the European Chapter of the Association for Computational Linguistics*, pp. 591-601. Association for Computational Linguistics.

Lopukhina, Anastasiya and Konstantin Lopukhin. 2016. Word sense induction methods: which one is better for Russian. Accessed October 1, 2016. https://www.academia.edu/26080939/Word_Sense_Induction_Methods_Which_One_Is_Better_for_Russian.

Nunberg, Geoff and Annie Zaenen. 1992. Systematic polysemy in lexicology and lexicography. *Proceedings of Euralex II*, pp. 387-395, Tampere, Finland.

Nunberg, Geoff. 1995. Transfers of meaning. *Journal of Semantics*, 12(2), pp. 109-132.

Paducheva, Elena V. 1998. Paradigms of semantic derivation for Russian verbs of sound. *Proceedings of Euralex VIII*, v. 1, pp. 231-238, Liège, Belgium.

Pustejovsky, James. 1995. *The Generative Lexicon.* The MIT Press, Cambridge, MA.

Shmelyov, Dmitrij N. 1966. On the analysis of word semantic structure. *Zeichen und System der Sprache.* Bd. 3. Berlin.

Uryson, Elena V. 2003. *Problems in linguistic worldview studies: Analogy in semantics.* Languages of Slavic Cultures, Moscow.

Vieu, Laure, Elisabetta Jezek, and Tim Van de Cruys. 2015. Quantitative methods for identifying systematic polysemy classes. *Proceedings of the 6th Conference on Quantitative Investigations in Theoretical Linguistics.* Tubingen.

Zaliznyak, Anna A. 2006. *Ambiguity in language and methods for its presentation.* Languages of Slavic Cultures, Moscow.

Path-based vs. Distributional Information
in Recognizing Lexical Semantic Relations

Vered Shwartz   **Ido Dagan**
Computer Science Department, Bar-Ilan University, Ramat-Gan, Israel
vered1986@gmail.com   dagan@cs.biu.ac.il

Abstract

Recognizing various semantic relations between terms is beneficial for many NLP tasks. While path-based and distributional information sources are considered complementary for this task, the superior results the latter showed recently suggested that the former's contribution might have become obsolete. We follow the recent success of an integrated neural method for hypernymy detection (Shwartz et al., 2016) and extend it to recognize multiple relations. The empirical results show that this method is effective in the multiclass setting as well. We further show that the path-based information source always contributes to the classification, and analyze the cases in which it mostly complements the distributional information.

1 Introduction

Automated methods to recognize the lexical semantic relation the holds between terms are valuable for NLP applications. Two main information sources are used to recognize such relations: path-based and distributional. Path-based methods consider the *joint* occurrences of the two terms in a given pair in the corpus, where the dependency paths that connect the terms are typically used as features (A. Hearst, 1992; Snow et al., 2004; Nakashole et al., 2012; Riedel et al., 2013). Distributional methods are based on the *disjoint* occurrences of each term and have recently become popular using word embeddings (Mikolov et al., 2013; Pennington et al., 2014), which provide a distributional representation for each term. These embedding-based methods were reported to perform well on several common datasets (Baroni et al., 2012; Roller et al., 2014), consistently outperforming other methods (Santus et al., 2016; Necsulescu et al., 2015).

While these two sources have been considered complementary, recent results suggested that path-based methods have no marginal contribution over the distributional ones. Recently, however, Shwartz et al. (2016) presented HypeNET, an integrated path-based and distributional method for hypernymy detection. They showed that a good path representation can provide substantial complementary information to the distributional signal in hypernymy detection, notably improving results on a new dataset.

In this paper we present LexNET, an extension of HypeNET that recognizes *multiple* semantic relations. We show that this integrated method is indeed effective also in the multiclass setting. In the evaluations reported in this paper, LexNET performed better than each individual method on several common datasets. Further, it was the best performing system in the semantic relation classification task of the CogALex 2016 shared task (Shwartz and Dagan, 2016).

We further assess the contribution of path-based information to semantic relation classification. Even though the distributional source is dominant across most datasets, path-based information always contributed to it. In particular, path-based information seems to better capture the relationship between terms, rather than their individual properties, and can do so even for rare words or senses. Our code and data are available at https://github.com/vered1986/LexNET.

Proceedings of the Workshop on Cognitive Aspects of the Lexicon,
pages 24–29, Osaka, Japan, December 11-17 2016.

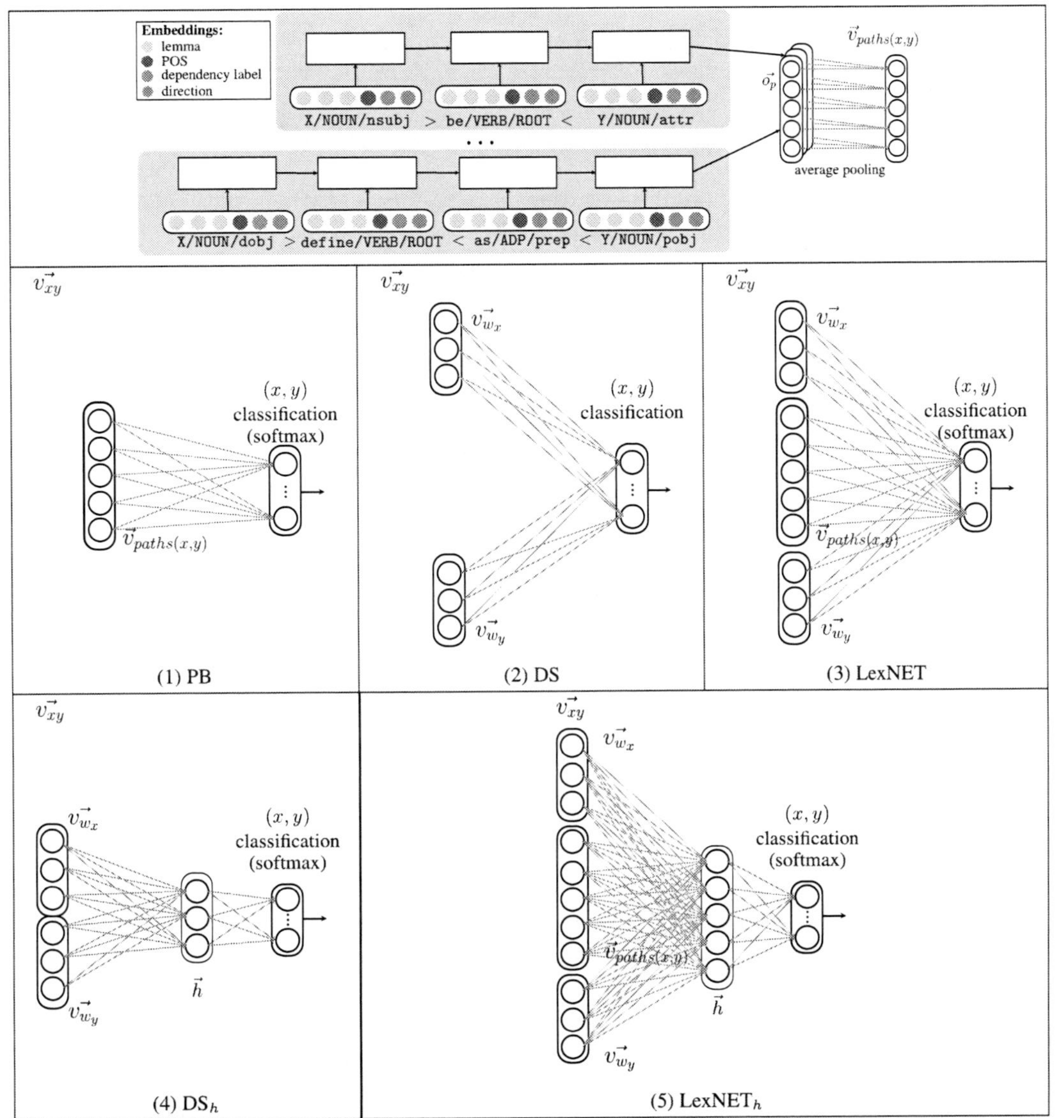

Figure 1: Illustrations of classification models. Top row: path-based component. A path is a sequence of edges, and each edge consists of four components: lemma, POS, dependency label and direction. Edge vectors are fed in sequence into the LSTM, resulting in an embedding vector $\vec{o_p}$ for each path. $\vec{v}_{paths(x,y)}$ is the average of (x,y)'s path embeddings.

2   Background: HypeNET

Recently, Shwartz et al. (2016) introduced HypeNET, a hypernymy detection method based on the integration of the best-performing distributional method with a novel neural path representation, improving upon state-of-the-art methods. In HypeNET, a term-pair (x, y) is represented as a feature vector, consisting of both distributional and path-based features: $\vec{v}_{xy} = [\vec{v}_{w_x}, \vec{v}_{paths(x,y)}, \vec{v}_{w_y}]$, where $\vec{v}_{w_x}$ and $\vec{v}_{w_y}$ are x and y's word embeddings, providing their distributional representation, and $\vec{v}_{paths(x,y)}$ is a vector representing the dependency paths connecting x and y in the corpus. A binary classifier is trained on these vectors, yielding $c = \mathrm{softmax}(W \cdot \vec{v}_{xy})$, predicting hypernymy if $c[1] > 0.5$.

Each dependency path is embedded using an LSTM (Hochreiter and Schmidhuber, 1997), as illustrated in the top row of Figure 1. This results in a path vector space in which semantically-similar paths (e.g. *X is defined as Y* and *X is described as Y*) have similar vectors. The vectors of all the paths that connect x and y are averaged to create $\vec{v}_{paths(x,y)}$.

dataset	dataset relations	#instances
K&H+N	hypernym, meroynym, co-hyponym, random	57,509
BLESS	hypernym, meroynym, co-hyponym, , event, attribute, random	26,546
ROOT09	hypernym, co-hyponym, random	12,762
EVALution	hypernym, meronym, attribute, synonym, antonym, holonym, substance meronym	7,378

Table 1: The relation types and number of instances in each dataset, named by their WordNet equivalent where relevant.

Shwartz et al. (2016) showed that this new path representation outperforms prior path-based methods for hypernymy detection, and that the integrated model yields a substantial improvement over each individual model. While HypeNET is designed for detecting hypernymy relations, it seems straightforward to extend it to classify term-pairs simultaneously to multiple semantic relations, as we describe next.

3 Classification Methods

We experiment with several classification models, as illustrated in Figure 1:

Path-based HypeNET's path-based model (PB) is a binary classifier trained on the path vectors alone: $\vec{v}_{paths(x,y)}$. We adapt the model to classify multiple relations by changing the network softmax output c to a distribution over k target relations, classifying a pair to the highest scoring relation: $r = \text{argmax}_i c[i]$.

Distributional We train an SVM classifier on the concatenation of x and y's word embeddings $[\vec{v}_{w_x}, \vec{v}_{w_y}]$ (Baroni et al., 2012) (DS).[1] Levy et al. (2015) claimed that such a linear classifier is incapable of capturing interactions between x and y's features, and that instead it learns separate properties of x or y, e.g. that y is a *prototypical hypernym*. To examine the effect of non-linear expressive power on the model, we experiment with a neural network with a single hidden layer trained on $[\vec{v}_{w_x}, \vec{v}_{w_y}]$ (DS$_h$).[2]

Integrated We similarly adapt the HypeNET integrated model to classify multiple semantic relations (LexNET). Based on the same motivation of DS$_h$, we also experiment with a version of the network with a hidden layer (LexNET$_h$), re-defining $c = \text{softmax}(W_2 \cdot \vec{h} + b_2)$, where $\vec{h} = \tanh(W_1 \cdot \vec{v}_{xy} + b_1)$ is the hidden layer. The technical details of our network are identical to Shwartz et al. (2016).

4 Datasets

We use four common semantic relation datasets that were created using semantic resources: K&H+N (Necsulescu et al., 2015) (an extension to Kozareva and Hovy (2010)), BLESS (Baroni and Lenci, 2011), EVALution (Santus et al., 2015), and ROOT09 (Santus et al., 2016).

Table 1 displays the relation types and number of instances in each dataset. Most dataset relations are parallel to WordNet relations, such as hypernymy (*cat, animal*) and meronymy (*hand, body*), with an additional *random* relation for negative instances. BLESS contains the *event* and *attribute* relations, connecting a concept with a typical activity/property (e.g. *(alligator, swim)* and *(alligator, aquatic)*). EVALution contains a richer schema of semantic relations, with some redundancy: it contains both meronymy and holonymy (e.g. for *bicycle* and *wheel*), and the fine-grained substance-holonymy relation. We removed two relations with too few instances: *Entails* and *MemberOf*.

To prevent the lexical memorization effect (Levy et al., 2015), Santus et al. (2016) added negative switched hyponym-hypernym pairs (e.g. *(apple, animal)*, *(cat, fruit)*) to ROOT09, which were reported to reduce this effect.

5 Results

Like Shwartz et al. (2016), we tuned the methods' hyper-parameters on the validation set of each dataset, and used Wikipedia as the corpus. Table 2 displays the performance of the different methods on all datasets, in terms of recall, precision and F_1.[3]

Our first empirical finding is that Shwartz et al.'s (2016) algorithm is effective in the multiclass setting as well (LexNET). The only dataset on which performance is mediocre is EVALution, which seems to be

---

[1] We experimented also with difference $\vec{v}_{w_x} - \vec{v}_{w_y}$ and other classifiers, but concatenation yielded the best performance.

[2] This was previously done by Bowman et al. (2014), with promising results, but on a small artificial vocabulary.

[3] Additional evaluation of the method is available in our CogALex 2016 shared task submission (Shwartz and Dagan, 2016).

	K&H+N			BLESS			ROOT09			EVALution		
method	P	R	F_1	P	R	F_1	P	R	F_1	P	R	F_1
PB	0.713	0.604	0.55	0.759	0.756	0.755	0.788	0.789	0.788	0.53	0.537	0.503
DS	0.909	0.906	0.904	0.811	0.812	0.811	0.636	0.675	0.646	0.531	0.544	0.525
DS_h	0.983	0.984	0.983	0.891	0.889	0.889	0.712	0.721	0.716	0.57	0.573	0.571
LexNET	0.985	0.986	0.985	0.894	**0.893**	**0.893**	**0.813**	0.814	0.813	**0.601**	**0.607**	**0.6**
$LexNET_h$	0.984	0.985	0.984	**0.895**	0.892	**0.893**	0.812	**0.816**	**0.814**	0.589	0.587	0.583

Table 2: Performance scores (precision, recall and F_1) of each individual approach and the integrated models. To compute the metrics we used scikit-learn (Pedregosa et al., 2011) with the "averaged" setup, which computes the metrics for each relation, and reports their average, weighted by support (the number of true instances for each relation). Note that it can result in an F_1 score that is not the harmonic mean of precision and recall.

dataset	#pairs	x	y	gold label	DS_h prediction	possible explanation
K&H+N	102	firefly	car	false	hypo	*(x, car)* frequent label is hypo
		racehorse	horse	hypo	false	out of the embeddings vocabulary
		larvacean	salp	sibl	false	rare terms *larvacean* and *salp*
BLESS	275	tanker	ship	hyper	event	*(x, ship)* frequent label is event
		squirrel	lie	random	event	*(x, lie)* frequent label is event
		herring	salt	event	random	non-prototypical relation
ROOT09	562	toaster	vehicle	RANDOM	HYPER	*(x, vehicle)* frequent label is HYPER
		rice	grain	HYPER	RANDOM	*(x, grain)* frequent label is RANDOM
		lung	organ	HYPER	COORD	polysemous term *organ*
EVALution	235	pick	metal	MadeOf	IsA	rare sense of *pick*
		abstract	concrete	Antonym	MadeOf	polysemous term *concrete*
		line	thread	Synonym	MadeOf	*(x, thread)* frequent label is MadeOf

Table 3: The number of term-pairs that were correctly classified by the integrated model while being incorrectly classified by DS_h, in each test set, with corresponding examples of such term-pairs.

inherently harder for all methods, due to its large number of relations and small size. The performance differences between LexNET and DS are statistically significant on all datasets with p-value of 0.01 (paired t-test). The performance differences between LexNET and DS_h are statistically significant on BLESS and ROOT09 with p-value of 0.01, and on EVALution with p-value of 0.05.

DS_h consistently improves upon DS. The hidden layer seems to enable interactions between x and y's features, which is especially noticed in ROOT09, where the hypernymy F_1 score in particular rose from 0.25 to 0.45. Nevertheless, we did not observe a similar behavior in $LexNET_h$, which worked similarly or slightly worse than LexNET. It is possible that the contributions of the hidden layer and the path-based source over the distributional signal are redundant.[4] It may also be that the larger number of parameters in $LexNET_h$ prevents convergence to the optimal values given the modest amount of training data, stressing the need for large-scale datasets that will benefit training neural methods.

6 Analysis

Table 2 demonstrates that the distributional source is dominant across most datasets, with DS performing better than PB. Although by design DS does not consider the relation between x and y, but rather learns properties of x or y, it performs well on BLESS and K&H+N. DS_h further manages to capture relations at the distributional level, leaving the path-based source little room for improvement on these two datasets.

On ROOT09, on the other hand, DS achieved the lowest performance. Our analysis reveals that this is due to the switched hypernym pairs, which drastically hurt the ability to memorize individual single words, hence reducing performance. The F_1 scores of DS on this dataset were 0.91 for co-hyponyms but only 0.25 for hypernyms, while PB scored 0.87 and 0.66 respectively. Moreover, LexNET gains 10 points over DS_h, suggesting the better capacity of path-based methods to capture relations between terms.

6.1 Analysis of Information Sources

To analyze the contribution of the path-based information source, we examined the term-pairs that were correctly classified by the best performing integrated model (LexNET/$LexNET_h$) while being incorrectly classified by DS_h. Table 3 displays the number of such pairs in each dataset, with corresponding term-pair examples. The common errors are detailed below:

---

[4] We also tried adding a hidden layer only over the distributional features of LexNET, but it did not improve performance.

Lexical Memorization   DS$_h$ often classifies (x, y) term-pairs according to the most frequent relation of one of the terms (usually y) in the train set. The error is mostly prominent in ROOT09 (405/562 pairs, 72%), as a result of the switched hypernym pairs. However, it is not infrequent in other datasets (47% in BLESS, 43% in EVALution and 34% in K&H+N). As opposed to distributional information, path-based information pertains to both terms in the pair. With such information available, the integrated model succeeds to overcome the most frequent label bias for single words, classifying these pairs correctly.

Non-prototypical Relations   DS$_h$ might fail to recognize non-prototypical relations between terms, i.e. when y is a less-prototypical relatum of x, as in *mero:(villa, guest)*, *event:(cherry, pick)*, and *attri:(piano, electric)*. While being overlooked by the distributional methods, these relations are often expressed in joint occurrences in the corpus, allowing the path-based component to capture them.

Rare Terms   The integrated method often managed to classify term-pairs in which at least one of the terms is rare (e.g. *hyper:(mastodon, proboscidean)*), where the distributional method failed. It is a well known shortcoming of path-based methods that they require informative co-occurrences of x and y, which are not always available. With that said, thanks to the averaged path representation, PB can capture the relation between terms even if they only co-occur once within an informative path, while the distributional representation of rare terms is of lower quality. We note that the path-based information of (x, y) is encoded in the vector $\vec{v}_{paths(x,y)}$, which is the averaged vector representation of all paths that connected x and y in the corpus. Unlike other path-based methods in the literature, this representation is indifferent to the total number of paths, and as a result, even a single informative path can lead to successful classification.

Rare Senses   Similarly, the path-based component succeeded to capture relations for rare senses of words where DS$_h$ failed, e.g. *mero:(piano, key)*, *event:(table, draw)*. Distributional representations suffer from insufficient representation of rare senses, while PB may capture the relation with a single meaningful occurrence of the rare sense with its related term. At the same time, it is less likely for a polysemous term to co-occur, in its non-related senses, with the candidate relatum. For instance, paths connecting *piano* to *key* are likely to correspond to the keyboard sense of *key*, indicating the relation that does hold for this pair with respect to this rare sense.

Finally, we note that LexNET, as well as the individual methods, perform poorly on synonyms and antonyms. The synonymy F_1 score in EVALution was 0.35 in LexNET and in DS$_h$ and only 0.09 in PB, reassessing prior findings (Mirkin et al., 2006) that the path-based approach is weak in recognizing synonyms, which do not tend to co-occur. DS$_h$ performed poorly also on antonyms ($F_1 = 0.54$), which were often mistaken for synonyms, since both tend to occur in the same contexts. It seems worthwhile to try improving the model using insights from prior work on these specific relations (Santus et al., 2014; Mohammad et al., 2013) or additional information sources, like multilingual data (Pavlick et al., 2015).

7   Conclusion

We presented an adaptation to HypeNET (Shwartz et al., 2016) that classifies term-pairs to one of multiple semantic relations. Evaluation on common datasets shows that HypeNET is extensible to the multi-class setting and performs better than each individual method.

Although the distributional information source is dominant across most datasets, it consistently benefits from path-based information, particularly when finer modeling of inter-term relationship is needed.

Finally, we note that all common datasets were created synthetically using semantic resources, leading to inconsistent behavior of the different methods, depending on the particular distribution of examples in each dataset. This stresses the need to develop "naturally" distributed datasets that would be drawn from corpora, while reflecting realistic distributions encountered by semantic applications.

Acknowledgments

This work was partially supported by an Intel ICRI-CI grant, the Israel Science Foundation grant 880/12, and the German Research Foundation through the German-Israeli Project Cooperation (DIP, grant DA 1600/1-1).

References

Marti A. Hearst. 1992. Automatic acquisition of hyponyms from large text corpora. In *COLING 1992 Volume 2: The 15th International Conference on Computational Linguistics*.

Marco Baroni and Alessandro Lenci. 2011. Proceedings of the gems 2011 workshop on geometrical models of natural language semantics. pages 1–10.

Marco Baroni, Raffaella Bernardi, Ngoc-Quynh Do, and Chung-chieh Shan. 2012. Entailment above the word level in distributional semantics. In *Proceedings of EACL 2012*, pages 23–32.

Samuel R Bowman, Christopher Potts, and Christopher D Manning. 2014. Learning distributed word representations for natural logic reasoning. *AAAI*.

Sepp Hochreiter and Jürgen Schmidhuber. 1997. Long short-term memory. *Neural computation*, 9(8):1735–1780.

Zornitsa Kozareva and Eduard Hovy. 2010. A semi-supervised method to learn and construct taxonomies using the web. In *Proceedings of EMNLP 2010*, pages 1110–1118.

Omer Levy, Steffen Remus, Chris Biemann, and Ido Dagan. 2015. Do supervised distributional methods really learn lexical inference relations? In *Proceedings of NAACL-HLT 2015*, pages 970–976.

Tomas Mikolov, Ilya Sutskever, Kai Chen, Gregory S Corrado, and Jeffrey Dean. 2013. Distributed representations of words and phrases and their compositionality. In *NIPS*, pages 3111–3119.

Shachar Mirkin, Ido Dagan, and Maayan Geffet. 2006. Integrating pattern-based and distributional similarity methods for lexical entailment acquisition. In *Proceedings of COLING/ACL 2006*, pages 579–586.

Saif M Mohammad, Bonnie J Dorr, Graeme Hirst, and Peter D Turney. 2013. Computing lexical contrast. *Computational Linguistics*, 39(3):555–590.

Ndapandula Nakashole, Gerhard Weikum, and Fabian Suchanek. 2012. Patty: A taxonomy of relational patterns with semantic types. In *Proceedings of the 2012 Joint Conference EMNLP and CoNLL*, pages 1135–1145.

Silvia Necsulescu, Sara Mendes, David Jurgens, Núria Bel, and Roberto Navigli. 2015. Reading between the lines: Overcoming data sparsity for accurate classification of lexical relationships. In *Proceedings of *SEM 2015*, pages 182–192.

Ellie Pavlick, Johan Bos, Malvina Nissim, Charley Beller, Benjamin Van Durme, and Chris Callison-Burch. 2015. Adding semantics to data-driven paraphrasing. In *Proceedings of ACL 2015 (Volume 1: Long Papers)*, pages 1512–1522.

F. Pedregosa, G. Varoquaux, A. Gramfort, V. Michel, B. Thirion, O. Grisel, M. Blondel, P. Prettenhofer, R. Weiss, V. Dubourg, J. Vanderplas, A. Passos, D. Cournapeau, M. Brucher, M. Perrot, and E. Duchesnay. 2011. Scikit-learn: Machine learning in Python. *Journal of Machine Learning Research*, 12:2825–2830.

Jeffrey Pennington, Richard Socher, and Christopher Manning. 2014. Glove: Global vectors for word representation. In *Proceedings of EMNLP 2014*, pages 1532–1543.

Sebastian Riedel, Limin Yao, Andrew McCallum, and M. Benjamin Marlin. 2013. Relation extraction with matrix factorization and universal schemas. In *Proceedings of NAACL-HLT 2013*, pages 74–84.

Stephen Roller, Katrin Erk, and Gemma Boleda. 2014. Inclusive yet selective: Supervised distributional hypernymy detection. In *Proceedings of COLING 2014*, pages 1025–1036.

Enrico Santus, Qin Lu, Alessandro Lenci, and Churen Huang. 2014. Unsupervised antonym-synonym discrimination in vector space.

Enrico Santus, Frances Yung, Alessandro Lenci, and Chu-Ren Huang. 2015. Proceedings of the 4th workshop on linked data in linguistics: Resources and applications. pages 64–69.

Enrico Santus, Alessandro Lenci, Tin-Shing Chiu, Qin Lu, and Chu-Ren Huang. 2016. Nine features in a random forest to learn taxonomical semantic relations. In *LREC*.

Vered Shwartz and Ido Dagan. 2016. Cogalex-v shared task: Lexnet - integrated path-based and distributional method for the identification of semantic relations. In *Proceedings of the 5th Workshop on Cognitive Aspects of the Lexicon (CogALex-V)*.

Vered Shwartz, Yoav Goldberg, and Ido Dagan. 2016. Improving hypernymy detection with an integrated path-based and distributional method. In *Proceedings of ACL 2016 (Volume 1: Long Papers)*, pages 2389–2398.

Rion Snow, Daniel Jurafsky, and Andrew Y Ng. 2004. Learning syntactic patterns for automatic hypernym discovery. In *NIPS*.

Semantic Relation Classification: Task Formalisation and Refinement

**Vivian S. Silva[1], Manuela Hürliman[2], Brian Davis[2],
Siegfried Handschuh[1] and André Freitas[1]**
[1]Department of Computer Science and Mathematics, University of Passau, Passau, Germany
[2] Insight Centre for Data Analytics, National University of Ireland, Galway, Ireland
{vivian.santossilva, siegfried.handschuh, andre.freitas}@uni-passau.de
{manuela.huerlimann, brian.davis}@insight-centre.org

Abstract

The identification of semantic relations between terms within texts is a fundamental task in Natural Language Processing which can support applications requiring a lightweight semantic interpretation model. Currently, semantic relation classification concentrates on relations which are evaluated over open-domain data. This work provides a critique on the set of abstract relations used for semantic relation classification with regard to their ability to express relationships between terms which are found in a domain-specific corpora. Based on this analysis, this work proposes an alternative semantic relation model based on reusing and extending the set of abstract relations present in the DOLCE ontology. The resulting set of relations is well grounded, allows to capture a wide range of relations and could thus be used as a foundation for automatic classification of semantic relations.

1 Introduction

The identification of abstract semantic relations between terms in text has emerged as a Natural Language Processing technique which is useful in a variety of tasks that depend on the extraction of key semantic relations from text. In essence, the task of semantic relation classification (SRC) consists in identifying common abstract relations such as causal, hypernymic and meronymic as relationships between terms in the text.

This definition puts semantic relation classification in the context of ontology extraction from text, where the emphasis is on the process of extracting more general and abstract relations, in contrast to more domain-specific relations.

However, despite the obvious intuition around the utility of the task, the justification on the scoping of the semantic relations set and their expressive coverage has not been fully grounded with regard to an ontological framework. In contrast to this situation, the set of relations expressed within foundational ontologies are more formally axiomatised and built under conceptually well grounded methodologies.

Complementarily, the semantic relation classification task provides a corpus-based analysis on the incidence of these semantic relations on discourse, providing the fine-grained semantic context in which these abstractions are instantiated. However, when projecting these semantic relations back to the corpora-level, it can be observed that the majority of the words within a text does not have a direct semantic relationship connecting them.

Recent semantic interpretation tasks targeting word prediction over broader discourse contexts (Paperno et al., 2016) may require the detection of broader and complex semantic relations. Addressing these interpretation tasks may strongly benefit from relating terms expressed into the sentence using compositions of semantic relations.

This work aims at improving the description and the formalisation of the semantic relation classification task by grounding it with a foundational ontology and by introducing the concept of composite semantic relations, in which the relations between terms within a text can be expressed using the composition of one or more relations.

Proceedings of the Workshop on Cognitive Aspects of the Lexicon,
pages 30–39, Osaka, Japan, December 11-17 2016.

This work focuses on the following contributions:

- Examination of the completeness of the set of semantic relations used for the evaluation of semantic relation classification (SRC) tasks in the context of a domain-specific corpus.

- Contrasting of the relations used in SRC tasks with regard to relations present in the foundational ontology DOLCE, in the context of a domain-specific corpora.

- Annotation of terms within sentences from a financial corpus with semantic relations, including composite semantic relations, and creation of a domain-specific test collection for relation classification.

The paper is organised as follows: Section 2 lists related work regarding the semantic relation annotation task. Section 3 presents an analysis of current sets of semantic relations, and describes the relations provided by the foundational ontology DOLCE. Section 4 describes the corpus-based analysis, followed by the conclusions and future work in Section 5.

2 The Semantic Relation Classification Task

Semantic Relation Classification is usually framed under the context of a supervised classification problem. Best practices for creating relation inventories have been subject to much discussion (O'Seaghdha, 2007). Inventories can either be organised under a hierarchical (Rosario and Hearst, 2001), (Nastase and Szpakowicz, 2003), (Masolo et al., 2003) or under a flattened approach (Moldovan et al., 2004).

The number of relations in a given inventory varies widely, ranging from binary classification (Lapata, 2002) to 35 classes (Moldovan et al., 2004) to open (inference-based) approaches (Sabou et al., 2008).

There are several test collections for Semantic Relation Classification. Task 8 in SemEval 2010 (Hendrickx et al., 2009) focuses on multi-way semantic relation classification between pairs of nouns. Nine relations with broad coverage were selected[1], with a focus on practical interest. Patterns were used to collect relation candidates from the web, which were then classified by two annotators. In the context of Distributional Semantics, BLESS (Baroni and Lenci, 2011) is a test collection which is designed to evaluate Distributional Semantic Models (DSMs) on the task of Semantic Relation Classification. BLESS provides a benchmark for evaluating the lexical semantic capabilities of DSMs: it provides *concept, relation, relatum* triples for a large range of common concepts. There are five lexical semantic relations (*co-hyponym, hypernym, meronym, attribute* and *event*) and three random relations (*random-noun, random-verb, random-adjective*), which provide additional value for discriminativeness assessments. Some work has been done on SRC for specific domains, with a focus on the medical domain. Stephens et al. (2001) distinguish 17 relations holding between genes. Rosario and Hearst (2001) classify relations between noun compounds in the medical domain, while Rosario et al. (2002) undertake a similar endeavour using the MeSH hierarchy. Rosario and Hearst (2004) explore SRC for biomedical texts, focusing on relations between treatments and diseases such as "prevents", "cures" or less specific effects.

3 A Critique of Existing Sets of Semantic Relations

3.1 SemEval-2010 Task 8

Although the Semeval-2010 Task 8 semantic relations set was developed with the aim of covering "real word" situations (Hendrickx et al., 2009), some of the constraints imposed to overcome the structural and lexical factors that can affect the truth of a relation, described next, can bring considerable limitations. In those cases, it is necessary to identify other classes of semantic relations between terms covering other lexical categories.

---

[1]Cause-Effect (CE), Instrument-Agency (IA), Product-Producer (PP), Content-Container (CC), Entity-Origin (EO), Entity-Destination (ED), Component-Whole (CW), Member-Collection (MC), Message-Topic (MT)

3.1.1 Focus on Nominals

The first point to be noted refers to the entities involved in the classification: the task focuses on semantic relations between pairs of nominals, that is, the relation arguments are only noun-phrases where the head is a common-noun.

3.1.2 Locality Constraint

The data used in the Semeval classification task also relies on a locality constraint, which means that only nominal expressions considered "local" to one another were chosen, excluding relations whose arguments occur in separate sentential clauses. Although in a few cases a long distance between the arguments can indeed indicate the absence of a proper relation, in our financial data we note many sentences where the concepts are not local to one another, and nevertheless it is possible to assign a relation to them. For example, consider the pair "debt" and "creditworthiness" in Example 1, or the concepts "credit union" and "caisse populaire" in Example 2.

(1) "Your debt problem won't go away, but your creditworthiness will. "

(2) "In Quebec 70 per cent of the population belongs to a caisse populaire, while in Saskatchewan close to 60 per cent belongs to a credit union".

In both cases, the concepts are located in different clauses within the sentences, but it is possible to identify a relation between them which could be *indirect reference* and *sibling concept*, respectively. In this case, no Semeval relation fits, and custom relations are necessary to better express the relationship.

3.1.3 Focus on Concrete Relations

Although not stated as a constraint, most Semeval relations seems to refer specifically to physical objects. For example, the relation *Content-Container (CC)* is described as "An object is physically stored in a delineated area of space". In *Instrument-Agency (IA)*, *Product-Producer (PP)*, *Entity-Origin (EO)* and *Entity-Destination (ED)*, all the mentioned examples involve physical objects as instruments, a material product being produced or a concrete objects physically moving to/from a place. This focus on concrete relations poses challenges to the classification of semantic relations within certain domains, since concepts representing abstract entities or quantitative/qualitative roles, such as "credit", "debit", "investment", "demand", "profit", "interest", "capital" or "price", to mention a few, are very frequent.

3.1.4 Conditionals

Finally, the exclusion of conditional clauses also imposes unnecessary generality constraints. The Semeval task considers, for example, that in Example 3 the presence of the "bleach solution" inside the "bottle" is a situation being described as holding in a counterfactual hypothetical world, so it is not possible to assign a relation that can be seen as true regardless of hypothesis confirmation.

(3) "Suppose you were given a bottle that contains 400 grams of a 3.0% bleach solution."

Conditional clauses are frequent in many domains, for example within the financial domain. This domain involves many variables and frequently a scenario is being described based on them and the possible values they can assume. Therefore, *condition* indeed seems to be a suitable relation between certain concepts, as in Example 4, where the relation arguments are "term" and "bought".

(4) "TIPS can be held to maturity and have a minimum term of ownership of 45 days if bought through TreasuryDirect"

In the light of these limitations, adopting a richer conceptual meta-model, such as the one provided by the DOLCE ontology (Masolo et al., 2003), allow us to cover a broader range of categories instead of focusing only on physical objects, and consequently bring us a wider variety of relations to link those categories. Since all relations have a well defined domain and range, we can also ensure that they are valid for a given pair of concepts. Our analysis of the dataset has also shown that a complementary set of custom relations is of substantial importance to express the correct relationship between domain-specific concepts or even between concepts that, although being very common, interact among them in

very domain-specific situations. In Section 3.2 below, we therefore describe the DOLCE ontology and
its relations.

3.2 DOLCE relations

DOLCE (Descriptive Ontology for Linguistic and Cognitive Engineering) is an upper level ontology
developed as a module of the WonderWeb library of foundational ontologies (Masolo et al., 2003). It has
a clear cognitive bias, that is, it aims at capturing the ontological categories underlying natural language
and human common sense.

The most fundamental distinction in DOLCE is that between *endurants* and *perdurants*. DOLCE
relations are organised in a hierarchical structure.There are two toplevel relations: *immediate-relation*,
defined as a relation that holds without mediating individuals, and *mediated-relation*, a relation that (implicitly) composes other relations. Two additional branches, namely *immediate-relation-i* and *mediated-
relation-i*, cover all the inverse relations (only 4 relations do not have an inverse, and 14 relations have
themselves as inverse, i.e., they are symmetric).

The *immediate-relation* branch has 23 sub-relations at its second level, many of them being also subdivided into further levels. Among them are worth highlighting: *part*, the most general meronym relation;
participant, the immediate relation holding between endurants and perdurants and which, through the
sub-relations of its sub-relation *functional-participant*, can define the role played by the endurant in the
perdurant, for instance: *patient, target, theme, performed-by, instrument, resource*, etc. ; and *references*,
a relation holding between non-physical objects and any other kind of entity (including non-physical
objects themselves), which can be seen as a type of association where the non-physical object carries
some kind of information that involves the referenced entity.

The *mediated-relation* branch has 25 sub-relations at its second level, with again some of them subdivided into further sub-relations. Among them are worth noting: *co-participates-with*, a relation between
two endurants participating in the same perdurant; *generic-location*, a relation defining the physical or
abstract location of an entity; and *temporal-relation*, a relation between perdurants which, through its
sub-relations, describe how two occurrences are related with respect to their temporal locations: *pre-
cedes, temporally-coincides, temporally-includes, temporally-overlaps*, etc.

The relations having more generic classes as domain and range, that is, classes at higher levels in the
hierarchy, proved to be more useful for the semantic annotation task (cp. Section 4 below). As most of
the relations have an inverse, it is almost always possible to assign a suitable property regardless of the
arguments order, without the need to indicate the direction of the relation.

DOLCE relations show to be a suitable set for SRC tasks because, as an upper level ontology, DOLCE
aims at covering entities in any domain of knowledge. Since any entity can be mapped to a DOLCE high
level category, it is always possible to find a relation (or a subset of candidate relations) between two
entities, which will be the relation(s) between their upper level DOLCE categories. When the relation
is defined specifically for a class, it determines in a meaningful way what kind of relationship this class
can have with another one. On the other hand, when the relation is inherited from an ancestor class,
the kind of relationship can become too general. To address this issue and avoid the use of semantically
vague relations, a small set of custom relations was proposed to complement the DOLCE relations set
(cp. Section 4.2.1). Notwithstanding, this complementary set was designed to be as domain-independent
as possible, in order to fit not only the context where it was defined, but to be also useful in any SRC
task.

4   Corpus-based Analysis

The analysis methodology presented in this section consists in the annotation of semantic relations with
the help of a corpus. The corpus focuses on financial discourse and was crawled considering two types
of discourse: glossaries and encyclopedic articles.

In the sections below, we describe the construction of our financial corpus including word pair selection and annotation (Section 4.1) and the extensive manual classification analysis (Section 4.2).

4.1 Corpus Construction

We created a financial corpus by crawling two distinct types of sources: a) definitions, comprising three sources: the Bloomberg financial Glossary[2] (8324 definitions; 212,421 tokens), SGM Glossary[3] (1007 definitions; 43,638 tokens) and Investopedia Definitions[4] (15476 definitions; 2,462,801 tokens), b) articles from two sources: Investopedia[5] (5890 articles; 5,129,793 tokens) and Wikipedia (articles on Investment[6] and Finance[7]; 8306 articles; 6,714,129 tokens). Overall, our corpus contains 14,580,803 tokens.

After the creation of the financial corpus, we selected word pairs for relation classification according to the following methodology: Splitting the corpus into sentences, the first word of the pair was randomly selected amongst the tokens in the sentence, with the only constraint that it was listed in one of the three financial glossaries. Then, the second word was manually selected. The sentence context was preserved for manual classification analysis (see Section 4.2 below).

4.2 Manual Classification Analysis

Our semantic relation classification comprised 300 pairs of words, each associated with a sentence context (see Section 4.1 above). First, for each pair, a class from the foundational ontology DOLCE (Masolo et al., 2003) was assigned to both concepts. These classes represent the primary, highest level category that the concept belongs to. This concept-ontology class alignment was performed with the aid of the WordNet-DOLCE alignment (Gangemi et al., 2003). For each concept, the correct sense and its corresponding DOLCE class were manually identified and assigned to it. For simplicity, all adjectives and adverbs were assigned the class *quality*.

After classifying both concepts, it is possible to search for the most suitable relation between them, which is a property from DOLCE having the classes assigned to the concepts as domain and range. For example, if one concept represents an *agent*, and the other one an *action*, the possible relations between them could be *performs*, meaning that the agent performs the action, or *prescribes*, signifying that the agent does not perform the action him/herself, but somehow causes it to happen and to be performed by other agent(s). Besides the domain and range information, the sentence context where the concepts appear also helps to identify the correct relation. This also means that the relation assigned represents the relationship between those concepts in a particular sentence; the same pair of words could have different meanings and/or show a different kind of relationship in other sentence. When no suitable relation could be found in DOLCE, a new relation or a composite relation was suggested. When suggesting a new relation, we tried to make it as general as possible, that is, not too tied to a specific context, so it could be later reused by other concept pairs. The manual classification was performed by an expert in conceptual modelling and later independently reviewed by a second expert.

Following this methodology, three scenarios occurred: (1) there was a direct relationship between the two concepts, so either a DOLCE relation or a custom suggested relation could be directly assigned to them; (2) there were no direct relations, but the concepts were indirectly related through other concepts, then a composition of (DOLCE or suggested) relations was drawn, building a path made of intermediate concept pairs linking the concepts; (3) no relation between the two concepts could be found at all, because they were too far away from each other in the same clause, or because they were in different clauses in a sentence, or in different sentences in a paragraph. In the final classification, 72. 67% (218 pairs) of the pairs were assigned a direct relation, 24.67% (74 pairs) were linked through an indirect relation, and only 2.66% (8 pairs) were not classified. The classification results are summarised in Table 1.

---

[2] http://www.isotranslations.com/resources/Bloomberg\%20Financial\%20Glossary.pdf
[3] http://www.sapient.com/content/dam/sapient/sapientglobalmarkets/pdf/
thought-leadership/SGM_Glossary_2014_final.pdf
[4] http://www.investopedia.com/terms/a/
[5] http://www.investopedia.com/articles/pf/
[6] https://en.wikipedia.org/wiki/Wikipedia:WikiProject_Investment
[7] https://en.wikipedia.org/wiki/Wikipedia:WikiProject_Finance

Table 1: Relation classification results

Relation type	DOLCE relations		Custom relations		Total	
	# of pairs	%	# of pairs	%	# of pairs	%
Direct	77	35.32	141	64.68	218	72.67
Composite[a]	36	48.65	38	51.35	74	24.67
Unclassified	-	-	-	-	8	2.66

[a]The numbers refer only to the first pair in each composite relation chain

4.2.1 Direct Relations

For most concept pairs it was possible to assign a direct semantic relation. Out of the 218 pairs where this scenario occurred, 35.32% (77 pairs) were assigned a DOLCE property as a semantic relation, and for 64.68% (141 pairs) of the pairs no DOLCE property fit, so a *suggested relation* was assigned to each of them. The suggested relations are listed in Table 2, and the DOLCE properties are well documented in the ontology itself[8].

Table 2: Descriptions and examples of suggested semantic relations

Relation	Description	Example
Common ownership	Both concepts have the same owner	Not only has the territory taken on increasing *debt* in the 21st century but it has less *revenue* coming in to pay that debt.
Condition	The existence or occurrence of one concept is conditioned by the existence or occurrence of the other concept, or by a broader condition involving that concept	If that's you, having a solid *credit history* can help you get funding for a start-up or establish a home-equity *line of credit* to get your project off the ground.
Co-occurring qualifier	Both qualifiers occur at the same time in the same entity	These models are based upon *historical market* data.
Coreference	Syntactic reference between concepts, where one of them (usually a relative pronoun) refers to the other one	[It] is one of two Federal Reserve Bank of Cleveland *branch* offices (the *other* is in Cincinnati).
Correlated variation	Both concepts represent measures, and the variation in one of them affects the variation in the other one	It also decreases the value of the *currency* - potentially stimulating exports and decreasing imports - improving the *balance of trade*.
Destination	One concept is the destination of the other one, which can be an (physical or abstract) object itself, or an event causing some object to move towards it	Through LIFFE CONNECT, LIFFE took its *market* to its *customers* wherever they were in the world.
Indirect ownership	One concept is a part or a kind of representation of an agent or organisation, who/which has the ownership of the other concept	When Birmingham Midshires became *part* of the Halifax in April 1999 it had savings balances of £5.9 billion and *mortgage* assets of £9.2 billion.
Indirect qualifier	One concept is a quality of something that has the other concept as a part or as a direct quality	The Crummey letter qualifies the transfer for the annual *gift* tax *exclusion* ....
Indirect reference	One concept makes some kind of reference to the other one, having other events and/or objects as intermediates	Characteristics and *risk* types of human capital differ for different *individuals*.
Indirect result	One concept indirectly produces the other one, having other events and/or objects as intermediates	The *acquisition* created the largest provider of brokerage and *investment* services in Greece.
Indirect target	One concept indirectly affects the other one through one or more events, which can also involve other (physical or abstract) objects	The *firm* employs shareholder activism to push for structural changes in *target companies*.
Instantiation	One concept is an instance of a class represented by the other one	The *FICO* score is the most commonly used of the *credit scores*.
Membership	One concepts is a member of a group or organisation represented by the other one	In 2004, Mary Mitchell, the *president* at the time, retired after a 60 year career at the *bank*, starting as a teller in 1944.
Opposition	One concept is an antonym of the other one	...and beggar thy neighbour policies that serve "*national* constituencies at the expense of *global* financial stability".
Ownership	One concept has the ownership of the other one	The *lessor* is the legal owner of the *asset*.
Qualifier	One concept is a quality of the other one	It's got speculators searching for *quick gains* in hot housing markets.
Represented in	One concept has some kind of (physical or abstract) representation expressed in/by the other one	All details of that *transaction* are stored in the one-time *code*.
Sibling concept	Both concepts belong to same category and play similar roles in a given context	Operating activities include net income, *accounts receivable, accounts payable* and inventory.
Source	One concept is the source of the other one, which can be an (physical or abstract) object itself, or an event causing some object to move from it	As of May 2014, AirHelp had raised a $400000 seed *round* from *business* angels.
Specialisation	One concept is a more specific subconcept of the other one	If a *value* other than *market value* is appropriate ....
Theme component	One concept is something that demands complementary information to make clear what it is about, and the other one is a piece of the whole information	The *downside* to this is that one *review* doesn't tell a customer very much about the product.
Used for	Both concepts represent (physical or abstract) objects, and one is used as an instrument to accomplish the other	Look for receipts for medical costs not covered by *insurance* or reimbursed by any other health plan , property taxes, and job-related and investment-related *expenses*.

[8]http://www.loa.istc.cnr.it/old/DOLCE.html

Value component	One concept represents a measure (something to which a value can be assigned), and the other one is something that, along with other parameters, determines its final value	Valuation of *life annuities* may be performed by calculating the actuarial *present value* of the future life contingent payments.
Affects	The existence or occurrence of one concept has some kind of effect on the other concept	If the option they have written gets *exercised* several things can happen: for both put and call *writers* if an option expires unexercised or is bought to close it is treated as a short-term capital gain.

Among the DOLCE relations, the most frequent ones are *patient* and its inverse *patient-of*, as well as *target* and its inverse *target-of*, covering around 42% (32 pairs) of the pairs in this scenario. These relations refer to the association between events and the (abstract or physical) objects they affect. The *patient* relation means that the object has a relatively static role in the event. *Target* is a specialisation of *patient*, and can be seen as an object to which an event is more intentionally directed.

This can give us an idea about the most frequent kind of concept that the events in this domain take as objects. The most common classes occurring as *patient* or *target* of an event are *legal-possession-entity*, such as "money", "loan", "shares", "income" or "investment", *description*, like "deal", "trend" or "agreement", and *situation*, such as "merger", "integration" or "asset management", being affected by events like "pay", "buy", "invest", "complete", "manage" and "deliver", for example.

The suggested relations provide an abstract structural framework to express unnamed (implicit) relations between concepts within the text, without the need to commit to a domain-specific ontological model. Among the suggested relations, the most recurrent ones are *qualifier*, *indirect target* and *ownership*, accounting for 47.5% (67 pairs) of the pairs in this scenario. The high frequency of the *qualifier* relation can give us a hint about what concepts commonly modifies/are modified by other concepts. Adjectives like "solvent", "failed" and "eligible" are usually associated with *social-roles*, like "company" or "bank", while nouns denoting *legal-possession*-entities frequently modifies other *legal-possession-entities*, specialising them, as in the pairs "mortgage" and "line [of credit]", and "capital" and "account".

The *indirect target* relation reinforces the high frequency of the "affecting-affected entity" pairs observed in the DOLCE-based classification, but in this case having some kind of intermediate between them, and also accepting (abstract or physical) objects, and not only events, as affecting entity. In this case, an event serves as intermediate, for example: "accountant" has as indirect target "funds", mediated by the event "examination", that is, "accountant" directly performs the action "examination", which in turn has as direct target "funds". Similarly, "liquidator" has as indirect target "company" through the event "liquidation", "recruiters" indirectly targets at "candidate" through "hire", and so on.

Another frequent suggested relation worth noting is *ownership*, which is very recurrent between *social-roles*, such as "company" and "bank", or *socially-constructed-persons*, like "employers", "sellers" or "manager" as the owner (both classes denote *roles*, the first being played by a juridical entity, and the second by a physical person), and *legal-possession-entities*, such as "assets", "funds", "insurance", "money" and "account" as the owned entity.

4.2.2 Relation Composition

When no direct relation between the two concepts could be found, the other concepts standing between them were analysed, and, instead of a single relation, a chain of concept pairs, each of them with its suitable direct relation, linked the two concepts from the original pair. Note that this scenario is different from the ones where direct, suggested relations such as *indirect target, indirect ownership* or *indirect qualifier*, for instance, were applied. In those cases, even having other events or objects as intermediates, a close relationship could be identified between the concepts. A composition of relations was necessary only when the only cohesive association from one concept to another is achieved by a direct mention of relation chains.

Considering the 74 concept pairs where only indirect relations applied, the average length of the relations chain is 2.66, that is, this is the average number of concept pairs necessary to link the concepts, where the first pair contains one of the concepts and the last one contains the other. For example, in Example 5, no direct relation between "type" and "month" can be inferred, but, analysing the intermediate concepts, the following chain can be drawn: "type [*references*] financing, financing [*used-in*] payments, payments [*happens-at*] month".

(5) "With another type of developer financing you make regular payments each month"

The most common classes in this scenario are *event* and *quality*, which means that, even in a short sentence, sometimes a concept is not affected by an event at all, having only a relatively weak relation to the one that does. For qualities, the most probable reason is the distance between the concepts, as qualities are more likely to appear close to the concepts they qualify, having no meaningful relation with concepts far away within the sentence.

Regarding the relations in the compositions, 53.3% (111 auxiliary pairs) of them were classified using DOLCE relations, and 43.7% (86 auxiliary pairs) using suggested relations. Again, *patient* and *target*, and their inverses *patient-of* and *target-of* are predominant, but here the relation *performs* also stands out. As all of these relations have *event* as domain or range, we can infer that, when no apparent relation exists between the concepts, possibly an event can help to explain why they co-occur. Among the suggested relations, *qualifier* and *ownership* were the most frequent semantic relations, again, due to the high occurrence of concepts belonging to the categories *quality*, what leads to the *qualifier* relation, and *social-role* and *socially-constructed-person*, which, along with the also frequent category *legal-possession-entity*, in this sample showed to be very likely to appear as the "owner-owned entity" pair.

4.3 Correlation between Semantic Relations and Semantic Relatedness

In order to further investigate the properties of the three relation categories *direct, composite, unassigned* we correlate them in terms of their semantic relatedness scores. Two human annotators scored each of the 300 concept pairs for semantic relatedness on a scale from 0 (unrelated) to 10 (identical or highly related), where the average of their scores was taken as the final score of the concept pair. Note that the relatedness scoring, unlike the semantic relation assignment, was done without reference to the sentence context in order to obtain a general semantic relatedness assessment (replicating the methodology of (Finkelstein et al., 2001)).

If we consider the types of direct relations with regard to semantic relatedness, we find that the most highly related ones are *Specialisation* (9.5; custom), *Component-of* (9; DOLCE), *Descriptive-place-of* (9; DOLCE), *Product* (9; DOLCE), *Use-of* (8.5; DOLCE), *Part-of* (8.25; DOLCE), *Unit-of* (DOLCE; 8.25). In more general lexical semantic terms, they are instances of hyponymy (*Specialisation*), meronymy (*Component-of, Part-of*), (abstract) location (*descriptive-place-of*), and association (*Unit-of, Use-of*) and thus scored as highly related in our annotation schema. The relations whose concepts on average display lowest relatedness are *Happens-at* (3; DOLCE), *Involves* (3.5; DOLCE), *Result* (3.5; DOLCE), *Source* (3.66; custom).*Happens-at* has temporal characteristics, which do not necessitate high relatedness. *Involves*, *Result* and *Source* have a low number of concept pairs in our data (one instance each for *Involves* and *Result*, three for *Source*), which is why these results do not generalise.

5 Conclusions and Future Work

The semantic relation classification (SRC) task is a fundamental step in the construction of lightweight semantic models for Natural Language Processing applications. Current SRC tasks focus on very general relations that deal well with common sense data, but whose expressivity proves to be limited when applied to domain-specific information. We presented an analysis of the semantic relations from SemEval-2010 (task 8), a widely used relations set in SRC tasks, evaluating its coverage and ontological soundness to assess its suitability to domain-specific data.

Given the drawbacks identified in our evaluation and guided by a corpus-based analysis, we proposed a set of semantic relations made up by the properties of the foundational ontology DOLCE, complemented by a set of custom relations, and used it to classify a set of 300 pairs of terms from a financial dataset. As a result, besides the direct ontology-based relations, we introduced the concept of composite relations, a combination of one or more relations intended to link terms for which no direct relationship exists. The direct relations show us how the concepts interact and the composite relations help us to explain how terms that seem to be unrelated interact within a given context.

In addition to the manual relation classification, the pairs also received a score to indicate their semantic relatedness, independent of the context where they appear. Comparing the results of both classifications, we noted that pairs in a direct relationship have, on average, the highest semantic relatedness scores. The most predominant scenarios express how concrete or abstract objects are targeted by an event, are owned by an agent, or are modified/qualified by other objects. In contrast, pairs involved in a composite relationship present, on average, the lowest semantic similarity scores, showing that their relatedness is highly dependent on the context and can only be determined through a set of intermediate terms.

This initial classification shows that a conceptually well-grounded set of relations based on an ontological model can bring more expressivity and more flexibility for domain-specific data than that provided by the Semeval relations set. As future work, we intend to expand our analysis also to the correlation between contextual semantic and syntactic relations, as well as to extend our dataset, annotating a larger number of concept pairs and using this data to train an automatic classifier, capable of identifying semantic relations in large-scale corpora.

Acknowledgements

This work is in part funded by the SSIX Horizon 2020 project (grant agreement No 645425). Vivian S. Silva is a CNPq Fellow – Brazil. 

References

Marco Baroni and Alessandro Lenci. 2011. How we blessed distributional semantic evaluation. In *Proceedings of the GEMS 2011 Workshop on GEometrical Models of Natural Language Semantics*, pages 1–10. Association for Computational Linguistics.

Lev Finkelstein, Evgeniy Gabrilovich, Yossi Matias, Ehud Rivlin, Zach Solan, Gadi Wolfman, and Eytan Ruppin. 2001. Placing search in context: The concept revisited. In *Proceedings of the 10th international conference on World Wide Web*, pages 406–414. ACM.

Aldo Gangemi, Nicola Guarino, Claudio Masolo, and Alessandro Oltramari. 2003. Sweetening wordnet with dolce. *AI magazine*, 24(3):13.

Iris Hendrickx, Su Nam Kim, Zornitsa Kozareva, Preslav Nakov, Diarmuid Ó Séaghdha, Sebastian Padó, Marco Pennacchiotti, Lorenza Romano, and Stan Szpakowicz. 2009. Semeval-2010 task 8: Multi-way classification of semantic relations between pairs of nominals. In *Proceedings of the Workshop on Semantic Evaluations: Recent Achievements and Future Directions*, pages 94–99. Association for Computational Linguistics.

Maria Lapata. 2002. The disambiguation of nominalizations. *Computational Linguistics*, 28(3):357–388.

Claudio Masolo, Stefano Borgo, Aldo Gangemi, Nicola Guarino, and Alessandro Oltramari. 2003. WonderWeb deliverable D18 ontology library (final). Technical report, IST Project 2001-33052 WonderWeb: Ontology Infrastructure for the Semantic Web.

Dan Moldovan, Adriana Badulescu, Marta Tatu, Daniel Antohe, and Roxana Girju. 2004. Models for the semantic classification of noun phrases. In *Proceedings of the HLT-NAACL Workshop on Computational Lexical Semantics*, pages 60–67.

Vivi Nastase and Stan Szpakowicz. 2003. Exploring noun-modifier semantic relations. In *Fifth international workshop on computational semantics (IWCS-5)*, pages 285–301.

Diarmuid O'Seaghdha. 2007. Designing and evaluating a semantic annotation scheme for compound nouns. In *Proc Corpus Linguistics*.

Denis Paperno, Germán Kruszewski, Angeliki Lazaridou, Quan Ngoc Pham, Raffaella Bernardi, Sandro Pezzelle, Marco Baroni, Gemma Boleda, and Raquel Fernández. 2016. The LAMBADA dataset: Word prediction requiring a broad discourse context. In *Proceedings of the 54th Annual Meeting of the Association for Computational Linguistics, ACL 2016, August 7-12, 2016, Berlin, Germany, Volume 1: Long Papers*.

Barbara Rosario and Marti Hearst. 2001. Classifying the semantic relations in noun compounds via a domain-specific lexical hierarchy. In *Proceedings of the 2001 Conference on Empirical Methods in Natural Language Processing*, pages 82–90.

Barbara Rosario and Marti A Hearst. 2004. Classifying semantic relations in bioscience texts. In *Proceedings of the 42nd annual meeting on association for computational linguistics*, page 430. Association for Computational Linguistics.

Barbara Rosario, Marti A Hearst, and Charles Fillmore. 2002. The descent of hierarchy, and selection in relational semantics. In *Proceedings of the 40th Annual Meeting on Association for Computational Linguistics*, pages 247–254. Association for Computational Linguistics.

Marta Sabou, Mathieu dâĂŹAquin, and Enrico Motta. 2008. Scarlet: semantic relation discovery by harvesting online ontologies. In *European Semantic Web Conference*, pages 854–858. Springer.

Matthew J Stephens, Mathew J Palakal, Snehasis Mukhopadhyay, Rajeev R Raje, Javed Mostafa, et al. 2001. Detecting gene relations from medline abstracts. In *Pacific Symposium on Biocomputing*, volume 6, pages 483–496.

The Power of Language Music: Arabic Lemmatization through Patterns

Mohammed Attia
Google Inc.
New York City
NY, 10011
`attia@google.com`

Ayah Zirikly and **Mona Diab**
Department of Computer Science
George Washington University
Washington, DC
`ayaz,mtdiab@gwu.edu`

Abstract

The interaction between roots and patterns in Arabic has intrigued lexicographers and morphologists for centuries. While roots provide the consonantal building blocks, patterns provide the syllabic vocalic moulds. While roots provide abstract semantic classes, patterns realize these classes in specific instances. In this way both roots and patterns are indispensable for understanding the derivational, morphological and, to some extent, the cognitive aspects of the Arabic language. In this paper we perform lemmatization (a high-level lexical processing) without relying on a lookup dictionary. We use a hybrid approach that consists of a machine learning classifier to predict the lemma pattern for a given stem, and mapping rules to convert stems to their respective lemmas with the vocalization defined by the pattern.

1 Introduction

Roots and patterns in Arabic are essential for understanding the derivational aspects of the lexicon. In Arabic, roots and patterns function like meta data. Lemmas or lexical entries recorded in dictionaries only represent a static lexicon at a fixed point in time, while roots and patterns (as part of the mental lexicon) have stronger dynamic role in the creation of new entries and the prediction of their semantic paradigms. So, derivation in Arabic is about the construction of a large semantic forests of concepts that are related through a single grand-parent or a super-lemma, that is the root.

The power of roots and patterns has not yet been fully utilized or understood in Natural Language Processing (NLP). They are traditionally considered as a convenient way for listing words in dictionaries or teaching Arabic for second language learners, but they have a great potential for automatic processing, due to their strong generalizing capacity and their function as an instrument for decomposing word forms. Roots and patterns are the hidden layers through which Arabic speakers organize, memorize and access the Arabic lexicon.

In many NLP tasks, using surface word forms is found to be inefficient as it significantly adds to sparsity, especially in highly inflected languages; thus, some form of normalization is necessary. Normalization in general, and lemmatization in particular, are meant to reduce the variability in word forms by collapsing related words. This has been shown to be beneficial for information retrieval (Larkey et al., 2002; Semmar et al., 2006), parsing (Seddah et al., 2010), summarization (Skorkovská, 2012; El-Shishtawy and El-Ghannam, 2014), document clustering (Korenius et al., 2004), keyphrase extraction (El-Shishtawy and Al-Sammak, 2012), and text indexing and classification (Hammouda and Almarimi, 2010).

From a lexical point of view, normalization can be conducted at the level of the root, stem or lemma. Lemmatization relates surface forms to their canonical base representations (or dictionary lookup form) (Attia and van Genabith, 2013). It is the inverse of inflection (Plisson et al., 2004), as it renders words to a default and uninflected form, or as is the case with Arabic, a least marked form. A lemma is the common denominator (Kamir et al., 2002) of a set of forms that share the same semantic, morphological and syntactic composition, where it represents the least marked word form without any inflectional affixes.

Proceedings of the Workshop on Cognitive Aspects of the Lexicon,
pages 40–50, Osaka, Japan, December 11-17 2016.

In Arabic, a verb lemma is chosen to be the perfective, indicative, 3rd person, masculine, and singular such as شَكَرَ $akara[1] "to thank". Whereas a nominal lemma (namely, nouns and adjectives) is in the nominative, singular, masculine (where possible), such as طالِب TAlib "student".

Stemming and lemmatization are quite distinct processes, albeit frequently confused the terms are sometimes used interchangeably (Brits et al., 2005). Stemming strips off prefixes and suffixes leaving a bare stem with no guarantee that the resulting form is a valid standalone word, while lemmatization renders word forms (inflected forms) in their dictionary citation forms. To illustrate this with an example, consider the Arabic verb form ينتظرون 'yanotaZiruwn' "they wait". Stemming will remove the present prefix 'ya' and the plural suffix 'uwn' and leave نتظر 'notaZir' which is a non-word in Arabic. By contrast, full lemmatization will reveal that the word has gone through a morphological alteration process and return the canonical انتظر 'AinotaZar' "to wait" as the base form.

The root, by contrast, is the three (or four) radical based form from which a word is formed, that is نظر nZr for the above example. Kamir et al. (2002) assume that the relationship between a root and a lemma is purely diachronic (related to the historical derivation of words and their semantic net). However, we show that the relationship is not only diachronic, but also synchronic related to inflection, as root radicals remain the pivots for inflectional affixes.

In our approach we treat the lemmatization as a classification problem relying mainly on word patterns. Unlike previous work, we do not use lexicons or morphological rules or analyzers. Our methodology is based on the powerful and instrumental component that patterns play in the Arabic morphology system. For example, verb lemmas are derived from roots selected from 10 morphological patterns and 35 phonological patterns, see Section 3.1. Additionally, verbs are also inflected for the imperfective, passive voice and imperative through patterns. Noun and adjective lemmas are similarly derived either from roots or from verbs through patterns. Nouns are also inflected for the plural (broken plural) selected from a large set of 83 phonological patterns.

This paper shows how the process of derivation is closely tied to a compact list of patterns with a backward and forward movement directions. For the benefit of the research community we make our list of morpho-phonological patterns publicly available for download[2].

1.1 Arabic Morphological System

Arabic words are originally formed from roots (triliteral or quadriliteral consonantal base), which are passed through different stages of derivation, inflection, and clitic attachment until they finally appear as surface forms. A root is not a word, as it does not carry vocalization or Part of Speech (POS) category, but it serves as an underlying representation of words, and the pivot on which morphological processes take place. Beside roots, patterns play a fundamental part in Arabic morphology, as they provide the vocalic mold (or scheme) for the root cardinals to be placed.

Patterns are divided into two paradigms: derivational and inflectional. Derivational patterns are responsible for the choice of syntactic (POS) and semantic structures, and they produce dictionary entries. Inflectional patterns are the ones that express morpho-syntactic features (such as gender, number, tense, mood, voice, etc.), i.e. creating variations within the same dictionary entry. For example درس drs is a root for the semantic net relating to studying/teaching; دَرَسَ darasa is a verb "to study" following the pattern $R_1aR_2aR_3a$, تَدْرُسُ tadorusu is an inflected verb "she studies" following the inflection pattern $taR_1oR_2uR_3u$, and so on. The root can be considered as the super-lemma relating words within the same semantic field (Kamir et al., 2002), while a lemma is realized by furnishing the root with a POS and derivational pattern, and the word form (or surface form) is realized by applying the inflectional patterns and attaching clitics.

Figure 1 shows the two layers and six tiers involved in the composition of the Arabic morphological system. The derivation layer is non-concatenative and opaque in the sense that it is a level of abstraction

---

[1] We use the Buckwalter Arabic Transliteration system (http://www.qamus.org/transliteration.htm).
[2] https://sourceforge.net/projects/arabicpatterns/

Derivation	Root	درس drs			
	POS	V			N
	Pattern	$R_1aR_2aR_3a$			$maR_1R_2aR_3ap$
	Lemma	daras 'study'			madrasap 'school'
Inflection	Pattern	$yaR_1oR_2iR_3$	$R_1aR_2aR_3$	$iR_1oR_2iR_3$	$maR_1AR_2iR_3$
	Inflected word	yadoris 'studies'	daras 'study'	{idoris 'study!'	madAris 'schools'

Table 1: Root and Pattern Interdigitation

that affects the choice of a POS, and it does not have a direct explicit surface manifestation. By contrast, the inflection layer is more transparent. It applies both concatenative and non-concatenative morphotactics. Non-concatenative morphotactics (or templates) are used to express the imperfective aspect, passive voice and the imperative mood for verbs as well as broken plural forms for nouns. Concatenative morphotactics are used to express number and gender for both verbs and nouns (in the case of dual and sound plurals) and person for verbs.

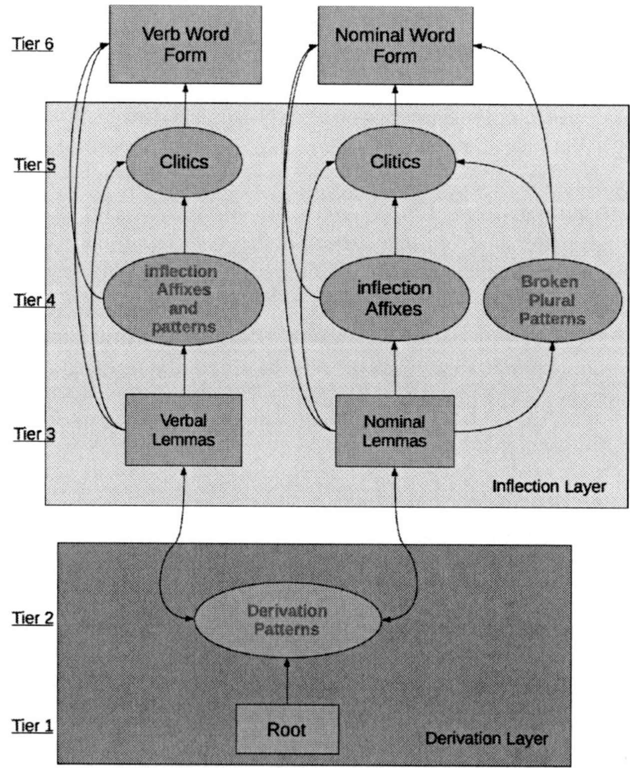

Figure 1: Multi-tier Structure of the Arabic Morphology

A pattern is a conso-vocalic scheme with empty slots, and a root is a sequence of ordered consonants (called radicals), and these radicals are the fillers which occupy the slots according to their linear order. This process of insertion is called interdigitation (Beesley and Karttunen, 2003). An example is shown in Table 1.

To show how the Arabic Lexicon is organized, we can examine the Buckwalter Morphological Analyzer (BAMA) (Buckwalter, 2004) that contains 40,657 entries words, 35,330 (or 87%) of which are derived from 4,494 roots (with an average 7.86 words per root). The remaining words (5,327 or 13%) are not derived and cover function, borrowed and other fixed words.

1.2 Vowelization

Arabic short vowels are pronounced in speech, but their representation (Diacritics, or vowel marks) are typically skipped in written text. The lack of diacritization in modern writing is the source of significant ambiguity. For example, the word علم "Elm" can be either عَلِمَ Ealima "to know", عَلَّمَ Eal~ama "to teach", عُلِمَ Eulima "be known", عُلِّمَ Eul~ima "be taught" or عَلَم Elam "flag". Arabic readers intuitively disambiguate based on context. For natural language processing tasks, this disambiguation is necessary, but at the same time not easily achievable.

The Arabic Treebank (ATB) comes with two versions: non-vowelized and fully vowelized. The Buckwalter Morphological Analyzer (BAMA) (Buckwalter, 2004) also provides possible vowelization for words. Together they allow the statistical systems to be trained on a model for vowelization.

Vowelization is an important aspect in the Arabic morphological patterns (which are sometimes referred to as vocalic scheme). Our list of 377 unique patterns is reduced to 175 patterns when vowel marks are removed.

Automatic vowelization, or diacritic restoration, has been discussed in a number of papers. For example, Bebah et al. (2014) describe a hybrid method for automatic vowelization using the Al-Khalil morphological analyzer and a hidden Markov model (HMM) to disambiguate. Some researchers use purely statistical methods for restoring diacritics (Nelken and Shieber, 2005; Elshafei et al., 2006; Ameur et al., 2015; Rashwan et al., 2011).

2 Related Work

Lemmatization has been discussed for morphologically rich languages, such as Setswana (Brits et al., 2005), Croatian (Tadić, 2006), Slovene, Serbian, Hungarian, Estonian, Bulgarian and Romanian (in addition to other languages) (Juršič et al., 2007), French (Seddah et al., 2010), Portuguese (da Silva, 2007), Finnish (Korenius et al., 2004), Turkish (Ozturkmenoglu and Alpkocak, 2012) and even English (Balakrishnan and Lloyd-Yemoh, 2014). Plisson et al. (2004) and Juršič et al. (2007) treat lemmatization as a machine learning problem and apply Ripple Down Rule (RDR) induction algorithm to a lexicon of words and their normalized forms to learn lemmatization rules.

Due to the high inflectional nature of the language, it is almost impossible to treat Arabic texts without some sort of normalization. From the implementation point of view, there are basically three approaches for normalizing Arabic: dictionary-based normalization, and statistical normalization, and hybrid normalization.

Dictionary-based normalization. The Buckwalter Arabic Morphological Analyser (BAMA) (Buckwalter, 2004) is the most widely used analyser in the literature. The Khoja stemmer (Khoja and Garside, 1999) is a mid-level analyser that falls between a full morphological analyser and a shallow stemmer. It recognizes prefixes and suffixes of a word, and uses patterns to determine the POS tag and extract the root. Hossny et al. (2008) develop an Arabic morphological rule induction system to predict morphological rules using inductive logic programming on sets of example pairs (stem and inflected form) with their feature vectors. El-Shishtawy and El-Ghannam (2012) build a rule-based system that exploits Arabic language knowledge in terms of roots, patterns, affixes, and a set of morpho-syntactic rules to generate lemmas for surface word forms.

Hybrid normalization. (Hajič, 2000) argues for the use of a dictionary as a source of morphological analyses for training a statistical POS and morphological tagger for inflectionally rich languages, such as Romanian, Czech, or Hungarian. The method was later applied to Arabic (Hajic et al., 2005). (Roth et al., 2008) develop a system (MADA) that uses statistical methods (SVM classifiers) to perform full morpho-syntactic tagging, along with lemmatization (LexChoice), by selecting the best candidate from the list of competing analyses generated by BAMA (Buckwalter, 2004).

Statistical normalization. The Stanford Tagger (Toutanova and Manning, 2000) is a Maximum Entropy POS tagger that has been extended for Arabic, but the problem with this tagger is that it does not perform segmentation of Arabic clitics. AMIRA 2.1 (Diab, 2007; Diab, 2009) uses a supervised SVM-based machine learning method for POS tagging, tokenization, and base phrase chunking. The

	Tokens	No alterations	Alterations %
Nouns	128,294	103,363	19.43
Verbs	31,667	16,276	48.60
Adjectives	53,177	32,599	38.70
Proper Nouns	22,245	20,840	6.32
Function Words	65,089	59,060	9.26
Total	300,472	232,138	22.74

Table 2: Frequency of alterations in Arabic words

tokenization in AMIRA 2.1 only separates clitics and does not split off inflectional affixes. Abdul-Mageed et al. (2013), develop ASMA, a Memory-Based Learning system that performs fine grained POS tagging and automatic segmentation (stemming) by splitting both inflectional morpheme and clitics, but, like AMIRA, it does not return the lemma of the word.

So far, purely statistical approaches succeeded at developing solutions for normalization at the root and stem levels, but they stopped short of lemmatization. In this paper we introduce the first attempt to treat lemmatization in Arabic as a machine learning classification problem.

3   Approach

The use of a machine learning (ML) classifier to directly map words to their lemmas is not feasible in Arabic, due to the fact that Arabic inflection contains change to the internal buildup of the word, as opposed to the straightforward suffixation and prefixation. Table 2 shows the frequency of mismatch between the stem and the lemma in the ATB (Maamouri et al., 2010). We notice that verbs have the highest rate of alterations, or mismatches, (48.6%) followed by adjectives then nouns.

In our work, we use a machine learning classifier to predict the pattern of the lemma for any given surface form (ideally if the words are diacritized and stemmed). In our view the pattern functions as the pivot, or the bridge, between the surface form and the lemma. Our lemmatization is based on two levels of mapping. First, we map the stem to the pattern of the lemma, then we map the pattern of the lemma to the actual lemma form, by extracting the radicals from the stem and filling the slots in the pattern. For training our model, we use the ATB which comes already annotated with lemmas.

Figure 2 shows the architecture of our system. The output to our system is tokenized and POS tagged words, which are then enriched with lemmas and formatted into features that are passed to our machine learning (ML) classifiers. The ML classifiers predict lemmas for given stems, which are then passed into our mapping rules to finally generate the lemmas by merging the stems with the predicted patterns.

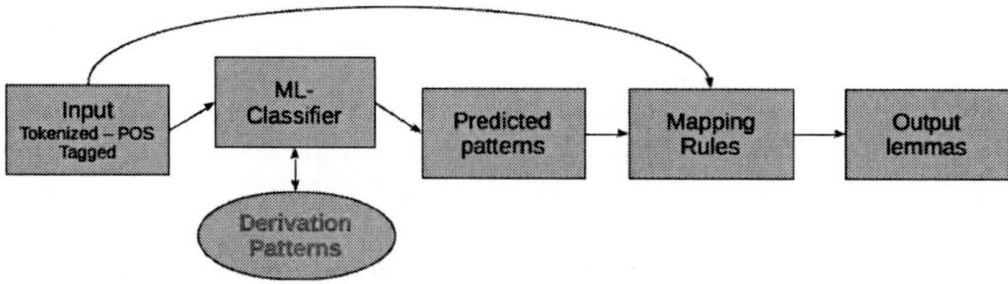

Figure 2: Architecture of the lemmatization system

3.1   The Pattern Database

We create a pattern database for all Arabic derivational and broken plural forms. The number of patterns in the database is 655. These are not unique patterns because of the many-to-many relationship between broken plural and singular patterns.

In our work we make a distinction between morphological patterns and phonological patterns. Phonological pattern makes allowance for alterations due to the existence of weak letters, gemination (doubling) and hamzah's (glottal stops). For example, the verb قال qAl "to say" will have the phonological

Word Type	No. of patterns	Example Pattern	Example word
Broken Plural	256 (87 unique)	$R_1aR_2A\}iR_3$	EajA}iz 'elderly'
Nouns taking broken plural	135	$R_1iR_2oR_3AR_4$	EimolAq 'giant'
Nouns taking feminine plural	26	$miR_1aR_2{\sim}ap$	miDax~ap 'pump'
Nouns taking no plural	20	$taR_1oR_2AR_3$	taokAr 'remembering'
Active participle اسم الفاعل	26	$muR_1AR_2iR_3$	muqAtil 'fighter'
Passive participle اسم المفعول	22	$muR_1aR_2{\sim}aR_3$	muwaj~ah 'directed'
Verbal nouns المصدر	42	$\{inoR_1iR_2AR_3$	{ino$iTAr 'spreading'
Nouns of instrument اسم الآلة	8	$miR_1oR_2AR_3$	mino$Ar 'saw'
Nouns of Instance اسم المرة	6	$<iR_1AR_2ap$	<iEAnp 'assistance'
Adjectives of hyperbole صيغ المبالغة	11	$R_1aR_2iyR_3$	xabiyr 'expert'
Attributive adjective الصفة المشبهة	21	$R_1aR_2oR_3$	Daxom 'huge'
Verbs	45	$\{iR1otaR2aR3$	{ijotamaE 'meet'
Names of place اسم المكان	3	$maR_1oR_2aR_3$	makotab 'office'
Elative Adjectives اسم التفضيل	3	$>aR_1oR_2aR_3$	>akoram 'more generous'
Miscellaneous	8	$maR_1oR_2aR_3An$	mahorajAn 'carnival'

Table 3: Categorization of Arabic patterns

pattern "R_1AR_3", while it has the morphological pattern "$R_1aR_2aR_3$". Matching via the phonological pattern is computationally more straightforward than matching against the morphological pattern.

The number of unique patterns is 379 (227 are purely morphological patterns, and 152 are purely phonological patterns). Phonological patterns are related to morpho-phonological alteration operations related to the existence of either weak letters or doubling. Weak letters are any of the long vowels (alif, waw, yaa) or hamzah (glottal stop). The traditional Arabic way of representing the root radicals is through the letters f, E, l in their respective order ($f = R_1$, $E = R_2$ and $l = R_3$). Morphological patterns are the representative productive and generic patterns that apply to the majority of words, while phonological patterns are exception sub-branches of the morphological patterns that apply to specific cases where a radical happens to be replaced by a weak letter (long vowel) or hamzah (glottal stop).

In our database we make a fine grained classification of patterns based on their morpho-syntactic functions. Table 3 shows the count of patterns for each type based on POS and plurality paradigm. It is to be noted that in our system proper nouns and foreign Arabized words that do not follow any of the known Arabic patterns and are passed without any further processing.

3.2 Dataset and Features

It is hard to directly predict lemmas from stems due to the very fine granularity level. Thus, we generate patterns for all stems and lemmas, which are relatively limited in numbers in comparison to the actual lexical items rendering the search space for the classifier, therefore more manageable. We have two types of patterns: a) automatic patterns generated by replacing all consonants in a word with placeholders, and b) morpho-phonological patterns which only replaces the consonantal base with placeholders. For example, the verb أنطلق inoTalaq will be replaced by .i.o.a.a. in the automatic pattern, while it will be replaced by ino.a.a. in the morpho-phonological patterns which correctly identifies the sequence ino outside of the consonantal base. The number of unique automatic lemma patterns is 77, the number of automatic stem patterns is 225, and the number of morpho-phonological lemma patterns is 43 for verbs and 209 for nominals. Then for each stem pattern, we predict the Lemma-pattern (either automatic or morpho-phonological pattern).

The features used in our classifier are the stem, autoStemPattern (the pattern automatically generated from the stem by replacing consonants with placeholders), and affixes ($PREF_0$, $PREF_1$, ..., $PREF_n$, $SUFF_0$, $SUFF_1$, ..., $SUFF_m$), where n and m are based on the maximum number of prefixes and suffixes, respectively, in the data.

Note that the prefixes and suffixes refer to both clitics (coordinating conjunctions, prepositions and particles) and morphological markers (related to number, gender, person, aspect, mood, etc.), as depicted

Affixes	Description	Type	List
PREF0	Conjunctions	pro-clitic	fa, wa
PREF1	Particle	pro-clitic	li, sa, la, mA
PREF2	Perfective marker	prefix	a, >u, na, nu, ta, tu, ya, yu, l
SUFF0	mood, number, and gender marker	suffix	A, Ani, a, at, atA, aw, awoA, awona, ayo, iy, iyna, nA, na, o, ta, ti, tu, tum, u, uw, uwA, uwna
SUFF1	Accusative pronouns	enclitic	hA, hi, him, himA, hu, hum, humA, ka, ki, kum, kumA, kun~a, nA, niy

Table 4: List of affixes for verbs

in Table 4 which shows the affixes for verbs.

Then we compare the performance of two machine learning classifiers to predict the morpho-phonological pattern or the automatic pattern of the lemma for each stem using the features specified above. The results are discussed in Section 4.

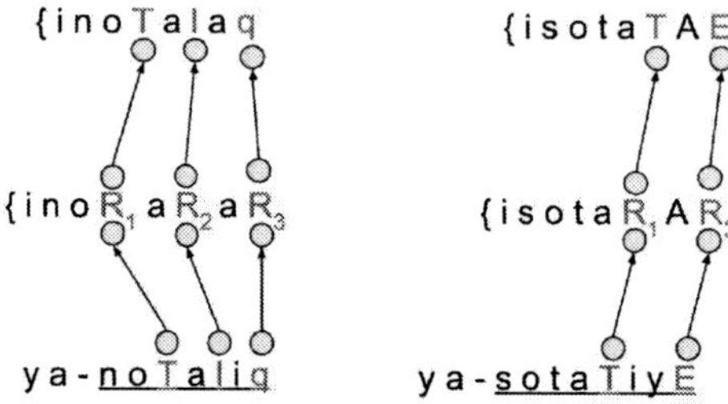

Figure 3: Stem-pattern-lemma Mapping

3.3 Mapping from lemma pattern to actual lemma

Using the ML classifier to predict the correct lemma pattern for each stem, we need, given the stem, to map the lemma pattern to the actual realization. We use deterministic rules to map the stem to the lemma using the predicted lemma pattern. We take the radicals from the stem and fill them in place of the pattern's slots in a reverse manner, i.e. starting from the end to the beginning of the string. The rules follow these procedures:

1. Remove prefixes and suffixes from stem

2. Remove diacritics (~, a, i, u, o) from stem

3. Remove weak letters (A, y, w)

4. From end to beginning replace the slot in the pattern with the radical from stem

For example, given the word yanoTaliq "set off" which has the lemma pattern $inoR_1aR_2aR_3$, first we remove the prefix ya, and the diacritics, that result in nTlq. Then, from the end to the beginning we fill the slots in the pattern with letters from the stem until all slots are consumed, thus replacing R_3 with q, R_2 with l, and R_1 with T. The same goes for yasotaTiyE, except that we additionally ignore the weak letters y and A. Figure 3 shows the mapping process for two words: the first with a morphological pattern (no weak letters), and the second with a phonological pattern (with weak letters).

4 Experiments and Evaluation

The method we develop is meant as a proof-of-concept that shows the usability of patterns in the sub-task of retrieving lemmas. It takes as input tokenized and POS-tagged texts. Due to the fact that we are not developing a full scale morphological processor, we cannot compare our results with state-of-the-art applications, such as MADA (Roth et al., 2008), and therefore we use intrinsic evaluation.

We evaluate our approach on the diacritized and undiacritized version of the ATB. For the baseline we consider the stem as the lemma without any further processing. Our data contains 128,293 nouns, 31,666 verbs, and 35,176 adjectives. We divide the data into 80% for training, 10% for development, and 10% for testing. The results in this section are reported against the test set.

Our method consists of two steps. First we use ML classifier to predict the lemma pattern for a given stem. For the ML step we notice that the results in general are remarkably better than the baseline. We conduct two classification experiments. In the first we take the set of morpho-phonological patterns (morphPtrn) as the prediction class, and in the second we use patterns automatically generated from the lemmas by removing cardinal letters (autoPtrn). For example, an autoPtrn can be generated from the lemma انتقال AinotiqAl "moving", which can be transformed into an autoPtrn by replacing all consonants with a placeholder "Ai.o.i.A.". This allows us to automatically generate a list of patterns without being constrained by a manually constructed list.

Baseline	72.35			
classifier/ template	**diac**		**nodiac**	
	tmpl_pred	lemma_mapping	tmpl_pred	lemma_mapping
Tree_morphPtrn	98.45	**98.23**	94.4	89.35
Tree_autoPtrn	98.67	94.12	94.34	**94.03**
extraTree_morphPtrn	97.73	92.98	90.38	77.36
extraTree_autoPtrn	99.05	90.14	94.28	81.54

Table 5: Verbs Results

We tested two ML algorithms: Decision Trees (C4.5) and Extra Trees classifier. We notice that using C4.5 produces significantly better results than Extra Trees. The second step is related to the reconstruction of the actual lemma from combining the stem and the predicted pattern using mapping rules. The results of this step show a marginal loss on the output of the prediction step. The experimental results are shown in Tables 5, 6, and 7, for verbs, nouns and adjectives respectively, and for both diacritized undiacritized words. The overall results are largely higher than the baseline with diacritized texts. For example, the baseline for verbs is 72.35% while our best result is 98.23%, with similar results for both adjectives and nouns.

With undiacritized words, the performance of the process varies with the type of entries. With verbs and nouns our results are higher than the baseline, with adjectives the prediction scores for patterns remains consistently high (mostly above 95%). But the mapping from pattern to lemma seems to fall below the baseline. Our justification is that adjectives do not undergo as many non-concatenative derivation. Moreover, mapping rules for undiacritized adjectives needs more improvement.

One of the interesting results we found in these experiments is that results with autoPtrn are comparable to (and sometimes even better than) morphPtrn which is an indication that patterns are machine learnable and that we do not need to rely solely on hand-crafted lists of Arabic templates.

Baseline	81.95			
classifier/ template	**diac**		**nodiac**	
	tmpl_pred	lemma_mapping	tmpl_pred	lemma_mapping
Tree_morphPtrn	97.93	**94.6**	96.48	**86.59**
Tree_autoPtrn	98.22	93.29	96.51	70.64
extraTree_morphPtrn	95.66	87.2	95.59	79.2
extraTree_autoPtrn	96.93	87.55	92.84	63.18

Table 6: Nouns Results

Baseline	93.10			
classifier/	diac		nodiac	
template	tmpl_pred	lemma_mapping	tmpl_pred	lemma_mapping
Tree_morphPtrn	93.32	*96.61*	97.04	79.60
Tree_autoPtrn	99.09	**97.92**	96.7	**86.20**
extraTree_morphPtrn	98.16	91.64	97.4	76.01
extraTree_autoPtrn	99.81	96.13	96.47	82.61

Table 7: Adjectives Results

5   Conclusion

We develop successful lemmatization method for Arabic without a dictionary or morphological analyzer. Our approach can serve as a plug-in to stemming applications and POS taggers. It needs to be fed the vowelized (diacritized) stem, the surrounding affixes and the POS tag to be able to return the correct lemma.

Although patterns have occupied center stage in traditional grammar and second language teaching for generations, they have been largely ignored in natural language processing. In this paper we have shown how the complex derivational and inflectional morphological system for Arabic can be modeled by machine learning methods when using patterns as an abstraction level to generalize on the variant surface forms. We also show how the cardinals of the root obey the linear order in various derivations and inflection, making filling the slots in the patterns a straightforward job. This paper describes the first attempt to relate surface forms to their lemmas in Arabic using probabilistic methods.

The recent few years have seen intense interest in deep learning and neural embeddings. In future work we want to handle the same problem with LSTM-based sequence-to-sequence models such as the neural encoder-decoder for morphological re-inflection explained in Kann and Schütze (2016), and test if direct mapping from words to lemmas is feasible, or patterns still represent a necessary component to mediate the process.

References

Muhammad Abdul-Mageed, Mona T Diab, and Sandra Kübler. 2013. Asma: A system for automatic segmentation and morpho-syntactic disambiguation of modern standard Arabic. In *RANLP*, pages 1–8.

Mohamed Seghir Hadj Ameur, Youcef Moulahoum, and Ahmed Guessoum. 2015. Restoration of Arabic diacritics using a multilevel statistical model. In *Computer Science and Its Applications*, pages 181–192. Springer.

Mohammed Attia and Josef van Genabith. 2013. A jellyfish dictionary for Arabic. In *Electronic lexicography in the 21st century: thinking outside the paper: proceedings of the eLex 2013 conference, 17-19 October 2013, Tallinn, Estonia*, pages 195–212.

Vimala Balakrishnan and Ethel Lloyd-Yemoh. 2014. Stemming and lemmatization: a comparison of retrieval performances. *Lecture Notes on Software Engineering*, 2(3):262.

Mohamed Bebah, Chennoufi Amine, Mazroui Azzeddine, and Lakhouaja Abdelhak. 2014. Hybrid approaches for automatic vowelization of Arabic texts. *arXiv preprint arXiv:1410.2646*.

Karien Brits, Rigardt Pretorius, and Gerhard B van Huyssteen. 2005. Automatic lemmatization in Setswana: Towards a prototype. *South African Journal of African Languages*, 25(1):37–47.

Tim Buckwalter. 2004. Buckwalter Arabic morphological analyzer version 2.0. linguistic data consortium, university of pennsylvania, 2002. ldc cat alog no.: Ldc2004l02. Technical report, ISBN 1-58563-324-0.

João Ricardo Martins Ferreira da Silva. 2007. Shallow processing of Portuguese: From sentence chunking to nominal lemmatization. *Master's thesis*.

Mona Diab. 2007. Improved Arabic base phrase chunking with a new enriched POS tag set. In *In Proceedings of the 2007 Workshop on Computational Approaches to Semitic Languages: Common Issues and Resources*, pages 89–96, Prague, Czech Republic.

Mona Diab. 2009. Second generation AMIRA tools for Arabic processing: Fast and robust tokenization, pos tagging, and base phrase chunking. In *In Proceedings of the Second International Conference on Arabic Language Resources and Tools*, pages 285–288, Cairo, Egypt.

Tarek El-Shishtawy and Abdulwahab Al-Sammak. 2012. Arabic keyphrase extraction using linguistic knowledge and machine learning techniques. *arXiv preprint arXiv:1203.4605*.

Tarek El-Shishtawy and Fatma El-Ghannam. 2012. An accurate Arabic root-based lemmatizer for information retrieval purposes. *arXiv preprint arXiv:1203.3584*.

Tarek El-Shishtawy and Fatma El-Ghannam. 2014. A lemma based evaluator for semitic language text summarization systems. *arXiv preprint arXiv:1403.5596*.

Moustafa Elshafei, Husni Al-Muhtaseb, and Mansour Alghamdi. 2006. Statistical methods for automatic diacritization of Arabic text. In *The Saudi 18th National Computer Conference. Riyadh*, volume 18, pages 301–306.

Jan Hajic, Otakar Smrz, Tim Buckwalter, and Hubert Jin. 2005. Feature-based tagger of approximations of functional Arabic morphology. In *Proceedings of the Workshop on Treebanks and Linguistic Theories (TLT), Barcelona, Spain*.

Jan Hajič. 2000. Morphological tagging: Data vs. dictionaries. In *Proceedings of the 1st North American chapter of the Association for Computational Linguistics conference*, pages 94–101. Association for Computational Linguistics.

Faten Khalfallah Hammouda and Abdelsalam Abdelhamid Almarimi. 2010. Heuristic lemmatization for Arabic texts indexation and classification 1.

Ahmad Hossny, Khaled Shaalan, and Aly Fahmy. 2008. Automatic morphological rule induction for Arabic. In *Proceedings of the LREC'08 workshop on HLT & NLP within the Arabic world: Arabic Language and local languages processing: Status Updates and Prospects*, pages 97–101.

Matjaž Juršič, Igor Mozetič, and Nada Lavrač. 2007. Learning ripple down rules for efficient lemmatization. In *Proceedings of the 10th international multiconference information society, IS*, pages 206–209.

Dror Kamir, Naama Soreq, and Yoni Neeman. 2002. A comprehensive NLP system for modern standard Arabic and modern Hebrew. In *Proceedings of the ACL-02 workshop on Computational approaches to semitic languages*, pages 1–9. Association for Computational Linguistics.

Katharina Kann and Hinrich Schütze. 2016. Single-model encoder-decoder with explicit morphological representation for reinflection. In *Proceedings of the 54th Annual Meeting of the Association for Computational Linguistics, Berlin, Germany*, pages 555–560.

Shereen Khoja and Roger Garside. 1999. Stemming Arabic text. *Lancaster, UK, Computing Department, Lancaster University*.

Tuomo Korenius, Jorma Laurikkala, Kalervo Järvelin, and Martti Juhola. 2004. Stemming and lemmatization in the clustering of Finnish text documents. In *Proceedings of the thirteenth ACM international conference on Information and knowledge management*, pages 625–633. ACM.

Leah S Larkey, Lisa Ballesteros, and Margaret E Connell. 2002. Improving stemming for Arabic information retrieval: Light stemming and co-occurrence analysis. In *Proceedings of the 25th annual international ACM SIGIR conference on Research and development in information retrieval*, pages 275–282. ACM.

Rani Nelken and Stuart M Shieber. 2005. Arabic diacritization using weighted finite-state transducers. In *Proceedings of the ACL Workshop on Computational Approaches to Semitic Languages*, pages 79–86. Association for Computational Linguistics.

Okan Ozturkmenoglu and Adil Alpkocak. 2012. Comparison of different lemmatization approaches for information retrieval on Turkish text collection. In *Innovations in Intelligent Systems and Applications (INISTA), 2012 International Symposium on*, pages 1–5. IEEE.

Joël Plisson, Nada Lavrac, Dunja Mladenic, et al. 2004. A rule based approach to word lemmatization. *Proceedings of IS-2004*, pages 83–86.

Mohsen Rashwan, Mohamed Al-Badrashiny, Mohamed Attia, Sherif Abdou, and Ahmed Rafea. 2011. A stochastic Arabic diacritizer based on a hybrid of factorized and unfactorized textual features. *Audio, Speech, and Language Processing, IEEE Transactions on*, 19(1):166–175.

Ryan Roth, Owen Rambow, Nizar Habash, Mona Diab, and Cynthia Rudin. 2008. Arabic morphological tagging, diacritization, and lemmatization using lexeme models and feature ranking. In *Proceedings of the 46th Annual Meeting of the Association for Computational Linguistics on Human Language Technologies: Short Papers*, pages 117–120. Association for Computational Linguistics.

Djamé Seddah, Grzegorz Chrupała, Özlem Çetinoğlu, Josef Van Genabith, and Marie Candito. 2010. Lemmatization and lexicalized statistical parsing of morphologically rich languages: The case of French. In *Proceedings of the NAACL HLT 2010 First Workshop on Statistical Parsing of Morphologically-Rich Languages*, pages 85–93. Association for Computational Linguistics.

Nasredine Semmar, Meriama Laib, and Christian Fluhr. 2006. Using stemming in morphological analysis to improve Arabic information retrieval. In *TALN 2006*, pages 317–326, Leuven, Belgium.

Lucie Skorkovská. 2012. Application of lemmatization and summarization methods in topic identification module for large scale language modeling data filtering. In *Text, Speech and Dialogue*, pages 191–198. Springer.

Marko Tadić. 2006. Croatian lemmatization server. In *Fifth International Conference Formal Approaches to South Slavic and Balkan languages (FASSBL)*.

Kristina Toutanova and Christopher D Manning. 2000. Enriching the knowledge sources used in a maximum entropy part-of-speech tagger. In *Proceedings of the 2000 Joint SIGDAT conference on Empirical methods in natural language processing and very large corpora: held in conjunction with the 38th Annual Meeting of the Association for Computational Linguistics-Volume 13*, pages 63–70. Association for Computational Linguistics.

Word Sense Disambiguation using a Bidirectional LSTM

Mikael Kågebäck,* Hans Salomonsson*
Computer Science & Engineering, Chalmers University of Technology
SE-412 96, Göteborg, Sweden
{kageback,hans.salomonsson}@chalmers.se

Abstract

In this paper we present a clean, yet effective, model for *word sense disambiguation*. Our approach leverage a *bidirectional long short-term memory* network which is shared between all words. This enables the model to share statistical strength and to scale well with vocabulary size. The model is trained *end-to-end*, directly from the raw text to sense labels, and makes effective use of word order. We evaluate our approach on two standard datasets, using identical hyperparameter settings, which are in turn tuned on a third set of held out data. We employ no external resources (e.g. knowledge graphs, part-of-speech tagging, etc), language specific features, or hand crafted rules, but still achieve statistically equivalent results to the best *state-of-the-art* systems, that employ no such limitations.

1   Introduction

Words are in general ambiguous and can have several related or unrelated meanings depending on context. For instance, the word *rock* can refer to both a stone and a music genre, but in the sentence "Without the guitar, there would be no *rock* music" the sense of *rock* is no longer ambiguous. The task of assigning a word token in a text, e.g. *rock*, to a well defined word sense in a lexicon is called *word sense disambiguation* (WSD). From the *rock* example above it is easy to see that the context surrounding the word is what disambiguates the sense. However, it may not be so obvious that this is a difficult task. To see this, consider instead the phrase "Solid rock" where changing the order of words completely changes the meaning, or "Hard rock crushes heavy metal" where individual words seem to indicate stone but together they actually define the word token as music. With this in mind, our thesis is that to do WSD well we need to go beyond *bag of words* and into the territory of sequence modeling.

Improved WSD would be beneficial to many natural language processing (NLP) problems, e.g. machine translation (Vickrey et al., 2005), information Retrieval, information Extraction (Navigli, 2009), and sense aware word representations (Neelakantan et al., 2015; Kågebäck et al., 2015; Nieto Piña and Johansson, 2015; Bovi et al., 2015). However, though much progress has been made in the area, many current WSD systems suffer from one or two of the following deficits. (1) Disregarding the order of words in the context which can lead to problems as described above. (2) Relying on complicated and potentially language specific hand crafted features and resources, which is a big problem particularly for resource poor languages. We aim to mitigate these problems by (1) modeling the sequence of words surrounding the target word, and (2) refrain from using any hand crafted features or external resources and instead represent the words using real valued vector representation, i.e. word embeddings. Using word embeddings has previously been shown to improve WSD (Taghipour and Ng, 2015; Johansson and Nieto Piña, 2015). However, these works did not consider the order of words or their operational effect on each other.

Proceedings of the Workshop on Cognitive Aspects of the Lexicon,
pages 51–56, Osaka, Japan, December 11-17 2016.

1.1 The main contributions of this work include:

- A purely learned approach to WSD that achieves results on par with state-of-the-art resource heavy systems, employing e.g. knowledge graphs, parsers, part-of-speech tagging, etc.

- Parameter sharing between different word types to make more efficient use of labeled data and make full vocabulary scaling plausible without the number of parameters exploding.

- Empirical evidence that highlights the importance of word order for WSD.

- A WSD system that, by using no explicit window, is allowed to combine local and global information when deducing the sense.

2 Background

In this section we introduce the most important underlying techniques for our proposed model.

2.1 Bidirectional LSTM

Long short-term memory (LSTM) is a gated type of *recurrent neural network* (RNN). LSTMs were introduced by Hochreiter and Schmidhuber (1997) to enable RNNs to better capture long term dependencies when used to model sequences. This is achieved by letting the model copy the state between timesteps without forcing the state through a non-linearity. The flow of information is instead regulated using multiplicative gates which preserves the gradient better than e.g. the logistic function. The bidirectional variant of LSTM, (BLSTM) (Graves and Schmidhuber, 2005) is an adaptation of the LSTM where the state at each time step consist of the state of two LSTMs, one going left and one going right. For WSD this means that the state has information about both preceding words and succeeding words, which in many cases are absolutely necessary to correctly classify the sense.

2.2 Word embeddings by GloVe

Word embeddings is a way to represent words as real valued vectors in a semantically meaningful space. *Global Vectors for Word Representation* (GloVe), introduced by Pennington et al. (2014) is a hybrid approach to embedding words that combine a log-linear model, made popular by Mikolov et al. (2013), with counting based co-occurrence statistics to more efficiently capture global statistics. Word embeddings are trained in an unsupervised fashion, typically on large amounts of data, and is able to capture fine grained semantic and syntactic information about words. These vectors can subsequently be used to initialize the input layer of a neural network or some other NLP model.

3 The Model

Given a document and the position of the target word, i.e. the word to disambiguate, the model computes a probability distribution over the possible senses corresponding to that word. The architecture of the model, depicted in Figure 1, consist of a softmax layer, a hidden layer, and a BLSTM. See Section 2.1 for more details regarding the BLSTM. The BLSTM and the hidden layer share parameters over all word types and senses, while the softmax is parameterized by word type and selects the corresponding weight matrix and bias vector for each word type respectively. This structure enables the model to share statistical strength across different word types while remaining computationally efficient even for a large total number of senses and realistic vocabulary sizes.

3.1 Model definition

The input to the BLSTM at position n in document $\mathcal{D}$ is computed as

$$\mathbf{x}_n = W^x \mathbf{v}(w_n), n \in \{1, \ldots, |\mathcal{D}|\}.$$

Here, $\mathbf{v}(w_n)$ is the *one-hot* representation of the word type corresponding to $w_n \in \mathcal{D}$. A one-hot representation is a vector with dimension V consisting of $|V| - 1$ zeros and a single one which index

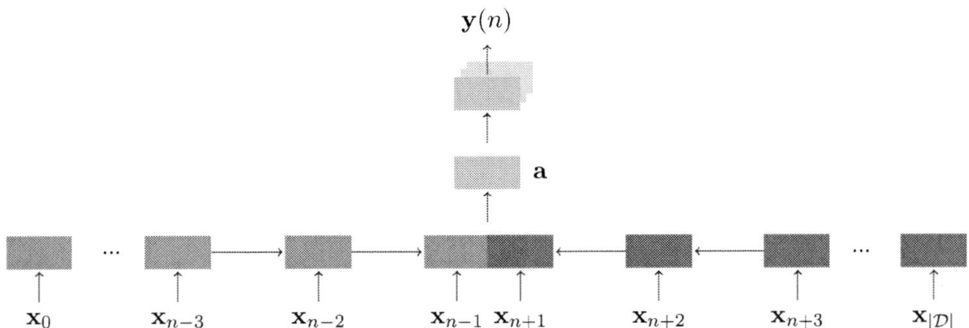

Figure 1: A BLSTM centered around a word at position n. Its output is fed to a neural network sense classifier consisting of one hidden layer with linear units and a softmax. The softmax selects the corresponding weight matrix and bias vector for the word at position n.

indicate the word type. This will have the effect of picking the column from W^x corresponding to that word type. The resulting vector is referred to as a word embedding. Further, W^x can be initialized using pre-trained word embeddings, to leverage large unannotated datasets. In this work GloVe vectors are used for this purpose, see Section 4.1 for details.

The model output,

$$\mathbf{y}(n) = \mathrm{softmax}(W_{w_n}^{ay}\mathbf{a} + \mathbf{b}_{w_n}^{ay}),$$

is the predicted distribution over senses for the word at position n, where $W_{w_n}^{ay}$ and $\mathbf{b}_{w_n}^{ay}$ are the weights and biases for the softmax layer corresponding to the word type at position n. Hence, each word type will have its own softmax parameters, with dimensions depending on the number of senses of that particular word. Further, the hidden layer $\mathbf{a}$ is computed as

$$\mathbf{a} = W^{ha}[\mathbf{h}_{n-1}^{L}; \mathbf{h}_{n+1}^{R}] + \mathbf{b}^{ha}$$

where $[\mathbf{h}_{n-1}^{L}; \mathbf{h}_{n+1}^{R}]$ is the concatenated outputs of the right and left traversing LSTMs of the BLSTM at word n. W^{ha} and $\mathbf{b}^{ha}$ are the weights and biases for the hidden layer.

Loss function The parameters of the model, $\Omega = \{W^x, \Theta_{BLSTM}, W^{ha}, \mathbf{b}^{ha}, \{W_w^{ay}, \mathbf{b}_w^{ay}\}_{\forall w \in V}, \}$, are fitted by minimizing the cross entropy error

$$L(\Omega) = -\sum_{i \in \mathcal{I}} \sum_{j \in S(w_i)} t_{i,j} \log y_j(i)$$

over a set of sense labeled tokens with indices $\mathcal{I} \subset \{1, \ldots, |\mathcal{C}|\}$ within a training corpus $\mathcal{C}$, each labeled with a target sense $\mathbf{t}_i, \forall i \in \mathcal{I}$.

3.2 Dropword

Dropword is a regularization technique very similar to *word dropout* introduced by Iyyer et al. (2015). Both methods are word level generalizations of dropout (Srivastava et al., 2014) but in word dropout the word is set to zero while in dropword it is replaced with a *<dropped>* tag. The tag is subsequently treated just like any other word in the vocabulary and has a corresponding word embedding that is trained. This process is repeated over time, so that the words dropped change over time. The motivation for doing dropword is to decrease the dependency on individual words in the training context. This technique can be generalized to other kinds of sequential inputs, not only words.

4 Experiments

To evaluate our proposed model we perform the *lexical sample task* of SensEval 2 (SE2) (Kilgarriff, 2001) and SensEval 3 (SE3) (Mihalcea et al., 2004), part of the SensEval (Kilgarriff and Palmer, 2000) workshops organized by *Special Interest Group on the Lexicon* at ACL. For both instances of the task training and test data are supplied, and the task consist of disambiguating one indicated word in a context. The words to disambiguate are sampled from the vocabulary to give a range of low, medium and high frequency words, and a gold standard sense label is supplied for training and evaluation.

4.1 Experimental settings

The hyperparameter settings used during the experiments, presented in Table 1, were tuned on a separate validation set with data picked from the SE2 training set. The source code, implemented using *TensorFlow* (Abadi et al., 2015), has been released as open source[1].

Hyperparameter	Range searched	Value used
Embedding size	$\{100, 200\}$	100
BLSTM hidden layer size	$[50, 100]$	$2 * 74$
Dropout on word embeddings $\mathbf{x}_n$	$[0, 50\%]$	50%
Dropout on the LSTM output $[\mathbf{h}^L_{n-1}; \mathbf{h}^R_{n+1}]$	$[0, 70\%]$	50%
Dropout on the hidden layer $\mathbf{a}$	$[0, 70\%]$	50%
Dropword	$[0, 20\%]$	10%
Gaussian noise added to input	$[0, 0.4]$	$\sim \mathcal{N}(0, 0.2\sigma_i)$
Optimization algorithm	-	Stochastic gradient descent
Momentum	-	0.1
Initial learning rate	-	2.0
Learning rate decay	-	0.96
Embedding initialization	-	GloVe
Remaining parameters initialized	-	$\in \mathcal{U}(-0.1, 0.1)$

Table 1: Hyperparameter settings used for both experiments and the ranges that were searched during tuning. "-" indicates that no tuning were performed on that parameter.

Embeddings The embeddings are initialized using a set of freely available[2] GloVe vectors trained on Wikipedia and Gigaword. Words not included in this set are initialized from $\mathcal{N}(0, 0.1)$. To keep the input noise proportional to the embeddings it is scaled by σ_i which is the standard deviation in embedding dimension i for all words in the embeddings matrix, W^x. σ_i is updated after each weight update.

Data preprocessing The only preprocessing of the data that is conducted is replacing numbers with a $< number >$ tag. This result in a vocabulary size of $|V| = 50817$ for SE2 and $|V| = 37998$ for SE3. Words not present in the training set are considered unknown during test. Further, we limit the size of the context to max 140 words centered around the target word to facilitate faster training.

4.2 Results

The results of our experiments and the state-of-the-art are shown in Table 2. 100JHU(R) was developed by Yarowsky et al. (2001) and achieved the best score on the English lexical sample task of SE2 with a F1 score of 64.2. Their system utilized a rich feature space based on raw words, lemmas, POS tags, bag-of-words, bi-gram, and tri-gram collocations, etc. as inputs to an ensemble classifier. htsa3 by Grozea (2004) was the winner of the SE3 lexical sample task with a F1 score of 72.9. This system was based mainly on raw words, lemmas, and POS tags. These were used as inputs to a regularized least square

---

[1]Source for all experiments is available at: `https://bitbucket.org/salomons/wsd`
[2]The employed GloVe vectors are available for download at: `http://nlp.stanford.edu/projects/glove/`

classifier. IMS+adapted CW is a more recent system, by Taghipour and Ng (2015), that uses separately trained word embeddings as input. However, it also relies on a rich set of other features including POS tags, collocations and surrounding words to achieve their reported result.

Our proposed model achieves the top score on SE2 and are tied with IMS+adapted CW on SE3. Moreover, we see that dropword consistently improves the results on both SE2 and SE3. Randomizing the order of the input words yields a substantially worse result, which provides evidence for our hypothesis that the order of the words are significant. We also see that the system effectively makes use of the information in the pre-trained word embeddings and that they are essential to the performance of our system on these datasets.

| | F1 score | |
Method	SE2	SE3
BLSTM (our proposed model)	**66.9**	**73.4**
100JHU(R)	64.2	-
htsa3	-	72.9
IMS+adapted CW	66.2	**73.4**
BLSTM without dropword	66.5	72.9
BLSTM without GloVe	54.6	59.0
BLSTM, randomized word order	58.8	64.7

Table 2: Results for Senseval 2 and 3 on the English lexical sample task.

5 Conclusions & future work

We presented a BLSTM based model for WSD that was able to effectively exploit word order and achieve results on *state-of-the-art* level, using no external resources or handcrafted features. As a consequence, the model is largely language independent and applicable to resource poor languages. Further, the system was designed to generalize to full vocabulary WSD by sharing most of the parameters between words.

For future work we would like to provide more empirical evidence for language independence by evaluating on several different languages, and do experiments on large vocabulary *all words WSD*, where every word in a sentence is disambiguated. Further, we plan to experiment with unsupervised pre-training of the BLSTM, encouraged by the substantial improvement achieved by incorporating word embeddings.

Acknowledgments

The authors would like to acknowledge the project *Towards a knowledge-based culturomics* supported by a framework grant from the Swedish Research Council (2012–2016; dnr 2012-5738). Further, the work was partly funded by the *BigData@Chalmers* initiative. Finally. the authors would like to thank the reviewers for their insightful and constructive feedback.

References

Martín Abadi, Ashish Agarwal, Paul Barham, Eugene Brevdo, Zhifeng Chen, Craig Citro, Greg S. Corrado, Andy Davis, Jeffrey Dean, Matthieu Devin, Sanjay Ghemawat, Ian Goodfellow, Andrew Harp, Geoffrey Irving, Michael Isard, Yangqing Jia, Rafal Jozefowicz, Lukasz Kaiser, Manjunath Kudlur, Josh Levenberg, Dan Mané, Rajat Monga, Sherry Moore, Derek Murray, Chris Olah, Mike Schuster, Jonathon Shlens, Benoit Steiner, Ilya Sutskever, Kunal Talwar, Paul Tucker, Vincent Vanhoucke, Vijay Vasudevan, Fernanda Viégas, Oriol Vinyals, Pete Warden, Martin Wattenberg, Martin Wicke, Yuan Yu, and Xiaoqiang Zheng. 2015. TensorFlow: Large-scale machine learning on heterogeneous systems. Software available from tensorflow.org.

Claudio Delli Bovi, Luis Espinosa-Anke, and Roberto Navigli. 2015. Knowledge base unification via sense embeddings and disambiguation. In *Proceedings of EMNLP*, pages 726–736.

Alex Graves and Jürgen Schmidhuber. 2005. Framewise phoneme classification with bidirectional lstm and other neural network architectures. *Neural Networks*, 18(5):602–610.

Cristian Grozea. 2004. Finding optimal parameter settings for high performance word sense disambiguation. In *Proceedings of Senseval-3 Workshop*.

Sepp Hochreiter and Jürgen Schmidhuber. 1997. Long short-term memory. *Neural computation*, 9(8):1735–1780.

Mohit Iyyer, Varun Manjunatha, Jordan Boyd-Graber, and Hal Daumé III. 2015. Deep unordered composition rivals syntactic methods for text classification. In *Proceedings of the Association for Computational Linguistics*.

Richard Johansson and Luis Nieto Piña. 2015. Combining relational and distributional knowledge for word sense disambiguation. *Nordic Conference of Computational Linguistics NODALIDA 2015*, page 69.

Mikael Kågebäck, Fredrik Johansson, Richard Johansson, and Devdatt Dubhashi. 2015. Neural context embeddings for automatic discovery of word senses. In *Proceedings of NAACL-HLT*, pages 25–32.

Adam Kilgarriff and Martha Palmer. 2000. Introduction to the special issue on senseval. *Computers and the Humanities*, 34(1-2):1–13.

Adam Kilgarriff. 2001. English lexical sample task description. In *The Proceedings of the Second International Workshop on Evaluating Word Sense Disambiguation Systems*, pages 17–20. Association for Computational Linguistics.

Rada Mihalcea, Timothy Anatolievich Chklovski, and Adam Kilgarriff. 2004. The senseval-3 english lexical sample task. Association for Computational Linguistics.

Tomas Mikolov, Wen-tau Yih, and Geoffrey Zweig. 2013. Linguistic regularities in continuous space word representations. In *HLT-NAACL*, pages 746–751.

Roberto Navigli. 2009. Word Sense Disambiguation: a survey. *ACM Computing Surveys*, 41(2):1–69.

Arvind Neelakantan, Jeevan Shankar, Alexandre Passos, and Andrew McCallum. 2015. Efficient non-parametric estimation of multiple embeddings per word in vector space. *arXiv preprint arXiv:1504.06654*.

Luis Nieto Piña and Richard Johansson. 2015. A simple and efficient method to generate word sense representations. In *Proceedings of Recent Advances in Natural Language Processing*, pages 465–472, Hissar, Bulgaria.

Jeffrey Pennington, Richard Socher, and Christopher D Manning. 2014. Glove: Global vectors for word representation. *Proceedings of the Empiricial Methods in Natural Language Processing (EMNLP 2014)*, 12:1532–1543.

Nitish Srivastava, Geoffrey Hinton, Alex Krizhevsky, Ilya Sutskever, and Ruslan Salakhutdinov. 2014. Dropout: A simple way to prevent neural networks from overfitting. *The Journal of Machine Learning Research*, 15(1):1929–1958.

Kaveh Taghipour and Hwee Tou Ng. 2015. Semi-supervised word sense disambiguation using word embeddings in general and specific domains. In *The 2015 Annual Conference of the North American Chapter of the Association for Computational Linguistics*, pages 314–323.

David Vickrey, Luke Biewald, Marc Teyssier, and Daphne Koller. 2005. Word-sense disambiguation for machine translation. In *Proceedings of the conference on Human Language Technology and Empirical Methods in Natural Language Processing*, pages 771–778. Association for Computational Linguistics.

David Yarowsky, Silviu Cucerzan, Radu Florian, Charles Schafer, and Richard Wicentowski. 2001. The johns hopkins senseval2 system descriptions. In *The Proceedings of the Second International Workshop on Evaluating Word Sense Disambiguation Systems*, SENSEVAL '01, pages 163–166, Stroudsburg, PA, USA. Association for Computational Linguistics.

Towards a resource based on *users' knowledge* to overcome the *Tip-of-the-Tongue* problem

Michael Zock
AMU (LIF, CNRS)
163 Avenue de Luminy
13288 Marseille / France
michael.zock@lif.univ-mrs.fr

Chris Biemann
Language Technology Group
Vogt-Kölln-Straße 30
22527 Hamburg / Germany
biemann@uni-hamburg.de

Abstract

Language production is largely a matter of words which, in the case of access problems, can be searched for in an external resource (lexicon, thesaurus). In this kind of dialogue the user provides the momentarily available knowledge concerning the target and the system responds with the best guess(es) it can make given this input. As tip-of-the-tongue (ToT)-studies have shown, people always have some knowledge concerning the target (meaning fragments, number of syllables, ...) even if its complete form is eluding them. We will show here how to tap on this knowledge to build a resource likely to help authors (speakers/writers) to overcome the ToT-problem. Yet, before doing so we need a better understanding of the various kinds of knowledge people have when looking for a word. To this end, we asked crowdworkers to provide some cues to describe a given target and to specify then how each one of them relates to the target, in the hope that this could help others to find the elusive word. Next, we checked how well a given search strategy worked when being applied to differently built lexical networks. The results showed quite dramatic differences, which is not really surprising. After all, different networks are built for different purposes; hence each one of them is more or less suited for a given task. What was more surprising though is the fact that the relational information given by the users did not allow us to find the elusive word in WordNet better than without it.

1   The problem : word access in language production

Communication is largely based on words which encode various sorts of information, *conceptual* (lexical semantics, encyclopedic knowledge), *linguistic* (word forms, part of speech), ... If ever we lack any of this information we may reach for a dictionary, a thesaurus or an encyclopedia in the hope to find what we are looking for. Information access works generally quite well for readers, but much less for authors. Obviously, readers and writers have different needs, and while both provide words as input, they clearly pursue different goals. Readers start from word forms in the hope to get meanings, while authors go the opposite direction: starting from meanings (or meaning fragments), broader topical categories (thesaurus) or specific target-related words (associations, co-occurrences) they hope to find the elusive word (target). We will be concerned here with this latter kind of search.

There are two major access modes, one being automatic, and the other deliberate. The former relies solely on our brain (on-line processing when speaking or writing) whereas the latter uses an additional, external resource (paper or electronic dictionary). In general we resort to this second strategy only if spontaneous access fails. Alas, most dictionaries are not very well suited for this purpose (see Section 3). Yet, even if we had such a dictionary, we are still faced with the problems of input and size. What information shall the user give to allow the resource to guess the elusive word? Since dictionaries are generally quite large, arises the question of how to reduce the entire set of words (scope of the lexicon) to one, the target. This leads to the next question: how to reduce quickly the initial space to a subspace which is neither too big nor too small, that is, how to ensure that the output contains only a reasonable set of candidates (not too big), yet still potentially relevant information? Inconsiderate filtering

Proceedings of the Workshop on Cognitive Aspects of the Lexicon,
pages 57–68, Osaka, Japan, December 11-17 2016.

might eliminate promising candidates, in which case the space gets too small. To answer these questions, it is interesting to take a look at the *Tip-of-the-Tongue* problem (Brown & McNeill, 1996), henceforth ToT.

2   The Tip-of-the-tongue problem

There are different sorts of impairment hindering wordfinding (aphasia, anomia, ...). One of the best known and most intensively studied ones is the ToT-problem (Brown, 1991). Someone is said to be in this state when he knows what to say, he also knows the corresponding form, but for some reason he simply is not able to access it in time, at the very moment of speaking or writing. To get a better understanding of the problem and process at hand, let us replace the task in its natural context, language production.[1] After all, words are generally used in this situation.

Language production involves three major tasks (Bock, 1996; Levelt, 1989), most of which apply not only for sentence generation, but also for the production of words. Hence, we start from an image or a concept ($Level_1$), which can be very abstract and be linguistically unspecified. Neither nor have information concerning part of speech, or phonology at this level. Indeed, at this stage we may have something like 'move' or 'reptile' but not their concrete lexical forms, for example: 'walk/limp/run'.

Hence, the speaker must add sufficient information to be able to decide whether, in the case of reptiles, he wants to refer to an 'alligator, 'caiman', or 'crocodile'. These are lexical concepts, i.e. entries in the mental lexicon, also called a *lemmas* ($Level_2$). Note that at this stage we have only an abstract form containing the meaning, part of speech and some general information concerning the phonological form (number of syllables, intonation, ...). Yet, it is only at the next step ($Level_3$) that the brain specifies the phonological form, to yield a *lexeme*, the word's concrete form. This allows us then to compute the required motor program to carry out the necessary steps to produce a written or spoken form. A tip-of-the-tongue state occurs if there is an interruption between $Level_2$ and $Level_3$.[2]

ToT problems can be seen as a puzzle which can be solved by providing or priming the missing elements. This can be done indirectly (cf. Abrams et al., 2007). James and Burke (2000) designed a protocol to do precisely this. They presented some pictures or definitions asking their subjects to find the corresponding word. Those who failed, but knew the word, i.e. those who were in a ToT-state, were used for the main part of the experiment. This group was then divided in two equal parts. Half of participants were asked to read aloud a list of words that cumulatively contained all of the syllables of the ToT word. Suppose someone failed to retrieve the target *abdicate*, in this case he would be asked to read the following list of ten words, *abstract, indigent, truncate, tradition* and *locate,* each of which contains a syllable of the target. The other half was also given a list of 10 words, but phonologically unrelated. Having done this exercise, participants were asked to try again to retrieve the target. And this time most of the members of the group being exposed to phonologically related words succeeded, while the other group did not.

Obviously, in a natural situation we can neither wait for the phonological primes to occur, nor can we provide them as James et al. did, as this would require knowledge of the target. Yet if we knew the target then we would give it, since this is what the author is looking for. To conclude, we cannot provide the missing parts or offer form-related cues (for example, phonological cues), what we can do though is to provide semantically related words, associations, i.e. words related to the user input.

3   Related work

Concerning lexical access, several communities are concerned: engineers from the natural language generation community (NLG), psychologists, computational linguists and lexicographers. Space constraints prevent us from referring to all this work. Hence, we will focus here mainly on the work

---

[1] For a broad view from a psycholinguistic or neuroscientist's perspective, see (Levelt, 1989; Rapp and Goldrick, 2006; Goldrick, et al., 2014). The equivalent, but from an engineering point of can be found in (Dale & Reiter, 2000, Krahmer and Theune, 2010). For a recent state of the art paper see (Bateman and Zock, 2016).

[2] Levelt's word production model (Levelt et al., 1999) is actually quite a bit more sophisticated. It requires the following six steps : (1) *conceptual preparation* → lexical concept ; (2) *lexical selection* (abstract word) → lemma; (3) *morphological encoding* → morpheme ; (4) *phonological encoding* (syllabification) → phonological word; (5) *phonetic encoding* → phonetic gestural code ; (6) *articulation* → sound wave. Note that it postulates two knowledge bases: the mental lexicon, vital for lemma retrieval, and the syllabary, important for phonetic encoding.

done in lexicography. Note though, that the problem addressed by the NLG community deals with 'lexical choice', but not with 'lexical access'. Yet, before choosing a word, one must have accessed it.

How words are stored and processed in the human mind has extensively been dealt with by psychologists (Aitchinson, 2003; de Deyne and Storms, 2015; deDeyne et al. 2016). Yet, while there are many papers dealing with the *tip-of-the-tongue phenomenon* (Brown & McNeill, 1996), or the problem of lexical access (Levelt et al. 1999), they do not consider the use of computers for helping people in their task (our goal).

Lexicographers bridge this gap. Unfortunately, until recently most of their tools have been built for the language receiver. Nevertheless, nowadays there are also some *tools* for the language producer. For example, Roget's thesaurus (Roget, 1852) or its modern incarnation built with the help of corpus linguistics (Dornseiff, 2003). There are also the Language Activator (Summers, 1993), the Oxford Learner's Wordfinder Dictionary (Trappes-Lomax, 1997), and various network-based lexical resources: *WordNet,* henceforth WN (Miller,1990), *Framenet* (Fillmore et al. 2003); *MindNet* (Richardson et al., 1998), and *HowNet* (Dong & Dong, 2006;). Finally, there are collocation dictionaries (Benson et al., 2010), and web-based tools like Lexical FreeNet[3] or Onelook (Beeferman, 2003), which, like BabelNet (Navigli & Ponzetto, 2012) combines a dictionary (WN) and an encyclopedia (Wikipedia), though putting the emphasis on onomasiological search, access by meaning. Reverse dictionaries have been built by hand (Bernstein, 1975) and with the help of machines (Dutoit and Nugues, 2002). In both cases, one draws on the words occurring in the definition. Thorat and Choudhari (2016) try to extend this idea by introducing a distance-based approach to compute word similarity. Given a small set of words they compare their approach with Onelook and with dense-vector similarity. While we adopt part of their methodology in our evaluation scheme, we are more reserved with respect to their architecture. Since it requires a fully computed similarity matrix for the entire vocabulary, their work cannot scale up: it is unreasonable to assume that the lexicon is stored in a fully connected similarity matrix, which grows quadratically in the size of the vocabulary. Note that while dense representations are easily compared, proximity search is not. It is computationally simply too expensive.

As one can see, a lot of progress has been made during the last two decades, yet more can be done especially with respect to indexing (organization of the data) and navigation.

4   Navigation, a fundamentally cognitive process

As we will show in this section, navigation in a lexical resource is above all a knowledge-based process. Before being able to use a word, we must have acquired it. It is only then that it has become part of our knowledge. Yet, storage does not guarantee access (Zock & Schwab, 2011). This fact has not received the attention it deserves by lexicographers. Note also that there are several kinds of knowledge: declarative, meta-knowledge (not necessarily linguistic) and knowledge states.

- *Declarative knowledge* is what we acquire when learning words (meaning, form, spelling, usage), and this is the information generally encoded in dictionaries. Obviously, in order to find a word or to find the information associated with it, they must be stored, though this is not enough.

- Next, there is *meta-knowledge,* which also needs to be acquired. Being generally unavailable for in(tro)spection, meta-knowledge reveals itself in various ways. For example, via the information available when we *fail to access* a *word* (Schwartz, 2006), or via the *query* we provide at the moment of launching a search. As word association experiments have shown (Aitchison, 2003) words always evoke something. Since this is true for all words one can conclude that all words are connected in our mind, which implies that all words are accessible from anywhere like in a fully connected graph.[4] All we have to do is to provide some input (source word, available information) and follow then the path linking this input to the output (target). Interestingly, people hardly ever start from words remotely related to the target. Quite to the contrary, they tend to start from a more or less direct neighbor of the target, the distance between the two, exceeding rarely the distance of 2.[5]

<hr>

[3] http://www.lexfn.com

[4] Note that this does not hold for WN, as WN is not a single network, but a set of networks. There are 25 for nouns, and at least one for all the other parts of speech

[5] This is probably one of the reasons why we would feel estranged if someone provided as cue 'computer', while his target 'mocha'. The two are definitely not directly connected, though, there is a path between them, eventhough it is not obvious

Also, dictionary users often know the type of relationship holding between the input (prime) and the target. These two observations clearly support our idea that people have a considerable amount of (meta-) knowledge concerning the organization of words in their mind, i.e. their mental lexicon.

- The idea of relationship has been nicely exploited by WN, which due to this feature keeps the search space, i.e. a set of candidates among which the user has to choose, quite small. The idea of relatedness has led lexicographers already in the past to build thesauri, collocation- and synonym dictionaries. Obviously an input consisting only of a simple word is hard to interpret. Does the user want a more general/specific word, a synonym or antonym? Is the input semantically or phonetically related to the target, or is it part of the target word's definition (dog-animal)? In each case the user is expecting a different word (or set of words) as output. Hence, in order to enable a system to properly interpret the users' goals we need this kind of metalinguistic information (neighbor of the target, i.e. source word + relation to the target) at the input.[6] If ever the user cannot provide it, the system is condemned to make a rough guess, presenting all directly connected words. Obviously, such a list can become quite large. This being so, it makes sense to provide the system this kind of information to produce the right set of words, while keeping the search space small.

- ***Knowledge states***, refer to the knowledge activated at a given point in time, for example, when launching a search. What has been primed? What is available in the user's mind? Not all information stored in our mind is equally available or prominent anytime. The fact that peoples' *knowledge states* vary is important, as it co-determines the way a user proceeds in order to find the information he is looking for. This being so, it is important to be taken into consideration by the system designer. In conclusion, all this knowledge must be taken into account as it allows us to determine the search space, reducing its scope, which otherwise is the entire lexicon.

The example here below illustrates to some extent these facts with regard to wordfinding in an electronic resource. Suppose you are looking for a word conveying the idea of a *large black-and-white herbivorous mammal of China*. Yet, for some reason you fail to retrieve the intended form, *Panda*, even though you know a lot concerning the target. People being in this state, called the ToT-problem, would definitely appreciate if the information they are able to access could be used to help them find the target. Figure 1 illustrates the process of getting from a visual stimulus to its expression in language via a lexical resource. Given an external stimulus (A) our brain activates a set of features (B) that ideally allow us to retrieve the target form. If our brain fails, we use a fallback strategy and give part of the activated information to a lexical resource (C) expecting it to filter its base (D) in the hope to find the target (panda) or a somehow related word (E). As one can see, we consider look-up basically as a two-step process. At step one the user provides some input (current knowledge) to which the system answers with a set of candidates, at step two the user scans this list to make her choice.

A: perceptual input, i.e. target	B: associated features in the brain		C: input to lexical resource	D: lexical resource	E: output of lexical resource
	type :	bear	bear China	aardvark ... ... *panda* ... ... theorem ... **zy**gote	*panda* polar bear
	lives_in :	China			
	features :	black patches			
	diet :	eats bamboo			

Figure 1: Lexical access a two-step process mediated by the brain and an external resource (lexicon).

5   A Framework for Dictionary Navigation

In this section we will try to answer briefly the following three questions: *What should a resource look like to allow for the search described in the figure here above? How to build and how to use it?*

(The chosen elements are always underlined.): *computer* → (*Java, Perl, Prolog ; mouse, printer ; Mac, PC*) ; (1) Java → (*island, programming language*) ; (2) Java (island) → (coffee; Kawa Igen); (3) coffee → (Cappucino, Mocha, Latte). Note that 'Java' could activate 'Java beans', a notion inherent to JAVA, the programming language. In this case it would lead the user directly to the class (hypernym) containing the desired target word (mocha).

[6] This has of course consequences with respect to the resource. To be able to satisfy the different user needs (goals, stratgies) we probably need to create different databases: Obviously, to find a target on the basis of sound (rhymes), meanings (meaning-fragments) or related words (co-occurrences), requires networks encoding a different kind of information.

(a) *What should a resource look like to allow for this?* We would need a fully connected graph, or, more precisely, an association thesaurus (AT) containing typed and untyped links. Both kinds of links are necessary for filtering, i.e. to ensure that the search space is neither too big (typed links), nor too small (untyped links). Untyped links are a necessary evil: they are necessary to address the fact that two words evoke each other eventhough we are not able qualify the nature of the link.

(b) *How to use it?* Imagine an author wishing to convey the name of a beverage typically served in coffee shops. Failing to evoke the desired form ('mocha'), he reaches for a lexicon. Since dictionaries are too huge to be scanned from cover (letter A) to cover (Z), we will try to reduce the search space incrementally. Having received some input from the user, say 'coffee', — which is the word coming to his mind while failing to access the target,— the system answers with a set of words among which the user chooses. Iff the input and the target are direct neighbors in the network, and iff the user knows the link between the two (source + target), then the search space is generally quite small. In the opposite case, that is, if the user cannot specify the link, then the system is condemned to make an exhaustive search, retrieving all direct neighbors of the input. However, the system could cluster the words by affinity and give names to these categories, so that the user, rather than navigating in a huge flat list navigates in a *categorial tree*, which avoids scanning long lists.

(c) *How to build it?* While there are quite a few resources, in particular, association thesauri, they are too small to allow us to solve the ToT-problem. Projected resource would still have to be built, and while one could imagine the use of combined resources, like Babelnet (Navigli and Ponzetto, 2012), or the combination of WN with other resources like topic maps (Agirre et al. 2001), Roget's Thesaurus (Mandala, 1999) or ConceptNet (Liu and Sing, 2004), it is not easy to tell which combination is best, all the more as besides encyclopedic knowledge, we also need episodic knowledge (Tulving, 1983).

One straightforward solution might be co-occurrences (Wettler & Rapp, 1993; Lemaire & Denhière, 2004; Schulte im Walde & Melinger, 2008). While co-occurring words contain many appropriate clue – target pairs, they also contain many unrelated terms that hamper access – even after application of appropriate significance measures. More severely, there are no structural elements that generalize across queries.

Another solution could be *lexical functions* (Mel'čuk, 1996) or semagrams (Moerdijk, 2008) which are reminiscent of the lexical-semantic networks produced by Fontenelle (1997) on the basis of the Collins-Robert dictionary enriched with Melcuk's lexical functions. Semagrams represent the knowledge associated with a word in terms of attribute-values. Each semantic class has its type template and corresponding slots. For instance, the type template for *animals* contains the slots 'parts, behavior, color, sound, size, place, appearance, function', etc., whereas the one for *beverages* has slots for 'ingredient, preparation, taste, color, transparency, use, smell, source, function, 'composition', etc. While it is unlikely that we can infer or mine semagrams automatically, chances are that we can populate them mechanically, which would then be seen as an alternative route of building an association thesaurus, but in a fairly controlled way.

6   Experimental Setup

In this section, we describe the experimental set-up to answer the following research questions: (a) *When being in the ToT-state what cues do people provide to help the system find the target?* (b) *How good are existing lexical resources for retrieving the targets by using these cues?* (c) *How big is the added value of knowing the relationship between the cue (source word) and the target?* Put differently, does it enhance retrieval precision and speed?

6.1   Lexical Graphs as Dictionaries

For our experiments we used three different lexical networks: WN, distributional semantic models using word similarity and word co-occurrence. They were chosen deliberately to cover different structural aspects, different amounts of effort to construct them manually, and different degrees of language-dependence. Note, that we could have chosen other resources, for example, the Edinburgh Association Thesaurus,[7] but the E.A.T lacks typed relations and it is quite old (Kiss et al. 1973),[8] covering only a subset of the words used in our experiment.

---

[7] Available at: http://www.eat.rl.ac.uk

- *WordNet:* WN 3.0 (Fellbaum, 1998) is a high-coverage, manually built lexical-semantic network of English. Words are organized in terms of synsets, i.e. sets of synonyms, which are linked in various ways depending on the part of speech. We used a subset of these links (synset, hyponymy, derivation, etc.) and domain categories in the hope to be able to retrieve the target.

- *Word Similarity:* We used the JoBimText distributional semantic model, its similarity score being based on common dependency parse contexts, which requires a language-specific parser. The JoBimText distributional thesaurus[9] (Biemann and Riedl, 2013) contains in ranked order the 200 most similar terms of a newswire corpus of 100 million sentences in English. We expect this resource to be suitable for most associative queries, that is to help us find words occurring in contexts like "X is somehow like a Y or a Z" (e.g. "a *panda* is somehow like a *koala* or a *grizzly*"). This example illustrates 'co-hyponymy', a relation not directly encoded in WordNet. Similarities (for example, panda/koala vs. panda/dog) are ranked by context overlap.

- *Word Co-occurrence*: We compute statistically significant sentence-based word co-occurrences using the same corpus as here above, and following the methodology of (Quasthoff et al., 2006)[10]. We expect this resource to be suited for free associations, i.e. cue words whose link to the target cannot be specified. This resource has by far the highest rate of relations across different word classes, as they may occur in patterns like "With $\underline{X}$s, especially with $\underline{Y}$ ones, you can $\underline{Z}$ and $\underline{W}$" (e.g. "with mochas, especially with iced ones, you can chill and have cookies"). Co-occurrences are ranked by the log-likelihood significance measure (Dunning, 1993).

6.2   Network Access

Given the structural differences of our resources, our networks are accessed with different query strategies. The general setup is to query the resource via a cue and to insert then the retrieved terms into a ranking. As long as the system has not found all the desired words, it will keep going by querying with words according to their rank, inserting previously un-retrieved terms below the ranking.

- *WordNet*: Having noticed that people tend to use *hypernyms* (flower) as cues to find the *hyponym* (rose, the target), we defined a heuristic supporting queries using this relation. We start by querying for 'synonyms' of the cue, putting results first in the ranking. Next, we proceed along the sense numbers, senses being ordered by frequency in WN, which ensures that we start with the most common senses. Third, we add (in this order) direct 'hyponyms', 'meronyms' and 'domain members'. This order seems to be justified by the fact that most people tend to go from general to specific, starting by a more general term when launching a search. Finally, we add other relations like 'similar', 'antonyms', 'hypernyms', 'holonyms, 'domains', etc. For example, for the cue "pronouncement", the target "affirmation" is found by first checking the cue's 'synonyms' ("dictum", "say-so"), before checking the direct *hyponym* and *hypernym* (directive, declaration). Next we navigate through directly related words of "dictum", synonym of "pronouncement", to find then the target as a direct *hypernym* of "say-so" in its first sense, resulting in rank 12.

- *Word Similarity*: We retrieve the most similar terms per query, ranked by their similarity. Note that due to structure limitations of the resource only 200 similar words can be retrieved per query.

- *Word Co-occurrence*: Having filtered out the 200 most frequent stopwords, we retrieve terms co-occurring at least twice with a minimum log-likelihood score of 6.63.

Each cue returns a ranking of the full vocabulary. Working with three cues per target (see Section 6.3), we explore two different combinations of target ranks (minimum rank and merged rank) from querying with the three cues. Regarding *minimum rank*, the rationale is that for each cue, a retrieval process

---

[8] For example, if you provide 'terrorism' as key, you will get the following list of ranked words as answer : Guerilla, Gun, Soldier, War, Guerrilla, Anarchist, Evil, Fear, Fighting, Rebel, Tyrant, Vandal, Vietnam, Abroad, Activities, Activity, Arab, Arson, Bandit, Blood, Bomb, Che, Che Guevara, Congo, Czech, Fight, Fighter, Gangster, Gorilla, Greek, Guerillas, Guns, Hooligan, Kill, Killer, Madness, Man, Mao, Maoist, Mexico, Night, Police, Regime, Revolution, Revolutionary, Rioter, Russian, Shoot, Terror, Tourist, Tree, Trotsky, Vietcong, Vietnamese, Wog. As one can see 'associations' change over time. The words we would associate nowadays with 'terrorism' are not the same as the ones people had associated in the seventees, the moment of history where this resource was built.

[9] Available at www.jobimtext.org

[10] Available at http://corpora.informatik.uni-leipzig.de

is started in parallel, terminating when the ToT target is encountered for the first time. Actually, only the rank of the 'best' cue is used. For *merged rank*, the rationale is as follows: we use all cues and merge the three rankings by a) adding the ranks per word and sorting by sum or b) multiplying the ranks and sorting by product. For more details, see Section 6.4.

6.3 Dataset

Since it is not trivial to put people in the ToT state, we have reformulated the problem in the following way: we ask people to describe a given target to other people who may not know the word (e.g. language learners), by providing three cues. Crowdworkers were asked to provide single-word cues rather than descriptions or definitions. Note that the idea was not the creation of a resource, but rather the creation of a set of data to see how well they would behave with respect to our three resources (section, 6.1). Also, in order to get a clearer picture concerning our third question, i.e. the added value of the relation between cue and target, we asked subjects to also specify the relationship between the target and each one of the given three cues. Relations were defined indirectly, i.e. via examples. They comprise synonyms, hypernyms/hyponyms, meronyms/holonyms, typical properties, typical roles (verb-subject, verb-object) and free associations.

Data acquisition was done via the Crowdflower crowdsourcing platform.[11] In order to check whether crowdworkers had given the right answer and understood the target, we presented the latter together with three definitions. For our experiment we used only trials that the crowdworkers had fully understood, that is, for which they had picked the correct definition. After data collection, we excluded data from crowdworkers that deliberately had ignored our instructions. For the targets and definitions we used the 208 common nouns listed in (Abrams et al., 2007; Harley and Bown, 1998), who examined the ToT state from a psychological angle. Full data, instructions and judgments are available online.[12]

Data collection yielded a total of 1186 cue triplets, provided by 65 participants, who worked on 3 to 132 targets. After manual correction of typos and lemmatization, cue triplets were filtered by eliminating words outside of the vocabulary of the respective resource used in the experiments. Inspection of the data revealed that crowdworkers generally chose the cues quite well, but many of them had a hard time to assign the appropriate relation, which is not all that surprising, as this requires quite a bit of metalinguistic knowledge. It is also possible that some participants had chosen the relation without taking the needed care since we did not perform any quality checks during the task. We probably need a different kind of experiment to validate this or measure the extent to which linguistically innocent users can accurately classify semantic relations.

Table 1 below shows the distribution of relations expressed in the first 200 cue triplets (target range 'a-c', i.e. abacus – calisthetics, in alphabetical order) containing also some manually assigned relations. The results show the importance of taxonomic relations, a fact well exploited by WN. Representing nearly 46% of the relations, they confirm the intuition that paradigmatic associations are an important means to access the desired word. However, the next largest class are *syntagmatic*, i.e. untyped, associations (37%). Note that about 17% of the cues come from a different word class than the targets.

Relation	associated	hyponym	synonym	quality	object	meronym	holonym	subject	hypernym
Ex.: cue - target	tea - afternoon	story - anecdote	horoscopy - astrology	white - albatross	share - anecdote	letters - anagram	day - afternoon	cheer - audience	zombie - cadaver
Typ. POS	N	N	N	A	V	N	N	V	N
%	36.8%	23.5%	13.3%	8.2%	5.2%	4.3%	4.2%	3.8%	0.6%

Table 1: Distribution of relations between target and cue, as well as typical part of speech (POS) for the cue (N: *Noun*, V: *Verb*, A: *Adjective*), manually assigned by the authors.

---

[11] www.crowdflower.com

[12] A full description of the crowdsourcing interface is contained in the 'Companion data', see https://www.inf.uni-hamburg.de/en/inst/ab/lt/resources/data/cogalex16-tot.html

6.4 Evaluation Methodology

Our methodology is very similar to the one of Thorat and Choudhari (2016): we query the lexical network with cues and retrieve then a ranked list of potential ToT targets. With more appropriate cues and better lexical resources, our targets will probably get a boost, appearing higher in the list.

Our vocabulary of WN comprises 139,784 terms, including multiwords, which can be mutually reached through the query procedure described above was used in the first experiment. The intersection of the vocabulary of the three networks consists of 34,365 terms, all of them being single words, just as the ones used in the second experiment. Here below are the criteria used in our evaluation:

- *Minimum rank per cue (MinRank)*: if all cues were processed strictly in parallel, when would the target appear for the first time?
- *Target rank in sum of ranks (+Rank)*: if the retrieval time depends on the average rank per cue, we sum the ranks of the three cues and sort the list of terms in ascending order, reporting the position of the target. Note that this score is strongly influenced by negative outlier cues.
- *Target rank in multiplication of ranks (*Rank)*: To model a multiplicative instead of an additive combination, we multiply the target ranks per cue, sort the list of terms by this score in ascending order, and report then the position of the target. This score is less sensitive to negative outliers.
- *Average Precision@*100 (P@100) measures the fraction of trials containing the target among the first 100 hits, for each of the above. While 100 is an arbitrary number, it seems a reasonable wordlist size to allow for the quick retrieval of a target.

Note that the *minimum rank* is not necessarily lower than the other two scores. It is possible, and it even happens in our data, that a target gets a low rank because all three cues rank it consistently low, while the targets preferred by single cues are ranked much less favorably than others. For example, the target "agnostic" was retrieved from WN (untyped) by its three cues "believer, god, atheist" with ranks 170, 890, respectively 25. Minimum Rank is thus 25, but ranking via sum of ranks lists the target at position 14, while the multiplicative combination results in rank 15.

In the next section, we will qualitatively assess the differences in rankings from our different semantic networks.

7 Results and Discussion

We ran two experiments. In the first we tried to find out whether the knowledge and usage of WN relations produces some added value in terms of retrieval. The goal of the second experiment was to compare the retrieval performance of our three dictionary resources.

7.1 Retrieval along Semantic Relations

To answer the question whether the usage of relations improves word access, i.e. retrieval, we used WN, as it is highly structured and our relations can be directly mapped to it. For incorporating relations, we adapted the following query procedure (cf. Section 6.2): we first query for the target relation and then for all the others. For example, for the target "abacus" and the clue "bead" of type *meronym*, we would first retrieve the *holonyms* of "bead", then all other relations in the order given in Section 6.2, for initial and subsequent queries. If the supplied relation between the cue and the target is directly given in WN, retrieval is quick. Since the WN hierarchy is quite fine-grained, and since a hyponym relation might be contained over several transitive steps, we keep this order throughout the entire query process.

strategy \ score	MinRank	P@100	+Rank	% top100	*Rank	P@100
WordNet untyped	12352.7	40.5%	**22403.2**	7.5%	17993.5	21.5%
WordNet relations	**11733.2**	**42.0%**	22722.7	**9.5%**	**17786.0**	**22.5%**
Random Baseline	35480.7	0.2%	70264.7	0.1%	70438.5	0.1%
(STDEV)	(514.8)		(636.0)		(777.1)	

Table 2: Scores for target retrieval in WordNet by using or ignoring relational information for 200 cue triples on a vocabulary of 139,784 terms

Both settings perform much better than the random baseline, which returns the vocabulary in random order irrespective of the dictionary's structure. The random baseline was obtained by running simulations over the same size of the dataset; we also provide the standard deviation on 10 runs in parenthesis where applicable. Since more than 40% of the targets are among the first 100 retrieved words in the MinRank setting, we conclude that WN is indeed suitable. A manual analysis statistically confirmed our intuition: WN is very good for retrieving targets based on taxonomically related cues (e.g. calculator – abacus), while it does not perform well at all for syntagmatically related words or for noun-noun cues (e.g. beads – abacus, gluten – allergy).

Regarding the added value of relations for retrieval, we conclude that typed relations only help to a small extent, if at all. Our data show fluctuations in the range of a relative -2% to +5% between the settings. Note that this may be a side effect of the sample size, which is quite small. Interestingly, the differences decreased when repeating the experiment with the smaller vocabulary from Experiment 2. Clearly, more work is needed here.

7.2   Comparison of the three Resources

In order to assess differences between our dictionary resources, we consider the 964 cue triplets per target matching, the common vocabulary of our three resources (see Table 3 below).

dictionary \ score	MinRank	P@100	+Rank	P@100	*Rank	P@100
Word Similarity	**523.6**	**61.0%**	**1945.9**	**40.6%**	**1040.2**	**55.7%**
Word Co-occurrence	1748.0	44.2%	4205.6	27.2%	3226.9	33.6%
WordNet	2615.4	51.2%	6132.9	13.0%	4247.2	30.3%
Random Baseline (STDEV)	8543.0 (189.7)	0.9%	17156.6 (260.7)	0.2%	17113.8 (252.0)	0.3%

Table 3: Scores for target retrieval in our resources for 964 cue triples
based on a common vocabulary of 34,365 words.

All dictionaries allow for much better retrieval than the random baseline. The results provide a clear picture: the *word similarity* resource achieves the lowest average ranks on all scores. In 61% of the cases, the target is among the top 100 retrieved words if we consider only the most effective cue (MinRank). Note that more than half of the targets are found in the top 100 for the multiplicative combination (*Rank). This is surprising, as the relations between the cues and the target are quite diverse (see Section 6.3), and Word Similarity mostly contains direct and indirect taxonomic relations, such as co-hyponyms. The second-best resource in this evaluation is the word co-occurrence network, which outperforms WN on all metrics except the P@100 of MinRank scores.

We also analyzed the differences qualitatively and looked at cue-target-pairs where the three networks perform very differently. As our findings show, different networks have different potentials with respect to the retrieval of ToT targets based on a given cue:

- *WordNet* good, *Co-occurrence* poor: Synonyms or near-synonyms, like javelin – spear, cadaver – corpse. These do not co-occur in sentences, also cf. (Biemann et al., 2012).
- *WordNet* poor, *Co-occurrence* good: associations, like hospital–doctor or hospital–sick. They are not encoded in WordNet, its associative relations are very spotty. Note that placing them first in the order of relations did not increase performance.
- *WordNet* good, *Similarity* poor: meronyms/holonyms, such as door–knob, road–asphalt. These are not similar at all from a distributional point of view.
- *WordNet* poor, *Similarity* good: relations that should be in WN, but for some reason are missing, e.g. torpedo–missile, calligraphy–art, gazebo–pavilion.
- *Co-occurrence* good, *Similarity* poor: associations, part-of and cross-POS-relations, such as orthodontist–braces, hospital–ER and growth–economic. Though being related, these words are not similar.
- *Co-occurrence* poor, *Similarity* good: (near) synonyms, such as mercenary–warrior, lampoon–caricature, orthodontist–dentist. Again, they rarely co-occur in the same sentence.

8   Final Comments and Conclusion

In this paper, we have examined the use of lexical semantic networks to overcome the ToT problem. After an analysis of the causes leading to this state, we have evaluated and analyzed three lexical networks meant to overcome the ToT problem: WordNet, a word similarity network and a word co-occurrence network. Our setup was to query the network with a cue and check whether this would allow us to retrieve the target. To see its relative efficiency, we measured the rank of the ToT target over the retrieved vocabulary.

A ToT state can be induced by describing a given target to another person by providing some cues and ask him then to name it. Something similar can be achieved via crowdsourcing. We assumed that the cues retrieved via this technique, are similar to the ones humans typically use for the target retrieval. In order to determine the added value of a cue, we asked subjects to specify also the relationship between the target and each one of the given three cues. It turned out that traditional X-'onym' relations (hyponym, hypernym, ...) represent about half of the relations, while the remainder are mainly associated terms, i.e. untyped relations.

While we could not successfully exploit relational information to enhance retrieval, we could show the relative efficiency of different lexical semantic networks with respect to word access. As expected, *WordNet* is very good for retrieving targets on the basis of synonyms or taxonomically related cues. *Word co-occurrence* excels in associations, qualities and typical actions. Yet, the best network in our experiment was the one based on *word similarity*, as, apart for meronym/holonym relations, it combines the advantages of the other two. It covers basically the same aspects as WN, but it is more complete, containing syntagmatically associated terms like the co-occurrence network.

The fact that WN does not perform well for syntagmatically related words suggests the usage of another resource like Mel'čuk's *Explanatory Combinatory Dictionaries* (ECD) (Mel'čuk, 2006). ECDs look like good candidates, possibly better suited for our task than WN. Being part of a language production theory, called 'Meaning-Text Model' (Mel'čuk, 2012), ECDs capture a larger range of lexical relations (50+ lexical functions) than WN. Alas, the problem we have with this option are coverage and availability. Though being extremely fine-grained the ECD covers so far only a subset of the words normally found in a lexicon. Also, the ECD is not available in digital form.

Other potentially interesting alternatives would be association networks. Unfortunately, these resources are either not free (Gavagai),[13] too old (Kiss, et al. 1973), not rich enough in terms of coverage (de Deyne, et al. 2016; Nelson, et al. 2004), or not in the needed language, English (Lafourcade, 2007, 2015). Probably the largest, and arguably the best association thesaurus at this moment is JeuxDeMots, a crowd-sourced resource created via a game, hence its name 'wordgames'.[14] Yet, as mentioned already, this resource is not available in English, which is probably the reason why it is so little known 'abroad'.

One last word concerning 'relations'. Since we do believe in the virtues of relational information, —they are a critical component of the input— we plan to re-visit the problem of navigation in lexical graphs, but on the basis of cues enriched with relational information. Relations provide a context for the input. Revealing the users' goal, they tell the information provider (human or system) what to do with the input: provide a synonym, hypernym, etc. Obviously, a user expects quite different outputs for the following inputs : ['similar_to' 'knife'], ['more general' than 'knife'], or ['part_of' 'knife']. Since our ultimate goal is the creation of a resource helping people to overcome the ToT problem, we plan to combine different types of corpora, to build then a hybrid semantic network, that is, an association thesaurus containing typed and untyped relations. The first to keep the search space small, the second to make it large enough to include potentially relevant words, possibly even our target.

References

Abrams, L., Trunk, D. L., and Margolin, S. J. (2007). Resolving tip-of-the-tongue states in young and older adults: The role of phonology. *In L. O. Randal (Ed.), Aging and the Elderly: Psychology, Sociology, and Health* (pp. 1-41). Hauppauge, NY: Nova Science Publishers, Inc.

Agirre, E., Ansa, O., Hovy, E., and Martinez, D. (2001). Enriching WordNet concepts with topic signatures. *In: SIGLEX workshop on WordNet and Other Lexical Resources: Applications, Extensions and Customizations,* Pittsburgh, PA, USA.

---

[13] https://explorer.gavagai.se and https://lexicon.gavagai.se
[14] http://www.jeuxdemots.org/jdm-accueil.php and http://www.jeuxdemots.org/AKI.php

Aitchison, J. (2003). *Words in the Mind: an Introduction to the Mental Lexicon*. Oxford, Blackwell. (original version, 1987)

Bateman J. and M. Zock. (2016) Natural Language Generation. In: *R. Mitkov (Ed.) Handbook of Computational Linguistics (2nd edition)*, Oxford University Press. Forthcoming.

Beeferman, D. (2003). Onelook reverse dictionary. http://onelook.com/reverse-dictionary.shtml.

Bernstein, T. (1975). *Bernstein's Reverse dictionary*. Crown, New York.

Biemann, C., Riedl, M. (2013). Text: Now in 2D! A Framework for Lexical Expansion with Contextual Similarity. *Journal of Language Modelling* 1(1):55-95.

Biemann, C., Roos, S., and Weihe, K. (2012). Quantifying Semantics Using Complex Network Analysis. In: *Proceedings of COLING-12*, Mumbai, India, pp. 263-278.

Bock, J.K. (1996). Language production: Methods and methodologies. *Psychonomic Bulletin & Review*, 3:395-421.

Brown, A. S. (1991). A review of the Tip-of-the-Tongue Experience. *Psychological Bulletin*, 109:204 – 223.

Brown, R and Mc Neill, D. (1966). The tip of the tongue phenomenon. *Journal of Verbal Learning and Verbal Behaviour*, 5:325-337.

de Deyne, S., and Storms, G. (2015). Word associations. In J. R. Taylor (Ed.), *The Oxford Handbook of the Word*. Oxford University Press, Oxford, UK.

de Deyne, S., Verheyen, S. and Storms, G. (2016). Structure and organization of the mental lexicon: A network approach derived from syntactic dependency relations and word associations. In: *Towards a Theoretical Framework for Analyzing Complex Linguistic Networks* (pp. 47-79). Springer Berlin Heidelberg.

Dong, Z. and Q. Dong. (2006). *HOWNET and the computation of meaning*. World Scientific, London.

Dornseiff, F. (2003). *Der deutsche Wortschatz nach Sachgruppen*. Berlin & New York: W. de Gruyter.

Dunning, T. (1993). Accurate methods for the statistics of surprise and coincidence. *Computational Linguistics*, 19(1):61–74.

Dutoit, D. and P. Nugues (2002): A lexical network and an algorithm to find words from definitions. In: *van Harmelen, F. (ed.): Proceedings of the 15th European Conference on Artificial Intelligence*, pp.450-454 Lyon, France.

Fellbaum, C. (Ed.) (1998). *WordNet: An electronic lexical database and some of its applications*. MIT Press.

Fillmore, C., Johnson, C., and Petruck, M. (2003). Background to FrameNet. *International Journal of Lexicography* 16:235–250.

Fontenelle, T. (1997). Using a bilingual dictionary to create semantic networks, International Journal of Lexicography, Vol.10, n°4, Oxford University Press, pp.275-303

Goldrick, M. A., Ferreira, V., and Miozzo, M. (2014). *The Oxford handbook of language production*. Oxford University Press.

Harley, T. A., and Bown, H. E. (1998). What causes a tip-of-the-tongue state? Evidence for lexical neighbourhood effects in speech production. *British Journal of Psychology*, 89:151–174.

James, L., and Burke, D. (2000). Phonological priming effects on word retrieval and tip-of-the-tongue experiences in young and older adults. *Journal of Experimental Psychology: Learning, Memory, and Cognition* 26:1378-1391.

Kiss, G.R., Armstrong, C., Milroy, R., and Piper, J. (1973). An associative thesaurus of English and its computer analysis. In: *A. Aitken, R. Beiley and N. Hamilton-Smith (eds.): The Computer and Literary Studies*. Edinburgh: University Press. pp. 153-16

Krahmer, E. and Theune, M. (Eds.) (2010). *Empirical Methods in Natural Language Generation-Data-oriented Methods and Empirical Evaluation*. Series: Lecture Notes in Computer Science, Vol. 5790, Springer Berlin Heidelberg.

Lafourcade, M., and Joubert, A. (2015). TOTAKI: A help for lexical access on the TOT Problem. In Gala, N., Rapp, R. et Bel-Enguix, G. (Eds). *Language Production, Cognition, and the Lexicon*. Festschrift in honor of Michael Zock. Series Text, Speech and Language Technology XI. Dordrecht, Springer, pp. 95-112

Lafourcade, M. (2007). Making people play for Lexical Acquisition with the JeuxDeMots prototype. In: *Proceedings of the 7th International Symposium on Natural Language Processing*, Pattaya, Chonburi, Thailand.

Lemaire, B. and Denhière, G. (2004). Incremental construction of an associative network from a corpus. *Proceedings of the 26th Annual Meeting of the Cognitive Science Society (CogSci'2004)*, 825-830

Levelt W., Roelofs A. and A. Meyer. (1999). A theory of lexical access in speech production. *Behavioral and Brain Sciences*, 22:1-75.

Levelt, W. (1989). Spe*aking: From intention to articulation*. Cambridge, MA: MIT Press.

Levelt, W. J. M. (1992). Accessing words in speech production: Stages, processes and representations. *Cognition*, 42:1-22.

Liu, H. and Singh, P. (2004). ConceptNet: A practical commonsense reasoning tool-kit. *BT Technology Journal* 22(4):211–226

Mandala, R., Tokunaga, T. and Tanaka, H. (1999). Complementing WordNet with Roget's and Corpus-based Thesauri for Information Retrieval. In: *Proceedings of EACL 99*, pp. 94-101, Bergen, Norway

Mel'čuk, I. (1996). Lexical Functions: A Tool for the Description of Lexical Relations in the Lexicon. In L. Wanner (ed), Lexical Functions in Lexicography and Natural Language Processing. Language Companion Series 31, Amsterdam/Philadelphia: John Benjamins, 37–102.

Mel'čuk, I. (2006). Explanatory Combinatorial Dictionary. In G. Sica (ed), Open Problems in Linguistics and Lexicography. Monza: Polimetrica, 225–355.

Mel'čuk, I. (2012). Semantics: From meaning to text. Volume 1, Studies in Language Companion Series 129, Amsterdam/Philadelphia: John Benjamins.

Miller, G.A. (ed.) (1990). WordNet: An On-Line Lexical Database. *International Journal of Lexicography*, 3(4):235-244.

Moerdijk F. (2008). Frames and semagrams; meaning description in the general Dutch dictionary. In: *Proceedings of the Thirteenth Euralex International Congress, EURALEX*, pp. 561-569, Barcelona, Spain.

Navigli, R. and Ponzetto, S. (2012), BabelNet: The Automatic Construction, Evaluation and Application of a Wide-Coverage Multilingual Semantic Network. *Artificial Intelligence* 193:217-250.

Nelson, D., McEvoy, C., and Schreiber, T. (2004). The university of South Florida free association, rhyme, and word fragment norms. *Behavior Research Methods* 36(3):402–407.

Quasthoff, U., Richter, M. and Biemann, C. (2006). Corpus Portal for Search in Monolingual Corpora. *In: Proceedings of LREC-06*, pp. 1799-1802, Genoa, Italy.

Rapp, B. and Goldrick, M. (2006). Speaking words: Contributions of cognitive neuropsychological research. *Cognitive Neuropsychology*, 23 (1):39-73.

Reiter, E. and Dale, R. (2000). *Building natural language generation systems* (Vol. 33). Cambridge: Cambridge University Press.

Richardson S, W., B. Dolan and L. Vanderwende. (1998). MindNet: Acquiring and Structuring Semantic Information from Text. In: *Proceedings of ACL-COLING'98*, pp. 1098-1102, Montreal, Canada.

Roget, P. (1852). *Thesaurus of English Words and Phrases*. Longman, London.

Schwartz, B. L. (2002). *Tip-of-the-tongue states: Phenomenology, mechanism, and lexical retrieval*. Mahwah. New Jersey: Lawrence Erlbaum Associates.

Schwartz, B. L. (2006). Tip-of-the-tongue states as metacognition. *Metacognition and Learning*, *1*(2), 149-158.

Schulte im Walde. S., and Melinger, A. (2008). An in-depth look into the co-occurrence distribution of semantic associates. *Rivista di Linguistica, Special Issue on From Context to Meaning: Distributional Models of the Lexicon in Linguistics and Cognitive Science*, 20(1):89-128.

Summers, D. (1993). *Language Activator: the world's first production dictionary*. Longman, London.

Thorat, S., and Choudhari, V. (2016). Implementing a Reverse Dictionary, based on word definitions, using a Node-Graph Architecture. In: *Proceedings of COLING 2016*, Osaka, Japan.

Trappes-Lomax, H. (1997). *Oxford Learner's Wordfinder Dictionary*. Oxford: Oxford University Press.

Tulving E. (1983). Elem*ents of Episodic Memory*. Oxford: Clarendon.

Wettler, M., and Rapp, R. (1993). Computation of word associations based on the co-occurrences of words in large corpora. In: *Proceedings of the 1st Workshop on Very Large Corpora*, pp. 84-93, Beijing, China.

Zock, M. and D. Schwab, (2011). Storage does not guarantee access. The problem of organizing and accessing words in a speaker's lexicon. *Journal of Cognitive Science* 12(3):233-258.

The CogALex-V Shared Task on the Corpus-Based Identification of Semantic Relations

Enrico Santus
The Hong Kong Polytechnic University
esantus@gmail.com

Anna Gladkova
The University of Tokyo, Japan
gladkova@phiz.c.u-tokyo.ac.jp

Stefan Evert
FAU Erlangen-Nürnberg, Germany
stefan.evert@fau.de

Alessandro Lenci
University of Pisa, Italy
alessandro.lenci@unipi.it

Abstract

The shared task of the 5th Workshop on Cognitive Aspects of the Lexicon (CogALex-V) aims at providing a common benchmark for testing current corpus-based methods for the identification of lexical semantic relations (*synonymy, antonymy, hypernymy, part-whole meronymy*) and at gaining a better understanding of their respective strengths and weaknesses. The shared task uses a challenging dataset extracted from EVALution 1.0 (Santus et al., 2015b), which contains word pairs holding the above-mentioned relations as well as semantically unrelated control items (*random*). The task is split into two subtasks: (i) identification of related word pairs vs. unrelated ones; (ii) classification of the word pairs according to their semantic relation. This paper describes the subtasks, the dataset, the evaluation metrics, the seven participating systems and their results. The best performing system in subtask 1 is GHHH ($F_1 = 0.790$), while the best system in subtask 2 is LexNet ($F_1 = 0.445$). The dataset and the task description are available at https://sites.google.com/site/cogalex2016/home/shared-task.

1 Introduction

Determining automatically if words are semantically related, and in what way, is important for Natural Language Processing (NLP) applications such as thesaurus generation (Grefenstette, 1994), ontology learning (Zouaq and Nkambou, 2008), paraphrase generation and identification (Madnani and Dorr, 2010), as well as for drawing inferences (Martinez-Gómez et al., 2016). Many NLP applications make use of handcrafted resources such as WordNet (Fellbaum, 1998). However, creating these resources is expensive and time-consuming; they are available for only a few languages, and their coverage inevitably lags behind the lexical and conceptual proliferation.

In the last decades, a number of corpus-based approaches have investigated the possibility of identifying lexical semantic relations by observing word usage. Even though these methods are still far from being able to provide a comprehensive model of how semantic relations work, pattern-based and distributional approaches (both supervised or unsupervised) have confirmed the existence of a strong connection between word meaning and word distribution.

The practical utility of this finding matches its theoretical significance. The connection between word meanings and their usage is gaining prominence in theories of the mental lexicon (Mikoajczak-Matyja, 2015) and language acquisition (Bybee and Beckner, 2015). The status of distributional semantics vis-à-vis linguistics and cognitive science (Lenci, 2008) depends on making progress in this area. To further assess and explore how much we can learn about semantic relations from word distribution, we propose a shared task as part of the 5th Workshop on Cognitive Aspects of the Lexicon (CogALex-V), co-located with COLING 2016 in Osaka, Japan.

The CogALex-V shared task is intended to provide a common benchmark for testing current corpus-based methods for the identification of lexical semantic relations in order to gain a better understanding of their respective strengths and weaknesses. It is articulated into two subtasks: (i) identification of semantically related word pairs vs. unrelated ones; (ii) classification of the word pairs according to their

Proceedings of the Workshop on Cognitive Aspects of the Lexicon,
pages 69–79, Osaka, Japan, December 11-17 2016.

semantic relation. Participants were provided with training and test datasets extracted from EVALution 1.0 (Santus et al., 2015b), as well as a scoring script for evaluating the output of their systems.

The shared task has been intended and designed as a "friendly competition": the goal was to identify strengths and weaknesses of various methods, rather than just "crowning" the best-performing model. In total, seven systems participated in the shared task. Most of them exploited Distributional Semantic Models (DSMs), either of the count-based or word-embedding type (Baroni et al., 2014). Most of them relied on distance or nearest neighbors in subtask 1, and on machine learning classifiers (e.g., Support Vector Machine (SVM), Convolutional Neural Network (CNN) and Random Forest (RF)) in subtask 2. Some systems enriched the DSM representation by adopting patterns (e.g., *LexNet*, the best system in subtask 2) or extracting distributional properties with unsupervised measures (e.g., ROOT18).

This paper reports the results achieved by the participating systems, providing insights about their respective strengths and weaknesses. It is organized as follows. Section 2 surveys similar shared tasks and provides an overview of existing methods for identifying lexical semantic relations. Section 3 introduces the task, the datasets, and the participating systems (each of them described in detail in a separate paper included in the workshop proceedings).[1] Section 4 lists the performance of the participating systems, analyzing it from several perspectives. Section 5 summarizes the findings, highlights the contribution of the shared task and suggests a few directions for future research.

2   Related Work

2.1   Shared Tasks on Semantic Relations Identification

The importance of efficient and accurate identification of different semantic relations for different NLP applications has already prompted several shared tasks, differing in the relations considered and the task definitions. These tasks are briefly surveyed in the current section.

SemEval-2007 shared task 4 (Girju et al., 2007) focused on seven "encyclopedic" semantic relations between nouns (*cause-effect, instrument-agency, product-producer, origin-entity, content-container, theme-tool, part-whole*). In order to disambiguate the senses, the participants could rely on WordNet synsets and/or on sentences in which the noun pairs were observed. The best system out of fifteen achieved 76.3% average accuracy.

SemEval-2010 shared task 8 (Hendrickx et al., 2010) considered the first five semantic relations of SemEval-2007 shared task 4, with the addition of *entity-destination, component-whole, member-collection, and message-topic*. These relations were annotated in sentence contexts. Given a sentence and two tagged nominals, the task was to predict the relation between those nominals and its direction. The best system out of twenty-eight achieved 82% accuracy. The participants were free to use various semantic, syntactic and morphological resources.

Related to the task of lexical semantic relation identification is the task of taxonomy construction, which essentially focuses on only one semantic relation: hypernymy (and its inverse, hyponymy). This task was explored in *SemEval-2015* (Bordea et al., 2015) and *SemEval-2016* (Buitelaar et al., 2016). The test data consisted of a list of domain terms that participants had to structure into a taxonomy (a list of pairs <term, hypernym>), possibly adding intermediate terms. The participating systems used lexical patterns, dictionary definitions, Wikipedia, knowledge bases, and vector space models. Also noteworthy is *SemEval-2016 Task 14* (Jurgens and Pilehvar, 2016), which asked participants to enrich WordNet taxonomy by determining, for a given new word, which synset it should be part of (thus combining detection of hypernyms with word sense disambiguation).

The present shared task differs from those listed above in the semantic relations it considers: *synonymy, antonymy, hypernymy, part-whole meronymy*, and *random* or "semantically unrelated". It also differs from SemEval-2010 task 8 and SemEval-2007 task 4 in the absence of sentence contexts for the pairs of target words. Most importantly, unlike the above tasks, the CogALex-V shared task forbids the use of any thesauri, knowledge bases, or semantic networks (particularly WordNet and ConceptNet), forcing the participating systems to rely exclusively on corpus data.

---

[1]Training and test data as well as further information about the shared task are available at `https://sites.google.com/site/cogalex2016/home/shared-task`.

2.2 Methods for the Identification of Semantic Relations

Up to this date, several corpus-based approaches to the identification of semantic relations have been proposed. Most of them, however, focus on a single semantic relation with the ambitious objective of isolating it from all the others. Dealing with multiple relations has been found particularly challenging, and few systems have attempted multi-class classifications. The exceptions include Turney (2008) and Pantel and Pennacchiotti (2006).

Early approaches rely on lexical-syntactic patterns (e.g. "tools *such as* hammers"). After the seminal work of Hearst (1992) who sketched methods for pattern discovery, Snow et al. (2004) adopted machine learning over dependency-paths-based features. While these approaches focused on hypernyms, Pantel and Pennacchiotti (2006) introduced *Espresso*, able to identify several semantic relations (i.e. *hypernymy, part-of, succession, reaction* and *production*) as well as to maximize recall by using the Web and precision by assessing the reliability of the patterns. Other pattern-based approaches to synonymy and antonymy are reported by Lin et al. (2003), Turney (2008), Wang et al. (2010) and Lobanova et al. (2010).

The major limitation of pattern-based approaches is that they require words to co-occur in the same sentence, strongly impacting the recall. Distributional approaches have therefore been adopted to reduce such limitations. They are based on the *Distributional Hypothesis* (Harris, 1954; Firth, 1957) that words occurring in similar contexts also bear similar meaning. Distributional approaches can be (i) unsupervised, generally consisting of mathematical functions that implement linguistic hypotheses about how and which contexts are relevant to identify specific relations (Kotlerman et al., 2010; Lenci and Benotto, 2012; Santus et al., 2014); or (ii) supervised, generally consisting of algorithms that automatically learn some distributional information about the words holding a specific relation (Weeds et al., 2014; Roller et al., 2014; Roller and Erk, 2016; Santus et al., 2016; Nguyen et al., 2016; Shwartz et al., 2016). While unsupervised approaches are commonly outperformed by supervised ones, the latter – which rely on distributional word vectors, either concatenated or combined through algebraic functions – seem to learn specific lexical properties of the words in the pairs rather than the general semantic relation existing between them (Weeds et al., 2014; Levy et al., 2015b). This has a negative impact on their performance on previously unseen words, lexically split datasets and unseen switched pairs (Santus et al., 2016).

One of the ongoing disputes in the NLP community concerns the relative merits and demerits of count-based distributional models and word embeddings (which are obtained by training neural networks rather than counting co-occurrence frequencies). While the latter seem to outperform the former in several tasks such as similarity estimation (Baroni et al., 2014), both types of models are subject to variation at the level of individual linguistic relations (Gladkova et al., 2016). Levy et al. (2015a) have also shown that optimization of hyperparameters can make a bigger difference than the choice between different models.

Finally, very recently, several scholars have investigated the possibility of integrating different kinds of information. Kiela et al. (2015) have used image generality for hypernymy detection, while Shwartz et al. (2016) have tried to identify the same relation by combining pattern-based and distributional information.

3 Shared task

3.1 Task description

The CogALex-V shared task was conducted as a "friendly competition" where participants had access to both training and testing datasets, released on the 8th and the 27th of September 2016, respectively. The participants were asked to evaluate the output of their system with the official evaluation script, released with the test set together with *random* and *majority* baselines. Each participant was furthermore requested to submit a description paper and the output of their system in the two subtasks by the 16th of October 2016. Two reviews for each paper were returned by the 25th of October 2016, and the camera-ready version was due on the 2nd of November. The shared task was split in two subtasks which are described below.

Subtask 1. For each word pair (e.g. *dog – fruit*), decide whether the terms are semantically related (TRUE) or not (FALSE). Given a TAB-separated input file with word pairs, participating systems must add a third column specifying their prediction. This subtask was evaluated in terms of precision, recall and F_1-score for the identification of related word pairs. The unrelated word pairs were considered as noise.

Subtask 2. For each word pair (e.g. *cat – animal*), decide which semantic relation (if any) holds between the two words. The options are *synonymy* (SYN), *antonymy* (ANT), *hypernymy* (HYPER), *part-whole meronymy* (PART_OF) and *random* (RANDOM) for pairs where none of the four relations holds (see section 3.2). The input file was the same as for subtask 1. Participant systems were expected to return a TAB-separated file, where each word pair is annotated with exactly one relation label. This subtask was evaluated in terms of precision, recall and F_1-score for each of the four semantic relations. The unrelated word pairs (RANDOM) were considered as noise and therefore not considered in the final weighted average.

As mentioned above, the participating systems were supposed to be entirely corpus-based, without recourse to any existing dictionaries, knowledge bases or semantic networks. However, there was no restriction on the corpora that could be used. The participants were free to use the provided training data for supervised machine learning or for developing or tuning an unsupervised system. For example, they could use purely handwritten knowledge patterns for relation mining or to learn knowledge patterns from the CogALex-V training data, but they could not bootstrap knowledge patterns from a different set of seed terms, and no other training data was allowed.

Each participant was asked to submit the output of the system whose results are reported in the description paper. Further post-hoc experiments were encouraged at the authors' discretion.

3.2 Datasets

The training and test datasets were constructed on the basis of EVALution 1.0 (Santus et al., 2015b), a dataset for evaluating distributional semantic models that was derived from WordNet 4.0 (Fellbaum, 1998) and ConceptNet 5.0 (Liu and Singh, 2004), and then refined through automatic filters and crowdsourcing.

EVALution 1.0 includes various parts of speech, both single words and multi-word units (e.g., *grow_up*).[2] Words have been stemmed (e.g. *feeling* appears as *feel*). This increases ambiguity in the dataset, but it is also consistent with the fact that semantic relations between lexical items are typically independent from their morphosyntactic realization (e.g. the hypernymic pair *anger – feel* now represents morphological variants such as *anger – feeling* and *anger – to feel*).

After being extracted from WordNet or ConceptNet, the pairs (e.g. *sweet* SYN *candy*) were evaluated by CrowdFlower workers in order to obtain native speaker judgments, which can be used as a proxy for the prototypicality of the relations. The crowdsourcing task was to rate the truthfulness of sentences generated from the word pairs (according to the templates presented in table 1) on a scale from 1 to 5, where 1=*completely disagree* and 5=*completely agree*. Five judgments were collected for each sentence.

The CrowdFlower workers also tagged the general domains in which the relata were found more appropriate, such as "nature", "culture" or "emotion". Unfortunately the reliability of these tags is fairly low, as some workers applied them randomly. We can therefore consider trustworthy only tags that were selected by a high number of voters. In addition to domains, EVALution contains other metadata, either concerning the pairs (e.g., from which resource the pair is inherited) or the single words (e.g., word frequency, capitalization distribution, morphological distribution, part-of-speech distribution, etc.). This metadata can be used for subsequent analysis of the performance of the systems.[3]

For this shared task, we extracted a subset of EVALution 1.0 that covers 747 target words (318 in the training set and 429 in the test set) with at least one of the following relata: *synonym, antonym, hypernym* and *part-whole meronym*; only pairs with average rating $\geq$ 4 were considered. In order to increase the difficulty of the identification task, for every target word we generated several random pairs by switching

---

[2]Multi-word units were filtered out for the shared task.

[3]Metadata is not available for the random pairs, but it is available for the individual words in the random pairs because they were generated exclusively from words contained in EVALution 1.0.

Relation	Tag	Template	Example	Training	Testing
Synonymy	SYN	W2 can be used with the same meaning as W1	*candy-sweet, apartment-flat*	167	235
Antonymy	ANT	W2 can be used as the opposite of W1	*clean-dirty, add-take*	241	360
Hypernymy	HYPER	W1 is a kind of W2	*cannabis-plant, actress-human*	255	382
Part-whole meronymy	PART_OF	W1 is a part of W2	*calf-leg, aisle-store*	163	224
Random word	RANDOM	None of the above relations apply	*accident-fish, actor-mild*	2228	3059

Table 1: Semantic relations in the shared task dataset

the relata. These pairs – approximately three times as many as related pairs – are intended to act as noise for the models. They may contain associated words (e.g. *coffee – cup, brick – build*), but pairs accidentally holding any of the four semantic relations above were filtered out manually.[4]

The dataset is particularly challenging for several reasons. First, it does not provide part-of-speech information for the words in the pairs, leaving the participant systems with the burden of disambiguation (e.g. *fire – shoot* are synonyms only when both are interpreted as verbs). Second, several words were interpreted in a specific meaning that does not always correspond to the dominant sense (e.g. *compact – car*, where *compact* is a noun referring to a specific kind of car). Third, it combines relations inherited from a lexical resource like WordNet with relations that were obtained by crowdsourcing and pattern-based extraction (in ConceptNet), making their definitions less consistent. Fourth, the terms in EVALution are stemmed, thereby denying systems the possibility of using morphological clues as features for the classification. Finding semantic relations between morphologically heterogeneous words is an additional challenge, but it is very likely that NLP applications (e.g. those for paraphrase generation and entailment verification) would benefit from the ability to focus on semantics while ignoring morphological differences. These difficulties sometimes appear together, e.g. in the hypernymic pair *stable – build*, where *stable* is used in the sense of "a building with stalls where horses, cattle, etc., are kept and fed"[5] and *build* is the stemmed form of *building*.

Although the above-mentioned difficulties could impact the possible performance of the competing systems, they stem from the very nature of natural language semantics. This is confirmed by the fact that CrowdFlower workers were clearly able to identify those pairs as semantically related. During the analysis of the systems, EVALution 1.0 metadata can be used for pinpointing the sources of problems.

3.3 Participants

The CogALex-V shared task had 7 participating teams in subtask 1, and 6 of these teams also took part in subtask 2. The methods and corpora used by these teams are summarized in table 2.

4 Results

4.1 Evaluation procedure

The participants were provided with a Python script for the evaluation. Given the gold standard and a system output file as input, it calculated precision, recall and their harmonic mean F_1 for related pairs (in subtask 1) or semantic relations (in subtask 2), ignoring the unrelated pairs. In subtask 2, for example, scores were computed for *synonymy* (SYN), *antonymy* (ANT), *hypernymy* (HYPER) and *part-whole meronymy* (PART_OF); the overall ranking of the systems was based on their weighted average.

---

[4]As the filtering was carried out by only two annotators, it is possible that a few such accidentally related pairs may have been overlooked.

[5]`http://www.wordreference.com/definition/stable` (retrieved on 3rd of November 2016)

Team	Method(s)	Corpus size	Corpus
GHHH	Word analogies, linear regression and multi-task CNN	100B	Google News (pre-trained word2vec embeddings, 300 dim.);
		6B	Wikipedia + Gigaword 5 (pre-trained GloVe embeddings, 300 dim.),
		840B	Common Crawl (pre-trained GloVe embeddings, 300 dim.)
Mach5	angular distance in SVD-reduced count-based DSM for subtask 1 and linear SVM classifier based on 1200 SVD dimensions in subtask 2	9.5B	ENCOW 2014, traditional dependency-based DSM
LexNet	multi-layer perceptron classifying feature vectors that consist of embeddings for two words and all dependency paths that connect them in a corpus	6B	Wikipedia + Gigaword 5 (pre-trained GloVe embeddings, 50-dim.);
		100B	Google News (pre-trained word2vec embeddings, 300 dim.)
ROOT18	random forest classifier trained on 18 features representing unsupervised distributional properties of the investigated relations	2B	UkWac, count-based BOW DSM
LOPE	cosine similarity, nearest neighbor position indexing, assuming the order synonymy-antonymy-hypernymy-meronymy-random	100B	Google News (pre-trained word2vec embeddings, 300 dim.)
HsH-Supervised	cosine similarity, classification based on SVM	2B	ukWaC (sparse PPMI-weighted vectors, 17400 features)
CGSRC	CNN-based relation classification	100B	Google News (pre-trained word2vec embeddings, 50–300 dim.)

Table 2: Description of the participating systems

The script requires that the gold standard and the output file contain exactly the same pairs, in the same order, and using the same annotation labels.

4.2 Results and ranks

Most of the participating systems obtained fairly good results in subtask 1. Performance was however much worse for all of them (even the best systems) in subtask 2, demonstrating once more that the identification of semantic relations is a hard task that calls for more attention from the community.

Team	Subtask 1		Team	Subtask 2
GHHH	0.790		LexNet	0.445
Mach5	0.778		GHHH	0.423
LexNet	0.765		Mach5	0.295
ROOT18	0.731		ROOT18	0.262
LOPE	0.713		CGSRC	0.252
HsH-Supervised	0.585		LOPE	0.247
CGSRC	0.431			

Table 3: Participating systems ranked by their F_1 scores in subtask 1 (left) and subtask 2 (right)

Table 3 ranks the participating systems according to their F_1-scores in subtask 1 and subtask 2. The best performing system in subtask 1 is GHHH ($F_1 = 0.790$), with the first 5 top systems being less than 10% behind, and Mach5 ($F_1 = 0.778$) and LexNet ($F_1 = 0.765$) less than 3%. This confirms that numerous corpus-based approaches are competitive in discriminating between related and unrelated word pairs. The situation is quite different for subtask 2, where the same three systems achieve the highest scores, but now LexNet comes first ($F_1 = 0.445$), GHHH second ($F_1 = 0.423$) with less than 3% difference, and Mach5 ($F_1 = 0.295$) lags behind much more than in subtask 1, achieving a score that is closer to the last three systems than to the first two.

As can be seen in Table 2, the top systems use very different approaches. GHHH investigates word analogies, linear regression and multi-task Convolutional Neural Networks (CNN) with 300-dimensional publicly available word embeddings trained on huge corpora (Google News, Common Crawl and Wikipedia + Gigaword 5). The authors found that linear regression works better in subtask 1 (i.e. binary classification), while multi-task CNN performs better in subtask 2, which involves multi-class classification. Analogy was instead found less appropriate for semantic relation identification.

LexNet relies on Wikipedia + Gigaword 5 and Google News corpora, leveraging the combination of distributional and path-based information. The authors merged the 50-dimensional GloVe pre-trained embeddings (Pennington et al., 2014) for the words in the pairs with the average embedding vector – created using a LSTM (Hochreiter and Schmidhuber, 1997) – of all the dependency paths that connect them in the corpus. In subtask 1, LexNet is combined with vector cosine (calculated on word2vec embeddings trained on Google News) through weights that were learned on a validation set. In subtask 2, in order to avoid a bias towards the majority class RANDOM, a Multi-Layer Perceptron (MLP) is trained and applied only on pairs that were classified as related in subtask 1.

The third system, Mach5, investigates the structure and hyperparameters of two traditional dependency-filtered and dependency-structured DSMs trained on a Web corpus of 9.5 billion words. The author sets most parameters according to Lapesa and Evert (2014), focusing on feature selection and optimization of SVD dimensions. Distance information is used directly in subtask 1, while for subtask 2 a linear SVM classifier is applied to 1200-dimensional vectors representing partial Euclidean distance in the two SVD-reduced spaces. Given the competitive results in subtask 1 and the much lower performance achieved in subtask 2, it is evident that Mach5 was optimized for identifying non-random pairs rather than for recognizing and discriminating specific semantic relations.

The other systems include ROOT18, which relies on several unsupervised features extracted from ukWaC that aim at identifying specific semantic relations. Like Mach5, the system performs relatively well in subtask 1, but is much worse in subtask 2. LOPE achieves similar performance to ROOT18 in both subtasks. It uses word2vec embeddings trained on Google News to determine the most similar words for each target; it classifies as related only the words appearing in the top-N nearest neighbors (with $N = 600$). In subtask 2, LOPE classifies the semantic relations according to the rank of the words in the nearest neighbors list, assuming that they are ranked decreasingly as synonyms-antonyms-hypernyms-meronyms-randoms.

The other two systems, CGSRC and HsH-Supervised, perform worse in subtask 1. CGSRC, however, obtains results comparable to ROOT18 in subtask 2, while HsH-Supervised did not participate in this task. CGSRC relies on a CNN architecture with four layer types: an input layer, a convolution layer, a max pooling layer and a fully connected softmax layer for term-pair relation classification. The CNN works on word2vec embeddings trained on about 100 billion words of Google News corpus. Finally, HsH-Supervised is an SVM classifier trained on the multiplication of the distributional vectors of the two words in the pairs extracted from ukWaC (similar to the approach of Mach5 in subtask 2). This method was reported to perform worse than cosine similarity on the same vectors.

As a rough summary, all systems relied on DSMs, in either "count" (Mach5, ROOT18 and HSH-Supervised) or "predict" form (GHHH, LexNet, LOPE and CGSRC). These DSMs were trained on corpora whose size ranges from 2 billion to 840 billion words (with "count" models relying on the

W1	W2	Gold	Prediction
cold	bad	FALSE	TRUE
combine	create	FALSE	TRUE
come	fill	FALSE	TRUE
dark	narrow	FALSE	TRUE
democracy	peace	FALSE	TRUE
depress	injure	FALSE	TRUE
desert	darkness	FALSE	TRUE
desert	landscape	FALSE	TRUE
enjoyment	quality	FALSE	TRUE
eye	lens	FALSE	TRUE

Table 4: Sample of pairs that were misclassified by the top three systems

W1	W2	Gold	Prediction
club	weapon	TRUE	FALSE
cold	friendly	TRUE	FALSE
commerce	deal	TRUE	FALSE
contract	grow	TRUE	FALSE
cook	action	TRUE	FALSE
crowd	desert	TRUE	FALSE
crowd	one	TRUE	FALSE
crown	base	TRUE	FALSE
cube	die	TRUE	FALSE
dart	action	TRUE	FALSE

Table 5: Sample of pairs that were misclassified by the top three systems

smaller corpora between 2 and 9.5 billion words). There seems to be a correlation between corpus size and system performance, even though it is not linear. GHHH, for example, obtains its highest performance in subtask 2 with embeddings trained on 840 billion words, but when embeddings trained on 6 billion words are used the performance is only slightly behind. The impact is much bigger when comparing systems based on 2 billion words with systems based on 6 billion words of corpus data.

Another observation is that vector distance or nearest neighbor information seems to be sufficient to obtain competitive results in subtask 1, but subtask 2 proves to be much more complex. Several classifiers have been adopted (SVM, Linear Regression, Random Forest and CNN), but none of them seems to have a clear edge on the others: the best two systems rely on a CNN (GHHH) and on a MLP (LexNet), but the CNN is also used by CGSRC with much less convincing results.

Further information about the systems and their parameters can be found in the respective description papers in this volume.

4.3   Analysis of results

In order to provide some insights about what went wrong in the systems and whether the dataset might have to be blamed for their relatively low performance in subtask 2, we investigated how many and which pairs were misclassified by the top three systems, separately for each subtask.

Subtask 1. As many as 162 pairs out of 4,260 were misclassified by all the top three systems: 60 of them are unrelated pairs wrongly classified as related (see Table 4 for examples), while the remaining 102 are related pairs in the gold standard that were not recognized by the systems (see Table 5). As can be seen from Table 4, many of the false positives carry some kinds of association (e.g. *cold – bad, combine – create, eye – lens*, etc.), which in very few cases might be due to an accidental semantic relationship not filtered out by the annotators (e.g. *desert – landscape* as hypernymy). In Table 5, instead, we notice that most of the false negatives include highly ambiguous words, mostly used in rare senses (e.g. the hypernymic *club – weapon*, the antonymous *crown – base*, etc.) and/or very general hypernyms (e.g. *dart – action* and *cook – action*).

Subtask 2. As many as 513 pairs out of 4,260 were misclassified by all the top three systems. 237 of them received the same label. In Table 6 we summarize the number of pairs per relation that were misclassified, both with different labels (on the left) and with the same ones (on the right). Among the 237 misclassified pairs, the large majority (i.e. 172) were misclassified as RANDOM, while the others were misclassified between the various relations. With respect to these ones, hypernyms were most often confused with synonyms (even native speakers may have a hard time discriminating them: e.g. *dessert – sweet*) and antonyms (as they might share similar distributional properties, cf. Santus et al. (2015a)). Also, hypernyms were sometimes confused with part-whole meronyms. This is particularly likely to happen if one of the words is semantically ambiguous (e.g. *sugar – candy*). Further errors should probably be attributed to the stemmed form of the words (e.g. the hypernymic *pride – feel(ing)*), to their ambiguity (e.g. *duck – move*), and to a large difference in generality between the related words

<table>
<tr><td colspan="2">Receiving any label</td><td colspan="2">Receiving the same label</td></tr>
<tr><td>143</td><td>ANT</td><td>62</td><td>ANT</td></tr>
<tr><td>140</td><td>HYPER</td><td>68</td><td>HYPER</td></tr>
<tr><td>85</td><td>PART_OF</td><td>50</td><td>PART_OF</td></tr>
<tr><td>22</td><td>RANDOM</td><td>9</td><td>RANDOM</td></tr>
<tr><td>123</td><td>SYN</td><td>48</td><td>SYN</td></tr>
<tr><td>513</td><td>total</td><td>237</td><td>total</td></tr>
</table>

Table 6: Pairs that were misclassified by the top three systems, organized by gold relation

(e.g. *cook – action*).

5 Conclusion

In this paper, we have described the shared task of the 5th Workshop on Cognitive Aspects of the Lexicon (CogALex-V), which aims at testing corpus-based methods for the identification of semantically related words on the same benchmark in order to gain a better understanding of how such methods can model the acquisition and manipulation of semantic relations.

A dataset extracted from EVALution 1.0 (Santus et al., 2015b), and split into a training and a test set, was provided at `https://sites.google.com/site/cogalex2016/home/shared-task` in September 2016, together with an evaluation script and two baselines (majority and random). Seven participants submitted their system output and their paper description in October 2016. The task was divided into two subtasks, respectively aiming at the binary classification of related vs. unrelated words and at the multi-class classification of synonyms, antonyms, hypernyms, meronyms and random pairs.

The systems achieved a reasonable F_1 score in the first subtask (GHHH was the best system with $F_1 = 0.790$), but a rather low performance in subtask 2 (LexNet was the best system with $F_1 = 0.445$). This is certainly due to the inherent difficulty of the multi-class setting, but compounded by a series of other difficulties rooted in the design of the dataset, which uses ambiguous and stemmed words without part-of-speech information. These results suggest that there is still need for improvement and we hope that this shared task has provided a challenging dataset and state-of-the-art baselines to support further investigation. We would also like to point out that our dataset includes metadata from EVALution 1.0 (i.e. semantic domain, word frequency, capitalization distribution, morphological distribution, part-of-speech distribution, etc.), which can be used to evaluate the performance of the system and to pinpoint the sources of problems.

As a general note to organizers of future shared tasks, we would suggest to keep the factors of variability in the participating systems as low as possible, or at least require explicit analyses of these factors. In fact, although we were able to draw some general conclusions about the participating systems (see section 4), it is hard to determine the precise impact of relevant factors such as corpus size, especially if these factors are not explicitly analyzed in all the system description papers.

References

Marco Baroni, Georgiana Dinu, and Germán Kruszewski. 2014. Don't count, predict! a systematic comparison of context-counting vs. context-predicting semantic vectors. In *ACL (1)*, pages 238–247.

Georgeta Bordea, Paul Buitelaar, Stefano Faralli, and Roberto Navigli. 2015. Semeval-2015 task 17: Taxonomy extraction evaluation (texeval). In *Proceedings of the 9th International Workshop on Semantic Evaluation (SemEval 2015)A*, volume 452, pages 902–910. Association for Computational Linguistics.

Paul Buitelaar, Georgeta Bordea, and Els Lefever. 2016. SemEval-2016 Task 13: Taxonomy Extraction Evaluation (TExEval-2). In *Proceedings of the 10th International Workshop on Semantic Evaluation (SemEval-2016)*, pages 1081–1091. Association for Computational Linguistics.

Joan L. Bybee and Clay Beckner. 2015. Usage-based theory. In Bernd Heine and Heiko Narrog, editors, *The Oxford Handbook of Linguistic Analysis*, pages 954–979. Oxford University Press.

Christiane Fellbaum, editor. 1998. *Wordnet: An Electronic Lexical Database*. Language, speech, and communication series. MIT Press Cambridge.

J. R. Firth. 1957. A synopsis of linguistic theory 1930-55. *Studies in Linguistic Analysis (special volume of the Philological Society)*, 1952-59:1–32.

Roxana Girju, Preslav Nakov, Vivi Nastase, Stan Szpakowicz, Peter Turney, and Deniz Yuret. 2007. Semeval-2007 task 04: Classification of semantic relations between nominals. In *Proceedings of the 4th International Workshop on Semantic Evaluations*, pages 13–18. Association for Computational Linguistics.

Anna Gladkova, Aleksandr Drozd, and Satoshi Matsuoka. 2016. Analogy-based detection of morphological and semantic relations with word embeddings: What works and what doesnt. In *Proceedings of naacl-hlt*, pages 8–15.

Gregory Grefenstette. 1994. *Explorations in Automatic Thesaurus Discovery*. Kluwer Academic Publishers.

Zellig Harris. 1954. Distributional structure. *Word*, 10(23):146–162.

Marti A. Hearst. 1992. Automatic acquisition of hyponyms from large text corpora. In *Proceedings of the 14th Conference on Computational Linguistics-Volume 2*, pages 539–545. Association for Computational Linguistics.

Iris Hendrickx, Su Nam Kim, Zornitsa Kozareva, Preslav Nakov, Diarmuid Ó Séaghdha, Sebastian Padó, Marco Pennacchiotti, Lorenza Romano, and Stan Szpakowicz. 2010. Semeval-2010 task 8: Multi-way classification of semantic relations between pairs of nominals. In *Proceedings of the 5th International Workshop on Semantic Evaluation, ACL 2010*, pages 33–38. Association for Computational Linguistics.

Sepp Hochreiter and Jürgen Schmidhuber. 1997. Long short-term memory. *Neural computation*, 9(8):1735–1780.

David Jurgens and Mohammad Taher Pilehvar. 2016. SemEval-2016 Task 14: Semantic Taxonomy Enrichment. In *Proceedings of SemEval-2016*, pages 1016–1026. Association for Computational Linguistics.

Douwe Kiela, Laura Rimell, Ivan Vulic, and Stephen Clark. 2015. Exploiting image generality for lexical entailment detection. In *Proceedings of the 53rd Annual Meeting of the Association for Computational Linguistics (ACL 2015)*. ACL.

Lili Kotlerman, Ido Dagan, Idan Szpektor, and Maayan Zhitomirsky-Geffet. 2010. Directional distributional similarity for lexical inference. *Natural Language Engineering*, 16(04):359–389.

Gabriella Lapesa and Stefan Evert. 2014. A large scale evaluation of distributional semantic models: Parameters, interactions and model selection. *Transactions of the Association for Computational Linguistics*, 2:531–545.

Alessandro Lenci and Giulia Benotto. 2012. Identifying hypernyms in distributional semantic spaces. In *Proceedings of the First Joint Conference on Lexical and Computational Semantics-Volume 1: Proceedings of the main conference and the shared task, and Volume 2: Proceedings of the Sixth International Workshop on Semantic Evaluation*, pages 75–79. Association for Computational Linguistics.

Alessandro Lenci. 2008. Distributional semantics in linguistic and cognitive research. 20(1):1–31.

Omer Levy, Yoav Goldberg, and Ido Dagan. 2015a. Improving distributional similarity with lessons learned from word embeddings. *Transactions of the Association for Computational Linguistics*, 3:211–225.

Omer Levy, Steffen Remus, Chris Biemann, and Ido Dagan. 2015b. Do supervised distributional methods really learn lexical inference relations? In *Proceedings of the 2015 Conference of the North American Chapter of the Association for Computational Linguistics â AS Human Language Technologies (NAACL HLT 2015), Denver, CO*.

Dekang Lin, Shaojun Zhao, Lijuan Qin, and Ming Zhou. 2003. Identifying synonyms among distributionally similar words. In *IJCAI*, volume 3, pages 1492–1493.

Hugo Liu and Push Singh. 2004. ConceptNeta practical commonsense reasoning tool-kit. 22(4):211–226.

Anna Lobanova, Gosse Bouma, and Erik Tjong Kim Sang. 2010. Using a treebank for finding opposites. In *Ninth International Workshop on Treebanks and Linguistic Theories*, page 139.

Nitin Madnani and Bonnie J. Dorr. 2010. Generating phrasal and sentential paraphrases: A survey of data-driven methods. 36(3):341–387.

Pascual Martinez-Gómez, Koji Mineshima, Yusuke Miyao, and Daisuke Bekki. 2016. ccg2lambda: A Compositional Semantics System. In *Proceedings of the 54th Annual Meeting of the Association for Computational Linguistics - System Demonstrations*, pages 85–90. Association for Computational Linguistics.

Nawoja Mikoajczak-Matyja. 2015. The Associative Structure of the Mental Lexicon: Hierarchical Semantic Relations in the Minds of Blind and Sighted Language Users. 19(1):1–18. [doi:10.1515/plc-2015-0001].

Kim Anh Nguyen, Sabine Schulte im Walde, and Ngoc Thang Vu. 2016. Integrating distributional lexical contrast into word embeddings for antonym-synonym distinction. *CoRR*, abs/1605.07766.

Patrick Pantel and Marco Pennacchiotti. 2006. Espresso: Leveraging generic patterns for automatically harvesting semantic relations. In *Proceedings of the 21st International Conference on Computational Linguistics and the 44th Annual Meeting of the Association for Computational Linguistics*, pages 113–120. Association for Computational Linguistics.

Jeffrey Pennington, Richard Socher, and Christopher D Manning. 2014. Glove: Global vectors for word representation. In *EMNLP*, volume 14, pages 1532–43.

Stephen Roller and Katrin Erk. 2016. Relations such as hypernymy: Identifying and exploiting hearst patterns in distributional vectors for lexical entailment. *arXiv preprint arXiv:1605.05433*.

Stephen Roller, Katrin Erk, and Gemma Boleda. 2014. Inclusive yet selective: Supervised distributional hypernymy detection. In *COLING*, pages 1025–1036.

Enrico Santus, Qin Lu, Alessandro Lenci, and Chu-Ren Huang. 2014. Unsupervised antonym-synonym discrimination in vector space. In *Proceedings of the First Italian Conference on Computational Linguistics CLiC-it 2014, 9-10 December 2014, Pisa*, volume 1, pages 328–333. Pisa University Press.

Enrico Santus, Alessandro Lenci, Qin Lu, and Chu-Ren Huang. 2015a. When similarity becomes opposition: Synonyms and antonyms discrimination in dsms. *Italian Journal on Computational Linguistics*, 1(1).

Enrico Santus, Frances Yung, Alessandro Lenci, and Chu-Ren Huang. 2015b. EVALution 1.0: An Evolving Semantic Dataset for Training and Evaluation of Distributional Semantic Models. In *Proceedings of the 4th Workshop on Linked Data in Linguistics (LDL-2015)*, pages 64–69.

Enrico Santus, Alessandro Lenci, Tin-Shing Chiu, Qin Lu, and Chu-Ren Huang. 2016. Nine features in a random forest to learn taxonomical semantic relations. *arXiv preprint arXiv:1603.08702*.

Vered Shwartz, Yoav Goldberg, and Ido Dagan. 2016. Improving hypernymy detection with an integrated path-based and distributional method. *ACL 2016*.

Rion Snow, Daniel Jurafsky, and Andrew Y. Ng. 2004. Learning syntactic patterns for automatic hypernym discovery. *Advances in Neural Information Processing Systems 17*.

Peter D. Turney. 2008. A uniform approach to analogies, synonyms, antonyms, and associations. In *Proceedings of the 22nd International Conference on Computational Linguistics (Coling 2008)*, pages 905–912.

Wenbo Wang, Christopher Thomas, Amit Sheth, and Victor Chan. 2010. Pattern-based synonym and antonym extraction. In *Proceedings of the 48th Annual Southeast Regional Conference*, page 64. ACM.

Julie Weeds, Daoud Clarke, Jeremy Reffin, David J Weir, and Bill Keller. 2014. Learning to distinguish hypernyms and co-hyponyms. In *COLING*, pages 2249–2259.

Amal Zouaq and Roger Nkambou. 2008. Building domain ontologies from text for educational purposes. 1(1):49–62.

CogALex-V Shared Task:
LexNET - Integrated Path-based and Distributional Method for the Identification of Semantic Relations

Vered Shwartz   **Ido Dagan**

Computer Science Department, Bar-Ilan University, Ramat-Gan, Israel

`vered1986@gmail.com`   `dagan@cs.biu.ac.il`

Abstract

We present a submission to the CogALex 2016 shared task on the corpus-based identification of semantic relations, using `LexNET` (Shwartz and Dagan, 2016), an integrated path-based and distributional method for semantic relation classification. The reported results in the shared task bring this submission to the third place on subtask 1 (word relatedness), and the first place on subtask 2 (semantic relation classification), demonstrating the utility of integrating the complementary path-based and distributional information sources in recognizing concrete semantic relations. Combined with a common similarity measure, `LexNET` performs fairly good on the word relatedness task (subtask 1). The relatively low performance of `LexNET` and all other systems on subtask 2, however, confirms the difficulty of the semantic relation classification task, and stresses the need to develop additional methods for this task.

1 Introduction

Discovering whether words are semantically related and identifying the specific semantic relation that holds between them is a key component in many NLP applications, such as question answering and recognizing textual entailment (Dagan et al., 2013). Automated methods for semantic relation identification are commonly corpus-based, and mainly rely on the distributional representation of each word.

The CogALex shared task on the corpus-based identification of semantic relations consists of two subtasks. In the first task, the system needs to identify for a word pair whether the words are semantically related or not (e.g. *True:(dog, cat), False:(dog, fruit)*). In the second task, the goal is to determine the specific semantic relation that holds for a given pair, if any (*PART_OF:(tail, cat), HYPER:(cat, animal)*).

In this paper we describe our approach and system setup for the shared task. We use `LexNET` (Shwartz and Dagan, 2016), an integrated path-based and distributional method for semantic relation classification. `LexNET` was the system with the overall best performance on subtask 2, and was ranked third on subtask 1, demonstrating the utility of integrating the complementary path-based and distributional information sources in recognizing semantic relatedness.[1]

To aid in recognizing whether a pair of words are related at all (subtask 1), we combine `LexNET` with a common similarity measure (cosine similarity), achieving fairly good performance, and a slight improvement upon using cosine similarity alone. Subtask 2, however, has shown to be extremely difficult, with `LexNET` and all other systems achieving relatively low F_1 scores. The conflict between the mediocre performance and the recent success of distributional methods on several other common datasets for semantic relation classification (Baroni et al., 2012; Weeds et al., 2014; Roller et al., 2014) could be explained by the stricter evaluation setup in this subtask, which is supposed to demonstrate more closely real-world application settings. The difficulty of the semantic relation classification task emphasizes the need to develop better methods for this task.

[1]`LexNET`'s code is available at `https://github.com/vered1986/LexNET`, and the shared task results are available at `https://sites.google.com/site/cogalex2016/home/shared-task/results`

Proceedings of the Workshop on Cognitive Aspects of the Lexicon,
pages 80–85, Osaka, Japan, December 11-17 2016.

2 Background

2.1 Word Relatedness

Recognizing word relatedness is typically addressed by distributional methods. To determine to what extent two terms x and y are related, a vector similarity or distance measure is applied to their distributional representations: $sim(\vec{v}_{w_x}, \vec{v}_{w_y})$. This is a straightforward application of the distributional hypothesis (Harris, 1954), according to which related words occur in similar contexts, hence have similar vector representations.

Most commonly, vector cosine is adopted as a similarity measure (Turney et al., 2010). Many other measures exist, including but not limited to Euclidean distance, KL divergence (Cover and Thomas, 2012), Jaccard's coefficient (Salton and McGill, 1986), and more recently neighbor rank (Hare et al., 2009; Lapesa and Evert, 2013) and APSyn (Santus et al., 2016a).[2] To turn this task into a binary classification task, where x and y are classified as either related or not, one can set a threshold to separate similarity scores of related and unrelated word pairs.

2.2 Semantic Relation Classification

Recognizing lexical semantic relations between words is valuable for many NLP applications, such as ontology learning, question answering, and recognizing textual entailment. Most corpus-based methods classify the relation between a pair of words x and y based on the distributional representation of each word (Baroni et al., 2012; Roller et al., 2014; Fu et al., 2014; Weeds et al., 2014). Earlier methods utilized the dependency paths that connect the joint occurrences of x and y in the corpus as a cue to the relation between the words (A. Hearst, 1992; Snow et al., 2004; Nakashole et al., 2012). Recently, Shwartz and Dagan (2016) presented LexNET, an extension of HypeNET (Shwartz et al., 2016). This method integrates both path-based and distributional information for semantic relation classification, which outperformed approaches that rely on a single information source, on several common datasets (Baroni and Lenci, 2011; Necsulescu et al., 2015; Santus et al., 2015; Santus et al., 2016b).

3 System Description

In LexNET, a word-pair (x, y) is represented as a feature vector, consisting of a concatenation of distributional and path-based features: $\vec{v}_{xy} = [\vec{v}_{w_x}, \vec{v}_{paths(x,y)}, \vec{v}_{w_y}]$, where $\vec{v}_{w_x}$ and $\vec{v}_{w_y}$ are x and y's word embeddings, providing their distributional representation, and $\vec{v}_{paths(x,y)}$ is the average embedding vector of all the dependency paths that connect x and y in the corpus. Dependency paths are embedded using a LSTM (Hochreiter and Schmidhuber, 1997), as described in Shwartz et al. (2016). This vector is then fed into a neural network that outputs the class distribution $\vec{c}$, and then the pair is classified to the relation with the highest score r:

$$\vec{c} = \text{softmax}(\text{MLP}(\vec{v}_{xy})) \tag{1a}$$

$$r = \text{argmax}_i \, \vec{c}[i] \tag{1b}$$

MLP stands for Multi Layer Perceptron, and could be computed with or without a hidden layer (equations 2 and 3, respectively):

$$\vec{h} = \tanh(W_1 \cdot \vec{v}_{xy} + b_1) \tag{2a}$$

$$\text{MLP}(\vec{v}_{xy}) = W_2 \cdot \vec{h} + b_2 \tag{2b}$$

$$\text{MLP}(\vec{v}_{xy}) = W_1 \cdot \vec{v}_{xy} + b_1 \tag{3}$$

where W_i and b_i are the network parameters and $\vec{h}$ is the hidden layer.

---

[2] See Lee (1999) for an extensive list of such measures.

	Method	Hyper-parameters	Corpus size	P	R	F_1
Subtask 1	Cos	word2vec, t: 0.3	100B	0.759	0.795	0.776
	LexNET	hidden layers: 0, dropout: 0.0, epochs: 3	6B	0.780	0.561	0.652
	LexNET+Cos	word2vec, $w_L = 0.3, w_C = 0.7, t = 0.29$	$\sim$100B	**0.814**	**0.854**	**0.833**
Subtask 2	Dist	dep-based, method: concat, classifier: SVM, L_1	3B	0.611	0.598	0.600
	LexNET	hidden layers: 0, dropout: 0.0, epochs: 5	6B	**0.658**	**0.646**	**0.642**

Table 1: Performance scores on the validation set along with hyper-parameters and effective corpus size (#tokens) used by each method. Subtask 2 results refer to the subset of related pairs, as detailed in § 4.2.

3.1 A Note About Word Relatedness

While path-based approaches have been commonly used for semantic relation classification (A. Hearst, 1992; Snow et al., 2004; Nakashole et al., 2012; Necsulescu et al., 2015), they have never been used for word relatedness, which is considered a "classical" task for distributional methods. We argue that path-based information can improve performance of word relatedness tasks as well (see Section 4.1). We train LexNET to distinguish between two classes: RELATED and UNRELATED, and combine it with the common cosine similarity measure to tackle subtask 1.

4 Experimental Settings

The shared task organizers provided a dataset extracted from EVALution 1.0 (Santus et al., 2015), which was split into training and test sets. As instructed, we trained and tuned our method on the training set, and evaluated it once on the test set. To tune the hyper-parameters, we split the training set to 90% train and 10% validation sets. Since the dataset contains only 318 different words in the x slot, we performed the split such that the train and the validation contain distinct x words.[3]

LexNET has several tunable hyper-parameters. Similarly to Shwartz and Dagan (2016), we used the English Wikipedia dump from May 2015 as an underlying corpus (3B tokens), and initialized the network's word embeddings with the 50-dimensional pre-trained GloVe word embeddings (Pennington et al., 2014), trained on Wikipedia and Gigaword 5 (6B tokens). We fixed this hyper-parameter due to computational limitations with higher-dimensional embeddings. For each subtask, we tuned LexNET's hyper-parameters on the validation set: the number of hidden layers (0 or 1), the number of training epochs, and the word dropout rate (see Shwartz et al. (2016) for technical details). Table 1 displays the best performing hyper-parameters in each subtask, along with the performance on the validation set, which is detailed below.

4.1 Subtask 1: Word Relatedness

We tuned LexNET's hyper-parameters on the validation set, disregarding the similarity measure at this point, and then chose the model that performed best on the validation set and combined it with the similarity measure.

We computed cosine similarity for each (x, y) pair in the dataset: $\cos(\vec{v}_{w_x}, \vec{v}_{w_y}) = \frac{\vec{v}_{w_x} \cdot \vec{v}_{w_y}}{\|\vec{v}_{w_x}\| \cdot \|\vec{v}_{w_y}\|}$, and normalized it to the range $[0, 1]$. We scored each (x, y) pair by a combination of LexNET's score for the RELATED class and the cosine similarity score:

$$\text{Rel}(x, y) = w_C \cdot \cos(\vec{v}_{w_x}, \vec{v}_{w_y}) + w_L \cdot \vec{c}[\text{RELATED}] \tag{4}$$

where w_C, w_L are the weights assigned to cosine similarity and LexNET's scores respectively, such that $w_C + w_L = 1$. We tuned the weights and a threshold t using the validation set, and classified (x, y) as related if $\text{Rel}(x, y) \geq t$. The word vectors used to compute the cosine similarity scores were chosen among several available pre-trained embeddings.[4] For completeness we also report the performance of two baselines: cosine similarity ($w_C = 1$) and LexNET ($w_L = 1$, fixed $t = 0.5$).

---

[3] A random split yielded perfect results on the validation set, which were due to lexical memorization (Levy et al., 2015).

[4] word2vec (300 dimensions, SGNS, trained on GoogleNews, 100B tokens) (Mikolov et al., 2013), GloVe (50-300 dimensions, trained on Wikipedia and Gigaword 5, 6B tokens) (Pennington et al., 2014), and dependency-based embeddings (300 dimensions, trained on Wikipedia, 3B tokens) (Levy and Goldberg, 2014).

	Method	P	R	F_1
Subtask 1	Random Baseline	0.283	0.503	0.362
	Majority Baseline	0.000	0.000	0.000
	`Cos`	**0.841**	0.672	0.747
	LexNET+Cos	0.754	**0.777**	**0.765**
Subtask 2	Random Baseline	0.073	0.201	0.106
	Majority Baseline	0.000	0.000	0.000
	`Dist`	0.469	0.371	0.411
	LexNET	**0.480**	**0.418**	**0.445**

Table 2: Performance scores on the test set in each subtask, of the selected methods and the baselines.

4.2   Subtask 2: Semantic Relation Classification

The subtask's train set is highly imbalanced towards random instances (roughly 10 times more than any other relation), and training any supervised method leads to overfitting to the random class. We therefore trained the model only on the related classes (excluding RANDOM pairs), for which the classes are more balanced. During inference time, we used the model from subtask 1 to assign a relatedness score to each pair, $Rel(x, y)$, and computed the class distribution using the model from subtask 2, only for pairs that were related according to this score.

Finally, we applied a heuristic that if for a word pair (x, y), the difference in scores between the top scoring classes is low (< 0.2), and the top class is SYN, then it is only classified as SYN if the number of paths between x and y is smaller than 3. This is due to the fact that synonyms are hard to recognize with both distributional and path-based approaches (Shwartz and Dagan, 2016), but it is known that they do not tend to co-occur.

To compare `LexNET`'s performance on the validation set with other methods' performances, we adapted the distributional baseline employed by Shwartz et al. (2016) and Shwartz and Dagan (2016), where a classifier is trained on the combination of x and y's word embeddings. We experimented with several combination methods (concatenation (Baroni et al., 2012), difference (Fu et al., 2014; Weeds et al., 2014), and ASYM (Roller et al., 2014)), regularization factors, and pre-trained word embeddings (Mikolov et al., 2013; Pennington et al., 2014; Levy and Goldberg, 2014). This time, we used cosine similarity (subtask 1) to separate related from unrelated pairs, and trained the classifier only to distinguish between the related classes. Similarly to subtask 1, we tune `LexNET` and the baseline's hyper-parameters on the validation set. The best performance is reported in Table 1.

5   Results and Analysis

Table 2 displays the performance of our methods and the baselines on the test set. In addition to the two baselines provided by the shared task organizers (majority and random), we report also the results of our baselines detailed in Section 4. The majority baseline classifies all the instances as UNREALTED (subtask 1) or RANDOM (subtask 2). Since these labels are excluded from the averaged F_1 computation, this baseline's performance metrics are all zero.

Subtask 1:   Word Relatedness   `Cos` achieves fairly good performance (F_1 = 0.747), and `LexNET+Cos` slightly improves upon it. To better understand `LexNET`'s contribution, we examined pairs that were correctly classified by `LexNET+Cos` while being incorrectly classified by `Cos`. Out of the 57 pairs that were true negative in `LexNET` and false positive in `Cos`, we judged only one as somehow related (*(death, man)*).

We sampled 25 (from the 184) true positive pairs in `LexNET+Cos` that were false negatives in `Cos`, and found that they were all connected via paths in the corpus, suggesting that `LexNET`'s contribution comes also from the path-based component, rather than only from adding distributional information. 12 of the pairs contained a polysemous term, for which the relation holds in a specific sense (e.g. *(fire, shoot)*). 5 other pairs had a weak relation, e.g. *(compact, car)*. While a *car* can be *compact*, non of these words is one of the most related words to the other.[5] As noted by Shwartz and Dagan (2016), these are

---

[5] *car* is mostly related to *driver*, *cars*, and *race*, and *compact* to *compactness* and *locally*.

	predictions						relation	P	R	F_1
	ANT	RANDOM	HYPER	PART_OF	SYN		ANT	0.450	0.403	0.425
ANT	40.28	30.28	5.56	5.83	18.06		RANDOM	0.897	0.931	0.914
RANDOM	2.35	93.07	1.31	1.37	1.90		HYPER	0.616	0.458	0.526
HYPER	10.21	22.77	45.81	6.02	15.18		PART_OF	0.510	0.478	0.493
PART_OF	2.23	37.05	6.70	47.77	6.25		SYN	0.278	0.319	0.297
SYN	25.96	20.43	14.47	7.23	31.91					

(The left table's rows are labeled "gold".)

Figure 1: Left: confusion matrix of LexNET's predictions to the subtask 2 test set. Rows indicate gold labels and columns indicate predictions. The value in $[i, j]$ is the percentage of pairs classified to relation j of those labeled i. Right: Per-relation F_1 scores of LexNET's predictions to the test set of subtask 2.

cases in which distributional methods may fail to identify the relation between the words, while even a single meaningful path connecting x and y can capture the relation between them.

Subtask 2: Semantic Relation Classification We note that the overall results on this task are low, in contrast to the success of several methods on common datasets (Baroni et al., 2012; Weeds et al., 2014; Roller et al., 2014; Shwartz and Dagan, 2016). One possible explanation is the stricter and more informative evaluation, that considers the RANDOM class as noise, discarding it from the F_1 average.[6] Additionally, the dataset is lexically split, disabling lexical memorization (Levy et al., 2015). However, the strict evaluation spots a light on the difficulty of this task, which was somewhat obfuscated by the strong results published so far, but might have been obtained thanks to dataset and evaluation peculiarities (Levy et al., 2015; Santus et al., 2016b; Shwartz and Dagan, 2016).

Figure 1 displays LexNET's per relation F_1 scores on the test set, with the corresponding confusion matrix. While the F_1 scores of individual classes are relatively low, the confusion matrix shows that pairs were always classified to the correct relation more than to any other class. A common error comes from subtask 1's model: while most unrelated pairs were classified as unrelated, many related pairs were also classified as unrelated. This may be solved in the future by learning the two subtasks jointly rather than applying a pipeline.

Among the other relations, the performance on synonyms was the worst. The path-based component is weak in recognizing synonyms, which do not tend to co-occur. The distributional information causes confusion between synonyms and antonyms, since both tend to occur in the same contexts. Moreover, synonyms were also sometimes mistaken with hypernyms, as the difference between the two relations is often subtle (Shwartz et al., 2016).

6 Conclusion

We have presented our submission to the CogALex 2016 shared task on corpus-based identification of semantic relations. The submission is based on LexNET (Shwartz and Dagan, 2016), an integrated path-based and distributional method for semantic relation classification. LexNET was the best-performing system on subtask 2, demonstrating the utility of integrating the complementary path-based and distributional information sources in recognizing semantic relatedness.

We have shown that subtask 1 (word relatedness) reaches reasonable performance with cosine similarity, and is slightly improved when combined with LexNET, especially when the relation between the words is non-prototypical. The performance on subtask 2, however, was relatively low for all systems that participated in the shared task, including LexNET. This demonstrates the difficulty of the semantic relation classification task, and emphasizes the need to develop improved methods for this task, possibly using additional sources of information.

Acknowledgments

This work was partially supported by an Intel ICRI-CI grant, the Israel Science Foundation grant 880/12, and the German Research Foundation through the German-Israeli Project Cooperation (DIP, grant DA 1600/1-1).

---

[6]When the random class is included in the averaged F_1 score, the results are: P = 0.780, R = 0.786, F_1 = 0.781.

References

Marti A. Hearst. 1992. Automatic acquisition of hyponyms from large text corpora. In *COLING 1992*.

Marco Baroni and Alessandro Lenci. 2011. Proceedings of the gems 2011 workshop on geometrical models of natural language semantics. pages 1–10.

Marco Baroni, Raffaella Bernardi, Ngoc-Quynh Do, and Chung-chieh Shan. 2012. Entailment above the word level in distributional semantics. In *Proceedings of EACL 2012*, pages 23–32.

Thomas M Cover and Joy A Thomas. 2012. *Elements of information theory*. John Wiley & Sons.

Ido Dagan, Dan Roth, and Mark Sammons. 2013. Recognizing textual entailment.

Ruiji Fu, Jiang Guo, Bing Qin, Wanxiang Che, Haifeng Wang, and Ting Liu. 2014. Learning semantic hierarchies via word embeddings. In *Proceedings of ACL 2014*, pages 1199–1209.

Mary Hare, Michael Jones, Caroline Thomson, Sarah Kelly, and Ken McRae. 2009. Activating event knowledge. *Cognition*.

Zellig S Harris. 1954. Distributional structure. *Word*.

Sepp Hochreiter and Jürgen Schmidhuber. 1997. Long short-term memory. *Neural computation*.

Gabriella Lapesa and Stefan Evert. 2013. Evaluating neighbor rank and distance measures as predictors of semantic priming. In *ACL Workshop on Cognitive Modeling and Computational Linguistics (CMCL 2013)*.

Lillian Lee. 1999. Measures of distributional similarity. In *Proceedings of ACL 1999*.

Omer Levy and Yoav Goldberg. 2014. Dependency-based word embeddings. In *Proceedings of ACL 2014*, pages 302–308.

Omer Levy, Steffen Remus, Chris Biemann, and Ido Dagan. 2015. Do supervised distributional methods really learn lexical inference relations? In *Proceedings of NAACL-HLT 2015*, pages 970–976.

Tomas Mikolov, Ilya Sutskever, Kai Chen, Gregory S Corrado, and Jeffrey Dean. 2013. Distributed representations of words and phrases and their compositionality. In *NIPS*, pages 3111–3119.

Ndapandula Nakashole, Gerhard Weikum, and Fabian Suchanek. 2012. Patty: A taxonomy of relational patterns with semantic types. In *Proceedings of the 2012 Joint Conference EMNLP and CoNLL*, pages 1135–1145.

Silvia Necsulescu, Sara Mendes, David Jurgens, Núria Bel, and Roberto Navigli. 2015. Reading between the lines: Overcoming data sparsity for accurate classification of lexical relationships. In *Proceedings of *SEM 2015*, pages 182–192.

Jeffrey Pennington, Richard Socher, and Christopher Manning. 2014. Glove: Global vectors for word representation. In *Proceedings of EMNLP 2014*, pages 1532–1543.

Stephen Roller, Katrin Erk, and Gemma Boleda. 2014. Inclusive yet selective: Supervised distributional hypernymy detection. In *Proceedings of COLING 2014*, pages 1025–1036.

Gerard Salton and Michael J McGill. 1986. Introduction to modern information retrieval.

Enrico Santus, Frances Yung, Alessandro Lenci, and Chu-Ren Huang. 2015. Proceedings of the 4th workshop on linked data in linguistics: Resources and applications. pages 64–69.

Enrico Santus, Emmanuele Chersoni, Alessandro Lenci, Chu-Ren Huang, and Philippe Blache. 2016a. Testing apsyn against vector cosine on similarity estimation. *PACLIC*.

Enrico Santus, Alessandro Lenci, Tin-Shing Chiu, Qin Lu, and Chu-Ren Huang. 2016b. Nine features in a random forest to learn taxonomical semantic relations. In *LREC*.

Vered Shwartz and Ido Dagan. 2016. Path-based vs. distributional information in recognizing lexical semantic relations. *Proceedings of the 5th Workshop on Cognitive Aspects of the Lexicon (CogALex-V)*.

Vered Shwartz, Yoav Goldberg, and Ido Dagan. 2016. Improving hypernymy detection with an integrated path-based and distributional method. In *Proceedings of ACL 2016*, pages 2389–2398.

Rion Snow, Daniel Jurafsky, and Andrew Y Ng. 2004. Learning syntactic patterns for automatic hypernym discovery. In *NIPS*.

Peter D Turney, Patrick Pantel, et al. 2010. From frequency to meaning: Vector space models of semantics. *Journal of artificial intelligence research*, 37(1):141–188.

Julie Weeds, Daoud Clarke, Jeremy Reffin, David Weir, and Bill Keller. 2014. Learning to distinguish hypernyms and co-hyponyms. In *Proceedings of COLING 2014*, pages 2249–2259.

CogALex-V Shared Task: GHHH - Detecting Semantic Relations via Word Embeddings

Mohammed Attia
Google Inc.
New York City
NY, 10011
attia@google.com

Suraj Maharjan
Dept. of Computer Science
University of Houston
Houston, TX, 77004
smaharjan2@uh.edu

Younes Samih and **Laura Kallmeyer**
Dept. of Computational Linguistics
Heinrich Heine University,
Düsseldorf, Germany
samih,kallmeyer@phil.hhu.de

Thamar Solorio
Dept. of Computer Science
University of Houston
Houston, TX, 77004
solorio@cs.uh.edu

Abstract

This paper describes our system submission to the CogALex-2016 Shared Task on Corpus-Based Identification of Semantic Relations. Our system won first place for Task-1 and second place for Task-2. The evaluation results of our system on the test set is 88.1% (79.0% for TRUE only) f-measure for Task-1 on detecting semantic similarity, and 76.0% (42.3% when excluding RANDOM) for Task-2 on identifying finer-grained semantic relations. In our experiments, we try word analogy, linear regression, and multi-task Convolutional Neural Networks (CNNs) with word embeddings from publicly available word vectors. We found that linear regression performs better in the binary classification (Task-1), while CNNs have better performance in the multi-class semantic classification (Task-2). We assume that word analogy is more suited for deterministic answers rather than handling the ambiguity of one-to-many and many-to-many relationships. We also show that classifier performance could benefit from balancing the distribution of labels in the training data.

1 Introduction

Finding semantic relatedness between words is of crucial importance for natural language processing as it is essential for tasks like query expansion in information retrieval. So far, systems have relied mainly on manually constructed semantic hierarchies, such as ontologies and knowledge graphs. With the recent interest in neural networks and word embeddings, there are attempts to find semantic relations automatically from texts in an arithmetic fashion by measuring the distance between words in the vector space, assuming that words that are similar to each other will tend to have similar contextual embeddings.

This paper describes our system for the CogALex-V Shared Task on Corpus-Based Identification of Semantic Relations. We evaluated three methods for semantic classification based on word embeddings: word analogy, linear regression, and multi-task CNNs. In all these methods, we use publicly available pre-trained English word vectors.

2 Related Work

Semantic relatedness between single words (excluding phrases, sentences and multilingual parallel data) has been addressed in a number of shared tasks before, including relational similarity in SemEval-2012 (Jurgens et al., 2012), word to sense matching in SemEval-2014 (Jurgens et al., 2014), hyponym-hypernym relations in SemEval-2015 (Bordea et al., 2015), semantic taxonomy (hypernymy) in SemEval-2016 (Bordea et al., 2016), and semantic association in CogALex-2014 (Rapp and Zock, 2014).

Proceedings of the Workshop on Cognitive Aspects of the Lexicon,
pages 86–91, Osaka, Japan, December 11-17 2016.

The idea of representing words as vectors has been studied for about three decades (Hinton et al., 1986; Rumelhart et al., 1986; Elman, 1990; Bengio et al., 2003; Kann and Schütze, 2008; Mikolov et al., 2013b). The interest in word embeddings has intensified recently with the introduction of the new log linear architecture of Mikolov et al. (2013a). This architecture provided an efficient and simplified training methodology that minimizes computational complexity by doing away with the non-linear hidden layer, enabling training on much larger data than were previously possible. The public availability of word embedding training programs such as word2vec (Mikolov et al., 2013a) and GloVe (Pennington et al., 2014) allowed researchers to create models with different parameters and dimensionality sizes for different purposes.

The evaluation data[1] used in the development of the Google Continuous Bag of Words (CBOW) and skip-gram vectors (Mikolov et al., 2013a) focused on semantic similarities and coarse-grained semantic relations in the form of deterministic answers by analogy. These relationships were one-to-one including, for example, capitals (Athens: Greece - Baghdad: Iraq), currencies (India: rupee - Iran: rial), gender (king: queen - man: woman), derivation (amazing: amazingly - safe: safely), and inflection (enhance: enhancing - generate: generating). The evaluation data provided in the CogALex-V Shared Task includes five different semantic relations within the same training and test data, where the relationship between words is one-to-many. For example, while it is relatively easy to predict 'queen' as the answer to this query $x = king - man + woman$, you cannot expect 'contract' as the answer to the query $x = shoe - boot + lease$ with the same level of confidence if the relationship is expected to be either synonymy, antonymy, hyponymy, or hypernymy.

In this paper we try three different methods for handling semantic classification in the shared task: word analogy, linear regression and multi-task CNN. Using word analogy for identifying semantic relations has been discussed in a number of papers including (Levy et al., 2015; Gladkova et al., 2016; Vylomova et al., 2015). The basic idea is to use vector-oriented reasoning based on the offsets between words (Mikolov et al., 2013b) assuming that pairs of words that share a certain semantic relation will have similar cosine distance.

Linear regression classifiers, including Naive Bayes, Logistic Regression and Support Vector Machines, have been used for the identification of semantic relations. For example, GuoDong et al. (2005) used SVM to extract semantic relationships between entities relying on features extracted from lexical, syntactic, and semantic knowledge. Hatzivassiloglou and McKeown (1997) used a log-linear regression model to predict the similarity of conjoined adjectives. Snow et al. (2004) use a logistic regression classifier for hypernym pair identification. Costello (2007) used Naive Bayes to learn associations between features extracted from WordNet and predict relation membership categories. In our work, we do not use any lexical, syntactic or semantic features, other than the word embeddings and we score similarity using the well known cosine similarity metric.

CNNs have also been applied to the task. Zeng et al. (2014) use a convolutional deep neural network (DNN) to extract lexical features learned from word embeddings and then fed into a softmax classifier to predict the relationship between words. Similar approaches have been applied in (Santos et al., 2015) and (Xu et al., 2015).

3 Data Description

3.1 Shared Task Data

The shared task organizers provide a training set of 3,054 word pairs for 318 target words. In Task-1, we are given a pair of words and we need to determine if the words are semantically related or not. Some examples of Task-1 are shown in 1. In Task-2 participants are required to detect the type of the relationship: HYPER, PART_OF, SYN, ANT, or RANDOM.

3.2 Pre-Trained Word Vectors

In our experiments we experimented with three large-scale, publicly available pre-trained word vectors:

---

[1] http://www.fit.vutbr.cz/ imikolov/rnnlm/word-test.v1.txt

Word 1	Word 2	Task-1: Related?	Task-2: Which Relation?
lease	contract	TRUE	HYPER
brain	head	TRUE	PART_OF
cheat	deceive	TRUE	SYN
move	rest	TRUE	ANT
bright	mature	FALSE	RANDOM
...	...	...	...

Table 1: Training data for Task-1 and Task-2.

Task	Prec.	Rec.	F1
Task-1	75.3	61.1	63.0
Task-2	68.1	34.0	42.6

Table 2: Word Analogy results

Google News[2]. This is built with the word2vec architecture from a news corpus of 100B words (3M vocabulary entries) with 300 dimensions, negative sampling, using continuous bag of words and window size of 5.

Common Crawler[3]. This is built with the GloVe architecture from a corpus of 840B words (2.2M vocabulary entries) with 300 dimensions, and applying the adaptive gradient algorithm (AdaGrad) (Duchi et al., 2011).

Wikipedia + Gigaword 5[4]. This is built with the GloVe architecture from a corpus of 6B words (400K vocabulary entries) with 300 dimensions, and applying AdaGrad with context size of 20.

4 Experiments and Results

In this section we outline the experiments and report the results for the three approaches we tested: word analogy, linear regression and multi-task CNN. The results reported in this section are on the training set for all labels including "FALSE" for Task-1 and "RANDOM" for Task-2. Results on the test set of our selected systems are reported in Section 5.

4.1 Word Analogy

In word analogy, similar to Levy et al. (2014), we query the word vector directly to obtain the closest match to the given example using the formula: $predicted\_word = example\_word1 - example\_word2 + target\_word$. We iterate the query over all the examples in the training set and limit the search scope to the vocabulary items within the set (a set is the target word and all potentially related words). Then we take the average of the responses. The results in Table 2 show that this approach does not work as well for this current task. As we will show, the scores are much lower than those of the other approaches we explored here.

4.2 Linear Regression

We extract similarity distance between words from word vectors, then we use a number of ML classifiers to detect labels based only on the numerical value of the similarity distance. In the initial stage, Table 3, we compare ML algorithms (using 10-fold cross validation) trained on the similarity cosine distance extracted from Google News vectors as the only feature.

We notice from Table 3 that Simple Logistic and Multi-task CNNs have the best score for Task-1 and Task-2 respectively. Now we compare the performance on the three word vector resources: Google News, Common Crawler and Wikipedia + Gigaword 5. Table 4 shows that the best results are obtained by Common-Crawler for Task-2, and by combining the similarity scores from two models of Google News and Wiki+Gigaword for Task-1. We combined them by feeding into the classifier the cosine distance from each word embedding as a feature.

We observe that the classes in the training data are highly imbalanced, where 27% of the pairs are related, while 73% are unrelated. We assume that this disproportion could bias the classifier to prefer

---

[2]https://drive.google.com/file/d/0B7XkCwpI5KDYNlNUTTlSS21pQmM/
[3]http://nlp.stanford.edu/data/glove.6B.zip
[4]http://nlp.stanford.edu/data/glove.840B.300d.zip

Classifier	Task-1	Task-2
Logistic Regression	77.2	56.6
Simple Logistic	**89.0**	70.1
Decision Trees (J48)	87.7	61.5
NaiveBayes	88.5	**77.4**
LazyIBk	83.5	74.0
LazyKStar	87.8	70.1
Single task CNN	81.8	75.3
Multi-task CNN	83.2	**77.4**

Table 3: F1 Score (%) comparison of ML classifiers.

Classifier (Word Vectors)	Task-1	Task-2
Simple Logistic (G)	89.0	70.1
Simple Logistic (WG)	86.6	75.5
Simple (CC)	89.0	76.0
Simple Logistic (G+WG)	**89.4**	77.2
NaiveBayes (CC)	86.9	76.6
NaiveBayes (G+WG)	88.7	77.8
Multi-task CNN (G)	83.2	77.4
Multi-task CNN (WG)	85.1	78.0
Multi-task CNN (CC)	86.0	**78.4**

Table 4: Comparison of word vectors (G=Google News, WG=Wikipedia+Gigaword and CC=Common Crawler).

Limit	TRUE	FALSE	Average	Diff
1	91.8	79.5	88.3	12.3
2	89.1	86.5	88.1	2.6
3	86.6	89.1	88.0	**2.5**
4	83.6	90.1	87.5	6.5
5	82.2	91.4	88.2	9.2
No limit	79.3	93.1	89.4	13.8

Table 5: Results for different limits of unrelated pairs.

Method	Task-1	Task-2
SimpleLogistic	**79.0**	28.7
Multi-task CNN	71.0	**42.3**

Table 6: Final F1 Scores (%) on the test set.

the majority labels over the minority ones. We try to correct this imbalanced distribution by reducing the number of unrelated pairs and see if this can improve the performance of the classifiers. We conduct our experiments using our best model so far for Task-1 (SimpleLogistic) over different limits of the unrelated words (1, 2, 3, 4, 5 and all) as shown in Table 5. We choose limit 3 as our best model as it has the smallest difference between the f-score for TRUE and FALSE. For Task-2, reduction of unrelated words did not lead to any improvement in the system, so we apply it only to Task-1.

4.3 Multi-task Convolution Neural Network (CNN)

The CNN architecture is similar to the one used by Collobert and Weston (2008). We first feed the pair of input words to the embedding layer, which is initialized with the pre-trained embeddings discussed in Section 3.2. Next in the model is a stack of convolution modules with 500 filters each for filter sizes 1 and 2. We then apply 1-MaxPooling operation, after which we have a Dense layer with 32 neurons. Finally, we have two softmax classifiers since our system uses a multitask approach to jointly learn both tasks. More precisely, the loss function L combines the loss for Task-1 and Task-2, as defined in Equation 1. Here, y_i^{task1}, y_j^{task2}, $\hat{y}_i^{task1}$ and $\hat{y}_j^{task2}$ represent the labels and prediction probabilities for Task-1 and Task-2 respectively. Multitask architectures are preferred over single task ones as the constituent tasks can act as regularizers (Ian Goodfellow and Courville, 2016). There are dropouts after Embedding, Convolution and Dense layers to regularize the network.

$$L(X,Y) = -\sum_i \left(y_i^{task1} \ln \hat{y}_i^{task1} \right) - \sum_j \left(y_j^{task2} \ln \hat{y}_j^{task2} \right) \tag{1}$$

Parameter tuning: We used 20% of the training data as parameter tuning dataset and used it to tune various hyper-parameters like dropout ranges, filters and filter sizes of CNN modules and learning rate. We then use the best model's parameters to perform 10-fold cross-validation experiments with the training data. The results are shown in Table 3 and 4. Additionally, we also experimented with models specific to either Task-1 or Task-2. The results show that the multi-task setting yields better performance than the single task setting.

Label	Precision	Recall	F-Score
RND	87.4	91.1	89.2
SYN	20.9	20.0	20.4
ANT	47.8	42.2	44.8
HYP	50.6	47.6	49.1
PRT	57.6	43.8	49.7
All	75.6	76.7	76.0

Table 7:   Detailed results for Task-2 labels.

Label	RND	SYN	ANT	HYP	PRT
RND	2787	85	78	78	31
SYN	86	47	50	41	11
ANT	132	39	152	26	11
HYP	112	42	27	182	19
PRT	70	12	11	33	98

Table 8:   Confusion Matrix for Task-2.

5 Final Results

In order to preserve the integrity of the test data, we do not apply any fine-tuning or measure performance improvement by iterating on the test set. We apply only our best performing systems on the training data, which are Simple Logistic trained on Google News and Wikipedia + Gigaword 5 for Task-1, and CNN for Task-2. The results are reported by the shared task evaluation script for the related pairs only (i.e. excluding 'FALSE' and 'RANDOM') and are shown in Table 6. We achieve 79.0% and 42.3% F-score For Task-1 and Task-2 respectively. Tables 7 and 8 present the detailed performance per label in Task-2 and the confusion matrix. We notice that synonyms are the hardest to distinguish among all other labels. This is reminiscent of the philosophical question of the non-existence of exact synonyms (Carstairs-McCarthy, 1994). By contrast, the system performs best in detecting hypernym and part-of relations.

6 Conclusion

In this paper we have presented our systems for identifying and classifying semantic relations between single words. We used linear regression trained only on the cosine distance between word embedding representations. This method gives better results for Task-1. For task2, multi-task CNN method performs better. Our system performs relatively well for the binary classification of similarity between pairs of words, but the performance significantly decreases for the multi-class classification of four semantic relations. This is probably due to the ambiguity in one-to-many and many-to-many relationships.

References

Y. Bengio, R. Ducharme, and P. Vincent. 2003. A neural probabilistic language model. *Journal of Machine Learning Research*, 3:1137–1155.

Georgeta Bordea, Paul Buitelaar, Stefano Faralli, and Roberto Navigli. 2015. Semeval-2015 task 17: Taxonomy extraction evaluation (texeval). In *Proceedings of the 9th International Workshop on Semantic Evaluation (SemEval 2015)*, pages 902–910, Denver, Colorado.

Georgeta Bordea, Els Lefever, and Paul Buitelaar. 2016. Semeval-2016 task 13: Taxonomy extraction evaluation (texeval-2). In *Proceedings of the 10th International Workshop on Semantic Evaluation*. Association for Computational Linguistics.

Andrew Carstairs-McCarthy. 1994. Inflection classes, gender, and the principle of contrast. *Language*, pages 737–788.

Ronan Collobert and Jason Weston. 2008. A unified architecture for natural language processing: Deep neural networks with multitask learning. In *Proceedings of the 25th international conference on Machine learning*, pages 160–167. ACM.

Fintan J Costello. 2007. Ucd-fc: Deducing semantic relations using wordnet senses that occur frequently in a database of noun-noun compounds. In *Proceedings of the 4th International Workshop on Semantic Evaluations*, pages 370–373. Association for Computational Linguistics.

John Duchi, Elad Hazan, and Yoram Singer. 2011. Adaptive subgradient methods for online learning and stochastic optimization. *Journal of Machine Learning Research*, 12:2121–2159.

J. Elman. 1990. Finding structure in time. *Cognitive Science*, 14:179–211.

Anna Gladkova, Aleksandr Drozd, and Satoshi Matsuoka. 2016. Analogy-based detection of morphological and semantic relations with word embeddings: What works and what doesn't. In *Proceedings of naacl-hlt*, pages 8–15.

Zhou GuoDong, Su Jian, Zhang Jie, and Zhang Min. 2005. Exploring various knowledge in relation extraction. In *Proceedings of the 43rd annual meeting on association for computational linguistics*, pages 427–434. Association for Computational Linguistics.

Vasileios Hatzivassiloglou and Kathleen R McKeown. 1997. Predicting the semantic orientation of adjectives. In *Proceedings of the eighth conference on European chapter of the Association for Computational Linguistics*, pages 174–181. Association for Computational Linguistics.

G.E. Hinton, J.L. McClelland, and D.E. Rumelhart. 1986. Distributed representations. *In: Parallel distributed processing: Explorations in the microstructure of cognition*, 1.

Yoshua Bengio Ian Goodfellow and Aaron Courville. 2016. Deep learning. Book in preparation for MIT Press.

David A. Jurgens, Saif M. Mohammad, Peter D. Turney, and Keith J. Holyoak. 2012. Semeval-2012 task 2: Measuring degrees of relational similarity. In *First Joint Conference on Lexical and Computational Semantics (SEM)*, pages 356–364, Montreal, Canada.

David Jurgens, Mohammad Taher Pilehvar, and Roberto Navigli. 2014. Semeval-2014 task 3: Cross-level semantic similarity. In *Proceedings of the 8th International Workshop on Semantic Evaluation (SemEval 2014)*, pages 17–26, Dublin, Ireland.

Katharina Kann and Hinrich Schütze. 2008. A unified architecture for natural language processing: Deep neural networks with multitask learning. In *Proceedings of the 25th International Conference on Machine Learning*, pages 160–167.

Omer Levy, Yoav Goldberg, and Israel Ramat-Gan. 2014. Linguistic regularities in sparse and explicit word representations. In *CoNLL*, pages 171–180.

Omer Levy, Yoav Goldberg, and Ido Dagan. 2015. Improving distributional similarity with lessons learned from word embeddings. *Transactions of the Association for Computational Linguistics*, 3:211–225.

Tomas Mikolov, Kai Chen, Greg Corrado, and Jeffrey Dean. 2013a. Efficient estimation of word representations in vector space. In *In Proceedings of International Conference on Learning Representations (ICLR) 2013. arXiv:1301.3781v3*, pages 746–751, Scottsdale, AZ.

Tomas Mikolov, Wen tau Yih, and Geoffrey Zweig. 2013b. Linguistic regularities in continuous space word representations. In *Proceedings of NAACL-HLT 2013*, pages 746–751, Atlanta, Georgia.

Jeffrey Pennington, Richard Socher, and Christopher D. Manning. 2014. Glove: Global vectors for word representation. In *Proceedings of the 2014 Conference on Empirical Methods in Natural Language Processing (EMNLP)*, pages 1532–1543, Doha, Qatar.

Reinhard Rapp and Michael Zock. 2014. The cogalex-iv shared task on the lexical access problem. In *Proceedings of the 4th Workshop on Cognitive Aspects of the Lexicon*, pages 1–14, Dublin, Ireland.

D. E. Rumelhart, G. E. Hinton, and R. J. Williams. 1986. Learning internal representations by backpropagating errors. *Nature. 323:533.536.*

Cicero Nogueira dos Santos, Bing Xiang, and Bowen Zhou. 2015. Classifying relations by ranking with convolutional neural networks. *arXiv preprint arXiv:1504.06580.*

Rion Snow, Daniel Jurafsky, and Andrew Y. Ng. 2004. Learning syntactic patterns for automatic hypernym discovery. In *Advances in Neural Information Processing Systems (NIPS 2004)*, November. This is a draft version from the NIPS preproceedings; the final version will be published by April 2005.

Ekaterina Vylomova, Laura Rimmel, Trevor Cohn, and Timothy Baldwin. 2015. Take and took, gaggle and goose, book and read: Evaluating the utility of vector differences for lexical relation learning. *arXiv preprint arXiv:1509.01692.*

Kun Xu, Yansong Feng, Songfang Huang, and Dongyan Zhao. 2015. Semantic relation classification via convolutional neural networks with simple negative sampling. *arXiv preprint arXiv:1506.07650.*

Daojian Zeng, Kang Liu, Siwei Lai, Guangyou Zhou, Jun Zhao, et al. 2014. Relation classification via convolutional deep neural network. In *COLING*, pages 2335–2344.

CogALex-V Shared Task: Mach5
A traditional DSM approach to semantic relatedness

Stefan Evert
Corpus Linguistics Group
Friedrich-Alexander-Universität Erlangen-Nürnberg
Bismarckstr. 6, 91054 Erlangen, Germany
stefan.evert@fau.de

Abstract

This contribution provides a strong baseline result for the CogALex-V shared task using a traditional "count"-type DSM (placed in rank 2 out of 7 in subtask 1 and rank 3 out of 6 in subtask 2). Parameter tuning experiments reveal some surprising effects and suggest that the use of random word pairs as negative examples may be problematic, guiding the parameter optimization in an undesirable direction.

1   Introduction

It is generally assumed that traditional "count"-type distributional semantic models (DSM) are good at identifying attributionally similar words, but cannot distinguish between different semantic relations (e.g. synonyms, antonyms, hypernyms) and work poorly for other forms of semantic relatedness such as meronymy (Baroni and Lenci, 2011). Moreover, DSMs based on syntactic dependency relations are supposed to achieve better results than window-based models (Padó and Lapata, 2007). The goal of the present paper is to test how well traditional DSMs can be tuned to identify different types of semantic relations in the CogALex-V shared task. It can thus be seen as a strong baseline against which more specialized approaches can be compared. The system developed here is nicknamed マッハ号, or Mach5[1] in English.

According to the distributional hypothesis (Harris, 1954), semantically related words should have a smaller distance in a distributional space than unrelated words, especially if they are attributionally similar. This suggests a simple strategy for the identification of semantically related words in subtask 1: candidate pairs are predicted to be related if their distributional distance is below a specified threshold value θ. The choice of θ determines the trade-off between precision and recall as visualized in the left panel of Fig. 1, where the thin dotted line shows precision (P) and the thin dashed line shows recall (R) for different values of θ. The optimal threshold $\theta^* = 80.7°$ – indicated by a circle and a thin vertical line – is chosen to maximize F_1-score, the harmonic mean of precision and recall, which is also the main evaluation criterion in the CogALex-V task. In this example, the DSM achieves $P = 76.27\%$, $R = 74.38\%$ and $F_1 = 75.31\%$ on the training data.

DSM distances cannot be used in the same way to discriminate between semantic relations in subtask 2 because antonyms, synonyms, hypernyms, etc. will all be relatively close in semantic space and their distance distributions are similar (Baroni and Lenci, 2011; Santus et al., 2015). Therefore, Mach5 implements a simple machine learning approach for this subtask, as described in Sec. 3. Parameters of the underlying DSM are tuned based on the overall identification of semantically related words (Sec. 2).

2   The Mach5 DSM

The Mach5 distributional model is based on ENCOW 2014, a large English Web corpus (Schäfer and Bildhauer, 2012) with a size of approx. 9.5 billion tokens after sentence deduplication. A particular

---

[1]https://en.wikipedia.org/wiki/Mach_Five

Proceedings of the Workshop on Cognitive Aspects of the Lexicon,
pages 92–97, Osaka, Japan, December 11-17 2016.

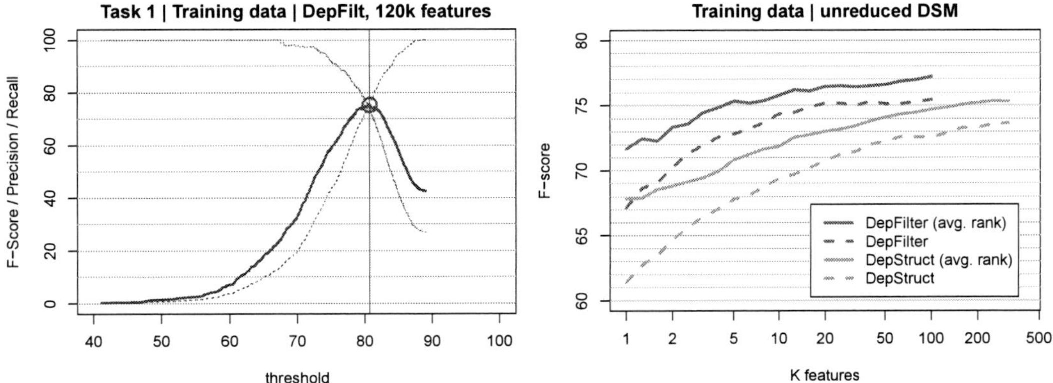

Figure 1: Left panel: Application of DSM distances (angles) to the identification of semantically related words. Right panel: Performance in subtask 1 depending on the number of feature dimensions used.

advantage of this huge corpus is its full coverage of the CogALex-V training and test sets, so that no special handling of unseen words is required. Both a dependency-filtered and a dependency-structured DSM were compiled from syntactic dependencies obtained with the robust C&C parser (Curran et al., 2007). The target vocabulary of 26,450 lemmas extends the vocabulary of Distributional Memory (Baroni and Lenci, 2010) with all words in the training and test sets of the shared task. Similar to the gold standard, the DSM uses lemmatized words (from TreeTagger) but does not distinguish between homonyms with different parts of speech (such as *clear*$_{\text{ADJ}}$ and *clear*$_{\text{VERB}}$). The 120,000 most frequent lemmas were extracted as features for the dependency-filtered model (henceforth DepFilt); the 300,000 most frequent relation-lemma combinations (e.g. OBJ=*cat*) were extracted as features for the dependency-structured model (henceforth DepStruct).

Some basic parameters were set according to the recommendations of Lapesa and Evert (2014): sparse (i.e. non-negative) simple log-likelihood (simple-ll) is used as an association measure for feature weighting and an additional log transformation is applied to the simple-ll scores. The models use angular distance (equivalent to cosine similarity) and explore logarithmic neighbour rank as an index of semantic (dis)similarity. Other parameters are tuned incrementally on the training data, as described in the following subsections. The main tuning criterion is the F_1 score achieved by an optimal cutoff threshold on the training data of subtask 1.

2.1 Feature selection

A first step is to determine how many feature dimensions are required in order to achieve good results and whether the dependency-filtered or the dependency-structured model is superior. The right panel of Fig. 1 plots F_1-scores in subtask 1 against the number of most frequent features and the other parameters. The graphs show clearly that more features produce better results and that further improvements may be expected from an even larger number of features, especially for DepStruct. Average logarithmic neighbour rank (solid lines) as an index of relatedness outperforms angular distance (dashed lines) by a large margin (forward and backward rank fall somewhere in between and have been omitted for clarity). DepFilt (blue, best $F_1 = 77.2\%$) is also considerably better than DepStruct (green, best $F_1 = 75.3\%$), even with a much smaller number of features.

Some authors suggest that medium-frequency features are the most informative for DSMs (Kiela and Clark, 2014), which motivates experiments with feature windows of 10,000–50,000 features in different frequency ranges. Fig. 2 shows the starting point of the feature window (i.e. the number of most frequent features skipped) on the x-axis and different window sizes in different colours.

For DepFilt (left panel), excluding the most frequent dimensions has a strong negative effect on angular distance. However, neighbour rank improves up to $F_1 = 78.03\%$ if the first 20,000–50,000 features are skipped, and it deteriorates much more slowly afterwards. The number of features in the window

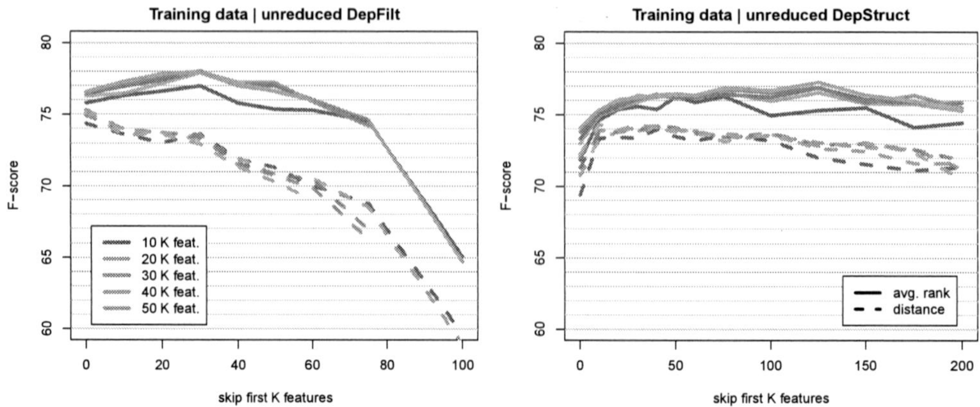

Figure 2: Performance of different feature windows in subtask 1 for DepFilt (left) and DepStruct (right). The x-axis shows how many thousands (K) of features are skipped.

seems to make little difference, especially for neighbour rank where as few as 20,000 features are sufficient.[2] The observations for DepStruct (right panel) are similar, but even more striking. Angular distance improves considerably if up to 50,000 high-frequency features are skipped, then declines only slowly. For neighbour rank, performance continues to improve and achieves $F_1 = 77.25\%$ when more than 100,000 features are skipped; in other words, a relatively small window of lower-frequency features seems to yield the best results. Contrary to what Fig. 1 suggested, DepFilt and DepStruct now achieve similar F_1-scores with a suitably chosen window of less than 50,000 words; both results are better than those reported above for the full feature sets.

For further experiments involving dimensionality reduction, somewhat larger feature windows are selected because the latent dimensions might be able to exploit shared information unlike the unreduced models evaluated here. DepFilt uses feature ranks 20,000–70,000 (with $1292 \leq f \leq 12720$) to achieve $F_1 = 77.25\%$ in subtask 1; DepStruct uses feature ranks 50,000–150,000 (with $1796 \leq f \leq 11040$) to achieve $F_1 = 76.52\%$.[3]

2.2 Dimensionality reduction by SVD

Most evaluation studies find that dimensionality reduction, which is traditionally carried out by an efficient sparse truncated singular value decomposition (SVD), improves DSM representations. Lapesa and Evert (2014) report consistently better results across a wide range of evaluation tasks and parameter settings. The following experiments explore how many latent dimensions are required and whether skipping the first latent dimensions is beneficial (Bullinaria and Levy, 2012; Lapesa and Evert, 2014). In addition, we look at a parameter that has only recently become popular: Caron's (2001) power scaling coefficient P for the SVD dimensions.[4] Bullinaria and Levy (2012) report a substantial improvement in model performance if P is set close to 0, especially for the TOEFL synonym task.

The DepFilt and DepStruct vectors selected in Sec. 2.1 are normalized according to the Euclidean norm, then SVD is applied to project them into 1000 latent dimensions for each model. The left panel of Fig. 3 shows that power scaling with $P < 1$ leads to a substantial improvement. For both models, $P = 0$ is a nearly optimal and theoretically motivated choice. It is particularly fascinating that power scaling evens out most of the differences between angular distance and neighbour rank as well as between DepStruct and DepFilt, with DepStruct performing slightly better now. Fixing $P = 0$, additional

---

[2]It is interesting to note that Schütze (1998) and several other early papers use 20,000 feature dimensions.

[3]In a 100-million-word corpus like the British National Corpus, this would correspond to frequencies between approx. 10 and 150 occurrences, i.e. a range of words that are normally excluded from distributional models.

[4]$P = 1$ corresponds to standard SVD, $P > 1$ gives more weight to the first latent dimensions (capturing the strongest correlation patterns), and $P < 1$ equalizes the dimensons. In particular, for $P = 0$ each latent dimension makes the same average contribution to distances between the word vectors (under certain additional circumstances).

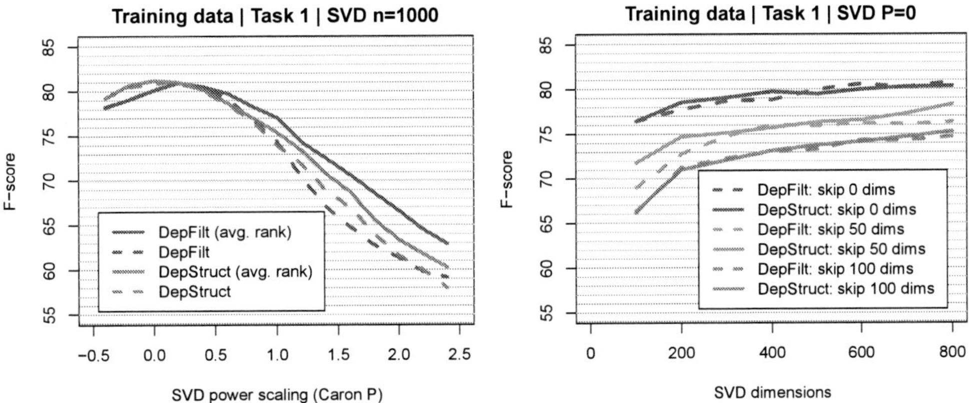

Figure 3: Effect of power scaling on SVD dimensions (Caron's P, left panel) and of further truncation of SVD as well skipping the first latent dimensions (for $P = 0$, right panel).

experiments show that skipping the first SVD dimensions does not lead to a further improvement, but rather to a considerably decrease in quality (left panel of Fig. 3). This surprising effect appears to be caused by feature equalization: without power scaling (i.e. $P = 1$), F_1 improves when skipping up to 50 SVD dimensions (not shown). Further truncation of the SVD to less than 600 dimensions also decreases quality, but performance seems to stabilize if at least 600 dimensions are used (blue lines in right panel).

The final Mach5 DSMs are based on the first 600 SVD dimensions with Caron's $P = 0$, equalizing the relative importance of the latent dimensions. Computationally cheaper distance values are used as an index of semantic relatedness, since they perform only marginally worse than average neighbour rank.

3 The Mach5 system

Run 1 of the Mach5 system only uses distance information from the DepFilt and DepStruct DSMs tuned in Sec. 2. For subtask 1, an optimal cutoff threshold is determined to maximize F_1 on the training data (DepFilt: 86.4°, DepStruct: 87.0°). For subtask 2, a SVM classifier with RBF kernel is applied to six-dimensional feature vectors containing angular distance as well as forward and backward neighbour rank from both DepFilt and DepStruct. Metaparameters (C and class weights) were tuned manually by cross-validation of weighted average F_1-scores on the training data.[5] Evaluation results on the training and test sets are shown in Table 1.

Run 2 explores the possibility that different types of semantic relations might be encoded in different SVD dimensions, which can be exploited by changing the weights of the dimensions when computing semantic distances. As a computationally efficient approximation, we apply a linear SVM classifier to feature vectors containing the contribution $(x_i - y_i)^2$ of each latent dimension i to the Euclidean distance between the pre-normalized vectors $\mathbf{x}$ and $\mathbf{y}$ of a word pair.[6] Features from DepFilt and DepStruct are concatenated for a total of 1,200 feature dimensions. Both subtasks can be approached in this way, training either a binary (substak 1) or a five-way (subtask 2) SVM classifier. Again, metaparameters were manually tuned on the training data. It turned out to be crucial to set the cost parameter to a low value $C \leq .01$ in order to ensure strong regularization and avoid overfitting.

For the official submission, the runs performing best on the training data were selected, shown in bold in Table 1. Competition results are thus $F_1 = 77.88\%$ in subtask 1 and $\bar{F}_1 = 29.59\%$ in subtask 2. All models were implemented in R using the `wordspace` package for distributional semantics (Evert, 2014)

---

[5]Cross-validation uses a round-robin scheme grouped by target word in order to avoid item-specific learning. Without this precaution, cross-validated performance on the training data might be highly optimistic in some cases. For example, a simple round-robin scheme yielded $\bar{F}_1 = 39.88\%$ for run 2 in subtask 2, while the more realistic grouped cross-validation yields $\bar{F}_1 = 32.37\%$. Differences are much smaller for the simpler models of run 1.

[6]These features gave slightly better performance than contribution $x_i y_i$ to cosine similarity.

| | Run | Subtask 1 | | Subtask 2 | |
		Train F_1	Test F_1	Train $\bar{F}_1$	Test $\bar{F}_1$
run 1	DepFilt	**80.59**	**77.88**	—	—
	DepStruct	79.98	76.80	—	—
	both	—	—	26.47	23.76
run 2	both	78.12	72.76	**32.37**	**29.59**
run 3	both	*80.88*	*78.93*	—	*31.97*

Table 1: Evaluation results of different Mach5 runs on the training data (10-fold cross-validation) and test data, using the official F_1-scores in subtask 1 and weighted average $\bar{F}_1$ across the four semantic relations in subtask 2. Runs selected for the competition are shown in bold font, the best results obtained in follow-up experiments are shown in italics.

and the LibSVM classifier from package `e1071`. Mach5 can be downloaded as an R script together with the original co-occurrence data from `http://www.collocations.de/data/#mach5`.

4 Discussion

The optimal cutoff angles determined for subtask 1 are surprisingly high – close to orthogonality – which suggests a possible problem with the use of random word pairs as negative examples in the gold standard (and many other DSM evaluation tasks that also use random word pairs as a control). As a consequence, the parameter tuning in Sec. 2 was guided towards recognizing random word pairs rather than clearly defined semantic relations. The distribution of DSM distances for different semantic relations in the left panel of Fig. 4 supports this interpretation: the distances between semantically related words spread over a wide range and can become very large (sometimes even above $90°$), while most random word combinations are almost precisely orthogonal. For a DSM with conventional state-of-the-art parameter settings[7] (right panel of Fig. 4), the distribution shows a much larger spread of the random word pairs.

It seems plausible that this "conventional" DSM may contain useful information for the discrimination between different semantic relations, while the Mach5 DSM has been tuned to identify random word pairs as accurately as possible. Therefore, a combined approach was implemented after the competition as run 3 of the Mach5 system. It uses an SVM classifier with RBF kernel, based on the six-dimensional features vectors from run 1, for distinguishing between related and unrelated word pairs in subtask 1. For the discrimination between semantic relations, a linear SVM classifier is trained only on related word pairs, using partial Euclidean distances from the conventional DepFilt model and partial inner products from the conventional DepStruct model as features (similar to run 2). In subtask 2, the first (binary) classifier identifies RANDOM pairs, while the second (four-way) classifier selects a relation label for the remaining word pairs. As can be seen from the bottom row of Table 1, run 3 performs noticeably better than the submitted system,[8] although it would still have ranked in second and third place, respectively, in the competition. These results provide additional support for the hypothesis that the wide-spread use of random word pairs as negative examples poses the risk of misguiding DSM parameter tuning.

References

Marco Baroni and Alessandro Lenci. 2010. Distributional Memory: A general framework for corpus-based semantics. *Computational Linguistics*, 36(4):673–712.

Marco Baroni and Alessandro Lenci. 2011. How we BLESSed distributional semantic evaluation. In *Proceedings of the GEMS 2011 Workshop on GEometrical Models of Natural Language Semantics*, pages 1–10, Edinburgh, UK.

---

[7]DepFilt with 50,000 features (except for the 150 most frequent lemmas), reduced to first 600 SVD dimensions without power scaling ($P = 1$); DepStruct with 100,000 features (except for 400 most frequent ones) and same SVD projection.

[8]$F_1 = 78.93\%$ vs. 77.88% in subtask 1 and $\bar{F}_1 = 31.97\%$ vs. 29.59% in subtask 2

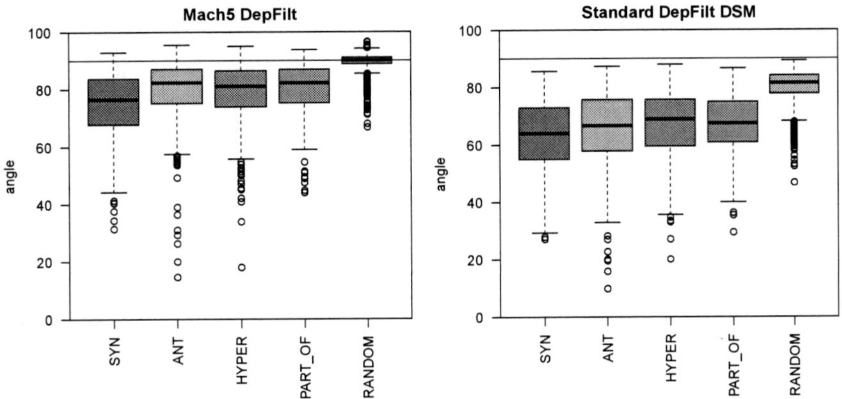

Figure 4: Distribution of DSM distances across the four semantic relations and the random controls in the test data for CogALex-V subtask 2, comparing the tuned Mach5 model (left panel) against a dependency-filtered DSM with conventional state-of-the-art parameter settings (right panel).

John A. Bullinaria and Joseph P. Levy. 2012. Extracting semantic representations from word co-occurrence statistics: Stop-lists, stemming and SVD. *Behavior Research Methods*, 44(3):890–907.

John Caron. 2001. Experiments with LSA scoring: Optimal rank and basis. In Michael W. Berry, editor, *Computational Information Retrieval*, pages 157–169. Society for Industrial and Applied Mathematics, Philadelphia, PA, USA.

James Curran, Stephen Clark, and Johan Bos. 2007. Linguistically motivated large-scale NLP with C&C and Boxer. In *Proceedings of the 45th Annual Meeting of the Association for Computational Linguistics, Posters and Demonstrations Sessions*, pages 33–36, Prague, Czech Republic.

Stefan Evert. 2014. Distributional semantics in R with the wordspace package. In *Proceedings of COLING 2014, the 25th International Conference on Computational Linguistics: System Demonstrations*, pages 110–114, Dublin, Ireland, August.

Zellig Harris. 1954. Distributional structure. *Word*, 10(23):146–162. Reprinted in Harris (1970, 775–794).

Douwe Kiela and Stephen Clark. 2014. A systematic study of semantic vector space model parameters. In *Proceedings of the 2nd Workshop on Continuous Vector Space Models and their Compositionality (CVSC)*, pages 21–30, Gothenburg, Sweden.

Gabriella Lapesa and Stefan Evert. 2014. A large scale evaluation of distributional semantic models: Parameters, interactions and model selection. *Transactions of the Association for Computational Linguistics*, 2:531–545.

Sebastian Padó and Mirella Lapata. 2007. Dependency-based construction of semantic space models. *Computational Linguistics*, 33(2):161–199.

Enrico Santus, Frances Yung, Alessandro Lenci, and Chu-Ren Huang. 2015. EVALution 1.0: an evolving semantic dataset for training and evaluation of distributional semantic models. In *Proceedings of the 4th Workshop on Linked Data in Linguistics: Resources and Applications*, pages 64–69, Beijing, China.

Roland Schäfer and Felix Bildhauer. 2012. Building large corpora from the web using a new efficient tool chain. In *Proceedings of the Eighth International Conference on Language Resources and Evaluation (LREC '12)*, pages 486–493, Istanbul, Turkey. ELRA.

Hinrich Schütze. 1998. Automatic word sense discrimination. *Computational Linguistics*, 24(1):97–123.

CogALex-V Shared Task: ROOT18

Emmanuele Chersoni
Aix-Marseille University
emmanuelechersoni@gmail.com

Giulia Rambelli
University of Pisa
rambelligiulia@gmail.com

Enrico Santus
The Hong Kong Polytechnic University
esantus@gmail.com

Abstract

In this paper, we describe ROOT 18, a classifier using the scores of several *unsupervised distributional measures* as features to discriminate between semantically related and unrelated words, and then to classify the related pairs according to their semantic relation (i.e. *synonymy, antonymy, hypernymy, part-whole meronymy*). Our classifier participated in the CogALex-V Shared Task, showing a solid performance on the first subtask, but a poor performance on the second subtask. The low scores reported on the second subtask suggest that distributional measures are not sufficient to discriminate between multiple semantic relations at once.

1 Introduction

The system described in this paper has been designed for the CogALex-V Shared Task, focusing on the corpus-based identification of semantic relations. Since Distributional Semantic Models (henceforth DSMs) were proposed as a special topic of interest for the current edition of the CogALex workshop, we decided to base our classifier on a number of distributional measures that have been used by past Natural Language Processing (NLP) research to discriminate between a specific semantic relation and other relation types.

The task is splitted into the following subtasks:

- for each word pair, the participating systems have to decide whether the terms are semantically related or not (TRUE and FALSE are the only possible outcomes);

- for each word pair, the participating systems have to decide which semantic relation holds between the terms of the pair. The five possible semantic relations are synonymy (SYN), antonymy (ANT), hypernymy (HYPER), meronymy (PART_OF) and no semantic relation at all (RANDOM).

Our system managed to achieve good results in discriminating between related and random pairs in the first subtask, but unfortunately it struggled in the second one, also due to the high difficulty of the task itself. In particular, the recall for some of the semantic relations of interest seems to be extremely low, suggesting that our unsupervised distributional measures do not provide sufficient information to characterize them, and that it could be probably useful to integrate such scores with other sources of evidence (e.g. information on lexical patterns of word co-occurrence).

The paper is organized as follows: in section 2, we summarize related works on the task of semantic relation identification; in section 3, we introduce our system, by describing the classifier and the features. Finally, in section 4 we present and discuss our results.

2 The Task: Related Work

Distinguishing between related and unrelated words and, then, discriminating among semantic relations are very important tasks in NLP, and they have a wide range of applications, such as textual entailment, text summarization, sentiment analysis, ontology learning, and so on. For this reason, several systems

Proceedings of the Workshop on Cognitive Aspects of the Lexicon,
pages 98–103, Osaka, Japan, December 11-17 2016.

over the last few years have been proposed to tackle this problem, using both unsupervised and supervised approaches (see the works of Lenci and Benotto (2012) and Shwartz et al. (2016) on hypernymy; Weeds et al. (2014) and Santus et al. (2016a) on hypernymy and co-hyponymy; Mohammad et al. (2013) and Santus et al. (2014) on antonymy). However, many of these works focus on a single semantic relation, e.g. antonymy, and describe methods or measures to set it apart from other relations. There have not been many attempts, at the best of our knowledge, to deal with corpus-based semantic relation identification in a multiclass classification task. Few exceptions include the works by Turney (2008) on similarity, antonymy and analogy, and by Pantel and Pernacchiotti (2006) on Espresso, a weakly supervised, pattern-based algorithm. Both these systems are based on patterns, which are known to be more precise than DSMs, even though they suffer from lower recall (i.e. they in fact require words to co-occur in the same sentence). DSMs, on the other hand, offer higher recall at the cost of lower precision: while they are strong in identifying distributionally similar words (i.e. nearest neighbors), they do not offer any principled way to discriminate between semantic relations (i.e. the nearest neighbors of a word are not only its synonyms, but they also include antonyms, hypernyms, and so on).

The attempts to provide DSMs with the ability of automatically identifying semantic relations include a large number of unsupervised methods (Weeds and Weir, 2003; Lenci and Benotto, 2012; Santus et al., 2014), which are unfortunately far from achieving the perfect accuracy. In order to achieve higher performance, supervised methods have been recently adopted, also thanks to their ease (Weeds et al., 2014; Roller et al., 2014; Kruszewski et al., 2015; Roller and Erk, 2016; Santus et al., 2016a; Nguyen et al., 2016; Shwartz et al., 2016). Many of them rely on distributional word vectors, either concatenated or combined through algebraic functions. Others use as features either patterns or scores from the above-mentioned unsupervised methods. While these systems generally obtain high performance in classification tasks involving a single semantic relation, they have rarely been used on multiclass relation classification. On top of it, some scholars have questioned their ability to really learn semantic relations (Levy et al., 2015), claiming that they rather learn some lexical properties from the word vectors they are trained with. This was also confirmed by an experiment carried out by Santus et al. (2016a), showing that up to 100% synthetic switched pairs (i.e. *banana-animal*; *elephant-fruit*) are misclassified as hypernyms if the system is not provided with some of these negative examples during training.

Recently, count based vectors have been substituted by prediction-based ones, which seem to slightly improve the performance in some tasks, such as similarity estimation (Baroni et al., 2014), even though Levy et al. (2015) demonstrated that these improvements were most likely due to the optimization of hyperparameters that were instead left unoptimized in count-based models (for an overview on word embeddings, see Gladkova et al. (2016)). On top of it, when combined with supervised methods, the low interpretability of their dimensions makes it even harder to understand what the classifiers actually learn (Levy et al., 2015).

Finally, the recent attempt of Shwartz et al. (2016) of combining patterns and distributional information achieved extremely promising results in hypernymy identification.

3 System description

Our system, ROOT18, is a Random Forest classifier (Breiman, 2001) and it is based on the 18 features described in the following subsections. The system in its best setting makes use of the Gini impurity index as the splitting criterion and has 10 as the maximum tree depth. The half of the total number of features were considered for each split.

3.1 Data

Our data come from *ukWaC* (Baroni et al., 2009), a 2 billion tokens corpus of English built by crawling the .uk Internet domain. For the extraction of our features, we generated several distributional spaces, which differ according to the window size and to the statistical association measure that was used to weight raw co-occurrences. Since we obtained the best performances with window size 2 and Positive Pointwise Mutual Information (Church and Hanks, 1990), we report the results only for this setting.

3.2 Features

Frequency It is a basic property of words and it is a very discriminative information. In this type of task, it proved to be competitive in identifying the directionality of pairs of hypernyms (Weeds and Weir, 2003), since we expect hypernyms to have higher frequency than hyponyms. For each pair, we computed three features: the frequency of each word (*Freq1,2*) and their difference (*DiffFreq*).

Co-occurrence We compute the co-occurrence frequency (*Cooc*) between the two terms in each pair. This measure has been claimed to be particularly useful to spot antonyms (Murphy, 2003), since they are expected to occur in the same sentence more often than chance (e.g. *Are you friend or foe?*).

Entropy In information theory, this score is related to the informativeness of a message: the lower its entropy, the higher its informativeness (Shannon, 1948). Moreover, subordinate terms tend to have higher amounts of informativeness than superordinate ones. We computed the entropy of each word in the pair (*Entr1,2*), plus the difference between entropies (*DiffEntr*).

Cosine similarity It is a standard measure in DSMs to compute similarity between words (Turney and Pantel, 2010). This measure is very useful to discriminate between related and unrelated terms.

$$sim(\vec{u}, \vec{v}) = \frac{\vec{u} \cdot \vec{v}}{\|\vec{u}\| \cdot \|\vec{v}\|}$$

LinSimilarity LinSimilarity (Lin, 1998) is a different similarity measure, computed as the ratio of shared context between u and v to the contexts of each word:

$$Lin(\vec{u}, \vec{v}) = \frac{\sum_{c \in \vec{u} \cap \vec{v}} [\vec{u}[c] + \vec{v}[c]]}{\sum_{c \in \vec{u}} \vec{u}[c] + \sum_{c \in \vec{v}} \vec{v}[c]}$$

Directional similarity measures We extracted several directional similarity measures that were proposed to detect hypernyms, such as *WeedsPrec*, *cosWeeds*, *ClarkeDe* and *invCL* (for a review, see Lenci and Benotto (2012)). They are all based on the *Distributional Inclusion Hypotesis*, according to which if a word u is semantically narrower to v, then a significant number of the salient features of u will be included also in v.

APSyn This measure and the following *APAnt* do not rely on the full distribution of words, but on the top N most related contexts of the words according to some statistical association measure. APSyn (Santus et al., 2016b) computes a weighted intersection of the top N context of the target words:

$$APSyn(w_1, w_2) = \sum_{f \in N(F_1) \cap N(F_2)} \frac{1}{(rank_1(f) + rank_2(f))/2}$$

That is, for every feature f included in the intersection between the top N features of w_1 and w_2 ($N(F_1)$, $N(F_2)$ respectively), the measure adds 1 divided by the average rank of the feature in the rankings of the top N features of w_1 and w_2.

APAnt *APAnt* (Santus et al., 2014) is defined as the inverse of APSyn. This unsupervised measure tries to discriminate between synonyms and antonyms by relying on the hypothesis that words with similar distribution (i.e. high vector cosine) that do not share their most relevant contexts (i.e. what APSyn computes) are likely to be antonyms. For each pair, we computed APSyn and APAnt for the top 1000 and for the top 100 contexts.

Same POS We realized that many of the random pairs in the data included words with different parts of speech. Therefore, we decided to add a boolean value to our set of features: 1 if the most frequent POS of the words in the pair were the same, 0 otherwise.

3.3 Evaluation dataset

The task organizers provided a training and a test set extracted from EVALution 1.0, a resource that was specifically designed for evaluating systems on the identification of semantic relations (Santus et al., 2015). EVALution 1.0 was derived from WordNet (Fellbaum, 1998) and ConceptNet (Liu and Singh, 2004) and it consists of almost 7500 word pairs, instantiating several semantic relations.

The training and the test set included, respectively, 3054 and 4260 word pairs and they are lexical-split, that is, the two sets do not share any pair. Since words were not tagged, we performed POS-tagging with the TreeTagger (Schmid, 1995).

4   Results

Model	P (task1)	R (task1)	F (task1)	P (task2)	R (task2)	F (task2)
Random Baseline	0.283	0.503	0.362	0.073	0.201	0.106
Cosine Baseline	0.589	0.573	0.581	0.170	0.165	0.167
ROOT18(100)	0.818	0.657	0.729	0.304	0.213	0.249
ROOT18(500)	0.818	0.650	0.724	0.313	**0.227**	**0.262**
ROOT18(1000)	**0.823**	**0.657**	**0.731**	**0.343**	0.218	0.261

Table 1: Precision, Recall and F-measure scores for subtask 1 and 2. The numbers between parentheses in the ROOT18 rows refer to the number of estimators used by the classifier.

As it can be seen from table 1, ROOT18 has a solid performance on the subtask 1, and it is quite accurate in separating related terms from unrelated ones. Generally speaking, we noticed that the classifier performs better when Gini impurity index is used as a splitting criterion instead of entropy. The model with 1000 estimators is our best performing one, with Precision = 0.823, Recall = 0.657 and F-score = 0.731. Concerning the contribution of the features, APSyn1000 and vector cosine have the highest relative importance, with respective contributions of 0.29 and 0.12 to the prediction function. This is not at all surprising, since APSyn and cosine already proved to be strong predictors of semantic similarity.

Relation	Precision	Recall	F-measure
SYN	0.309	0.179	0.226
ANT	0.298	0.206	0.243
HYPER	0.397	0.343	0.368
PART-OF	0.200	0.116	0.147

Table 2: Precision, recall and F-measure for each relation in subtask 2 (ROOT-18 with 500 estimators).

Relation	SYN	ANT	HYPER	PART-OF	RANDOM
SYN	42	29	58	24	82
ANT	29	74	38	23	196
HYPER	32	46	131	30	143
PART-OF	15	43	59	26	81
RANDOM	18	56	44	27	2914

Table 3: Confusion matrix for subtask 2 (ROOT-18 with 500 estimators).

Results are much less convincing for subtask 2. In particular, the recall values are extremely low, especially for some of the semantic relations: part_of, for example, is often below 0.15. For such relation we have no dedicated features in our system, so the difficulty in identifying meronyms are not a surprise. On the other hand, ROOT18 showed the benefits of the inclusion of several measures targeting hypernymy, since the latter is the most accurately recognized relation (precision often > 0.4), recording also the higher recall (always > 0.3, even in the worst performing models).

The performance did not show any particular improvement by increasing the number of the decision trees, so that our best overall results are obtained by the model with 500 estimators (precision = 0.343, recall = 0.218 and F-score = 0.261). As for the contributions of the single features, APSyn1000 (0.19) and cosine (0.09) are still the top ones, followed by cosWeeds (0.07) and APAnt1000 (0.06).

Table 4 describes the confusion matrix, which shows that randoms are properly working as distractors for the model, leading to a large number of misclassification. Synonyms are often confused with hypernyms and this might be due to the fact that the difference between the two is subtle. These results suggest that measures based on the Distributional Inclusion Hypothesis are not always efficient in discriminating between synonyms and hypernyms.

Antonyms are confused with hypernyms and *vice versa*, which might be due to the fact that neither share their most relevant features, obtaining therefore similar APAnt scores (Santus et al., 2015b). Meronyms, finally, are mostly confused with hypernyms, which is almost surely due to the generality spread that characterize both relations and that is captured by both frequency and entropy in our system.

4.1 Conclusions

Our results clearly highlight the difficulty of DSMs in discriminating between several semantic relations at once. Such models, in fact, rely on a vague definition of semantic similarity (i.e. distributional similarity) which does not offer any principled way to distinguish among different types of semantic relations.

Nonetheless, it is still feasible for traditional DSMs to achieve good performances on the recognition of taxonomical relations (Santus et al., 2016a), for which metrics can be defined on the basis of feature inclusion, of context informativeness etc. For other relations, such as antonymy and meronymy, it is not easy to define measures based on distributional similarity (for the latter relation, it is difficult even to find an univocal definition: see Morlane-Hondère (2015)): APAnt works relatively well in discriminating antonyms from synonyms, but – as noticed by Santus et al. (2015b) – this measure has also a bias towards hypernyms, which explains why these are often confused. A possible solution, in our view, would be the integration of DSMs with pattern-based information, in a way that is already being shown by some of the current state-of-the-art systems (see, for example, Shwartz et al. (2016)). Such integration has the advantage of combining the precision of the patterns with the high recall of DSMs.

Finally, we may assume that also the configuration of the original dataset could contribute to our results, since some pairs in the dataset have ambiguous words and the target relations hold for only one of the their meanings. Disambiguating the pairs, at least by Part-Of-Speech, would certainly help in improving the results. A simple method might consist in computing the vector cosine for the pairs with the target words declined in all possible POS (i.e. VV, NN, JJ) and then maintain in the dataset only the pair with the higher value.

5   Acknowledgements

This work has been carried out thanks to the support of the A*MIDEX grant (n ANR-11-IDEX-0001-02) funded by the French Government "Investissements d'Avenir" program.

References

Marco Baroni, Silvia Bernardini, Adriano Ferraresi, and Eros Zanchetta. 2009. The WaCky wide web: a collection of very large linguistically processed web-crawled corpora. *Language resources and evaluation*, 43(3):209-226.

Baroni, Marco, Georgiana Dinu and German Kruszewski. 2014. Don't count, predict! A systematic comparison of context-counting vs. context-predicting semantic vectors. *Proceedings of ACL*, Vol (1).

Leo Breiman. 2001. Random forests. *Machine Learning*, 45(1):5-32.

Kenneth Ward Church and Patrick Hanks 1990. Word association norms, mutual information, and lexicography. *Computational linguistics*, 16(1):22-29.

Christiane Fellbaum. 1998. WordNet. Wiley Online Library.

Anna Gladkova, Aleksandr Drozd and Satoshi Matsuoka 2016. Analogy-based detection of morphological and semantic relations with word embeddings: what works and what doesn't *Proceedings of SRW@HLT-NAACL*

German Kruszewski, Denis Paperno and Marco Baroni. 2015. Deriving Boolean structures from distributional vectors. *TACL*, Vol.3: 375-388

Alessandro Lenci and Giulia Benotto. 2012. Identifying hypernyms in distributional semantic spaces. *Proceedings of *SEM*.

Omer Levy, Steffen Remus, Chris Biemann and Ido Dagan Do Supervised Distributional Methods Really Learn Lexical Inference Relations? *Proceedings of NAACL HLT*

Omer Levy, Yoav Goldberg and Ido Dagan. 2015. Improving distributional similarity with lessons learned from word embeddings. *TACL, Vol. 3: 211-225*

Dekang Lin. 1998. An information-theoretic definition of similarity. *ICML*, 98:296-304.

Hugo Liu and Push Singh 2004. ConceptNet: a practical commonsense reasoning toolkit. *BT technology journal*, 22(4):211-226.

Saif M. Mohammad, Bonnie J. Dorr, Graeme Hirst and Peter D. Turney. 2013. Computing Lexical Contrast. *Computational Linguistics*, Vol. 39(3): 555–590. MIT Press.

François Morlane-Hondère. 2015. What can distributional semantic models tell us about part-of relations? *Proceedings of NetWordS*: 46-50.

Lynne G Murphy. 2003. Semantic relations and the lexicon: Antonymy, synonymy and other paradigms. Cambridge University Press.

Kim Anh Nguyen, Sabine Schulte im Walde, and Ngoc Thang Vu. 2016. Integrating Distributional Lexical Contrast into Word Embeddings for Antonym-Synonym Distinction. *Proceedings of ACL*.

Patrick Pantel and Marco Pennacchiotti Espresso: Leveraging Generic Patterns for Automatically Harvesting Semantic Relations *Proceedings of COLING ACL*: 113–120

Stephen Roller, Katrin Erk and Gemma Boleda. 2014. Inclusive yet Selective: Supervised Distributional Hypernymy Detection. *Proceedings of COLING*: 1025-1036.

Stephen Roller and Katrin Erk. 2016. Relations such as Hypernymy: Identifying and Exploiting Hearst Patterns in Distributional Vectors for Lexical Entailment. *Proceedings of EMNLP*.

Enrico Santus, Qin Lu, Alessandro Lenci and Chu-Ren Huang. 2014. Taking antonymy mask off in vector space. *Proceedings of PACLIC*.

Enrico Santus, Frances Yung, Alessandro Lenci and Chu-Ren Huang. 2015. EVALution 1.0: an Evolving Semantic Dataset for Training and Evaluation of Distributional Semantic Models. *Proceedings of the ACL Workshop on Linked Data in Linguistics*: 64-69.

Enrico Santus, Alessandro Lenci, Qin Lu and Chu-Ren Huang. 2015. *Italian Journal on Computational Linguistics* aAccademia University Press

Enrico Santus, Alessandro Lenci, Tin-Shing Chiu, Qin Lu, and Chu-Ren Huang. 2016. Nine Features in a Random Forest to Learn Taxonomical Semantic Relations. *Proceedings of LREC*.

Enrico Santus, Tin-Shing Chiu, Qin Lu, Alessandro Lenci and Chu-Ren Huang. 2016. What a Nerd! Beating Students and Vector Cosine in the ESL and TOEFL Datasets. *Proceedings of LREC*.

Helmut Schmid. 1995. Treetagger: a language independent part-of-speech tagger. *Institut für Maschinelle Sprachverarbeitung, Universität Stuttgart*.

Claude Shannon. 1948. A Mathematical Theory of Communication. *Bell System Technical Journal*, 27: 379-423 and 623-656.

Vered Shwartz, Yoav Goldberg, and Ido Dagan. 2016. Improving hypernymy detection with an integrated path-based and distributional method. *Proceedings of ACL*.

Peter Turney. 2008 A uniform approach to analogies, synonyms, antonyms, and associations *Proceedings of the 22nd International Conference on Computational Linguistics (Coling 2008)*: 905-912.

Peter Turney and Patrick Pantel. 2010. From frequency to meaning: Vector Space Models for semantics. *Journal of Artificial Intelligence Research*, 37: 141-188.

Julie Weeds and David Weir. 2003. A general framework for distributional similarity. *Proceedings of EMNLP*: 81-88.

Julie Weeds, Daoud Clarke, Jeremy Reffin, David J Weir and Bill Keller. 2014. Learning to Distinguish Hypernyms and Co-Hyponyms. *Proceedings of COLING*: 2249-2259.

CogALex-V Shared Task: CGSRC - Classifying Semantic Relations using Convolutional Neural Networks

Chinnappa Guggilla

chinna.guggilla@gmail.com

Abstract

In this paper, we describe a system (CGSRC) for classifying four semantic relations: synonym, hypernym, antonym and meronym using convolutional neural networks (CNN). We have participated in CogALex-V semantic shared task of corpus-based identification of semantic relations. Proposed approach using CNN-based deep neural networks leveraging pre-compiled word2vec distributional neural embeddings achieved 43.15% weighted-F1 accuracy on subtask-1 (checking existence of a relation between two terms) and 25.24% weighted-F1 accuracy on subtask-2 (classifying relation types).

1 Introduction

Discovering semantic relations and the corresponding relation types between word pairs is an important task in Natural Language Processing (NLP) with a wide range of applications, such as automatic Machine Translation, Question Answering Systems, Ontology Learning, Paraphrase Generation, etc. Corpus-driven automated methods for semantic relation identification have been promising an efficient and scalable solution in the recent past.

To discover semantic relations such as synonym, hypernym and antonym, most of the existing methods (Hearst, 1992; Snow et al., 2004) employed lexical patterns or distributional hypothesis, and suffer from sparsity and low accuracy problems. Moreover, many of these methodologies model individual semantic relations using external knowledge sources such as thesauri, WordNet, etc. Although semantic networks like WordNet[1] define semantic relations such as synonym, hypernym, antonym and part-of between word types, however they are limited in scope and domain.

Recently, few approaches based on distributional word embeddings (Shwartz et al., 2016; Baroni et al., 2012; Ono et al., 2015; Leeuwenberg et al., 2016) reported significant improvements in identifying various lexical semantic relations such as hypernymy, antonymy, synonymy etc. Distributional representations of words learned from a large corpus capture linguistic regularities and collapse similar words into groups (Mikolov et al., 2013b).

Inspired by these approaches, we propose a lexical semantic relation detection system using CNN-based deep neural networks by leveraging word2vec[2] distributional word embeddings as part of 5th edition of CogALex shared task . The shared task proposed two subtasks namely, relation detection and relation type identification. Subtask-1 aims at detecting a relation between two given terms and subtask-2 aims at identifying semantic relations such as synonym, hypernym, antonym, and part-of between two terms if a relation exists. This task is particularly challenging as local context for term pairs is not available in the training corpus.

The rest of the paper is organized as follows: in section 2, we describe related work and in section 3, we introduce deep learning-based supervised classification technique for identifying semantic relations. We describe datasets and the experimental results in section 4. In section 5, we analyze various types of errors in relation classification and conclude the paper.

[1]http://wordnetweb.princeton.edu/perl/webwn/
[2]https://code.google.com/archive/p/word2vec/

Proceedings of the Workshop on Cognitive Aspects of the Lexicon,
pages 104–109, Osaka, Japan, December 11-17 2016.

2 Related Work

For discovering semantic relations between term pairs, several researchers have employed various methods such as pattern-based, distributional, unsupervised and supervised approaches. Several methods that have been developed for synonym extraction employed distributional hypothesis (Saveski and Trajkovski, 2010; Pak et al., 2015) approach. Van der Plas and Tiedemann (2006) combined distributional word similarity, and word-alignment context for synonym extraction in Dutch.

More recently, Leeuwenberg et al. (2016) proposed minimally supervised synonym extraction approach based on neural word embeddings that are compiled using continuous bag-of-words model (CBoW) and the skip-gram model (SG). They analyzed word categories that are similar in the vector space using various combinations of similarity measures with part of speech (POS) information for extracting synonyms from the corpus.

Shwartz et al. (2016) proposed an integrated approach based on deep neural networks by combining path-based and distributional methods for hypernymy detection. Initially, authors experimented with path-based model using dependency paths as embedding features and reported good improvement over prior path-based methods and comparable performance with the superior distributional methods. Later, they extended deep neural networks with distributed signals and showed significant improvement over state-of-the-art approaches. Our proposed approach is similar to this approach in employing deep neural networks and uses word2vec embeddings instead of dependency-based embeddings and also models other semantic relations synonymy, meronymy and antonymy along with hypernymy relation.

Most of the existing approaches (Yih et al., 2012; Zhang et al., 2014) for antonym extraction leveraged thesauri information for distinguishing antonyms from synonyms. Ono et al. (2015) proposed a word embedding-based approach using supervised synonym and antonym information from thesauri, and distributional information from large-scale unlabeled text data and reported improved results.

Shoemaker and Ganapathi (2005) system for automatically discovering meronyms (part-whole) from text corpora using supervised SVM classifier based on empirical distribution over dependency relations as features. vor der Brück and Helbig (2010) proposed semantic-oriented approach for meronymy relation extraction based on semantic networks using automated theorem prover.

3 Methodology

Deep neural networks, with or without word embeddings, have recently shown significant improvements over traditional machine learning–based approaches when applied to various sentence- and relation-level classification tasks.

Kim (2014) have shown that CNNs outperform traditional machine learning-based approaches on several tasks, such as sentiment classification, question type classification, etc. using simple static word embeddings and tuning of hyper-parameters. Zhou et al. (2016) proposed attention-based bi-directional LSTM networks for relation classification task. More recently, (Shwartz et al., 2016) proposed LSTM-based integrated approach by combining path-based and distributional methods for hypernymy detection and shown significant accuracy improvements.

3.1 CNN-based Relation Classification

Following Kim (2014), we present a variant of the CNN architecture with four layer types: an input layer, a convolution layer, a max pooling layer, and a fully connected softmax layer for term pair relation classification as shown in figure 1. Each term pair (sentence) in the input layer is represented as a sentence(relation) comprised of distributional word embeddings. Let $v_i \in \mathbb{R}^k$ be the k-dimensional word vector corresponding to the ith word in the term pair. Then a term pair S of length ℓ is represented as the concatenation of its word vectors:

$$S = v_1 \oplus v_2 \oplus \cdots \oplus v_\ell. \tag{1}$$

In the convolution layer, for a given word sequence within a term pair, a convolutional word filter P is defined. Then, the filter P is applied to each word in the sentence to produce a new set of features. We use

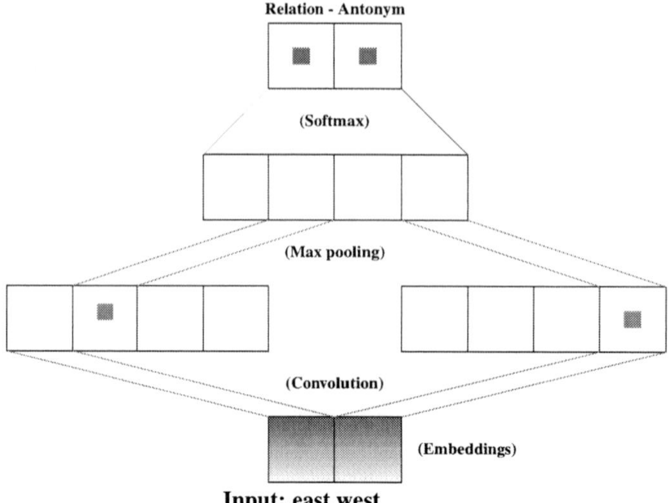

Figure 1: Illustration of an example term pair relation classification using convolutional neural networks

a non-linear activation function such as rectified linear unit (ReLU) for the convolution process and max-over-time pooling (Collobert et al., 2011; Kim, 2014) at pooling layer to deal with the variable sentence size. After a series of convolutions with different filters with different heights, the most important features are generated. Then, this feature representation, Z, is passed to a fully connected penultimate layer and outputs a distribution over different relation labels:

$$y = \mathrm{softmax}(W \cdot Z + b), \tag{2}$$

where y denotes a distribution over different relation labels, W is the weight vector learned from the input word embeddings from the training corpus, and b is the bias term.

3.2 Experimental Setup

We model the relation classification as a sentence classification task. We use the CogALex-V 2016 shared task dataset in our experiments which is described in the next section. This dataset consisting of term pairs is tokenized using white space tokenizer. We performed both binary and multi-class classification on the given data set containing two binary and five multi-class relations from subtask-1 and subtask-2 respectively. We used Kim's (2014) Theano implementation of CNN[3] for training the CNN model. We use word embeddings from word2vec which are learned using the skipgram model of Mikolov et. al (2013a,b) by predicting linear context words surrounding the target words. These word vectors are trained on about 100 billion words from Google News corpus. As word embeddings alone have shown good performance in various classification tasks, we also use them in isolation, with varying dimensions, in our experiment. We performed 10-fold cross-validation (CV) on the entire training set for both the subtasks in random and word2vec embedding settings. We initialized random embeddings in the range of $[-0.25, 0.25]$. We did not use any external corpus for training our model but used pre-compiled word2vec embeddings trained on about 100 billion words from Google News corpus. We used a stochastic gradient descent-based optimization method for minimizing the cross entropy loss during the training with the Rectified Linear Unit (ReLU) non-linear activation function.

Tuning Hyper Parameters. The hyper-parameters we varied are the drop-out, batch size, embedding dimension and hidden node sizes for training our models in cross-validation setting for finding

---

[3]`https://github.com/yoonkim/CNN_sentence`

	TRUE	FALSE	Total
Train	826	2228	3054
Test	1201	3059	4260
Total	2027	5287	7314

Table 1: Training and test data sets: Subtask-1 of CogALex-V shared task

	ant	hyper	part_of	random	syn	Total
Train	241	255	163	2228	167	3054
Test	360	382	224	3059	235	4260
Total	601	637	387	5287	402	7314

Table 2: Training and test data sets: Subtask-2 of CogALex-V shared task

CNN	Relation	Precision	Recall	F1
random emb.	true	41.23	37.26	39.00
	false	77.45	80.26	78.80
weighted		41.23	37.26	**39.00**
word2vec emb.	true	58.15	52.69	54.99
	false	82.94	85.96	84.37
weighted		58.15	52.69	**54.99**

Table 3: Avg. 10-fold cross-validation results on subtask-2 with rand. & word2vec embeds.

	Relation	Precision	Recall	F1
CNN	true	35.21	55.70	43.15
	flase	77.46	59.76	67.47
weighted		35.21	55.70	**43.15**
Rand.baseline	true	28.33	50.29	36.24
	flase	71.95	50.05	59.03
weighted		8.33	50.29	**36.24**

Table 4: Subtask-1 test set results word2vec embedding setting Vs. Random baseline.

the optimal model using training set. We performed grid search over these value ranges for the mentioned hyper parameters: drop out{0.1,0.2,0.3,0.4,0.5,0.6}, batch size{12,24,32,48,60}, embedding dimension{50,100,150,200,250,300} and hidden node sizes{100,200,300,400,500}. Optimal results are obtained using drop out-0.5, batch size-32,embedding size-300 and hidden node size-300 for subtask-1 and dropout-0.5, batchSize-24, embedding size-300 and hidden node size-400 for subtask-2 in cross validation setting as shown in tables 3 and 5. We used fixed context-window sizes set at [1,2] as max length of the term pair in given corpus is 2 for both the tasks. We also used fixed number of 25 iterations with default learning rate (0.95) for training our models.

4   Datasets and Evaluation Results

In this section, we describe CogALex-V 2016 shared task data sets and the experimental results.

Datasets.   We used a dataset extracted from EVALution 1.0 (Santus et al., 2015), which was developed from WordNet and ConceptNet, and which was further filtered by native speakers in a CrowdFlower task. This data set is split into training and test sets. The distribution of training and test splits are shown in tables 1 and 2. The samples in the subtask-1 and subtask-2 test set are unbalanced and majority of relation classes are "FALSE" and "random" in the given train and test sets.

Evaluation and Results.   We evaluated results on test sets using trained models with the optimal parameters for both the tasks and compared results against random baseline results as shown in tables 4 and 6. CogALex-V shared task results are evaluated using weighted-F1 measure on both the tasks. Weighted F-1 values for all the relations except for "random" relation are computed and reported on subtask-2. On subtask-1, i.e. for relation detection, in the cross-validation setting, it is shown that CNN with word2vec embedding setting performed (16%F1) better than the random embeddings. On test set, CNN with word2vec embeddings outperformed (13%) the random baseline results. On subtask-2, i.e for relation type detection, in the cross-validation setting, it is shown that CNN with word2vec embedding setting performed (14.63%F1) better than the random embeddings learned from the training set. On the test set, CNN with word2vec embeddings outperformed (14.64%) the random baseline results. These results suggest that word2vec-based distributional embeddings significantly contributed in improving the relation classification performance.

CNN	Rel.type	Precision	Recall	F1
random emb.	syn	22.61	16.46	18.01
	ant	17.84	13.09	14.67
	hyper	14.05	32.80	35.63
	part_of	40.87	27.98	32.08
weighted		27.82	20.01	**22.68**
	random	69.65	77.15	73.15
word2vec emb.	syn	21.36	12.30	15.03
	ant	39.10	33.08	35.30
	hyper	51.89	48.89	49.61
	part_of	49.24	39.11	42.63
weighted		42.09	34.93	**37.31**
	random	81.89	87.84	84.66

Table 5: Avg. 10-fold cross-validation results on subtask-2 with rand. & word2vec embeds.

	Rel.type	Precision	Recall	F1
	syn	06.96	13.62	09.21
CNN	ant	20.21	31.39	24.59
	hyper	30.71	40.84	35.06
	part_of	25.20	27.68	26.38
weighted		21.89	30.22	**25.24**
	random	77.40	62.93	69.42
	syn	05.89	20.85	09.18
Rand.baseline	ant	07.77	19.17	11.06
	hyper	08.83	20.42	12.33
	part_of	05.31	20.09	08.40
weighted		07.28	20.07	**10.60**
	random	71.57	18.93	29.94

Table 6: subtask-2 results in word2vec embedding setting vs Random baseline.

		Predicted	
		true	**false**
Actual	**true**	669	532
	false	1231	1828

Table 7: Confusion matrix of subtask-1 test set results

		Predicted				
		random	**syn**	**ant**	**hyper**	**part-of**
	random	1925	336	363	280	155
	syn	118	32	47	30	8
Actual	**ant**	190	39	113	12	6
	hyper	145	35	31	156	15
	part_of	109	18	5	30	62

Table 8: Confusion matrix of subtask-2 test set results

5 Discussion and Conclusion

We can assess the degree of confusion between various relation classes from the confusion matrix of CNN classification model as shown in tables 7 and 8. On subtask-1, 44% of the term pairs are false-negatives and 40% of the term pairs are reported as false-positives. On subtask-2, the "synonym" relation is mostly confused with the "antonym" and "hypernym" and less confused with the "part_of" relation. We also observe a significant amount of confusion between "part_of" and the "hypernym" relations. The relations– "antonym" and "hypernym" are less confused with the "meronym" relation but both are confused with the "synonym" relation. We also observe that majority of the identified relation classes largely confused with the majority "random" class.

In our proposed approach, our system showed that distributional embeddings learned from the large corpus improve relation classification. There are a number of potential directions to improve relation classification accuracy. One possible future work might be to compile the common vocabulary among most confusing relation classes and for the vocabulary compile embeddings from large, unlabeled relation corpora using neural networks, and encode both syntactic and semantic properties of words in the network representation.

Learning embeddings from sense-annotated larger relation corpus might improve the relation detection and relation-type classification accuracy further. Incorporation of dependency embeddings might also improve the relation classification as syntactic contexts can help in distinguishing different terms for identifying appropriate relation type on subtask-2. As antonyms and synonyms fall on the same side in the vector space due to the frequent co-occurrences in the similar contexts, embeddings learned from extra contexts can also improve the relation-type classification performance.

References

Marco Baroni, Raffaella Bernardi, Ngoc-Quynh Do, and Chung-chieh Shan. 2012. Entailment above the word level in distributional semantics. In *Proceedings of the 13th Conference of the European Chapter of the Association for Computational Linguistics*, pages 23–32. Association for Computational Linguistics.

Ronan Collobert, Jason Weston, Léon Bottou, Michael Karlen, Koray Kavukcuoglu, and Pavel Kuksa. 2011. Natural language processing (almost) from scratch. *The Journal of Machine Learning Research*, 12:2493–2537.

Marti A Hearst. 1992. Automatic acquisition of hyponyms from large text corpora. In *Proceedings of the 14th conference on Computational linguistics-Volume 2*, pages 539–545. Association for Computational Linguistics.

Yoon Kim. 2014. Convolutional neural networks for sentence classification. In *Proceedings of the 2014 Conference on Empirical Methods in Natural Language Processing*, pages 1746–1751.

Artuur Leeuwenberg, Mihaela Vela, Jon Dehdari, and Josef van Genabith. 2016. A minimally supervised approach for synonym extraction with word embeddings. *The Prague Bulletin of Mathematical Linguistics*, 105(1):111–142.

Tomas Mikolov, Ilya Sutskever, Kai Chen, Greg S Corrado, and Jeff Dean. 2013a. Distributed representations of words and phrases and their compositionality. In *Advances in Neural Information Processing Systems 26*, pages 3111–3119.

Tomas Mikolov, Wen-tau Yih, and Geoffrey Zweig. 2013b. Linguistic regularities in continuous space word representations. In *Proceedings of the 2013 Conference of the North American Chapter of the Association for Computational Linguistics: Human Language Technologies*, pages 746–751.

Masataka Ono, Makoto Miwa, and Yutaka Sasaki. 2015. Word embedding-based antonym detection using thesauri and distributional information. In *Proc. of NAACL*.

Alexander Alexandrovich Pak, Sergazy Sakenovich Narynov, Arman Serikuly Zharmagambetov, Sholpan Nazarovna Sagyndykova, Zhanat Elubaevna Kenzhebayeva, and Irbulat Turemuratovich. 2015. The method of synonyms extraction from unannotated corpus. In *Digital Information, Networking, and Wireless Communications (DINWC), 2015 Third International Conference on*, pages 1–5. IEEE.

Enrico Santus, Frances Yung, Alessandro Lenci, and Chu-Ren Huang. 2015. Evalution 1.0: an evolving semantic dataset for training and evaluation of distributional semantic models. In *Proceedings of the 4th Workshop on Linked Data in Linguistics: Resources and Applications, Association for Computational Linguistics, Beijing, China*, pages 64–69.

Martin Saveski and Igor Trajkovski. 2010. Automatic construction of wordnets by using machine translation and language modeling. In *13th Multiconference Information Society, Ljubljana, Slovenia*.

Austin Shoemaker and Varun Ganapathi. 2005. Learning to automatically discover meronyms.

Vered Shwartz, Yoav Goldberg, and Ido Dagan. 2016. Improving hypernymy detection with an integrated path-based and distributional method. In *Proceedings of the 54th Annual Meeting of the Association for Computational Linguistics, ACL 2016, August 7-12, 2016, Berlin, Germany, Volume 1: Long Papers*.

Rion Snow, Daniel Jurafsky, and Andrew Y Ng. 2004. Learning syntactic patterns for automatic hypernym discovery. *Advances in Neural Information Processing Systems 17*.

Lonneke Van der Plas and Jörg Tiedemann. 2006. Finding synonyms using automatic word alignment and measures of distributional similarity. In *Proceedings of the COLING/ACL on Main conference poster sessions*, pages 866–873. Association for Computational Linguistics.

Tim vor der Brück and Hermann Helbig. 2010. Meronymy extraction using an automated theorem prover. *JLCL*, 25(1):57–81.

Wen-tau Yih, Geoffrey Zweig, and John C Platt. 2012. Polarity inducing latent semantic analysis. In *Proceedings of the 2012 Joint Conference on Empirical Methods in Natural Language Processing and Computational Natural Language Learning*, pages 1212–1222. Association for Computational Linguistics.

Jingwei Zhang, Jeremy Salwen, Michael R Glass, and Alfio Massimiliano Gliozzo. 2014. Word semantic representations using bayesian probabilistic tensor factorization. In *EMNLP*, pages 1522–1531.

Peng Zhou, Wei Shi, Jun Tian, Zhenyu Qi, Bingchen Li, Hongwei Hao, and Bo Xu. 2016. Attention-based bidirectional long short-term memory networks for relation classification. In *The 54th Annual Meeting of the Association for Computational Linguistics*, page 207.

CogALex-V Shared Task: LOPE

Kanan Luce
University of California,
Berkeley
`kanan.luce@berkeley.edu`

Jiaxing Yu
Nanjing University

`jiaxinguy@gmail.com`

Shu-Kai Hsieh
National Taiwan University

`shukaihsieh@ntu.edu.tw`

Abstract

This paper attempts the answer two questions posed by the CogALex shared task: How to determine if two words are semantically related and, if they are related, which semantic relation holds between them. We present a simple, effective approach to the first problem, using word vectors to calculate similarity, and a naive approach to the second problem, by assigning word pairs semantic relations based on their parts of speech. The results of the second task are significantly improved in our post-hoc experiment, where we attempt to apply linguistic regularities in word representations (Mikolov 2013b) to these particular semantic relations.

1 Introduction

Automatic discovery of semantically-related words is one of the most important NLP tasks, and has great impact on the theoretical psycholinguistic modeling of the mental lexicon. In this shared task, we employ the *word embeddings model* (Mikolov 2013a) to reflect paradigmatic relationships between words. Previous work has shown that word representations extracted from simple recurrent neural networks could hierarchically categorize words based on their collocational distribution (Elman 1990). Word representations also hold other regularities. More recently, Mikolov et al. (2013b) showed that word vectors could be added or subtracted to isolate certain semantic and syntactic features. The well-known example is to take the representations for *king*, subtract *man*, and add *woman*. This produces a vector very near by *queen*. This method was tweaked by Levy and Goldberg (2014) by representing the same idea as three pairwise similarities, and is the basis for the post hoc revisions to our system.

The particular semantic relations we are concerned with in this paper are synonymy, antonymy, hypernymy, and meronymy. The shared task consists of two subtasks. The first is to, given a pair of words, identify if they are semantically related. The second task is to determine, if the pair is related, what relation there is between them. We will present first our official system for each subtask, followed by our post-hoc changes.

2 Subtask 1

Subtask 1 was to see if two words were semantically related. For our system, we returned true if word 2 was in the top *n* similar word vectors for word 1, or vice versa. We used the pretrained Google News vectors (Mikolov 2013a), which are 300 dimensions, and contain a vocabulary of 3 million words, and used the Gensim Word2Vec library (Rehurek and Sojka 2010) to manipulate the data.

We found that the best results were achieved when we considered the top 600 similar words. This number had the best coverage without suffering from too many false positives. We also found it helpful to limit the vocabulary from 3 million to only the top 50,000 most frequently occurring tokens, which eliminated unlikely candidate word-forms.

Proceedings of the Workshop on Cognitive Aspects of the Lexicon,
pages 110–113, Osaka, Japan, December 11-17 2016.

Initially, we found the 600 most similar words by building a dictionary of each word in the training data and its corresponding related words. Because we used the same dictionary made from the training data when running the finalized version on test data, our official submission only looked up words that occurred in the training data. In our post-hoc experiment for subtask 1, we use all the words from the test data as well. The results of both systems are below.

LOPE	P = 0.596	R = 0.886	F1 = 0.713
LOPE-PH	P = 0.623	R = 0.884	F1 = 0.731

Table 1: Compares F1 scores of the original (LOPE) and post-hoc (LOPE-PH) systems on Subtask 1

While the performance of the post-hoc system was slightly better, it did not make substantial gains on the original system. The recall for the two systems was almost the same despite the original system not containing the test data, because as long as one of the two words in a pair was in the dictionary, the system could still find related words.

3   Subtask 2

Subtask 2 asks us to take the related pairs from subtask 1 and determine what their relation is: either synonyms, antonyms, hypernyms, or meronyms. Our original system used a crude method to categorize the pairs based on their parts of speech. In the training data, nouns, verbs, and adjectives occurred at different frequencies for each relation, and we used that information to sort them into their mostly likely categories. Noun-noun pairs were sorted as hypernyms, adjective-adjective pairs were sorted as antonyms, and verb-verb pairs were split between antonyms and synonyms based on where the word pair occurred in the list of 600 similar words. If the word occurred in the first 100 most similar it was sorted as a synonym, otherwise it was sorted as an antonym. The part of speech information of each pair was determined by finding the most frequent shared part of speech between the two words as they appeared in the Brown corpus. While this approach was better than a random baseline, it is not helpful in that it does not provide us with any useful information and the results were lackluster.

We significantly improved our results in the post hoc system by completely changing approach and using a method inspired by Mikolov et al.'s method (2013b) of finding linguistic regularities in word representations. We were curious if this method could be applied to this particular problem of finding differences between synonyms, antonyms, hypernyms, and meronyms.

We initially implemented a method inspired by Levy and Goldberg (2014). We used three word representations, one related pair from the training data and one word from the input pair, in order to predict the other word from the input pair as one of the most similar vectors. The idea being that the cosine similarity of the target fourth word will be different in the case where the semantic relation of the input pair matches that of the training pair.

This assumption was incorrect, and we had to revise our approach. We instead started to find the cosine similarity between the two sets of words (the input set, and a related set from the training data). The cosine similarity was often higher if the two sets shared a relation. While this was inconsistent when comparing only two sets, we found that we could compare (find the cosine similarity of) an input set to each antonym, synonym, hypernym and meronym set in the training data, average the results for each semantic relation, and then assign the input pair to the class that had the highest average.

LOPE	P	R	F1
SYN	0.304	0.191	0.235
ANT	0.417	0.217	0.285
HYPER	0.328	0.406	0.363
PART_OF	0.000	0.000	0.000
Subtask 2	0.289	0.231	0.247

LOPE-PH	P	R	F1
SYN	0.089	0.438	0.148
ANT	0.447	0.405	0.425
HYPER	0.199	0.514	0.287
PART_OF	0.411	0.365	0.387
Subtask 2	0.373	0.414	0.374

Table 2: Compares F1 scores of the original (LOPE) and the post-hoc (LOPE-PH) system on Subtask 2

So if the average of the input pair compared to all of the antonym pairs was higher than it was for the same comparison to all of the synonym, hypernym, and meronym sets, then the input pair was assigned the relation antonym. Using this method, we were able to significantly increase our F1 score for the task and our coverage of which relations we were able to get right (we completely ignored meronyms in the first system). However, we still struggled with some relations more than others. Synonyms in particular had a very poor precision, and the accuracy of the system on synonyms was much lower than for the other three relations.

4   Conclusion

There were two mistakes in the initial version of our system. First, the there was no reason not to use the test data rather than the training data when looking at the top 600 similar representations for each word in a pair. The difference, however, in the results was relatively small. A much more significant error was our original system for solving subtask 2, which was both relatively ineffective and didn't show anything interesting..

Despite these errors, we were able to propose a system that while very simplistic and easy to implement, was able to achieve good results compared to the rest of the field. Table 3 shows the results of the various systems in the shared task on both subtask 1 and subtask 2.

<table>
<tr><td colspan="2" align="center">Subtask 1</td></tr>
<tr><td>Team</td><td>F1</td></tr>
<tr><td>GHHH</td><td>0.790</td></tr>
<tr><td>Mach5</td><td>0.778</td></tr>
<tr><td>LexNET</td><td>0.765</td></tr>
<tr><td>ROOT18</td><td>0.731</td></tr>
<tr><td>LOPE-PH</td><td>0.731</td></tr>
<tr><td>LOPE</td><td>0.713</td></tr>
<tr><td>HsH-Supervised</td><td>0.585</td></tr>
<tr><td>CGSRC</td><td>0.431</td></tr>
</table>

<table>
<tr><td colspan="2" align="center">Subtask 2</td></tr>
<tr><td>Team</td><td>F1</td></tr>
<tr><td>LexNET</td><td>0.445</td></tr>
<tr><td>GHHH</td><td>0.423</td></tr>
<tr><td>LOPE-PH</td><td>0.374</td></tr>
<tr><td>Mach5</td><td>0.295</td></tr>
<tr><td>ROOT18</td><td>0.262</td></tr>
<tr><td>CGSRC</td><td>0.252</td></tr>
<tr><td>LOPE</td><td>0.247</td></tr>
</table>

Table 3: Results of the different systems in the CogALex shared task, with the addition of our post-hoc system

In particular, our method of comparing the input pair to each related pair in the training data, averaging the results in each relational category, and assigning the input pair the relation with the highest average, appears to be effective at categorizing pairs according to their semantic relationship. Although our exact method was different than that of Mikolov et al. and Levy and Goldberg, it shows that the linguistics regularities they found in word embeddings are useable to find this kind of paradigmatic information about the semantic relationships synonymy, antonymy, hypernymy, and meronymy.

While not at the top of the table for either subtask, we believe we were able to put up respectable results for a simple system. It is possible that with a more complex expansion of the system, we could improve the results even more, particularly by finding ways to increase the accuracy of synonym detection in subtask 2.

4.1   Further Study

As a further study, we would like to attempt the task in Chinese. We argue that relation extraction is a task that could be language/writing system dependent. For example, in Chinese, it would be possible to exploit morpho-semantic relations and the character radical ontology (paradigmatic information embedded in the characters) to re-conduct subtask 2. We are currently underway creating original Chinese language data from Chinese Word Net to mirror the English data, so as to avoid translating polysemous words in English that aren't polysemous in Chinese, such as *cell* (a *cell* could be a small room or a part of an organism).

Reference

Jeffrey Elman. 1990 . Finding structure in time. Cognitive Science, 14, 179-211

Omar Levy and Yoav Goldberg. 2014. Linguistic regularities in sparse and explicit word representations. In Proceedings of the Eighteenth Conference on Computational Language Learning, pages 171-180, Baltimore, Maryland USA, June 26-27 2014. Association for Computational Linguistics

Tomas Mikolov, Kai Chen, Greg Corrado, and Jeffrey Dean. 2013a. Efficient estimation of word representations in vector space. CoRR, abs/1301.3781.

Tomas Mikolov, Wen-tau Yih, and Geoffrey Zweig. 2013b. Linguistic regularities in continuous space word representations. In Proceedings of the 2013 Conference of the North American Chapter of the Association for Computational Linguistics: Human Language Technologies, pages 746–751, Atlanta, Georgia, June. Association for Computational Linguistics.

Radim Rehurek and Petr Sojka. 2010. Software framework for topic modeling with large corpora. In Proceedings of the LREC 2010 Workshop on New Challenges for NLP Frameworks, pages 45-50, Valletta, Malta, May 22. ELRA

Enrico Santus, Frances Yung, Alessandro Lenci, and Chu-Ren Huang. 2015. EVALution 1.0: An evolving semantic dataset for training and evaluation of distributional semantic models. In Proceedings of the 4th Workshop on Linked Data in Linguistics, Beijing

CogALex-V Shared Task: HsH-Supervised – Supervised similarity learning using entry wise product of context vectors

Rosa Tsegaye Aga and **Christian Wartena**
Hochschule Hannover
Hanover, Germany
{rosa-tsegaye.aga, christian.wartena}@hs-hannover.de

Abstract

The CogALex-V Shared Task provides two datasets that consists of pairs of words along with a classification of their semantic relation. The dataset for the first task distinguishes only between related and unrelated, while the second data set distinguishes several types of semantic relations. A number of recent papers propose to construct a feature vector that represents a pair of words by applying a pairwise simple operation to all elements of the feature vector. Subsequently, the pairs can be classified by training any classification algorithm on these vectors. In the present paper we apply this method to the provided datasets. We see that the results are not better than from the given simple baseline. We conclude that the results of the investigated method are strongly depended on the type of data to which it is applied.

1 Introduction

In distributional semantics words are represented by a large number context features. In most cases, words context features are based on co-occurrences number or probabilities with other words. It turns out that words with similar vectors of co-occurrence based features are semantically related. A simple approach to decide whether two words are semantically related or not, can be based directly on the similarity of their associated vectors. This approach has been used in a large number of studies.

In order to improve on the quality reached by this simple approach, a number of papers recently proposed to use derived distributional features to represent each pair of words by a large distributional feature vector. Such a vector can be constructed by taking the pairwise sum or pairwise product of the vectors of two words. Now, the similarity between two words can be learned by a supervised classification method. In the following, we will see, how this method can be applied to the first part of the shared task. Since we have feature representations for each pair of words, we can also try to learn several different relations. We will do so for the second part of the task.

The rest of the paper is organized as follows. Section 2 discusses the related works. In section 3 we will have a short look at the data and the shared task. Section 4 explains the distributional feature construction, pairwise feature generation and the classification methods. In section 5 and 6, we present and discuss the results.

2 Related Work

Supervised approaches have not been used extensively in combination with distributional features. Shimizu et al. (2008) used a learned Mahalanobis distance to rank pairs of synonyms and unrelated words. In order to make the learning computationally feasible they reduced the number of context features massively by selecting the most promising features. Hagiwara (2008) follows a different approach. He constructed features to represent each pair of words. Subsequently a Support Vector Machine is used to learn which pairs are pairs of synonyms and which pairs are not. The features for the pair of words are constructed by pairwise addition or multiplication of the features of each word. Similar approaches are followed by Weeds et al. (2014) and Aga et al. (2016).

Proceedings of the Workshop on Cognitive Aspects of the Lexicon,
pages 114–118, Osaka, Japan, December 11-17 2016.

Alternatively, a pair of words can be represented by a small number of features. These features either represent properties of one of both words, or a property of the pair, e.g. the pointwise mutual information of these words. Possible features include also similarity measures based on the co-occurrence features. The use of such a set of features is followed by Bär et al. (2012), Wartena (2013) and Santus et al. (2016) for example. Turney (2014) combines these type of aggregated features with simple co-occurrence features.

3   Task and data

The CogALex shared task consist of two parts. For the first task pairs of words have to be classified as semantically related or not related. For the second task the type of relation for the related pairs has to be classified further into 4 semantic relations. For both tasks a test and a training set is provided.

The training data for both tasks contain 3054 pair of words. From these pairs 826 are semantically related, the remaining 2228 pairs are not related. The test data consists of 4260 pairs, 1201 of which are related and 3059 are not. In contrast to many other datasets, the words in this set are very heterogeneous: the set contains nouns, adjectives, verbs and even pronouns. For the second task, the relation between the related words is classified into 4 classes: synonymy, antonymy, hypernymy and meronymy. Especially, the combination of different part of speech and antonymy gives rises to unexpected pairs of related words, like *burn–cool* or *anger-calm*. Moreover, pairs like *arm–leg* or *vegetable-meat* are considered as anontonyms and hence related words, while other pairs, that are related somewhat more indirectly, like *breast-leg*, *vegetable-apple* (both co-meronyms) or *run-athlete* (we could consider athletics as a hypernym of running) are classified as unrelated. Thus it becomes clear that the dataset is far from trivial and is a real challenge for automatic classification.

For the construction of the context vectors of the words we use the UKWaC-Corpus (Baroni et al., 2009).

4   Methodology and Experiment

In this section, we will explain the task description, the feature construction for the words, and our approach to the task.

4.1   Feature construction

In DS the meaning of a word is represented by a vector of context features. As context features co-occurrence data with other words in a large text corpus are used.

There are a number of choices that have to be made when building the context vectors for each word. In the following we will use the choices that turned out to yield the best results in a number of different tasks in recent studies by Bullinaria and Levy (2007; 2012) and Kiela and Clark (2014).

First it has to be determined what words are used as context features, i.e. for what words co-occurrence statistics have to be computed. Generally, it is found that mid frequency words are most effective. After some preliminary experiments we found that including all words in the frequency range from $4 \cdot 10^3$ to $1 \cdot 10^6$ in the UKWaC Corpus is a good compromise between optimal results and acceptable storage and computing efforts. Therefore, context words which have frequency range from $4 \cdot 10^3$ to $1 \cdot 10^6$ in the UKWaC Corpus have been considered to construct the context vector for each words. Then each word is now represented by a vector of 17 400 features.

Next we have to determine the size of the window for co-occurrence. If the training corpus is large enough all studies show that smaller windows yield better results. We first remove all stop words and then use a window size of two words on the preprocessed text, respecting sentence boundaries. Syntactic relations are not used to determine the context of a word.

Finally, we use positive pointwise mutual information (PPMI) as a feature weighting, since it was shown to give better results than raw co-occurrence probabilities in a number of different studies. For a context words c and a (target) word t the PPMI is defined as

$$ppmi(c, t) = \max\left(\log \frac{p(c|t)}{p(c)}, 0\right). \tag{1}$$

Task	Method	Precision	Recall	F-score	Accuracy
Task 1	All True (Majority)	0.282	1.000	0.440	0.282
	Cosine	0.590	0.713	0.646	0.780
	Supervised (Addition)	0.362	0.094	0.149	0,698
	HsH-Supervised (Multiplication)	0.577	0.593	0.585	0,760
Task 2	All hypernym (Majority)	0.0897	0.318	0.140	0.0897
	HsH-Supervised (Multiplication)	0.506	0.154	0.229	0,753

Table 1: Performance of the HsH-Supervised method and two baselines for both tasks on the test set

4.2 Representation of word pairs

The similarity of words can be computed by comparing their feature vectors. In order to decide whether two words are semantically related, Hagiwara (2008) proposed a novel approach which is learning an SVM model by taking the distributional features as an input, that were constructed by addition of the context vectors of both words. In addition, recently, distributional features have also been used directly to train classifiers that classify pairs of words as being synonymous or not (Weeds et al., 2014; Aga et al., 2016) and showed good performance on the applied tasks. For the shared task, we have also followed this approach which is using distributional features directly on classifiers. To construct the feature vector for each pair of words, we use multiplication. Pairwise multiplication was shown to give good results in (Weeds et al., 2014) and (Aga et al., 2016).

As a baseline we have been considering the classical cosine similarity between the context vectors of the two words. On the training data, the optimal split has been learned between the related and non-related pairs. For the test data, we thus consider pairs with context vectors that have a cosine above 0.0842 to be semantically related.

As a further simple baseline for the first task we use a classifier that considers each pair as semantically related. In fact, this is a type of majority classifier, that always assigns the largest *evaluated* category.[1] For the second task the largest evaluated category in the training data is the hypernym relation (255 pairs). Thus this classifier assigns hypernym to each pair.

4.3 Supervised Similarity Learning

We have used linear SVM from the liblinear package to learn a model and classify the word pairs represented by one feature vector. Liblinear is very efficient and fast for training large-scale problems as showed by Fan Fan et al. (2008). To find the best combination of parameter values for the cost parameter C and the kernel parameter γ we used grid search. We tested for $-5 \leq \log_2 C \leq 15$ and $-15 \leq \log_2 \gamma \leq 2$ n steps of 0.05. Using cross validation on the training data we found $C = 32$ and $\gamma = 0,00781$ as optimal values. The right selection of the hyper-parameters should minimize the risk of overfitting.

5 Results

The results of the supervised method and our two baselines are given in Table 1. For the first task the supervised method based on the Hadamard-Product of context vectors could not give better results than the simple cosine similarity baseline. The multiplication, however, is much better than addition of vectors and also clearly better than the naive baseline, that considers each pair as related.

For the second task the F1-score of the supervised method is very low, but still far above the naive baseline. Remarkably, the precision is quite high: half of the pairs found for one of the four semantic relations indeed have this relation.

---

[1] As an anonymous reviewer pointed out, in the special case of task 1 the largest class that is taken into account in the evaluation, happens to be the smallest class. Thus this baseline could also be coined "minority classifier".

6 Discussion and conclusions

In a number of papers pairwise multiplication of context vectors has been used to represent pair of words. The feature vectors for the pairs of words created by multiplication (or another operation of two numbers) then is used to train a supervised model that learns whether the words in the pair are semantically related or not. We have applied this method to the CogALex shared task.

At first sight it is quite surprising that the supervised method stays behind the simple cosine similarity approach, since various publications have reported that this method that we applied is slightly better than cosine similarity.

The main reason for the bad performance of the SVM is probably that the model is overfitting the training data. We expected the SVM with carefull selection of the C-parameter to be quite robust against overfitting. In (Aga et al., 2016) we used the same number of features and could improve a lot over the cosine baseline. In the present study, however, the model clearly is overfitting the training data: when we apply the learned model to the training data we get a result with an accuracy of about 99%, showing that the model indeed overfits the training data.

Furthermore, we used a standard SVM that optimizes for overall accuracy, while the official evaluation for the task is the F1-Score of a small class. In fact the accuracy is quite high and the difference in accuracy between the simple cosine based method and the supervised method is very small. For a discussion on the differences between optimizing on F-Score and accuracy see e.g. Ye et al. (2012)

Finally, we have the impression that the method is successful in recognizing a loose semantic relatedness, but is not able to distinguish between very closely related words (like synonyms) and more loosely related words: In Aga et al. (2016), we studied relatedness of terms in a thesaurus. Here the supervised method also performs well on pairs of terms that are related to each other by some thesaurus relations via at most one intermediate concept. The performance is worst on pairs build from alternative labels for the same concept. Here we have a similar situation, in which we only want to find words with a specific and precise defined semantic relation, while other words, that have other or more loose semantic relations are classified as unrelated. Thus it seems that the findings of the present experiment are in-line with previous results for the same approach.

For future work we will apply dimensionality reduction in order to reduce the number of features and to prevent the SVM from overfitting.

References

Rosa Tsegaye Aga, Christian Wartena, Lucas Drumond, and Lars Schmidt-Thieme. 2016. Learning thesaurus relations from distributional features. In Nicoletta Calzolari (Conference Chair), Khalid Choukri, Thierry Declerck, Sara Goggi, Marko Grobelnik, Bente Maegaard, Joseph Mariani, Helene Mazo, Asuncion Moreno, Jan Odijk, and Stelios Piperidis, editors, *Proceedings of the Tenth International Conference on Language Resources and Evaluation (LREC 2016)*, Paris, France, may. European Language Resources Association (ELRA).

Daniel Bär, Chris Biemann, Iryna Gurevych, and Torsten Zesch. 2012. UKP: Computing Semantic Textual Similarity by Combining Multiple Content Similarity Measures. In *Proceedings of the Sixth International Workshop on Semantic Evaluation (SemEval-2012)*, pages 435–440.

Marco Baroni, S. Bernardini, A. Ferraresi, and E. Zanchetta. 2009. The WaCky Wide Web: A Collection of Very Large Linguistically Processed Web-Crawled Corpora. *Language Resources and Evaluation 43 (3): 209-226*, 43(3):209–226.

John A. Bullinaria and Joseph P. Levy. 2007. Extracting semantic representations from word co-occurrence statistics: A computational study. *Behaviour Research Methods*, 39(3):510–526.

John A. Bullinaria and Joseph P. Levy. 2012. Extracting Semantic Representations from Word Co-occurrence Statistics: Stop-lists, Stemming and SVD. *Behaviour Research Methods*, 44(3):890–907.

Rong-En Fan, Kai-Wei Chang, Cho-Jui Hsieh, Xiang-Rui Wang, and Chih-Jen Lin. 2008. Liblinear: A library for large linear classification. *J. Mach. Learn. Res.*, 9:1871–1874, June.

Masato Hagiwara. 2008. A Supervised Learning Approach to Automatic Synonym Identification Based on Distributional Features for Computational Linguistics, June 15-20, 2008, Columbus, Ohio, USA, Student Research

Workshop. In *ACL 2008, Proceedings of the 46th Annual Meeting of the Association for Computational Linguistics*, pages 1–6.

Douwe Kiela and Stephen Clark. 2014. A Systematic Study of Semantic Vector Space Model Parameters. In *2nd Workshop on Continuous Vector Space Models and their Compositionality (CVSC)*, pages 21–30, Stroudsburg, PA, USA. Association for Computational Linguistics.

Enrico Santus, Alessandro Lenci, Tin-Shing Chiu, Qin Lu, and Chu-Ren Huang. 2016. Nine features in a random forest to learn taxonomical semantic relations. In Nicoletta Calzolari (Conference Chair), Khalid Choukri, Thierry Declerck, Sara Goggi, Marko Grobelnik, Bente Maegaard, Joseph Mariani, Helene Mazo, Asuncion Moreno, Jan Odijk, and Stelios Piperidis, editors, *Proceedings of the Tenth International Conference on Language Resources and Evaluation (LREC 2016)*, Paris, France, may. European Language Resources Association (ELRA).

Nobuyuki Shimizu, Masato Hagiwara, Yasuhiro Ogawa, Katsuhiko Toyama, and Hiroshi Nakagawa. 2008. Metric learning for synonym acquisition. In *COLING '08 Proceedings of the 22nd International Conference on Computational Linguistics*, pages 793–800.

Peter Turney. 2014. Distributional semantics beyond words: Supervised learning of analogy and paraphrase. *Transactions of the Association for Computational Linguistics*, 1:353–366.

Christian Wartena. 2013. HsH: Estimating semantic similarity of words and short phrases with frequency normalized distance measures. In *Proceedings of the 6th International Workshop on Semantic Evaluation (SemEval 2012), Atlanta, Georgia, USA*.

Julie Weeds, Daoud Clarke, Jeremy Reffin, David Weir, and Bill Keller. 2014. Learning to distinguish hypernyms and co-hyponyms. In *Proceedings of COLING 2014, the 25th International Conference on Computational Linguistics: Technical Papers*, pages 2249–2259, Dublin, Ireland, August. Dublin City University and Association for Computational Linguistics.

Nan Ye, Kian Ming Adam Chai, Wee Sun Lee, and Hai Leong Chieu. 2012. Optimizing f-measure: A tale of two approaches. In *Proceedings of the 29th International Conference on Machine Learning, ICML 2012*.

A Study of the *Bump* Alternation in Japanese from the Perspective of Extended/Onset Causation

Natsuno Aoki[1]   Kentaro Nakatani[2]

Konan University
8-9-1 Okamoto, Higashi-Nada
Kobe, Hyogo 658-8501, Japan
[1]1929na@gmail.com   [2]kentaron@konan-u.ac.jp

Abstract

This paper deals with a seldom studied object/oblique alternation phenomenon in Japanese, which. We call this the *bump* alternation. This phenomenon, first discussed by Sadanobu (1990), is similar to the English *with/against* alternation. For example, compare *hit the wall with the bat* [=immobile-as-direct-object frame] to *hit the bat against the wall* [=mobile-as-direct-object frame]). However, in the Japanese version, the case frame remains constant. Although we fundamentally question Sadanobu's acceptability judgment, we also claim that the causation type (i.e., whether the event is an instance of onset or extended causation; Talmy, 1988; 2000) could make an improvement. An extended causative interpretation could improve the acceptability of the otherwise awkward immobile-as-direct-object frame. We examined this claim through a rating study, and the results showed an interaction between the Causation type (extended/onset) and the Object type (mobile/immobile) in the direction we predicted. We propose that a perspective shift on what is moving causes the "extended causation" advantage.

1 Introduction

There are many types of object/oblique alternation. A representative one is *locative* alternation:

(1) a. Jack sprayed paint onto the wall.   [mobile/theme object]
    b. Jack sprayed the wall with paint.   [immobile/location object]

(Levin, 1993: 51)

Locative alternation is the alternation between a theme-object frame, in which the verb selects the mobile theme as the direct object, and a location-object frame, in which the verb selects the immobile location (goal) as the direct object.

The present paper deals with a much less studied alternation in Japanese, which we call the *bump* alternation. Sadanobu (1990) first studied this phenomenon under the label *tama-ate daikan* ('bullet-hit' alternation). We can regard this to be a variant of locative alternation because it is an alternation between a mobile theme and an immobile location. This is similar to what Levin (1993) called the *with/against* alternation, as illustrated below:

(2) a. Brian hit the stick against the fence.   [mobile object]
    b. Brian hit the fence with the stick.   [immobile object]

(Levin, 1993: 67)

However, what is peculiar about the Japanese version is that the case marking remains constant, as shown in (3).

Proceedings of the Workshop on Cognitive Aspects of the Lexicon,
pages 119–124, Osaka, Japan, December 11-17 2016.

(3) a. *Tama-o   mato-ni   ateru*   [mobile object]
       bullet-ACC target-DAT hit
       '(lit.) hit the bullet to the target' = 'make the bullet hit the target'
    b. *Mato-o   tama-ni   ateru*   [immobile object]
       target-ACC bullet-DAT hit
       '(lit.) hit the target to a bullet' = 'hit the target with a bullet'

(Sadanobu, 1990)

The English translation for (3a) is awkward, but Japanese *ateru* means 'to cause something to hit somewhere.' This is much more natural with a mobile/theme object, whereas the immobile/location object (3b) sounds more awkward (we will get back to this issue shortly). In this sense, *ateru* may be closer to English *bump* than *hit*, which is the reason why we tentatively call this alternation the *bump* alternation. In any case, what is peculiar here is that in (3b), the accusative-dative frame remains constant. Sadanobu (1990) claims that both frames denote the same event in which the agent causes the mobile object to move, and then bump into the immobile one. Thus, in this alternation, the case marking for the two objects is switchable without changing the interpretation. Such an alternation is crosslinguistically peculiar, and thus hard to translate directly in English. However, according to our intuition (as native speakers of Japanese), Sadanobu's acceptability judgment of (3b) is questionable. It sounds unacceptable when interpreted in the same way as (3a). Thus, the existence of this alternation is at stake.

If this alternation were simply an erroneous observation by Sadanobu, not much would be interesting about it. However, it seems to us that this type of alternation can be more acceptable by controlling the type of the mobile object. For example:

(4) a. *Doamiraa-o   dentyuu-ni   ateta/butuketa.*   [mobile object]
       door.mirror-ACC   utility.pole-DAT   hit/bumped
       'bumped the door mirror against the utility pole'
    b. *Dentyuu-o   doamiraa-ni   ateta/butuketa.*   [immobile object]
       utility.pole-ACC   door.mirror-DAT   hit/bumped
       'bumped the utility pole with the door mirror'

In (4), *doamiraa* 'door mirror' is the mobile entity and *dentyuu* 'utility pole' is the immobile one. Sentence (4b) sounds more acceptable than (3b) even though *dentyuu* 'utility pole' is obviously immobile. Why is it easier for immobile *dentyuu* 'utility pole' in (4b) to appear as the direct object than *mato* 'target' in (3b)?

In order to account for the difference in acceptability judgment between (3b) and (4b), we claim that different kinds of mobile themes induce different types of causation: namely, onset and extended causations (Talmy, 1988; 2000). The former type consists of two stages, i.e., the agent's causative action, followed by an autonomous event of the theme's movement.

(5)   The carton slid (all the way) across the grass from a (single) gust of wind blowing on it.

(Talmy, 2000: 493)

In (5), an autonomous event (the carton's movement) follows a causative situation (a single gust of wind blowing). This event consists of two such stages, so this is an *onset causation* event. On the other hand, the latter type, extended causation, depicts a situation where "the caused event takes place exactly during the duration of the causing event" (Talmy, 2000: 493–494).

(6)   The carton slid across the grass from the wind blowing on it (steadily).

(Talmy, 2000: 494)

The example in (6), unlike (5), depicts a situation in which the carton continues to move while the wind blows on it. Such synchronicity of the causative event and the movement of the theme are labeled *extended causation.*

In terms of the causation type, we can regard the event in (3) to be an instance of onset causation. The agent pulls the trigger of a gun, which is the causative event; after that, the bullet autonomously starts to move to the target, without help from the agent. Thus, the entire event can be construed as consisting of two stages, and thus can classify it as an instance of onset causation. By contrast, in (4), the door mirror, which is part of a car, keeps moving all the while the agent drives the car. The movement of the door mirror and the agent's causation always coincide. Thus, we can consider the event in (4) to be an instance of extended causation.

We hypothesize that the *bump* alternation (more specifically, the immobile object variant) is more acceptable when the sentence denotes an extended causation. The reason is as follows. In the case of extended causation, the agent moves together with the mobile theme. This could trigger a perspective shift such that it makes us perceive the immobile entity as if it were a mobile one. For example, when you are driving and you approach a huge billboard, you may perceive that the billboard is coming closer even though it is not moving. The same may apply to the *bump* alternation with extended causation. In (4), even though the agent moves toward the immobile utility pole while driving a car (with door mirrors), it may be possible to perceive this situation in such a way that it is the immobile entity (the utility pole) that is moving toward the agent, eventually hitting the door mirror. The baseline assumption is that the *bump* alternation is not really an alternation; the *bump* verbs in Japanese only allow mobile objects. An apparent "alternation" is possible only when the immobile entity can appear as a mobile one. That is, it can occur only if the sentence denotes extended causation, but not when it denotes onset causation. If this hypothesis is on the right track, it follows that the immobile object frame with extended causation such as (4b) is more acceptable than the one with onset causation such as (3b). Our research question is whether there is an interaction between the Causation type (whether the event's interpretation involves onset or extended causation) and the Object type (whether the direct object is the mobile theme or immobile entity). In particular, we would like to examine whether the difference in Causation type affects the acceptability of the immobile object frame.

2   Experiment

In order to examine the questions shown above, we conducted a questionnaire experiment through *Lancers,* a crowdsourcing service in Japan similar to Amazon Mechanical Turk. As mentioned above, the current research question is whether an interaction arises between Causation type (onset/extended) and Object type (mobile/immobile).

2.1   Methods

Materials
We prepared materials under a 2x2 factorial design. The first factor was the Causation type. We varied the mobile theme to permit interpretation of the causative event as either extended or onset causation. For example, if the mobile theme is an entity that someone is likely to throw, like a pebble or a ball, the event is likely an onset causation event. On the other hand, if the mobile theme is an entity that is likely to move along with the agent, such as a door mirror or a body part (like a shoulder or elbow), the event is interpreted as an extended causation event. The second factor was the Object type. In one situation, the accusative case *-o* marks the mobile theme, while the immobile is dative-marked with *–ni*. In another case, the immobile object is accusative-marked, with the mobile theme being dative-marked. The verbs used in this experiment were either *ateru* 'to make hit' or *butukeru* 'bump.' Some sample materials are shown below:

(7) Extended causation conditions:
    a. *Yopparai-ga*   *ganmen-o*   *kootuuhyoosiki-ni*   *ateta.*   [mobile object]
       drunken.man-NOM   face-ACC   traffic.sign-DAT   hit
       'A drunken man hit his face against the traffic sign.'
    b. *Yopparai-ga*   *kootuuhyoosiki-o*   *ganmen-ni*   *ateta.*   [immobile object]
       drunken.man-NOM   traffic.sign-ACC   face-DAT   hit
       'A drunken man hit the traffic sign with his face.'

Onset causation conditions:

    c. *Yopparai-ga*   *isitubute-o   kootuuhyoosiki-ni   ateta.*   [mobile object]
        drunken.man-NOM   pebble-ACC traffic.sigh-DAT   hit
        'A drunken man hit a pebble against the traffic sign (=made a pebble hit the sign).'

    d. *Yopparai-ga*   *kootuuhyoosiki-o isitubute-ni ateta.*   [immobile object]
        drunken.man-NOM   traffic.sign-ACC   pebble-DAT   hit
        'A drunken man hit the traffic sign with a pebble.'

(8) Extended causation conditions:

    a. *Musuko-ga kata-o   genkantobira-ni   butuketa.*
        son-NOM   shoulder-ACC   entrance.door-DAT   bumped
        'My son bumped his shoulder against the entrance door.'

    b. *Musuko-ga genkantobira-o   kata-ni   butuketa.*
        son-NOM   entrance.door-ACC shoulder-DAT   bumped
        'My son bumped the entrance door with his shoulder.'

Onset causation conditions:

    c. *Musuko-ga setubun-no mame-o   genkantobira-ni   butuketa.* [mobile object]
        son-NOM   *setubun*-GEN beans-ACC entrance.door-DAT bumped
        '(lit.) My son bumped beans for the *setubun* festival to the entrance door.'
        = 'My son threw beans for the *setubun* festival against the entrance door.'

    d. *Musuko-ga genkantobira-o   setubun-no mame-ni   butuketa.* [immobile object]
        son-NOM   entrance.door-ACC *setubun*-GEN beans-DAT   bumped
        '(lit.) My son bumped the entrance door with beans for the *setubun* festival.'
        = 'My son hit the entrance door with beans for the *setubun* festival.'

Participants and Procedures

Participants were 105 native speakers of Japanese, recruited on-line via *Lancers*. They were asked to rate the naturalness of each sentence on a five-point Likert scale by clicking one of radio buttons numbered 1-5, with '5' corresponding to 'natural' and '1' to 'unnatural'. They were instructed to rate each item quickly following their intuitions. 54 yen was paid for each participant after the task.

The total of 16x4 sentences were evenly distributed into four lists with a Latin square design. Each list also included the same 32 fillers, among which 11 sentences were unacceptable and 21 were acceptable. The total of 48 sentences were shuffled in a fixed, pseudo-random order. Additional four lists that contained the sentences in a reverse order were prepared to counterbalance potential ordering effects. Each participant was assigned one of the eight lists. Each list was rated by 10 to 15 participants.

2.2   Predictions

Because *ateru* 'hit' and *butukeru* 'bump' both by default select a mobile theme as the direct object, we predicted there would be no significant difference in the acceptability of the mobile object conditions between the two causation types. The immobile object conditions were generally less acceptable. However, our hypothesis predicted that the possibility of interpreting the event as extended causation should improve the acceptability, compared with the onset causation conditions.

2.3   Results and Discussion

The data from one subject was excluded from the analyses because all sentences were rated 5. The grand mean of all items was 2.9. The mean rating of each condition is shown in Figure 1.

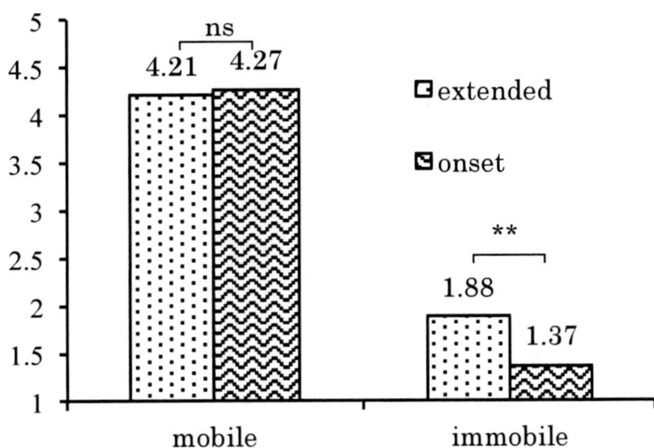

Figure 1: Mean Acceptability Ratings for Four Conditions

It is obvious from the figure that the mean ratings of the immobile object conditions were overall much lower than the means of the mobile object conditions. This fits our intuition that these *bump* verbs in Japanese select the mobile-object frame by default. A linear mixed effects model analysis conducted with maximal random effects structure (cf. Barr et al., 2013) revealed main effects of the onset type (t=19.45) and the causative type (t=2.32), as in Table 1. Most importantly, there was a significant interaction (t=-2.70). Planned paired comparisons revealed a highly significant main effect of the Causation type in the immobile conditions (t=3.91), but no significant effect in the mobile conditions (t=-0.42). These findings conform to our hypothesis that the extended causation may improve the acceptability of an otherwise very awkward immobile-as-direct-object frame in the *bump* alternation in Japanese. We assume that the reason for this is that the extended causation can trigger a perspective shift such that the immobile object comes across as a mobile entity.

	Estimate	Standard Error	t value
Intercept	2.94	0.06	50.67
Object (mobile)	1.30	0.06	19.45
Causation (extended)	0.11	0.04	2.32
Object:Causation	-0.14	0.05	-2.70

Table 1: Linear Mixed Effects Model Coefficients

	Estimate	Standard Error	t value
Intercept	1.63	0.08	20.92
Causation (extended)	0.26	0.07	3.91

Table 2: Causation Contrast in Immobile Object Conditions

	Estimate	Standard Error	t value
Intercept	4.24	0.10	43.18
Causation (extended)	-0.03	0.08	-0.42

Table 3: Causation Contrast in Mobile Object Conditions

3 Conclusion

The results revealed a significant interaction between Causation type and Object type in the *bump* alternation in Japanese. This extended causation makes the immobile object more acceptable compared with the case of onset causation. We interpret this result to be evidence for our hypothesis that extended causation could let us interpret the immobile object as if it were a mobile object. This occurs because the agent moves with the mobile object toward the immobile object, enabling a perspective shift with respect to what is moving. This in turn improves the acceptability of the immobile-as-direct-object frame in the *bump* alternation, due to reinterpretation of the immobile as mobile. In other words, the immobile-as-direct-object frame comes across as the mobile-as-direct-object frame. Onset causation does not trigger such a perspective shift.

Our finding also raises questions about the validity of introspective acceptability judgments regarding various alternation phenomena reported in linguistics literature (see Bresnan et al., 2007 for a criticism in this line). For example, in our case, we found a significant improvement in the acceptability of the immobile object frame by introducing extended causation. However, the mean acceptability rate was 1.88 for the immobile object × the extended causation condition, which is very low. Thus, it is not clear if we can state that this *bump* alternation phenomenon in Japanese really exists. We may also find other cases where quantitative studies do not support the acceptability judgments reported in theoretical literature of alternation phenomena.

Another implication of this finding is that previous theoretical literature may have focused too closely on analyzing the semantics of verbs when it comes to alternation phenomena. A finer-grained analysis is desirable, especially on the effects of pragmatic interpretation induced by combining the verb and its arguments. This study demonstrated that simply changing the type of mobile theme could influence the acceptability judgment. Future research should shed more light on the contribution of nominal semantics to the interpretation of alternation phenomena.

Acknowledgments

The research reported here is partially supported by JSPS KAKENHI Grant Number 26370519. Part of this work was presented at the 32nd annual meeting of Konan English Literary Society, and we thank the audience for their comments.

References

Barr, D. J., Levy, R., Scheepers, C., and Tily, H. (2013). Random Effects Structure for Confirmatory Hypothesis Testing: Keep It Maximal. *Journal of Memory and Language, 68*, 255–278.

Bresnan, J., Cueni, A., Nikitina, T., and Baayan, R. H. (2007). Predicting the Dative Alternation. In G. Boume, I. Kraemer, and J. Zwarts (Eds.), *Cognitive Foundations of Interpretation,* (pp. 69–94). Amsterdam: Royal Netherlands Academy of Science.

Levin, B. (1993). *English Verb Classes and Alternations: A Preliminary Investigation.* Chicago, IL: University of Chicago Press.

Sadanobu, T. (1990). Bun no 'Taishoosee' to Meeshiku no Soogokookan [On the case marking system of Japanese motive verbal predicate sentences]. *Gengogakukenkyuu*, Vol. 9, 1–57. Kyoto: Kyoto University Linguistics Circle.

Talmy, L. (1988). Force Dynamics in Language and Cognition. *Cognitive Science* 12, 49–100.

Talmy, L. (2000). *Toward a Cognitive Semantics. Volume I: Concept Structuring System.* Cambridge, MA: MIT Press.

G$_h$oSt-PV: A Representative Gold Standard of German Particle Verbs

Stefan Bott, Nana Khvtisavrishvili, Max Kisselew, Sabine Schulte im Walde
Institute for Natural Language Processing
University of Stuttgart, Germany
{stefan.bott,nana.khvtisavrishvili,max.kisselew,schulte}@ims.uni-stuttgart.de

Abstract

German particle verbs represent a frequent type of multi-word-expression that forms a highly productive paradigm in the lexicon. Similarly to other multi-word expressions, particle verbs exhibit various levels of compositionality. One of the major obstacles for the study of compositionality is the lack of representative gold standards of human ratings. In order to address this bottleneck, this paper presents such a gold standard data set containing 400 randomly selected German particle verbs. It is balanced across several particle types and three frequency bands, and accomplished by human ratings on the degree of semantic compositionality.

1 Introduction

German particle verbs (PVs), such as *auf|schauen* (*to look up*) represent a type of multi-word expression composed of a particle and a base verb (BV). As example (1) shows, they may be written together or syntactically separated but they always form one semantic unit.

(1) a. Das Kind **sah**   seine Mutter **an**.
          The child looked his/her mother an-PRT.
          'The child looked at his/her mother.'

      b. .... dass das Kind seine Mutter **an|sah**.
          ... that the child his/her mother looked|an-PRT.
          '... that the child looked at his mother.'

In German, PVs are particularly frequent and form a highly productive paradigm in the lexicon, which often leads to neologisms and is subject to creative language use in puns and word plays (Springorum et al., 2013). Like many other multi-word expressions, PVs differ with respect to their compositionality. Some PVs can be deduced entirely from the meaning of the BV but others have meanings which are totally distinct. Most PVs fall on a continuum in between the two extremes. Some examples are the following:

FULLY COMPOSITIONAL: *an|leuchten* (*to illuminate*); the BV *leuchten* means *to shine*, and *an* expresses directionality (among other senses), cf. (2-a).

SEMI-COMPOSITIONAL: *ab|segnen* means *to approve*; literally, *segnen* means *to bless*. The two verb meanings are related, but a meaning shift occurred (cf. (2-b)). Semi-compositional PVs are usually part of a productive paradigm. In our case, *ab|segnen* patterns with verbs like *ab|nicken* (also meaning *to approve*, where the BV means *to nod*), and *ab|zeichnen* (*to give the approval signature*, where *zeichnen* means *to sign*).

NON-COMPOSITIONAL: *nach|schlagen* means *to look up* (e.g. *a reference*) or *to consult* (e.g. *a dictionary*); the BV *schlagen* means *to beat* (cf. (2-c)).

(2) a. Peter **leuchtete** das Bild   mit der Taschenlampe **an**.
          Peter shined   the picture with the flashlight   an-PRT.
          'Peter illuminated the picture with the flashlight.'

      b. Der Chef **segnete** die Pläne **ab**.
          The boss blessed the plans ab-PRT.
          'The boss approved the plans.'

      c. Stella **schlug** das Wort im   Wörterbuch **nach**.
          Stella beat   the word in-the dictionary   nach-PRT.
          'Stella looked up the word in the dictionary.'

125

The compositionality of PVs has received some attention in Computational Linguistics. For example, the assessment of compositionality grades has been studied for English (Baldwin et al., 2003; McCarthy et al., 2003; Bannard et al., 2003; Bannard, 2005; Reddy et al., 2011; Salehi and Cook, 2013; Salehi et al., 2014) and German (Hartmann et al., 2008; Kühner and Schulte im Walde, 2010; Bott and Schulte im Walde, 2014), mostly with the use of methods from distributional semantics. A central requirement for such studies is the availability of gold standards of human ratings which can serve as the basis for evaluation.

Only few gold standards of this kind are available (cf. section 2), and they tend to require a high amount of human work to create. While humans have relatively clear intuitions on the grade of compositionality of PVs, the ambiguity of PVs often represents a problem both for the elicitation of ratings and automatic assessment. Most of the studies that are dedicated to PV compositionality have created their own gold standards, but both the workload and the issue of comparability among studies make larger, public ally available data sets highly desirable. In addition, the availability of standard resources is a prerequisite for inter-study comparability. In this paper we present such a resource containing 400 German PVs. The gold standard was designed as a target selection which is balanced over different types of particles and various ranges of corpus frequency. A subset of the gold standard has already been used in Bott and Schulte im Walde (2015) for the assessment of PV-compositionality. The data set has been created in a larger project which also produced $G_h$ost-NN (Schulte im Walde et al., 2016), a gold standard for German noun-noun Compounds with a similar design and a similar rating collection process. The resource is available to the research community under a Creative Commons License.[1]

In the remainder of this paper, section 2 discusses the availability of similar existing resources. In section 3 we describe the criteria which were important for the design of the new resource. In sections 4 and 5 we describe the creation and the properties of the gold standard.

2   Previously Existing Data

The only comparable previously existing data set which contains human ratings on German PVs can be found in Hartmann (2008). This data set is balanced over 8 frequency bands and rated by 3 expert raters, but it only contains 99 PVs, corresponding to 11 particles. The collection of this data set considered polysemy by asking raters to indicate ambiguities and, if they noticed any, to disambiguate them in their own words. The ambiguity was not a criterion for the selection of the PVs in that data set, and the compositionality ratings did not distinguish between different word senses. This inability to distinguish between word senses for annotation is a problem with no obvious solution, as we will argue in section 4.4 below. We found that this resource, even if highly valuable, was too small for many purposes, especially because statistic significance depends highly on the size of the sample.

Also for English particle verbs, a limited number of data sets do exist. Bannard et al. (2003) present a corpus-based approach to the semantics of particle verb constructions in English. To this end they collected a gold standard containing 40 randomly selected phrasal verbs which were rated by 26 annotators. This gold standard contains ratings on compositionality for each particle verb construction with respect to both the BV and the particle. Ratings were given regarding only three levels: *yes*, *no* and *don't know*. For our new gold standard we wanted to avoid a simple binary classification, cf. the discussion in the previous section (2).

Somewhat related to our topic is the data set created by Cook and Stevenson (2006) for the evaluation of the prediction of particle senses. This gold standard consists of a list of of 389 English particle verb constructions with *up* balanced over three different frequency bands. Each of the PVs was annotated by two annotators for four different particle senses. The focus of their research was, however, not the study of compositionality, but the classification of particle meanings, and specified for one particle type.

3   Considerations for the Creation of the Gold Standard

For the creation of the gold standard we defined a series of properties which we wanted to find reflected in the data set, based on theoretical considerations and previous experiences.

- *Scalar judgments on compositionality:* As we already argued, the degree of compositionality falls on a continuum from fully compositional and non-compositional. For this reason we wanted scalar compositionality judgments.

- *Random selection:* In order to avoid bias we wanted to obtain a random sample from all existing PVs, but we also wanted different PV properties reflected in our selection, such as frequency and ambiguity levels.

- *Balanced over frequency bands:* From earlier studies (Bott and Schulte im Walde, 2014) we know that both very frequent and very sparse PVs tend to present special problems in comparison to mid-frequency PVs: high-frequency items tend to be strongly lexicalized and ambiguous, while low-frequency items are often

---

[1]`http://www.ims.uni-stuttgart.de/data/ghost-pv`

subject to problems that can be attributed to data sparseness. So we were faced with an inherent conflict between a strict balancedness of the GS –which would require us to represent PVs from the extreme ends of the frequency spectrum proportionally– and the goal to select PVs with prototypical behavior –which is contradicted by the fact that we know a priori that extremely frequent and extremely infrequent PVs tend to behave idiosyncratically.

- *Different ambiguity levels:* Polysemy is a factor which influences both human ratings and automatic computational assessment. We thus wanted semantic ambiguity levels to represent a feature in the data set. Ideally, we wanted compositionality ratings which correspond to different word senses. In section 4.4 below we discuss the complications this point brings about.

- *Selection of particles:* We were interested in de-prepositional particles which are semantically ambiguous and abstract (Lechler and Roßdeutscher, 2009; Haselbach, 2011; Kliche, 2011; Springorum, 2011). We chose to sample PVs corresponding to 11 verb particles, which were already used in (Hartmann et al., 2008): *an, auf, aus, nach, ab, zu, ein, über, unter, um, durch.* These particles are all de-prepositional, and their semantics are all highly ambiguous and show a high proportion of abstract readings.

4 Creation of the Gold Standard

The creation of the gold standard involved a number of steps: We collected a list of all PVs across particle types, as found in a large corpus. From this list a random selection was created automatically, which was balanced over three different frequency ranges. This initial list was manually filtered and finally this data set was annotated by human raters for PV compositionality. In the following, we describe these steps in some detail.

$G_h$ost-PV was designed with similar goals and similar desired properties in mind as $G_h$ost-NN (Schulte im Walde et al., 2016), a gold standard of German noun-noun compounds which was compiled within the same research project and in a very similar crowdsourcing process. Both PVs and noun-noun compounds are multi-word-expressions, but their different nature required also some different design-decisions which makes the two gold standards comparable, but not not entirely parallel.

4.1 Compilation of a Complete List of Existing PVs

We wanted to select PVs out of a list of all PVs that could be attested in German corpora. This required the compilation of a full corpus-extracted list of PVs. We only targeted PVs which are built with one of the particles we mentioned in section 3. An automatic detection of adequate candidate lemmas is not entirely trivial for three reasons.

1. If the lemma of a PV starts with the string that coincides with one of the particles, this can produce false positive PVs because also non-PVs start with the same string. For example, the simplex verb *zupfen* (*to pluck/pick*) happens to start with the character sequence that is idiomorphic to the particle *zu*.

2. Lemmatizers and parsers tend to produce errors in the detection and treatment of PVs, especially in the case of syntactically separate occurrences. This is problematic since prepositions may be wrongly interpreted as syntactically separated particles.

3. Some particles have counterparts which act as verb prefixes, so prefix verbs may be confounded with PVs. Some complex verbs are even ambiguous between a prefix verb and a particle verb, e.g. the verb *umfahren* in (3), which can be a PV which means *to drive over* or a prefix verb with the meaning of *to drive around*. Prefix verbs resemble particle verbs, but behave syntactically very different because they are never separated from the BV, as exemplified in example (3-b).

    (3)   a.   Er **fuhr** den Baum **um**.
                    He drove the tree   um-PRT.
                    'He knocked over the tree (with a car).'

            b.   Er **umfuhr**   den Baum.
                    He over-drove the tree.
                    'He drove around the tree.'

In order to exclude prefix verbs, we looked for combinations of verbs and particles which occurred both syntactically separated and written together as one word, relying on a dependency-parsed version of the *SdeWaC* corpus (Bohnet, 2010; Faaß and Eckart, 2013).

4.2 Selection of the Particle Verbs

Since our goal was to create a random but balanced selection of PVs, we automatically selected 938 PVs from the list obtained in the previous step. We aimed for a selection of 990 PVs (11 particles, 3 frequency bands and 30 PVs per combination), but for one particle (*unter*) the corpus only contained 38 PVs. We sampled from three different frequency ranges: Frequency tertiles were used to determine the three frequency bands: L(ow), M(id) and H(igh). Since the frequencies of PVs are not independent from the particles they correspond to, the tertiles were computed for each particle separately.

The frequencies were obtained as the harmonic mean of frequencies obtained from four different corpora: *SdeWaC* (Faaß and Eckart, 2013), *DECOW12* (Schäfer and Bildhauer, 2012), *HGC* (Fitschen, 2004) and the German *Wikipedia* (dump `dewiki-20110410`). The calculation of word frequency over different corpora was done to balance out known and suspected deficits in the balancedness of each corpus.

4.3 Cleaning of the Gold Standard

Since the original list of PVs was created randomly, the gold standard of 938 PVs still contained a certain amount of noisy entries. To remedy this problem we created a reduced gold standard which eliminated problematic entries. The most noticeable problem was the fact that some of the listed verbs were either ambiguous between homophone versions as a prefix verb and a particle verb (cf. example (3)) or only existed as prefix verbs. This means that we had to eliminate such verbs which were not detected by the filters described in section 4.1.

A second problem was that the automatically harvested PVs often contained wrong entries which were produced by parsing or lemmatization errors. We eliminated all verbs for which no consensus among the authors could be obtained on the basis of their graphic form whether they are existing PVs or not. In the same process also PVs were deleted which could be attested, but only for a very specific and limited domain, such as the verb *ab|teufen* (*to sink*), which could be attested for highly technical domains, but was not known by all authors.

Finally we considered all highly frequent and highly infrequent PVs as not desirable for practical experiments, as we found out in earlier experiments (Bott and Schulte im Walde, 2014). For this reason we excluded the 20 PVs with the highest and lowest frequency for each particle type. As a result of the manual filtering, the balance over frequency bands changed, as the number of mid-frequency PVs in the final gold standard is now higher than the number of low-frequency and high-frequency PVs. The distribution across particle types was however kept similar, because we removed the same number of PVs from the gold standard across particle types. We consider the manual cleaning more beneficial than harming since it excludes problematic entries while it retains those which are most prototypical and especially interesting for the task of compositionality assessment. The three parts of Table 1 present the final numbers of PV elements for each particle, frequency band and ambiguity level.

Particle	an	auf	aus	nach	ab	zu	über	unter	ein	um	durch
	47	45	48	45	47	37	9	12	45	37	28

Frequency Level	H	M	L
	88	238	74

Ambiguity Level	A1	A2	A3	AG3
	141	143	56	60

Table 1: Number of items per particle, frequency band and ambiguity band (A1 refers to one PV sense (i.e., monosemy); ambiguity of >3 is coded as AG3) after the manual selection process.

4.4 Collection of Compositionality Ratings

We collected compositionality ratings via Amazon Mechanical Turk (AMT)[2], allowing only for German native speakers as raters. Raters were asked to evaluate in how far the meaning of the PV is related to the meaning of its base verb. Each item was rated by 7 to 31 raters, with an average of 16.14 raters per item. Rating was done on a scale from 1 to 6, with 6 representing the maximum rating for compositionality. Raters with an insufficient level of German were detected by the inclusion of non-existing verbs which had to be detected in the rating process. If participants did not recognize the fake words, all of their ratings were rejected.

One problematic aspect of the collection of ratings on compositionality is the treatment of polysemy. It is evident that different readings of PVs correspond to different ambiguity levels. For example, the PV *zu|schlagen* has at least two meanings: *to strike* and *to take advantage of a good offer/bargain*. In addition, it can mean *to slam a door* and *to hit quickly and hard*. The BV *schlagen* means *to hit*. It is evident that the *strike* meaning is closely related

---

[2]`https://www.mturk.com`

to the meaning of the BV, and even more so the meaning of *hit-quickly*, while the meaning of *take advantage* is less compositional. But how many readings are there exactly? Is *striking* and *hitting* one sense or two? Which sense is predominant, and does the predominant sense exist in terms of frequency or in terms of some cognitive aspect? We found that these aspects are extremely hard to assess and even more so in a data collection based on crowd-sourcing. For this reason, we tried not to bias the raters choices by providing them contextual information, or any other information to disambiguate the target PV. We are aware of the fact that this is problematic, but we considered any other alternative even more problematic. Items were thus presented without context, and the rated word sense was assumed to be the predominant word sense as perceived by the raters. Our ongoing and future work explores alternative methods of data collection which addresses this problem, but which is necessarily more costly and more limited in scope.

5 Properties of the Gold Standard

The resulting gold standard data set contains 400 PVs accomplished by the following information:

- PV lemma
- Harmonic mean of PV corpus frequencies across four corpora
- The PV frequency band (low, mid, high)
- The PV level of ambiguity (ambiguities of 1, 2, 3 or greater than 3)
- The number of human ratings for the PV
- The mean compositionality rating for each PV
- The standard deviation of ratings among raters, as a measure of agreement
- The proportions of syntactically separated and syntactically non-separated appearances of the PV

The degree of semantic ambiguities is represented as the average grade of semantic ambiguity according to four lexical resources: GermaNet, Duden online, DictCC and Wiktionary. Any resource shows cases of a) spurious sense distinctions and b) under-representation of word senses. We tried to overcome definition problems by combining different lexical resources. In practice it is of course still very difficult to find an optimal representative listing of the number of word senses. Table 2 shows some sample entries of PVs from different frequency and ambiguity bands.

PV	PV freq	freq band	ambig. band	no. raters	mean rating	std dev	prop. synt. sep.	prop. synt. non-sep.
abkratzen	39.80	M	AG3	14	5.29	2.52	0.16	0.84
absegnen	23.38	H	A1	14	4.07	1.90	0.09	0.91
anleuchten	6.37	L	A1	20	5.95	1.50	0.62	0.38
anstiften	7.92	M	A2	15	1.80	0.86	0.17	0.83
aufhorchen	74.58	H	A1	29	4.55	1.97	0.16	0.84
aufschneiden	43.31	H	AG3	14	6.07	1.73	0.32	0.68
ausreizen	19.35	M	A2	29	3.62	2.13	0.07	0.93
durchrosten	9.66	M	A1	14	6.29	0.73	0.31	0.69
einstampfen	33.34	H	A1	14	4.07	2.06	0.15	0.85
nachschicken	22.81	H	A1	15	6.00	1.07	0.29	0.71
nachtragen	3.97	L	A2	15	4.47	2.03	0.21	0.79
umplanen	14.44	M	A2	15	4.93	1.83	0.10	0.90
zukneifen	8.53	M	A2	14	4.71	1.77	0.33	0.67
zulegen	4.00	L	AG3	14	3.86	2.07	0.29	0.71

Table 2: Sample entries from the gold standard.

The data collection scenario via Amazon Mechanical Turk makes it difficult to calculate inter-annotator agreement. Items were annotated by a varying number of annotators and each annotator annotated a different set of items. In the gold standard we include the standard deviation per item as a measure of agreement for each PV. The average standard deviation per rating target was 1.82 points on a 6-point scale. In Figure 1, the distribution of standard deviation over items can be seen in the form of a histogram. The x-axis shows the standard deviation per PV, where PVs were binned into intervals of 0.2 points of standard deviation. The y-axis shows the count of PVs per bin.

The plot shows that the highest peak is reached at a standard deviation of approximately 2.3 on a 6-point scale. This reflects the difficulty of the annotation task but is also to a certain extent a consequence of the crowd-sourcing approach, which on the one hand allows for a larger collection of data, but on the other hand provides less control on the background of the raters. There is a strong tendency of PVs with a low deviation in rating –the ones that represent the tail to the left in Figure 1– to be monosemous, like *nach|reisen* (*to follow s.o. or s.th by traveling*) and *durch|rosten* (*to rust through*), and the ones with strongly deviating ratings to be polysemous. A good example for this is the PV *ab|kratzen*, which can either mean *to scratch off* or *to die*. Among the latter group we also find PVs which are clearly monosemous, like *nach|denken* (*to meditate on s.th.*) or *durch|rechnen* (*to thoroughly calculate*). The strong variation in the ratings for such cases is surprising. A final, more expected, tendency that can be observed is that PVs with strong deviation in ratings also tend be the least compositional ones like *unter|jubeln* (*to plant s.th. on s.o.*).

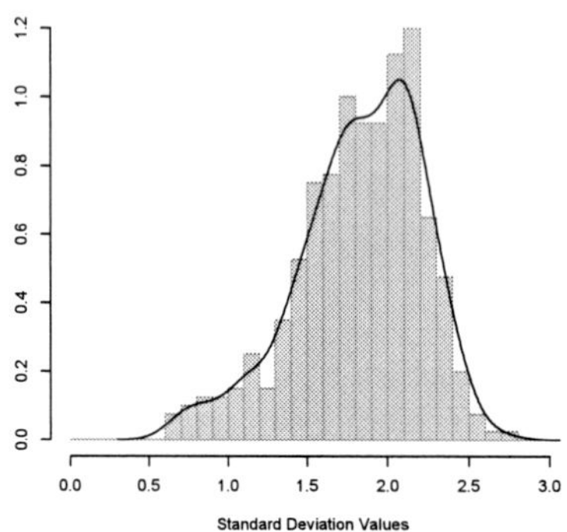

Figure 1: Histogram of the distribution and approximate density of standard deviation values for compositionality ratings across PVs. Standard deviation is provided to approximate inter-annotator agreement per item.

Figures 2 and 3 show the distribution of the obtained ratings and log-transformed word frequencies in relation to the different particles. The plots confirm some of the already known facts about the particles in question. For example, the particle *über* is predominantly locative and nearly always occurs in PVs which express some kind of movement or state (*über|streifen, to pull over*), even if it may be implicit (*über|schäumen, to foam over*). These PVs are always highly compositional, but not highly frequent. PV with *ab*, *an* and *ein* are much more varied in their semantics. Consequently, the corresponding PVs show a wider distribution in both frequency and compositionality. In general, the variation among particles is expected and thus confirmed by the gold standard.

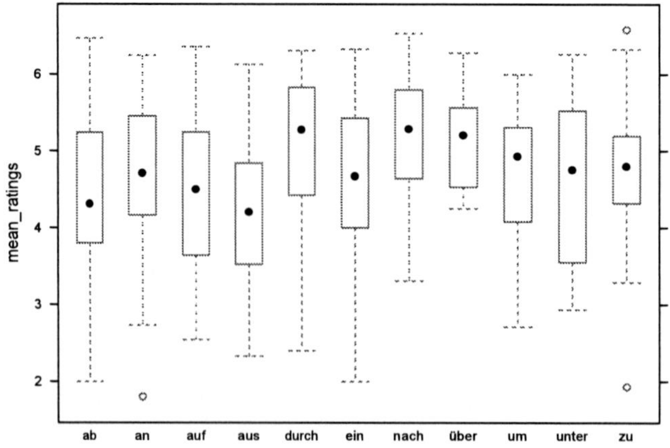

Figure 2: Mean ratings of particle verbs across particles types.

Figures 4 and 5 show the variation of ratings over frequency bands and ambiguity levels. We can observe little variation, which is good, since we intended the gold standard to be balanced. The ratings are quite evenly distributed over the different frequency bands. The mean value of the ratings is 4.67, which shows that PVs with a

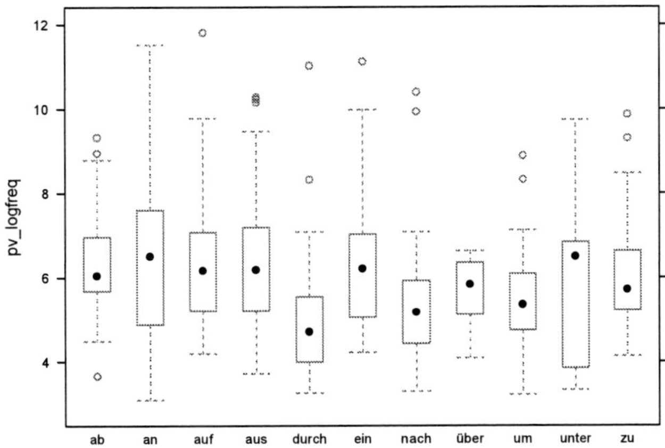

Figure 3: Log frequencies of particle verbs across particle types.

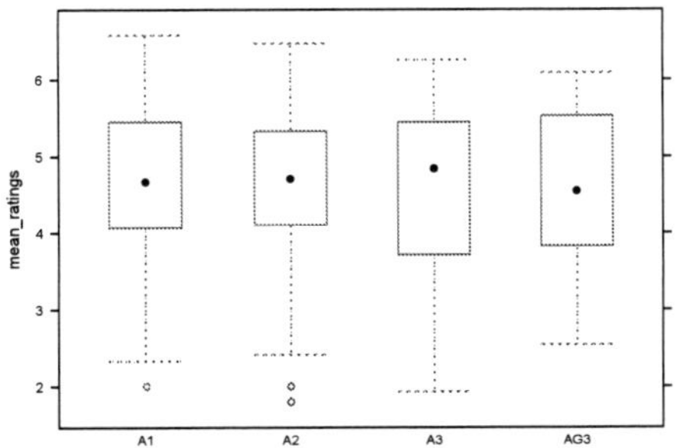

Figure 4: Mean compositionality ratings across frequency bands.

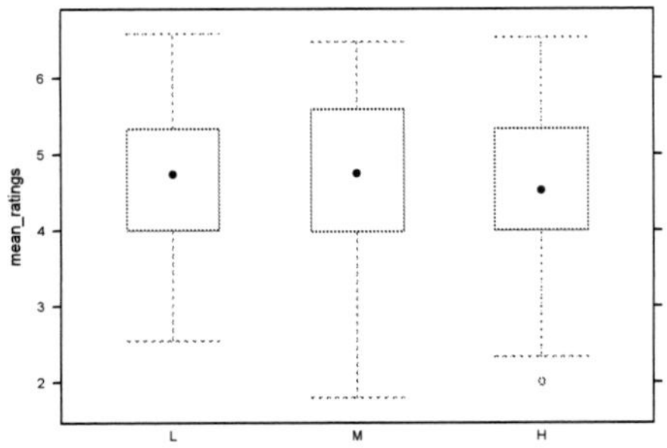

Figure 5: Mean compositionality ratings across ambiguity levels.

higher compositionality are slightly more dominant than those with low compositionality. Since the selection of PVs was done randomly we can assume that this reflects a general tendency of PVs to be compositional. Figure 4 shows the distribution of compositionality ratings for different ambiguity levels. The PVs with the highest polysemy (number of senses greater than 3) show a slight tendency to be rated in the medium range of compositionality. Highly ambiguous PVs tend to have senses with different levels of compositionality. They tend to mix word senses with different compositionality level, which should result in less PVs in the very high and the very low range. We expected this effect to be more pronounced than we could finally observe. We did not find a straightforward explanation for this, except for the already known fact that information on the grade of ambiguity extracted from lexical resources are never fully reliable, which might have caused the observed behavior.

6   Conclusion

This paper introduced a new gold standard for the evaluation of predicting German particle verb compositionality. The selection of particle verbs for this data set was carefully designed, especially in compiling a random selection of PVs which are balanced over different frequency bands. We provided some descriptive statistics which show that the data set is balanced in the distribution of PV compositionality across frequency and the grade of polysemy. The gold standard is available for research and education.

One of the problems which we could not resolve in a fully satisfactory way is the fact that the compositionality ratings per particle verb do not distinguish between different word senses. We have argued that this is a problem which is difficult to solve in a crowdsourcing approach for various reasons. Ongoing and future work addresses this specific aspect, but is necessarily limited to smaller amounts of target verbs and a smaller number of ratings.

References

Timothy Baldwin, Colin Bannard, Takaaki Tanaka, and Dominic Widdows. 2003. An Empirical Model of Multiword Expression Decomposability. In *Proceedings of the ACL-2003 Workshop on Multiword Expressions: Analysis, Acquisition and Treatment*, pages 89–96, Sapporo, Japan.

Colin Bannard, Timothy Baldwin, and Alex Lascarides. 2003. A Statistical Approach to the Semantics of Verb-Particles. In *Proceedings of the ACL Workshop on Multiword Expressions: Analysis, Acquisition and Treatment*, pages 65–72, Sapporo, Japan.

Collin Bannard. 2005. Learning about the Meaning of Verb–Particle Constructions from Corpora. *Computer Speech and Language*, 19:467–478.

Bernd Bohnet. 2010. Very High Accuracy and Fast Dependency Parsing is Not a Contradiction. In *Proceedings of the 23rd International Conference on Computational Linguistics*, pages 89–97, Beijing, China.

Stefan Bott and Sabine Schulte im Walde. 2014. Optimizing a Distributional Semantic Model for the Prediction of German Particle Verb Compositionality. In *Proceedings of the 9th International Conference on Language Resources and Evaluation*, pages 509–516, Reykjavik, Island.

Stefan Bott and Sabine Schulte im Walde. 2015. Exploiting Fine-grained Syntactic Transfer Features to Predict the Compositionality of German Particle Verbs. In *Proceedings of the 11th International Conference on Computational Semantics*, page 34–39, London, UK.

Paul Cook and Suzanne Stevenson. 2006. Classifying Particle Semantics in English Verb-Particle Constructions. In *Proceedings of the Workshop on Multiword Expressions: Identifying and Exploiting Underlying Properties*, pages 45–53, Sydney, Australia.

Gertrud Faaß and Kerstin Eckart. 2013. SdeWaC – A Corpus of Parsable Sentences from the Web. In *Proceedings of the International Conference of the German Society for Computational Linguistics and Language Technology*, pages 61–68, Darmstadt, Germany.

Arne Fitschen. 2004. *Ein computerlinguistisches Lexikon als komplexes System*. Ph.D. thesis, Institut für Maschinelle Sprachverarbeitung, Universität Stuttgart.

Silvana Hartmann, Sabine Schulte im Walde, and Hans Kamp. 2008. Predicting the Degree of Compositionality of German Particle Verbs based on Empirical Syntactic and Semantic Subcategorisation Transfer Patterns. In *Talk at the Konvens Workshop'Lexical-Semantic and Ontological Resources*.

Silvana Hartmann. 2008. Einfluss syntaktischer und semantischer Subkategorisierung auf die Kompositionalität von Partikelverben. Studienarbeit. Institut für Maschinelle Sprachverarbeitung, Universität Stuttgart.

Boris Haselbach. 2011. Deconstructing the Meaning of the German Temporal Verb Particle *'nach'* at the Syntax-Semantics Interface. In *Proceedings of Generative Grammar in Geneva*, pages 71–92, Geneva, Switzerland.

Fritz Kliche. 2011. Semantic Variants of German Particle Verbs with *"ab"*. *Leuvense Bijdragen*, 97:3–27.

Natalie Kühner and Sabine Schulte im Walde. 2010. Determining the Degree of Compositionality of German Particle Verbs by Clustering Approaches. In *Proceedings of the 10th Conference on Natural Language Processing*, pages 47–56, Saarbrücken, Germany.

Andrea Lechler and Antje Roßdeutscher. 2009. German Particle Verbs with *auf*. Reconstructing their Composition in a DRT-based Framework. *Linguistische Berichte*, (220):439–478.

Diana McCarthy, Bill Keller, and John Carroll. 2003. Detecting a Continuum of Compositionality in Phrasal Verbs. In *Proceedings of the ACL-SIGLEX Workshop on Multiword Expressions: Analysis, Acquisition and Treatment*, pages 73–80, Sapporo, Japan.

Siva Reddy, Diana McCarthy, and Suresh Manandhar. 2011. An Empirical Study on Compositionality in Compound Nouns. In *Proceedings of the 5th International Joint Conference on Natural Language Processing*, pages 210–218, Chiang Mai, Thailand.

Bahar Salehi and Paul Cook. 2013. Predicting the Compositionality of Multiword Expressions Using Translations in Multiple Languages. In *Proceedings of the 2nd Joint Conference on Lexical and Computational Semantics*, pages 266–275, Atlanta, GA.

Bahar Salehi, Paul Cook, and Timothy Baldwin. 2014. Using Distributional Similarity of Multi-way Translations to Predict Multiword Expression Compositionality. In *Proceedings of the 14th Conference of the European Chapter of the Association for Computational Linguistics*, pages 472–481, Gothenburg, Sweden.

Roland Schäfer and Felix Bildhauer. 2012. Building Large Corpora from the Web Using a New Efficient Tool Chain. In *Proceedings of the 8th International Conference on Language Resources and Evaluation*, pages 486–493, Istanbul, Turkey.

Sabine Schulte im Walde, Anna Hätty, Stefan Bott, and Nana Khvtisavrishvili. 2016. G$_h$ost-NN: A Representative Gold Standard of German Noun-Noun Compounds. In *Proceedings of the 10th International Conference on Language Resources and Evaluation*, pages 2285–2292, Portoroz, Slovenia.

Sylvia Springorum, Sabine Schulte im Walde, and Antje Roßdeutscher. 2013. Sentence Generation and Compositionality of Systematic Neologisms of German Particle Verbs. Talk at the 5th Conference on Quantitative Investigations in Theoretical Linguistics.

Sylvia Springorum. 2011. DRT-based Analysis of the German Verb Particle *"an"*. *Leuvense Bijdragen*, 97:80–105.

Discovering Potential Terminological Relationships from Twitter's Timed Content

Mohammad Daoud
Department of Computer Science
American University of Madaba
Madaba, Jordan
m.daoud@aum.edu.jo

Daoud Daoud
Department of Computer Science
Princess Sumaya University for Technology
Amman, Jordan
d.daoud@psut.edu.jo

Abstract

This paper presents a method to discover possible terminological relationships from tweets. We match the histories of terms (frequency patterns). Similar history indicates a possible relationship between terms. For example, if two terms (t1, t2) appeared frequently in Twitter at particular days, and there is a 'similarity' in the frequencies over a period of time, then t1 and t2 can be related. Maintaining standard terminological repository with updated relationships can be difficult; especially in a dynamic domain such as social media where thousands of new terms (neology) are coined every day. So we propose to construct a raw repository of lexical units with unconfirmed relationships. We have experimented our method on time-sensitive Arabic terms used by the online Arabic community of Twitter. We draw relationships between these terms by matching their similar frequency patterns (timelines). We use dynamic time warping as a similarity measure. For evaluation, we have selected 630 possible terms (we call them preterms) and we matched the similarity of these terms over a period of 30 days. Around 270 correct relationships were discovered with a precision of 0.61. These relationships were extracted without considering the textual context of the term.

1   Introduction

Internet users are producing 10,000 Microposts on average every second (internetlivestats 2015). Microposts are short messages containing few sentences written in several languages. These messages tend to talk about time sensitive topics (Grinev, Grineva et al. 2011) (Kwak, Lee et al. 2010). Microposts are rich with terminology (Uherčík, Šimko et al. 2013), not only old and well defined terminology but also newly coined terms (Becker, Naaman et al. 2011).

Building and maintaining an up-to-date terminological repository is very important for several applications (Daoud, Boitet et al. 2010), like machine translation (Vasconcellos, Avey et al. 2001), information retrieval (Peñas, Verdejo et al. 2001)… However, finding terminology (terms and relationships) is a very difficult task (Cabre and Sager 1999), especially for poorly equipped languages, and when the domain is active and changing everyday (new concepts appear every day). Classical approaches in building terminology depend heavily on terminologists and subject-matter experts (Hartley and Paris 1997, Kim, Yang et al. 2005). This approach is very expensive (Gaussier and Langé 1997, Davidson 1998), and it achieves poor coverage (Daoud 2010) because terminologists have limited capability and subject matter experts are rare for contemporary domains. Statistical approaches on the other hand are less expensive, but they need large and processed corpus/corpora. Besides, statistical methods might find a list of candidate terms without relationships, so mapping these terms into a lexical network can be difficult. Microblogs are massive and can solve the problem of the availability of a large textual corpus, however, these microblogs have little textual context (A micropost in Twitter is 140 characters only) and they are usually poorly written (Cornolti, Ferragina et al. 2013).

Proceedings of the Workshop on Cognitive Aspects of the Lexicon,
pages 134–144, Osaka, Japan, December 11-17 2016.

We are working on analyzing terms that appear on microblogs over a period of time to monitor their evolutions. Our idea is that terms with similar histories (frequency patterns over a period of time) are probably similar. For example, if two terms are peaking at the same dates then there is a chance that these terms are used by the internet users synonymously. That way rather than using textual context (which is almost nonexistent in microblogs), we are using historical context to relate between terms. And that will make social media a legitimate source of terminology (terms and relationships). Building a terminological database is still challenging (Roche, Calberg-Challot et al. 2009), because terminology must be standardized and must have a formal body to approve it. We are proposing to extract unconfirmed terminological relationships (preterminology relationships) (Daoud, Boitet et al. 2009, Daoud, Boitet et al. 2009, Daoud, Kageura et al. 2010) rather than standard terminology. Preterminology is considered as raw material for terminology that can be refined to produce standard terminology.

Matching timelines for terms is a classical time series problem, where time series are searched for similarities. There are several approaches to search time series. The performance of these approaches depends on the application (Agrawal, Faloutsos et al. 1993). We use an algorithm originally used for speech recognition called Dynamic Time Warping algorithm (Sakoe and Chiba 1978) with a normalized Euclidean distance function. This approach will not only measure the distance between timelines, but it will consider the slight shifts in the timelines. And this is very suitable for our application because related terms might not peak on the exact same days.

This article is organized as follows; the following section introduces terminology evolution in big data. The third section presents our approach in finding historical similarity between terms. The fourth section shows our data collection method. The fifth section shows the experimental results and evaluation, and finally we will draw some conclusions.

2   Terminology and Preterminology in Big Data

A term is a sign to describe a thought in a particular domain (Sager 1990); this sign is a lexical unit that corresponds to one or more words (Kageura 2002). According to the extended semantic triangle (Suonuuti 1997), a term corresponds to a concept and must have a definition. A terminology is the vocabulary (set of signs) of a domain. Building a term base involves finding precise definitions for each term and connecting terms with relationships. Such process is difficult to achieve in dynamic domains and mediums (Gaussier and Langé 1997, Davidson 1998, Roche, Calberg-Challot et al. 2009). Therefore, we propose to collect preterminology rather that terminology (Daoud 2010). Preterminology is considered as raw material for terminology that can be refined to produce standard terminology. Preterminology incorporates neology (Cabré and Nazar 2011) of new concepts with no standard terms.

Social media posters associate a new concept with a sign (preterm) (Giannakidou, Vakali et al. 2014). This association was not approved by a standardization body and this preterm may not have a specific definition. That is why we call it a preterm rather than a term. A preterm can be processed to produce a term. Social media content may associate two terms (preterms), which can lead to an actual terminological relationship. That is why in this paper we are investigating possible terms (preterms) and their relationships (preterminological relationships). Preterminology can be convenient for useful application such as IR and opinion mining, moreover, it can be used to produce actual terminology.

Extracting knowledge from big data, such as social media generated content, is attracting more and more researchers (Chen, Chiang et al. 2012). Data provided by internet users can be used to find new trends, prevent diseases (Yang, Horneffer et al. 2013), detect crimes (Kandias, Stavrou et al. 2013), and predict future events(Bothos, Apostolou et al. 2010). Extracting terminology or other lexical semantic information from Twitter (Twitter 2015) or social media in general is an ambitious task (Federmann, Gromann et al. 2012). Many succeeded in extracting trending lexical units, finding collocations, classifying tweets, and analyzing positivity/negativity of terms and tweets (Speriosu, Sudan et al. 2011, Zhao, Jiang et al. 2011, Daoud, Alkouz et al. 2015). These attempts consider the textual context of lexical units. However, there is a limitation in using Twitter's textual context as natural language processing of tweets is difficult, especially for Arabic. Therefore, while there is a need and a possibility to extract real-time terminology from tweets, attempts are faced with challenges.. We are proposing a method that considers the textual and the historical context to extract terminological information and relationships.

Traditional terminology has a specific definition that disallows the integration of unconventional resources. That is why a classical standard terminological repository suffers from a lack of linguistic and informational coverage (Gallego Hernández and Herrero Díaz 2014), and it cannot deal flexibly with hidden or absent terminology (Daoud 2010). We suggest extracting unconfirmed terminological relationship between terms (preterms). These possible relationships will have a similarity weight indicating a possible relationship (translation, synonymy, acronym, hyponymy, antonymy, or other).

3   Timeline Similarity

We monitor the frequencies of possible terms each day. We create a timeline for each one. The timeline shows the daily frequencies of the preterm. These timelines illustrate the peaks, bottoms, and possibly the coining date of a preterm. Figure (1) shows the timeline for "اقتحام لاقصى" (Al-Aqsa raid). We can see that the term has peaked on 13 September 2015 with 11,800 frequencies.

The tool used to produce the figure is an online Arabic social media monitoring platform built by the second author. We studied a small set of Arabic preterms and we observed similarities between the timelines of related ones. Figure (2) shows the timelines of "اسعار النفط , اوبك" (OPEC, oil prices). We can see similarity in the frequencies during the period from 25 August 2015 to 29 September 2015. The similarity between terms can occur due to one of the following reasons:

1.   Term collocation: terms that co-occur to convey certain meaning, figure 3 shows an example.
2.   Event co-occurrence: separate events happened at the same time. Each event has related terms that might produce similar timelines.
3.   Same event with different concepts (related terms); Figure (4) shows an example.
4.   Same or similar concept with different lexical units (translation, synonymy, acronym, hyponymy, antinomy, hypernymy). Figure (5) shows an example.

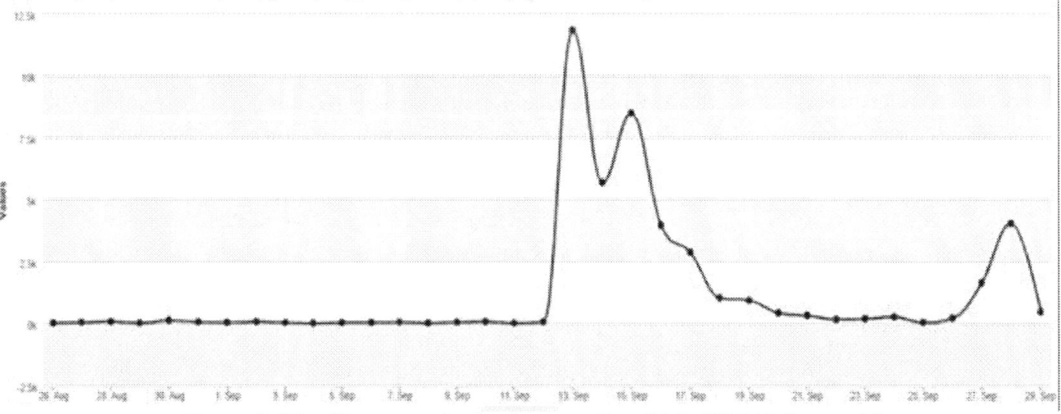

Figure 1. Timeline example for the term "اقتحام لاقصى" (Al-Aqsa raid)

Our objective based on these observations is to search for similar timelines to build a candidate set of relationships between new terms (preterms) extracted from the community of Arabic social media.

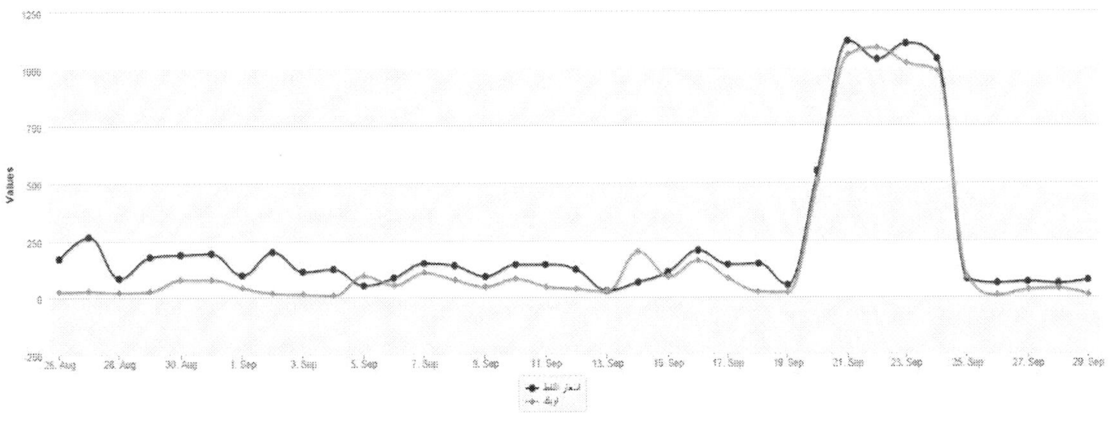

Figure 2. Timelines of "اوبك ,اسعار النفط"

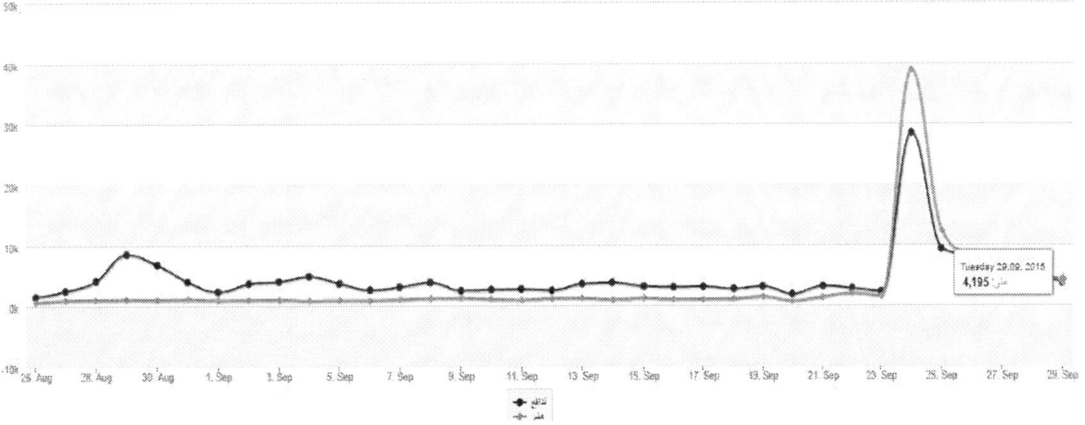

Figure 3. Timeline example (Term collocation)

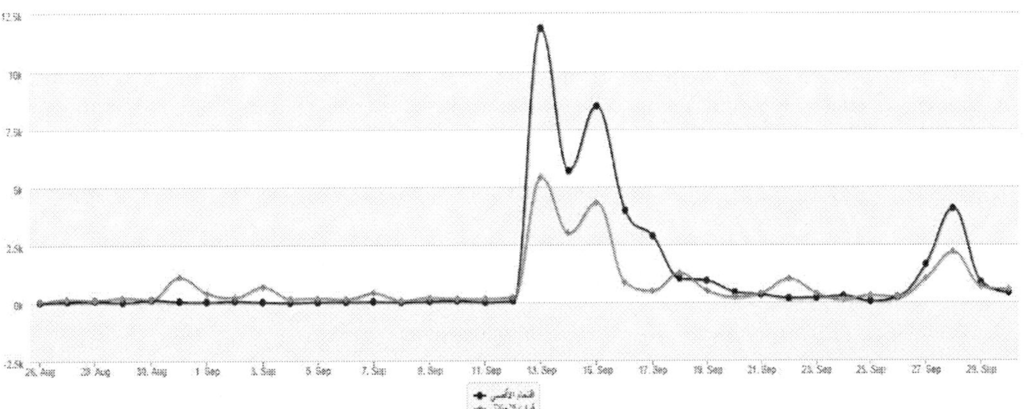

Figure 4. Event co-occurrence

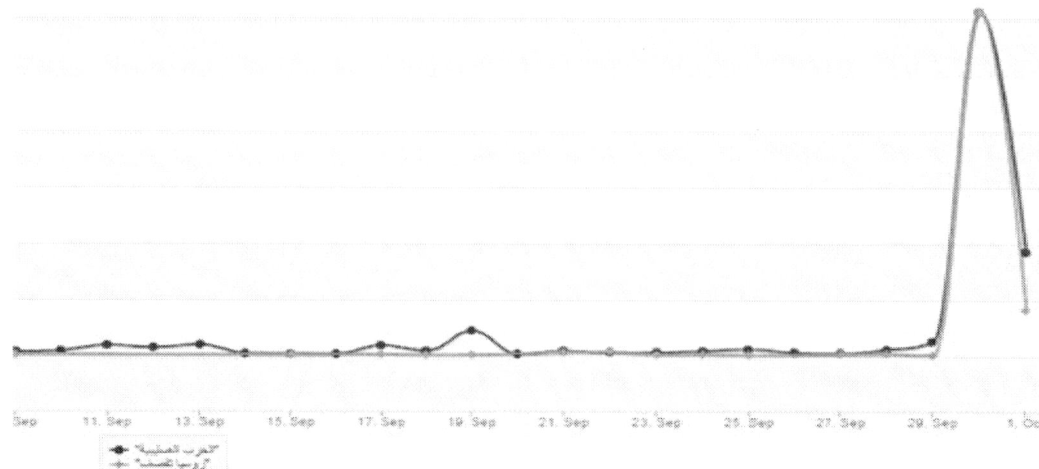

Figure 5. Community generated synonym

3.1 Time-series similarity search

Similarity search in timelines (time-series) is an interesting research direction to analyze stock prices data, weather forecast, biomedical measurements, etc. While there are several methods to find similarity between time series, the choice of a particular method is an application-dependent. Therefore, we are testing our hypothesis with a standard Dynamic Time Warping (Berndt and Clifford 1994) algorithm to measure the similarity between terms. There are several approaches that depend on the application. In our case the approach we need to use must consider the following assumptions:

1. Suppose that *t1* and *t2* are two timelines for two terms. *t1* and *t2* are similar if they have similar shapes. For example, figure (4, from 12/9 to 17/9) shows different frequencies between the two timelines. However, the shapes are similar.
2. Similar terms might not peak in the exact same day. *t1* could peak in a particular day and the other *t2* might peek in the next day. *t1* and *t2* are considered similar if they have similar peaks.
3. The presence of the peaks is more important that their magnitudes.

Dynamic time warping (DTW) is a technique that aligns two time series in which one time serie may be "warped" by stretching or shrinking its time axis. This alignment can be used to find corresponding regions or to determine the similarity between the two time series.

DTW focuses on aligning the peaks of the time lines without focusing on their magnitudes and it matches peaks even if they did not appear at the exact same time. This satisfies the assumptions mentioned above. DTW would consider *t1* and *t2* in figure (6) to be similar.

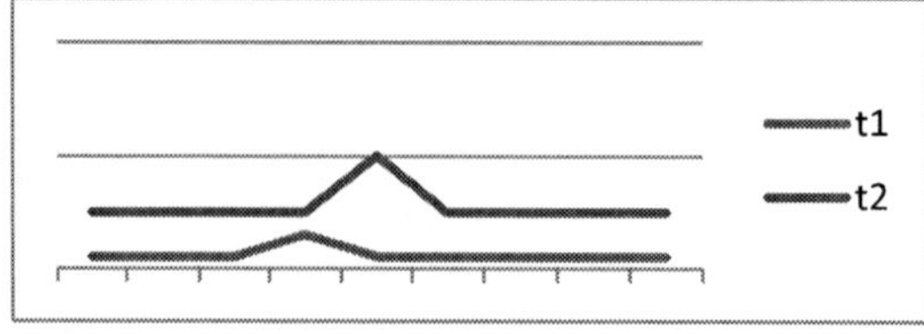

Figure 6. Two similar time series

3.2 DTW algorithm

DTW is a time series alignment algorithm that was originally used in voice recognition (Sakoe and Chiba 1978) It relates two time series of feature vectors by warping the time axis of one series onto another. Given two time series X and Y, Where:

$$X = x_1 + x_2 + x_3 + \ldots + x_i + \ldots + x_n$$
$$Y = y_1 + y_2 + y_3 + \ldots + y_i + \ldots + y_n$$

Algorithm 1 will produce the cost of aligning X and Y (warping them) the cost will be low if the two time series are similar.

```
int standardDWT(X, Y) {
// Where X = x₁ + x₂ + x₃ + . . . + xᵢ + . . . + xₙ and Y = y₁ + y₂ + y₃ + . . . + yᵢ + . . . + yₙ
  Create DTW[0..n, 0..m]
  Set the first row and column of DTW to infinity
  DTW[0, 0] = 0
  for i = 1 to n
    for j = 1 to m
      DTW[i, j] = d(X[i], Y[j])+ minimum(DTW[i-1, j] ,
                                         DTW[i , j-1],
                                         DTW[i-1, j-1])
  return DTW[n, m]
}
```

Algorithm 1. Standard DWT

We start by filling a distance matrix DTW which has n × m elements; each element represents the warping distance between every two points in the time series. The warping distance between x_i and y_j is measured according to the following equation:

$$DTW(x_i, y_j) = d(x_i, y_j)+ minimum(DTW(x_{i-1}, y_j), DTW(x_i, y_{j-1}), DTW(x_{i-1}, y_{j-1}))$$

Where $d(x_i, y_i)$ is a distance function to calculate the distance between x_i and y_i. This version of DTW satisfies the monotonicity, continuity, boundary constrains demonstrated by (Sakoe and Chiba 1978, Keogh and Ratanamahatana 2004, Salvador and Chan 2007). We use the Euclidian distance as a distance function between x_i, y_i. So the distance will be calculated as follows:

$$d(x_i, y_j) = | x_i - y_i |$$

Frequency reading must be normalized to achieve meaningful results and to give more importance to peaks in relation to the average readings of a particular timeline. A frequency reading f is measured according to this equation:

$$Norm(f) = f - m$$

Where m is the average of frequencies for that term and the returned value from the algorithm indicates the cost of aligning the two normalized timelines. The similarity score described below indicates the possible similarity between the two timeline:

$$Similarity(X, Y) = 1 - cost/max(n, m)$$

Where *cost* is the returned value from the algorithm, n and m are the lengths of X and Y respectively. High similarity score means the probability that the two terms are related is high.

4   Data Collection

We are testing our approach with timelines collected by an online platform that addresses Arabic social media content and provides a platform to collect, search, monitor and analyze social media content. The platform has many functions. However, we are interested in the production of timelines which are archived through the following steps:

1. Data collection: Arabic tweets are collected using Twitter API. The online platform receives live feed from Twitter. Any non-Arabic tweets will be filtered.
2. Indexing: tweets are analyzed and indexed according to the terms they carry. Arabic analysis component is used for stemming and tokenization.

3. Reporting: the platform reports the frequencies for each term per time interval. Thus, we can build a timeline for each term.

The online system is available currently at "http://45.33.23.107". We are using its produced time-lines and terms for our experiment.

5 Experimentation and Evaluation

Arabic tweets collected by the online platform during the month of May 2016 were analyzed. We selected 630 timelines for the most popular preterms in that month. Then we searched for similarities between them. The produced relationships were evaluated based on precision and recall.

The top 1108 relationships were rated by 2 evaluators (E1 and E2). Relationship between $t1$ and $t2$ is considered correct if the two evaluators found that $t1$ and $t2$ are event related or if they found that there is a terminological relationship (synonymy, acronym, hyponymy, antinomy, and hypernymy) between them. Using Cohen's Kappa coefficient (Cohen 1960) the inter-agreement score was 0.93 which indicates a substantial agreement between the evaluators.

5.1 Precision

We are trying to evaluate the precision of the similarity score according to this equation:

$$Precision = C_{th}/T_{th}$$

Where C_{th} is number of correct relationships with a score greater than the threshold th. T_{th} is total number of produced relationships with a score that is greater that th. When th is small the produced set of relationships increases but precision might decrease. When $th = 0.85$ the precision is 0.92. Figure (7) shows the precision in relation to the threshold.

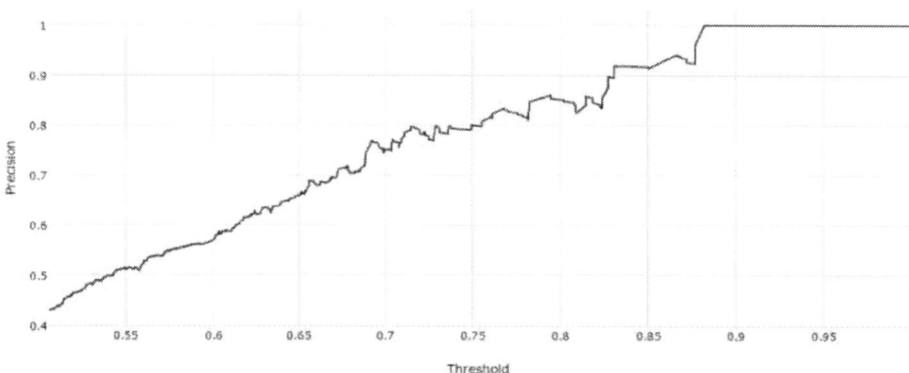

Figure 7. Precision

As you can see the precision starts to decline when th is below 0.5. The similarity score proved to be a good indicator of a relationship between preterms.

5.2 Recall

Recall is measured in terms of number of correct relationships extracted by our approach. When the threshold is 0.65 number of correct relationships is 200. Figure (8) shows the recall in relation to the threshold. When the threshold is 0.6 the precision is 0.61 and 270 correct relation were extracted from 630 preterm.

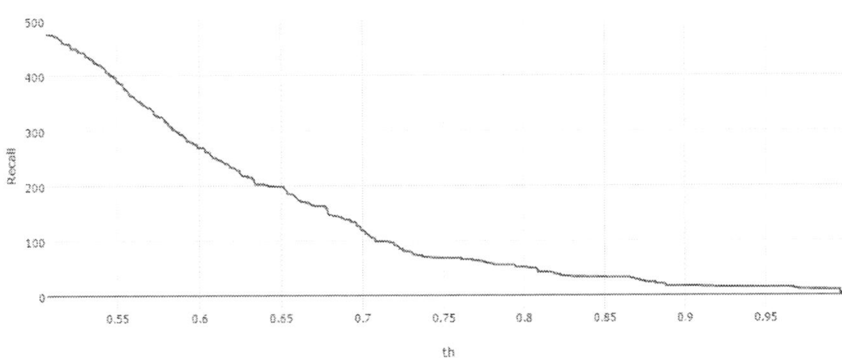

Figure 8. Recall

5.3 Assessment and sample results

Our approach has correctly identified terminological relationships between time sensitive preterms without analyzing the textual context; Table (2) shows sample results.

Table 2. Sample results

T1	T1 - English Translation	T2	T2 - English Translation	Similarity	Note
الثورة العربية الكبرى	The great Arab revolt	الثورة العربية	The Arab re-volt	0.98	correct
ولي ولي العهد	Deputy crown prince	الرؤية السعودية 2030	Saudi vision 2030	0.96	correct
منوية الثورة	Revolt Centennial	الثورة العربية الكبرى	The great Ar-ab revolt	0.89	correct
الاحتلال الإسرائيلي	Israeli occupation	قوات الاحتلال	Occupation forces	0.88	correct
عيد الاستقلال	Independence day	الاعياد الوطنية	National holi-day	0.88	correct
العراق	Iraq	الحشد الشعبي	Popular Mobi-lization Forces	0.83	correct
جرائم حرب	War Crimes	الحشد الشعبي	Popular Mobi-lization Forces	0.81	correct
الشرطة	Police	وزارة الداخلية	Ministry of interior affairs	0.8	correct
ولي العهد	Crown prince	خادم الحرمين	Custodian of the Two Holy Mosques	0.8	correct
ولي ولي العهد	Deputy crown prince	محمد بن سلمان	Mohammad bin Salman	0.8	correct
القصف الروسي	Russian bombing	العدوان الروسي	Russian ag-gression	0.76	correct
وزارة الصحة	Ministry of health	البترول	Petrol (oil)	0.73	incorrect
الثورة العربية الكبرى	The great Arab revolt	ولي ولي العهد	Deputy crown prince	0.7	incorrect

Extracting relationships between terms is a challenging task that needs large corpora, and specialists. The challenge increases when the terms are time sensitive Arabic terms. Our approach extracted 480 of relationships from 630 preterms with high precision; these relationships can be used in many applications, such as:

1. Extracted relationships can be post edited by specialists to enrich Arabic term bases.
2. Lexicon for social media analysis: auto microblogs classifications, auto tagging, sentiment analysis. In fact, we intend to use these relationships to dynamically extend a polarized lexicon for Arabic sentiment analysis.
3. These relationships can locate newly coined terms on an ontological resource.

The approach will be used on a larger scale to automatically discover related terms on-the-fly by analyzing online microblog feeds. The importance of this approach is that it does not rely on textual context; in fact many extracted relations were between terms that did not appear in the same tweet. Most of the wrongly extracted relationships were between key terms describing two separate events that took place at the same time. These errors can be reduced when the timeline is longer than 30 days.

6   Conclusions

We have presented an approach to extract terminological relationships between time-sensitive Arabic preterms. Our hypothesis is that terms that have similar history (timeline) are similar or related. We used Dynamic Time Warping algorithm to measure the similarity between terms. Our experiment produced 270 correct relationships out of 630 preterms with a precision of 0.61. The extracted information is crucial because it maps time-sensitive terms into a wider terminological map. The approach can be used to identify and connect terminology on-the-fly by analyzing microblogs feeds online, without relying on textual context (which is very limited in the case of online microblogs).

References

Agrawal, R., et al. (1993). Efficient Similarity Search In Sequence Databases. <u>Proceedings of FODO</u>. Illinois, USA.

Becker, H., et al. (2011). "Beyond trending topics: Real-world event identification on Twitter." <u>In Proceedings of the Fifth International Conference on Weblogs and Social Media</u>.

Berndt, D. J. and J. Clifford (1994). <u>Using Dynamic Time Warping to Find Patterns in Time Series</u>. KDD workshop, Seattle, WA.

Bothos, E., et al. (2010). "Using social media to predict future events with agent-based markets."

Cabre, M. T. and J. C. Sager (1999). "Terminology: Theory, methods, and applications." J. Benjamins Publishing: xii, 247 p.

Cabré, T. and R. Nazar (2011). <u>Towards a new approach to the study of neology</u>. Neology and Specialised Translation 4th Joint Seminar Organised by the CVC and Termisti.

Chen, H., et al. (2012). "Business Intelligence and Analytics: From Big Data to Big Impact." <u>MIS quarterly</u> **36**(4): 1165-1188.

Cohen, J. (1960). "A coefficient of agreement for nominal scales." <u>Educational and Psychological Measurement</u> **20**(1): 37-46.

Cornolti, M., et al. (2013). <u>A framework for benchmarking entity-annotation systems</u>. Proceedings of the 22nd international conference on World Wide Web, International World Wide Web Conferences Steering Committee.

Daoud, D., et al. (2015). "Time-Sensitive Arabic Multiword Expressions Extraction from Social Networks." <u>INTERNATIONAL JOURNAL OF SPEECH TECHNOLOGY</u>.

Daoud, M. (2010). "Utilisation de ressources non conventionnelles et de méthodes contributives pour combler le fossé terminologique entre les langues en développant des" préterminologies" multilingues."

Daoud, M., et al. (2009). Constructing Multilingual Preterminological Graphs using various online-community resources. The Eighth International Symposium on Natural Language Processing (SNLP09), Thailand, Bangkok, IEEE.

Daoud, M., et al. (2009). "Constructing multilingual preterminological graphs using various online-community resources". the Eighth International Symposium on Natural Language Processing (SNLP2009), Thailand: pp. 116 - 121.

Daoud, M., et al. (2010). "Building Specialized Multilingual Lexical Graphs Using Community Resources." Lecture Notes in Computer Science - Resource Discovery **Volume 6162**: pp 94-109.

Daoud, M., et al. (2010). "Passive and Active Contribution to Multilingual Lexical Resources through Online Cultural Activities". NLPKE10, Beijing, China: 4 p.

Davidson, L. M. (1998). "Knowledge extraction technology for terminology."

Federmann, C., et al. (2012). Multilingual terminology acquisition for ontology-based information extraction. Proceedings of the 10th Terminology and Knowledge Engineering Conference (TKE 2012).

Gallego Hernández, D. and S. Herrero Díaz (2014). "Terminology and French-Spanish business translation: evaluating terminology resources for the translation of accounting documents." MonTI : Monografías de Traducción e Interpretación **6**.

Gaussier, É. and J.-M. Langé (1997). "Some methods for the extraction of bilingual terminology." 1997). New Methods in Language Processing: 145-153.

Giannakidou, E., et al. (2014). Towards a Framework for Social Semiotic Mining. Proceedings of the 4th International Conference on Web Intelligence, Mining and Semantics (WIMS14), ACM.

Grinev, M., et al. (2011). "Analytics for the RealTime Web." Proceedings of the VLDB Endowment **Volume 4**: pp 1391-1394.

Hartley, A. and C. Paris (1997). "Multilingual Document Production: from Support for Translating to Support for Authoring." Machine Translation 12 (1-2), pp. 109-29.

internetlivestats (2015). "Internet Live Stats - Internet Usage & Social Media Statistics." Retrieved 1/2/2015, 2015, from http://www.internetlivestats.com/one-second/.

Kageura, K. (2002). "The Dynamics of Terminology: A descriptive theory of term formation and terminological growth", Terminology and Lexicography Research and Practice 5, 322 p.

Kandias, M., et al. (2013). Proactive insider threat detection through social media: The YouTube case. Proceedings of the 12th ACM workshop on Workshop on privacy in the electronic society, ACM.

Keogh, E. and C. Ratanamahatana (2004). "Exact indexing of dynamic time warping." Knowledge and Information Systems: 358-386.

Kim, Y. G., et al. (2005). "Terminology construction workflow for Korean-English patent MT". MT Summit X. Phuket, Thailand: 5 p.

Kwak, H., et al. (2010). What is Twitter, a Social Network or a News Media? The 19th International World Wide Web (WWW) Conference, Raleigh NC (USA).

Peñas, A., et al. (2001). Corpus-based terminology extraction applied to information access. Proceedings of Corpus Linguistics, Citeseer.

Roche, C., et al. (2009). <u>Ontoterminology: A new paradigm for terminology</u>. International Conference on Knowledge Engineering and Ontology Development.

Sager, J. C. (1990). <u>A Practical Course in Terminology Processing</u> Amesterdam/Philadelphia, John Benjamins Publishing Company, 266 p.

Sakoe, H. and S. Chiba (1978). "Dynamic programming algorithm optimization for spoken word recognition." <u>IEEE Transactions on Acoustics, Speech and Signal Processing</u>: 43- 49.

Salvador, S. and P. Chan (2007). "Toward accurate dynamic time warping in linear time and space." <u>Intelligent Data Analysis</u>: 561 - 580.

Speriosu, M., et al. (2011). "Twitter polarity classification with label propagation over lexical links and the follower graph." <u>EMNLP '11 Proceedings of the First Workshop on Unsupervised Learning in NLP</u>: 53-63

Suonuuti, H. (1997). " Guide to Terminology." <u>Nordterm 8. Helsinki:TSK</u>.

Twitter (2015). "Twitter." Retrieved 1/2/2015, 2015, from twitter.com.

Uherčík, T., et al. (2013). "Utilizing Microblogs for Web Page Relevant Term Acquisition." <u>SOFSEM 2013: Theory and Practice of Computer Science - Lecture Notes in Computer Science</u> **Volume 7741**: pp 457-468.

Vasconcellos, M., et al. (2001). "Terminology and machine translation." <u>Handbook of terminology management</u> **2**: 697-723.

Yang, Y. T., et al. (2013). "Mining social media and web searches for disease detection." <u>Journal of public health research</u> **2**(1): 17.

Zhao, W. X., et al. (2011). "Topical keyphrase extraction from Twitter." <u>HLT '11 Proceedings of the 49th Annual Meeting of the Association for Computational Linguistics: Human Language Technologies - Volume 1</u> **379-388**.

Lexfom: a lexical functions ontology model

Alexsandro Fonseca
Université du Québec à Montréal
201 Président Kennedy Avenue
H2X 3Y7, Montreal, Canada
affonseca@gmail.com

Fatiha Sadat
Université du Québec à Montréal
201 Président Kennedy Avenue
H2X 3Y7, Montreal, Canada
sadat.fatiha@uqam.ca

François Lareau
Université de Montréal
C.P. 6128 succursale Centre-Ville
Montreal, Canada
francois.lareau@umontreal.ca

Abstract

A lexical function represents a type of relation that exists between lexical units (words or expressions) in any language. For example, the antonymy is a type of relation that is represented by the lexical function *Anti*: *Anti(big)* = *small*. Those relations include both paradigmatic relations, i.e. vertical relations, such as synonymy, antonymy and meronymy and syntagmatic relations, i.e. horizontal relations, such as objective qualification (*legitimate demand*), subjective qualification (*fruitful analysis*), positive evaluation (*good review*) and support verbs (*pay a visit, subject to an interrogation*). In this paper, we present the *Lexical Functions Ontology Model* (lexfom) to represent lexical functions and the relation among lexical units. Lexfom is divided in four modules: *lexical function representation* (lfrep), *lexical function family* (lffam), *lexical function semantic perspective* (lfsem) and *lexical function relations* (lfrel). Moreover, we show how it combines to *Lexical Model for Ontologies* (lemon), for the transformation of lexical networks into the semantic web formats. So far, we have implemented 100 simple and 500 complex lexical functions, and encoded about 8,000 syntagmatic and 46,000 paradigmatic relations, for the French language.

Keywords: lexical functions, lexical ontology, lexical network, collocations

1 Introduction

We present in this paper the Lexical Functions Ontology Model (lexfom), a model for the representation of lexical functions (Mel'čuk, 1998) of the Meaning-Text Theory (MTT) (Mel'čuk, 1997).

A lexical ontology uses the semantic web formalism (RDF/OWL languages) to represent different aspects of the lexicon, such as meaning, morphology, part of speech, as well as the relation among lexical units, such as syntactic, semantic and pragmatic relations.

We show in this paper how our ontology can be used to represent relations among lexical units in lexical networks. This is an important aspect since most of the existing lexical networks do not implement syntagmatic information (Schwab et al., 2007) provided by some Lexical Functions (LFs). Moreover, we show how this model can be used to represent collocations in a lexical network since the relation among lexical units in a collocation is a syntagmatic relation (Mel'čuk 1998).

We do not intend to recreate lexical representations already realized by previous works, such as lemon (McCrae et al., 2012), LexInfo (Buitelaar, 2009) or LMF (Francopoulo, 2007). Our proposal is to use, whenever possible, the lexical information already implemented by those models, such as the

Proceedings of the Workshop on Cognitive Aspects of the Lexicon,
pages 145–155, Osaka, Japan, December 11-17 2016.

classes "LexicalEntry" and "LexicalSense" in the lemon model, and create the necessary classes for the implementation of lexical functions information.

The present paper is organized as follows: in the Section 2, we report state-of-the-art related to the problem. Section 3 presents our proposed scheme for an ontology to represent LFs. In Section 4 we give a summary of the lexical functions and lexical relations encoded within our model. Finally, Section 5 summarizes our work and gives future perspective.

2 Foundations and Related Work

We present in this section the theoretical information about LFs and related work, as follows: In Section 2.1, we give the definition of collocation adopted in this paper. Section 2.2 explains LFs and gives some examples. In Section 2.3, we discuss the *French Lexical Network* (in French, *Réseau Lexical du Français*), which is based on LFs. In Section 2.4, we present a semantic classification for LFs. Finally, in Section 2.5, we discuss the lemon model and how we intend to combine it with our model to represent sense relations in a lexical network.

2.1 Definition of collocation

Before giving the definition of collocation, we present an example to show how frequent collocations are and the importance of treating them in computer applications. This example was taken from Mel'čuk (2004):

> Government troops have spread a DRAGNET across the country in a SEARCH for three heavily ARMED guerrillas. The FARC has claimed RESPONSIBILITY for the ATTACK launched Tuesday in which four ROCKETS were fired at an ARMY camp.

In this example, each underlined expression is a collocation. The capitalized word is the base or keyword of the collocation and the non capitalized word is the collocate. Note that collocates have a more idiomatic than prototypical meaning in each collocation and ignoring them can cause problems in machine translation, information retrieval and text generation applications.

A phrase is unrestrictedly constructed when the rules used in its construction are not obligatory. For example, instead of saying "pay for a lunch" we could say "pay for a meal". In contrast, an expression such as "pay attention" is fixed. We cannot say "pay care", even if it is grammatically correct. Therefore, "pay attention" is a phraseme, since it is not unrestrictedly constructed.

A phase is regularly constructed when its words are combined according to general rules of a grammar and its sense can be derived exclusively from sense of its constituent words. The phrase "red house" is regularly constructed because it follows the rules of the English grammar and its sense can be obtained from its constituent words. On the other hand, the expression "red neck" is not regularly constructed: it follows the rules of the English grammar. However, its sense cannot be completely derived from its constituent words.

A collocation is a kind of phraseme, as defined by Mel'čuk (1998). There are two types of phrasemes: pragmatic phrasemes or pragmatemes and semantic phrasemes, as defined by Morgan (1978). The pragmatemes are defined as:

- Expressions whose signified and signifier (Saussure, 1983) are not unrestrictedly constructed, even if they are regularly constructed. For example: "all you can eat", "see you later";
- Expressions whose signified only is not unrestrictedly constructed. For example: greetings, technical expressions and phrases like "it is forbidden to smoke".

In semantic phrasemes, the signified is free (it is unrestrictedly constructed, although it may not be regularly constructed) and its signifier is not free. There are three types of semantic phrasemes:

- Idioms: the sense of the expression is larger than the sense of its constituent words, which are not included in the sense of the expression. Examples: "to kick the bucket", "to spill the beans";

- Quasi-phrasemes or quasi idioms: the signified of the expression includes the signified of its constituent words. However, it also contains a signified that goes beyond the signified of each isolated word. Example: "start a family", "bed and breakfast";
- Collocations: The signified of the expression includes the signified of one of its constituent words (w_1), which is freely chosen, and another word or expression, (w_2), which is chosen contingent to (w_1). There are different types of collocations (Manning and Schütze, 1999): light verbs constructions (*to pay attention, to make a decision*), phrasal verbs (to *take out, to give up*), etc.

According to Polguère (2000), a collocation is a semi-idiomatic expression having the form L_1+L_2, where one of the components, the collocate (L_2) is chosen to express a specific sense in a specific syntactic role contingent to the selection of the other component, the base or keyword (L_1). The selection of collocate depends strongly on the lexeme chosen as keyword (Heid and Raab 1989).

2.2   Lexical Functions

Bolshakov and Gelbukh (1998) defined a lexical function (LF) as a formalism for the description and use of combinatorial properties of individual lexemes. A more technical definition, given by Mel'čuk (1998), says that a *"Lexical Function f is a function that associates with a given lexical unit L, which is the argument, or keyword, of f, a set* $\{L_i\}$ *of (more or less) synonymous lexical expressions – the value of f –* that are selected contingent on *L* to manifest the meaning corresponding to *f*:

$$f(L) = \{L_i\}$$

The LFs considered in this paper are the standard ones, differentiated from the non-standard by the fact that the former can be coupled with a higher number of possible keywords and value elements (Mel'čuk 1998). For example, the LF *Bon*, which represents the sense "subjective qualifier", can be coupled with many keywords (e.g. cut_N, $struggle_N$, *proposal, service, place* and many others) to give different values : Bon(cut_N) = {*neatly, cleanly*}; Bon($struggle_N$) = *heroic*; Bon(*proposal*) = *tempting*; Bon(*service*) = *first-class*; Bon(*place*) = *prominent*; (Mel'čuk 1998). On the other hand, the sense *"additionné de..."* (with the addition of...) is a non-standard LF in French, because it can only be coupled with a few number of keywords (*café; fraises; thé*), to create the expressions: *café crème, fraises à la crème* (and not **café à la crème*, **fraises crème*); *café au lait; café arrosé; café noir; thé nature*; etc (Mel'čuk 1992). About 70 simple standard LFs have been identified (Kolesnikova, 2011).

LFs can be classified as paradigmatic or syntagmatic, according to the kind of lexical relation they model. The paradigmatic LFs model the vertical, "in absence" or "in substitution" relation among lexical units (Saussure, 1983). For example, antonymy, Anti(*big*) = *small*; synonymy, Syn(*car*) = *automobile*; hyponymy, Hypo(*feline*) = {*cat, tiger, lion,* etc.}. Syntagmatic LFs model the horizontal, "in presence" or "in composition" relations among lexical units (Saussure, 1983). For example: magnification, Magn(*committed*) = *deeply*; confirmation, Ver(*argument*) = *valid*; laudatory, Bon(*advice*) = {*helpful, valuable*}.

Another important concept is that of semantic actant (Sem-actant) (Mel'čuk, 2004). In logic, a predicate is a falsifiable assertion. Each predicate has one or more arguments. For example, in the assertion "Rome is the capital of Italy", we can define the predicate 'capital' having two arguments, 'Rome' and 'Italy': *capital(Italy, Rome)*.

In linguistics, the predicate is called "predicative sense" and the arguments are its "semantic actants". Each LF represents a different predicative sense and the semantic actants are represented by subscripts. For example, the LF *S* (actantial noun) gives the equivalent noun of the value to which it is applied. S_1 gives the first actant (the one who executes the action), S_2 gives the second actant (the object of the action) and S_3 gives the third actant (the recipient of the action): S_1(*to teach*) = *teacher*; S_2(*to teach*) = {*subject; matter*}; S_3(*to teach*) = {*pupil; student*}. Other subscripts give circumstantial information. For example: S_{loc} – local of the action/event; S_{instr} – instrument used; etc.

LFs can be classified according to their semantic or syntactic behaviour. For example, in (Mel'čuk, 1998) we find the following classification:
- Semantic derivatives: S_1(*to teach*) = *teacher*; S_3(*to teach*) = *pupil*; S_{loc}(*to fight*) = *battlefield*; S_{instr}(*murder*$_{V,N}$) = *weapon*; A_1(*anger*$_N$) = *angry*; Adv_1(*anger*) = *angrily*;

- Support verbs: $Oper_1(support) = [to]$ *lend* [~ *to N*]; $Oper_1(promise_N) = [to]$ *make* [ART ~];
  $Func_2(proposal) = concerns$ [*N*];
- Realization verbs: $Real_1(bus) = [to]$ *drive* [ART ~]; $Real_2(bus) = [to]$ *ride* [*on* ART ~];
  $Real_1(promise_N) = [to]$ *keep* [ART ~];
- Modifiers: $Magn(injury) =$ *serious*; $Ver(citizen) =$ *loyal*; $Bon(analysis) = fruitful$.

Complex LFs are formed by the combination of simple standard ones: for example, the LFs *Anti* and *Bon* can be combined to form the LF *AntiBon*: $AntiBon(hotel) =$ {*seedy, sleazy, //flea bag*}. The symbol "//" before "flea bag" represents a fused element: the keyword *hotel* does not compose with the value of the LF function to form a collocation. Compare to: *seedy hotel, sleazy hotel.*

The advantage of using LFs for modeling relations between lexical units are many. We present here some of them, as stated by Kolesnikova (2011):

- LFs are universal. They represent semantic relations that are present in virtually all languages. This allows us to use them for building representations in several languages for multilingual alignments, to be used in automatic translation applications, multilingual information search, ontology alignment in different languages, etc;
- LFs are idiomatic. This allows the representation of a "non-typical" sense that emerges only when certain words are found together. For example, in English we can say "to know firmly". In this expression, the sense of "know firmly" is idiomatic. One can use the LF *Magn* (magnification or intensification) to represent this relation: $Magn (know) =$ {*firmly*};
- Some LFs are the converse of one another, which can account for the paraphrase and passivization of collocations: $Oper_1 (analysis) =$ {[*to*] *carry out* DET ~} (*John carries out the analysis*); $Func_1 (analysis) =$ {DET ~ *is due* [*to*] N} (*The analysis is due to John*);

2.3   French Lexical Network

The *French Lexical Network* (FLN) (Lux-Pogodalla and Polguère, 2011) is based on the MTT, more specifically on the LFs. We extract from FLN the LFs that appear in lexical relations, in a total of about 100 simple LFs and 500 complex ones. The total number of LFs is elevated because, for instance, $Oper_1$, $Oper_2$, $Oper_3$ and $Oper_4$ are considered distinct LFs and there are many different complex LFs, for instance, $CausFinOper_1$ and $S_0SingReal_1$.

FLN has been built manually by a lexicographic team of around 15 persons. Luxpogodalla and Polguère (2011) explain that lexicographic strategies used to extract linguistic information from corpora are based on the Explanatory Combinatorial Lexicology (Mel'čuk et al, 1995) and that they also make extensive use of the *Trésor de la Langue Française informatisé* (Dendien and Pierrel, 2003) as a lexical database from which to extract lexicographic information.

An important idea we extracted from the FLN is the concept of LF family. For example, $Oper_1$, $Caus_1Oper_1$, $Caus_2Oper_1$, $Caus_3Oper_1$, $FinOper_1$, etc., all belong to the LF family $Oper_1$.

2.4   Semantic Perspective

Jousse (2010) presents a system for the classification of lexical functions in four different ways: a semantic, a syntactic, a combinatorial and a paradigmatic classification. We present here the semantic classification, the only one we have included in our model, to this date.

In the semantic classification, LFs are divided in twelve classes: action-event, causativity, element-set, equivalence, form (or way), location, opposition, participants, phase-aspect, qualification, semantically-empty-verb and support-verb. Each class is divided in one or more sub-classes. For example, action-event has nine sub-classes: attempt, creation, decrease/degradation, imminence, manifestation, etc., and location has two: spatial/temporal and typical place.

Each LF has at least one meaning associated to it, and then each LF is classified in one or more semantic perspective. For example, *Magn* (intensification) is associated with the class "qualification", sub-class "intensity", while the LF *Bon* is also associated with the class "qualification", however with the sub-class "judgement".

2.5 The lemon Model

lemon (McCrae et al., 2012) is a model for sharing lexical information on the semantic web. It is based on earlier models, such as LexInfo (Buitelaar, 2009) and LMF (Francopoulo, 2007). As its main advantages over these previous models, we cite:

- separation between the linguistic and the ontological information;
- linguistic information, such as "partOfSpeech" and "writenForm" are represented as RDF properties, differently of LMF, which represent them as attributes of a property, which makes easier the use of other resources, like the SPARQL query language;
- lemon uses ISOCat, data categories homologated by ISO (for example, "partOfSpeech", "gender" and "tense");
- lemon is an easily extensible model;
- there are already many linguistic resources in lemon format, like WordNet and DBPedia Wiktionary.

Lexical units are represented in the lemon model using the classes "LexicalEntry" and "LexicalForm". The "LexicalEntry" class is connected to the lexical unit sense, which is represented by the "LexicalSense" class. The connection between the lemon model and external ontologies are made through this last class.

In our model, the keyword and the value of a LF will be represented as a lemon "LexicalSense" class. In MTT, the different senses of a word are represented by subscripts, using Roman and Arabic numbers and Latin letters (Mel'čuk, 1995), which we illustrate here with an example. Consider the word *"ocean"*. It has concrete senses, like *"a body of water that covers the planet"* and abstract senses, like in *"ocean of people"*. In MTT, the concrete senses of *"ocean"* would be represented as "$Ocean_I$" and the abstract senses as "$Ocean_{II}$". Inside "$Ocean_I$" we could have subdivisions:

- $Ocean_{I.1a}$: *"extension of water that covers the planet"* (always in singular);
- $Ocean_{I.1b}$: the set of oceans in general (always in plural) – *"the oceans are polluted."*;
- $Ocean_{I.2}$: a part of $Ocean_{I.1a}$ in a specific region – *Atlantic Ocean, Pacific Ocean, Arctic Ocean*, etc.

In our model, the word *"ocean"* is represented by a lemon object "LexicalEntry" and $Ocean_I$, $Ocean_{I.1a}$, $Ocean_{I.1b}$, $Ocean_{I.2}$ and $Ocean_{II}$ are each represented by a "LexicalSense" lemon object. The reason for this is explained as follows: the semantic connection represented by an individual LF is between senses, and not between lexical forms or lexical entries. By doing so, we can have an already disambiguated lexical network when connecting lexical units with a LF.

3 The lexfom Model

This section presents our model for the representation of LFs. The lexical function ontology model (lexfom) is divided in four modules: lexical function representation (lfrep), lexical function family (lffam), lexical function semantic perspective (lfsem) and lexical function relations (lfrel). Each subsection presents one of these modules.

3.1 The lfrep Module

Figure 1 illustrates the lfrep module and its connection to lffam and lfsem. The central class in this module is "lexical_function". In this figure and in the following ones, a black arrow represents an object property relation between classes and a white arrow represents a sub-class relation.

In yellow, we have classes which represent characteristics of a LF, e.g. if it is simple or complex, standard or semi-standard, etc. In grey, we have classes representing constituent of a LF. Most of those classes are specific to some LF families. For example, the "spatial specification" appear in the LF *Loc*: Loc_{ab}, Loc_{ad} and Loc_{in} and "intensification dimension" in the LF *Magn*: *Magn_behaviour, Magn_height, Magn_size*, etc.

In this module we can indicate to which LF family a LF belongs, using the object property "belongsToLFF" and we can also connect a LF to the meaning it denotes, using the object property "hasSemanticPerspective". Each of this properties connects to classes which belongs to different modules, *lffam* (lexical function family) and *lfsem* (lexical function semantic perspective), respectively, which will be presented in the next two sections.

Figure 2(a) illustrates the part of the lfrep module used to represent complex LFs and Figure 2(b) shows an example of a complex LF (*AntiBon*) represented in RDF/OWL format (turtle dialect), following the general schema of Figure 2(a).

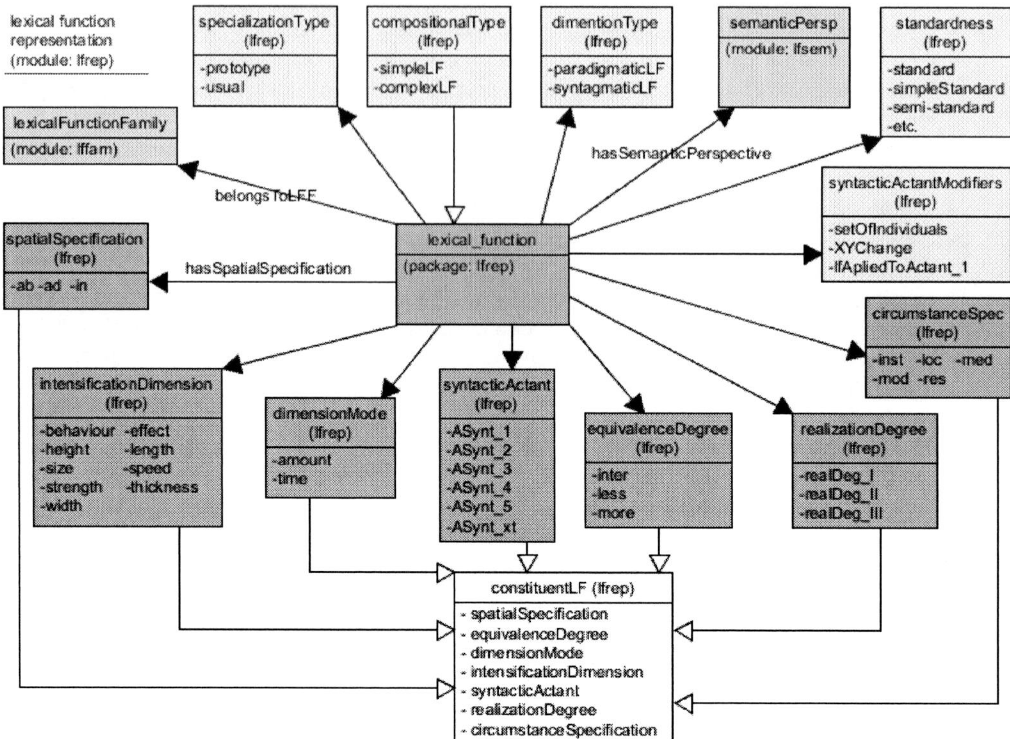

Figure 1: Module to represent a lexical function (lfrep) and its connection to lfsem and lffam.

3.2   The lffam Module

Figure 3 illustrates the module *lffam*. This module is used to cluster the LFs into families, according to their semantic/syntactic similarity, as introduced in Section 2.3. There are two main groups, the paradigmatic and the syntagmatic LF. The last one is subdivided in support verbs, phasal verbs (which indicate the start, continuation or finalization of an action), realization verbs, causation verbs (cause, permission and liquidation of an action) and some other functions which are not classified in any specific sub-group. The paradigmatic LFs are subdivided in nine groups, e.g. actantial nouns, adjectives and adverbs, circumstantial nouns, syntactic conversion, etc.

The concept of family was extracted from FLN. Complex LFs whose base LF is the same belong to the same family, as explained in Section 2.3. FLN contains about 100 LF families, each one roughly corresponding to a simple LF. It is important to note that similar LFs, differentiable one from another only by their syntactic actant, such as $Oper_1$, $Oper_2$, $Oper_3$, etc, is each one the head of a LF family. For example, we have the $Oper_1$ family (*$Oper_1$, $Caus_1Oper_1$, $Caus_2Oper_1$*), the $Oper_2$ family (*$Oper_2$, $Caus_1Oper_2$, $Caus_2Oper_2$, $Caus_3Oper_2$, $FinOper_2$*, etc.) and so on.

3.3   The lfsem Module

Figure 4 illustrates the LF semantic perspective module, as introduced in Section 2.4. Twelve semantic classes are represented, each one divided in one or many sub-classes. A LF can have one or more semantic perspective, depending on the context and on the lexical units it connects.

For example, the LF *Magn* (intensification) has the semantic perspective "qualification/intensity" and the LF *Syn* (synonymy) has the semantic perspective "equivalence/similar lexical units".

Figure 5 shows a RDF representation of the LF *Anti*. Note how the modules "lfrep", "lffam" and "lfsem" are used to represent it.

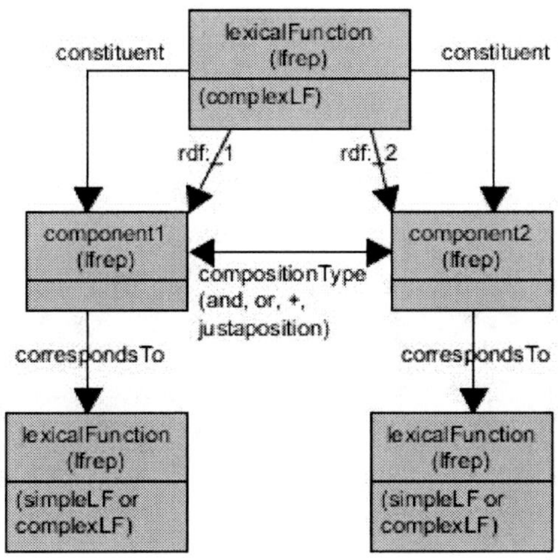


```
lfrlf:LF-AntiBon rdf:type
    lfrep:complexLF;
lfrep:constituentComplexLF
   :CCLF-AntiBon-Anti,
        CCLF-AntiBon-Bon.


:CCLF-AntiBon-Anti rdf:type
    lfrep:componentComplexLF;
lfrep:justapositionComposition
   :CCLF-AntiBon-Bon;
lfrep:correspondsTo lfrlf:LF-Anti.


:CCLF-AntiBon-Bon rdf:type
    lfrep:componentComplexLF;
lfrep:correspondsTo lfrlf:LF-Bon.
```

(a) Part of the lfrep module used to represent complex LFs.

(b) RDF/OWL representation of the complex LF *AntiBon*, using the module lfrep.

Figure 2: Representation of complex LFs.

3.4 The lfrel Module

Figure 6 illustrates the lexical function relation module (lfrel), which represents the way lexical units are connected by a LF.

We decided to connect the LF keyword and the LF value using an intermediate class (lfSenseRelation), which is a subclass of a the lemon class "SenseRelation", instead of connecting them directly with the LexicalFunction class because in this way we can connect to the lfSenseRelation information that is specific to the relation between two lexical units, independently of the LF connection them, and we can connect to a LF information that is independent of the lexical units that it connects. Also, the paradigmatic/syntagmatic information (LRType) is connected to the LexicalRelation class instead of being connected to the LexicalFunction class.

Although the LFs usually have a definite type (paradigmatic or syntagmatic), some of them do not have it, which will depend on the lexical units they model.

The property "hasGovPattern" is used to indicate the government pattern (GP) in the sense/lexical relation. For example, the collocation "receive an order from N", is modeled by the LF $Oper_3(order_N)$ = *receive* and its GP is [ART ~ *from* N]. For the moment, the GPs are represented by strings in our model, but we intend to create a module "lfgpat" with a hierarchy of the most commons GPs.

Figure 7 illustrates how the collocation "*close friend*" can be represented. It is modelled by the LF Magn (predicative sense = intensification): Magn($friend_{I.1}$) = $close_{III.1a}$; Since also Magn($friend_{I.1}$) = $good_{II}$, we could have another LexicalRelation (*Magn_02*) connecting the LexicalSense $good_{II}$ and the LexicalSense $friend_{I.1}$.

The lexical relation is connected to the value of the collocation using the property "hasLFValue" and to the keyword using the property "hasLFKeyword". The property "hasLRType" informs that the relation between "$close_{III.1a}$" and "$friend_{I.1}$", modelled by the LF "Magn", is a syntagmatic relation.

As explained in Section 2.5, it is important to note that the lexical units that appear in our example, "$friend_{I.1}$", and "$close_{III.1a}$" will be modeled as "LexicalSense" and not as a "LexicalEntry" lemon object. This means that our model will connect to the lemon model via the sense of the lexical units. This allows the construction of already disambiguated lexical networks. Finally, the lexical variations (e.g. plural) can be treated at the level of the LexicalEntry lemon object, already implemented by lemon.

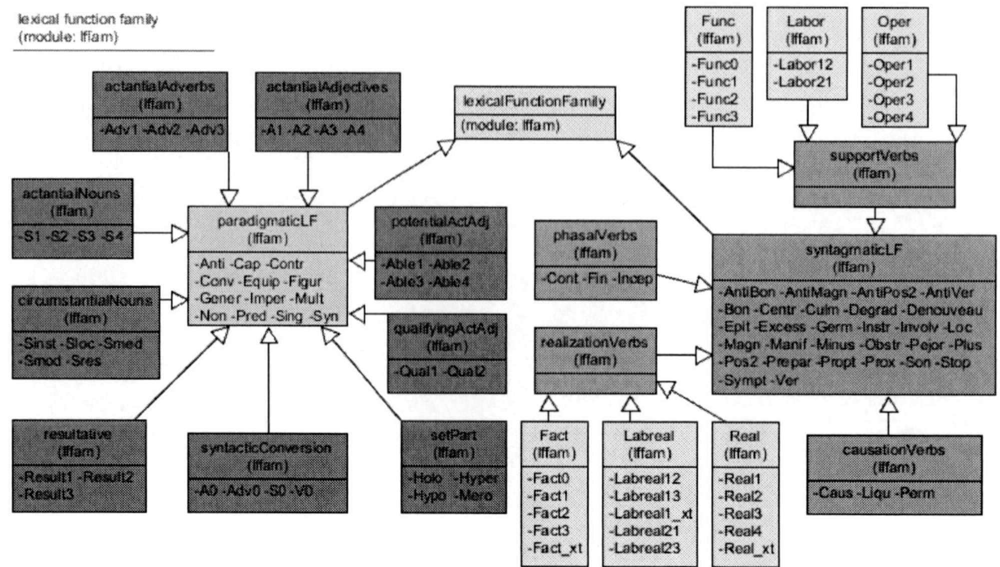

Figure 3: Module lffam, which represents the lexical functions families.

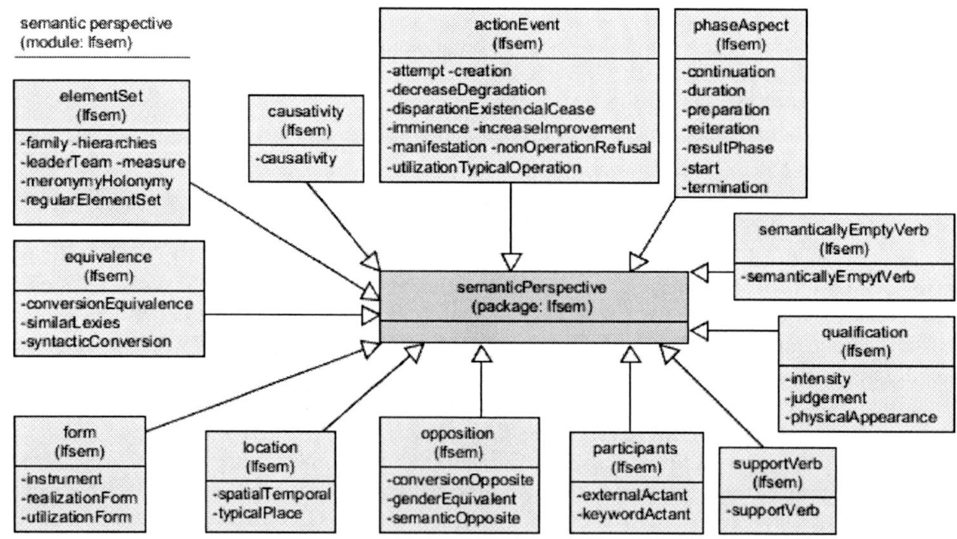

Figure 4: Semantic perspective module (lfsem) contains twelve classes used to indicate the semantics of a LF.

One advantage of representing lexical units as lemon LexicalSense/LexicalEntry is that lemon implements the Syntax and Semantics (synsem)[1] module, which can be used to connect its LexicalEntry class to syntactic and morphological information about lexical units.

For example, we can use the property "syntacticBehavior" to indicate that a lexical unit is a transitive verb, to indicate its direct object, etc. We can also indicate alternative spelling of a lexical unit (e.g. American/British spelling). lemon also implements the Variation and Translation (vartrans)[2], which can be used to connect a lexical unit to its translations in other languages.

Another advantage of using lemon is the following: it implements the connection of a LexicalSense to a concept defined by an external ontology, such DBPedia[3], through the "reference" property.

[1] https://www.w3.org/2016/05/ontolex/#syntax-and-semantics-synsem
[2] https://www.w3.org/2016/05/ontolex/#variation-translation-vartrans
[3] http://dbpedia.org/ontology/

```
lfrlf:LF-Anti rdf:type lfrep:simpleLF;
      lfrep:belongsToLFFamily lffam:LFF-par-Anti;
      lfrep:dimension lfrep:type-paradigmaticLF;
      lfrep:semanticPerspective lfsem:pSem-op-semanticOpposite.
```

Figure 5: RDF representation of the simple LF *Anti*, using the modules lfrep, lffam and lfsem.

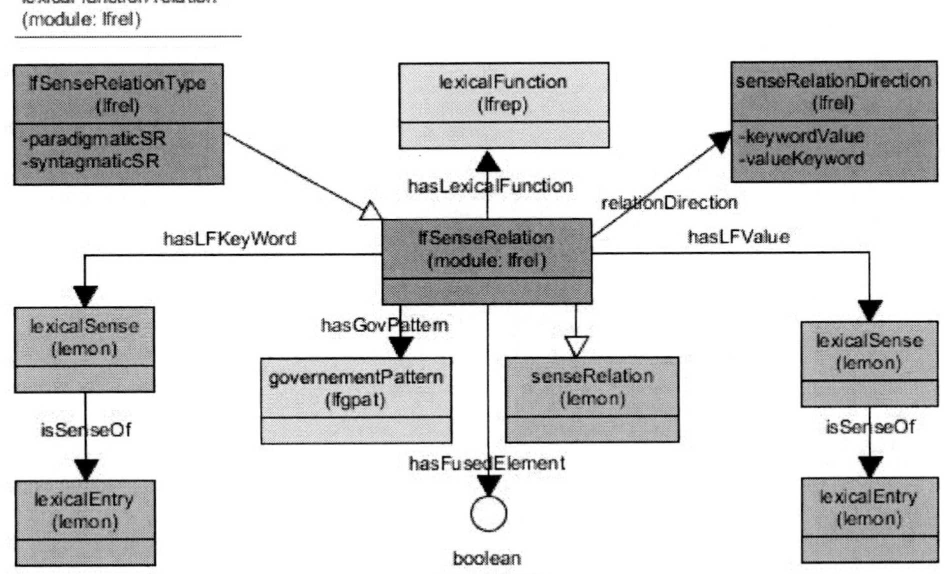

Figure 6: Lexical function relation module (lfrel).

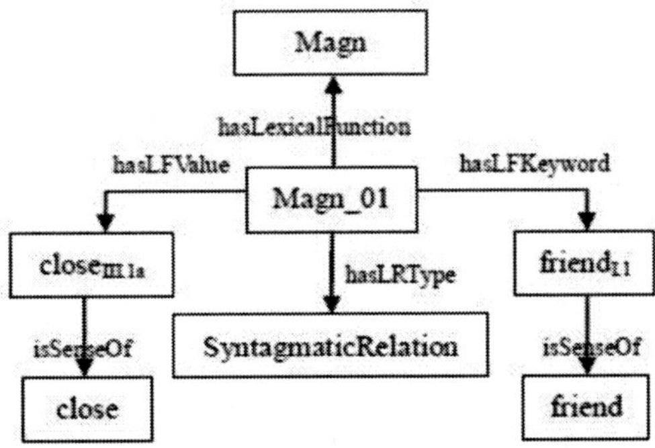

Figure 7: Representation of the collocation "close friend" using the lfrel module.

4   Application

The information about LFs, lexical units and the syntagmatic relation between lexical units were extracted from FLN. In this lexical network, this information is stored in a relational data bank and can be extracted by SLQ table dumps or SQL queries.

FLN has about 600 standard LFs (about 100 simple and 500 complex LFs) and we encoded all of them using lexfom.

We also encoded the lexical relations mediated by these standard LFs. So far we have encoded using the lexfom model about 54,000 relations, being 46,000 paradigmatic and 8,000 syntagmatic.

Figure 8 shows the RDF representation of the French collocation *porter un vêtement* (*to wear a clothe*). It is intermediated by the LF *Real$_I$*: Real$_I$ (*vêtement*) = {*porter*}. Each word is first represented as a lemon:LexicalEntry, and each sense of the words are represented as a lemon:LexicalSense. The

LF *Real$_1$* is represented with its properties, using the modules *lfrep*, *lffam* and *lfsem*. Finally, the module *lfrel* is used to represent the sense relation between *porter* and *vêtement*.

```
:lex_vêtement a ontolex:LexicalEntry,      :form_vêtement a ontolex:Form;
            ontolex:Word;                      ontolex:writtenRep "vêtement"@fr .
ontolex:canonicalForm:form_vêtement;
ontolex:sense :vêtement_sense_I.2;        vêtement_sense_I.2   a ontolex:LexicalSense.
ontolex:sense :vêtement_sense_I.1;        vêtement_sense_I.1   a ontolex:LexicalSense.
ontolex:sense :vêtement_sense_II;         vêtement_sense_II    a ontolex:LexicalSense.
ontolex:sense :vêtement_sense_III.1;      vêtement_sense_III.1 a ontolex:LexicalSense.
ontolex:sense :vêtement_sense_III.2;      vêtement_sense_III.2 a ontolex:LexicalSense.
rdfs:label "vêtement"@fr .
```
```
:lex_porter a ontolex:LexicalEntry,       :form_porter a ontolex:Form;
  ontolex:Word;                               ontolex:writtenRep "porter"@fr .
  ontolex:canonicalForm :form_porter;
  ontolex:sense :porter_sense_I;          porter_sense_I a ontolex:LexicalSense.
  ontolex:sense :porter_sense_II;         porter_sense_II a ontolex:LexicalSense.
  rdfs:label "porter"@fr .
```
```
LF-Real1 rdf:type lfrep:simpleLF,         :lfsr_11420 a
    lfrlf:Real1, owl:NamedIndividual;              lfrel:SyntagmaticLFSenseRelation;
lfrep:belongsToLFFamily                       lfrel:hasLexicalFunction lfrep:LF-Real1;
  lffam:LFF-synt-realV-Real1;             lfrel:hasLFKeyword
lfrep:hasSyntActant                               ontolex:vêtement_sense_I.2;
  lfrep:lfrep-const-sa-ASynt_1;           lfrel:hasLFValue ontolex:porter_sense_IV;
lfrep:dimension                           lfrel:hasGovPattern
  lfrep:lfrep-type-syntagmaticLF;               lfgpat:"DET ~s"^^xsd:string;
lfrep:semanticPerspective                 lfrel:relationDirection lfrel:valueKeyword;
  lfsem:pSem-ae-utilTypicalOperation.     lfrel:hasFusedElement "false"^^xsd:boolean.
```

Figure 8: RDF representation of the LF *Real$_1$*, the lexical units *vêtement* and *porter* and the sense relation between *vêtement* and *porter* to form the French collocation *porter un vêtement*.

5   Conclusion and Future Work

We present in this paper an ongoing project, called Lexical Functions Ontology Model (lexfom), aimed at the representation of the lexical functions of Meaning-Text Theory as a lexical ontology.

Most of the existing lexical networks lack important semantic information, especially the syntagmatic relations between lexical units. Lexical functions are a powerful tool for the representation of linguistic relations. In particular, syntagmatic lexical functions can fill the present gap in the representation of syntagmatic relations in lexical networks.

Moreover, the combination of the descriptive logic embedded in the OWL language with the semantic, syntactic, paradigmatic and combinatorial information, provided by lexical functions, creates a strong tool for studying human reasoning, the relation between lexical units and can be used by diverse natural language processing applications and tools.

Finally, this work can be seen as a new form of representation of collocations. It is important to observe that we deal with collocations as defined by Mel'čuk (1998), and not the definition usually employed in NLP articles, which usually states a collocation as "word cooccurrences whose idiosyncrasy is of statistical nature only" (Vincze et al., 2016).

Dealing with collocations, as stated in Section 2.1, is of vital importance for a real understanding and correct identification and representation of the relations between lexical units.

As a future work, we intend to use our model to transform the *French Lexical Network*, from its present relational database format to an ontology format. We have so far encoded about 100 simple LFs and 500 complex LFs, extracted from FLN, and also encoded about 54,000 lexical relations, being 46,000 paradigmatic and 8,000 syntagmatic relations.

Also, similarly to the lfsem module, new modules will be created to represent the remaining classifications presented by Jousse (2010): a syntactic, a combinatorial and a paradigmatic classification module.

Finally, we intend to combine the semantic information in our ontology with a word embeddings model to enhance the automatic construction of lexical networks.

References

Bolshakov, I. and Gelbukh, A. (1998). Lexical functions in Spanish. *Proceedings CIC-98, Simposium Internacional de Computación*, pp. 383-395. November 11-13, 1998, Mexico D.F., Mexico.

Buitelaar, P., Cimiano, P., Haase, P. et Sintek, M. (2009). Towards linguistically grounded ontologies. In *L. Aroyo et al. (Eds.): ESWC 2009, LNCS 5554*, pp. 111-125, Spring-Verlag Berlin. Heidelberg 2009.

Dendien, J. and Pierrel, J.-M. (2003). Le Trésor de la Langue Française informatisé: un exemple d'informatisation d'un dictionnaire de langue de référence. Traitement Automatique des Langues (T.a.l.), 44(2):11–37.

Francopoulo, G., Bel, N., Georg, M., Calzolari, N., Monachini, M., Pet, M. and Soria, C. (2007). Lexical markup framework: ISO standard for semantic information in NLP lexicons. In: *Proceedings of the Workshop of the GLDV Working Group on Lexicography at the Biennial Spring Conference of the GLDV*.

Jousse, A. (2010). Modèle de structuration des relations lexicales fondé sur le formalisme des fonctions lexicales. Thèse de doctorat. Université de Montréal et Université Paris Diderot (Paris 7), 340 p.

Kolesnikova, O. Automatic extraction of lexical functions, PhD Thesis (2011). Instituto Politecnico Nacional – Centro de Investigacion en Computacion, Mexico, D.F., Mexico, 116 p.

Lux-Pogodalla, V. and Polguère, A. (2011). Construction of a French lexical network: Methodological issues. In *Proceedings of the First International Workshop on Lexical Resources, WoLeR'11*. An ESSLLI 2011 Workshop, pp. 54-61, Ljubljana, Slovenia.

Manning, C. D. and Schütze, H. (1999). Foundations of Statistical Natural Language Processing. Cambridge, MA: The MIT Press, 1999, 680 p.

McCrae, J., Aguado-de-Cea, G., Buitelaar, P., Cimiano, P., Declerck, T., Gómez-Pérez, A., Gracia, J., Hollink, L., Montiel-Ponsoda, E., Spohr, D. and Wunner, T. (2012). Interchanging lexical resources on the Semantic Web. *Lang Resources & Evaluation (2012)* 46:701–719.

Mel'čuk, I. (2004). Actants in semantics and syntax, I: Actants in semantics. *Linguistics* 42(1):1-66.

Mel'čuk, I. (1998). Collocations and lexical functions - *A.P. Cowie (Ed.), Phraseology. Theory, Analysis and Applications*, Oxford: Clarendon Press, pp. 23-53.

Mel'čuk, I. (1997). Vers une linguistique Sens-Texte. Leçon inaugurale. Paris: Collège de France, 78 p.

Mel'čuk, I. (1996). Lexical functions: A tool for the description of lexical relations in the lexicon. In *L. Wanner (ed.): Lexical Functions in Lexicography and Natural Language Processing*, pp. 37-102, Amsterdam/Philadelphia: Benjamins.

Mel'čuk, I., Clas, A. et Polguère, A. (1995). *Introduction à la lexicologie explicative et combinatoire*, Coll. Champs linguistiques/Universités francophones, Louvain-la-Neuve/Paris, Éditions Duculot/AUPELF-UREF, 256 p.

Mel'čuk, I. (1992). Paraphrase et lexique: La théorie Sens-Texte et le *Dictionnaire explicatif et combinatoire* in Mel'cuk *et al.* 1992: 9-58.

Morgan, J. L. (1978), 'Two types of convention in Indirect Speech acts', in P. Cole (ed.), *Syntax and Semantics, v.9. Pragmatics* (New York *etc.*: Academic Press), 261-280.

Polguère (2000). Towards a theoretically-motivated general public dictionary of semantic derivations and collocations for French. In *Approaches to Lexical Combinatorics, Proceedings of Euralex 2000*, p. 517-527.

Heid, U. et Raab, S. (1989). Collocations in Multilingual Generation. In *Proceedings of the fourth conference on European chapter of the Association for Computational Linguistics* - EACL '89, pp. 130-136. Stroudsburg, PA, USA.

Saussure, F. de (1983). Course in general linguistics. Eds. Charles Bally and Albert Sechehaye. Trans. Roy Harris. La Salle, Illinois: Open Court. 1983, 236p.

Schwab, D., Tze, L. L. et Lafourcade, M. (2007). Les vecteurs conceptuels, un outil complémentaire aux réseaux lexicaux. TALN'07: Traitement Automatique des Langues Naturelles, pp. 293-302, Jun 2007, Toulouse, France, ATALA.

Vincze, V., Savary, A., Candito, M. and Ramisch, C. (2016). Annotation guidelines for the PARSEME shared task on automatic detection of verbal MultiWord Expresions. Version 5.0. http://typo.uni-konstanz.de/parseme/images/shared-task/guidelines/PARSEME-ST-annotation-guidelines-v6.pdf

A Proposal for combining "general" and specialized frames

Marie-Claude L'Homme
Observatoire de linguistique
Sens-Texte (OLST)
Université de Montréal
C.P. 6128, succ. Centre-ville
Montréal (Québec)
H3C 3J7, Canada
mc.lhomme@umontreal.ca

Carlos Subirats
Universitat Autónoma de
Barcelona
Facultad de Letras
Dept. Filología Española
08193 Bellaterra, Spain
carlos.subirats@gmail.com

Benoît Robichaud
Observatoire de linguistique
Sens-Texte (OLST)
Université de Montréal
C.P. 6128, succ. Centre-ville
Montréal (Québec)
H3C 3J7, Canada
benoit.robichaud@umontreal.ca

Abstract

The objectives of the work described in this paper are: 1. To list the differences between a general language resource (namely FrameNet) and a domain-specific resource; 2. To devise solutions to merge their contents in order to increase the coverage of the general resource. Both resources are based on Frame Semantics (Fillmore 1985; Fillmore and Baker 2010) and this raises specific challenges since the theoretical framework and the methodology derived from it provide for both a lexical description and a conceptual representation. We propose a series of strategies that handle both lexical and conceptual (frame) differences and implemented them in the specialized resource. We also show that most differences can be handled in a straightforward manner. However, some more domain specific differences (such as frames defined exclusively for the specialized domain or relations between these frames) are likely to be much more difficult to take into account since some are domain-specific.

1   Introduction

During the past two decades, Frame Semantics (Fillmore, 1985; Fillmore and Baker, 2010) has drawn the attention of an increasing number of scholars interested in accounting for the relationship between the lexicon and background knowledge that speakers of a language are assumed to share (details about Frame Semantics are given in Section 2.1). This led to the compilation of a number of lexical resources in different languages (English, German, Spanish, Japanese, Chinese, Portuguese, etc.)[1] to describe what we will call from now on the *general lexicon*. In this paper, we refer to the English resource FrameNet (Fillmore et al., 2003; Ruppenhofer et al., 2010).

Frame semantics is also increasingly cited in terminology and other fields focusing on specialized lexical items and has been used to describe terms in different domains, such as the environment, law, soccer and biomedicine (Schmidt, 2009; Faber, 2012, among others). Semantic frames are especially attractive in terminology since it is assumed that there is a connection between the conceptual structure of specialized fields of knowledge and the linguistic units used to convey this knowledge.

However, work on the general lexicon and specialized terms is usually carried out separately resulting in resources that could be linked but that seldom are. The objective of the work reported in this paper is twofold. Assuming that it would be productive to link existing resources (specialized and general) to increase the coverage of the lexicon contained in different kinds of texts:

1. List the differences observed between a domain-specific resource that contains terms related to the environment (the Framed DiCoEnviro, 2016; L'Homme and Robichaud, 2014) and the contents of FrameNet.

---

[1] Frame Semantics based projects are listed here:
https://framenet.icsi.berkeley.edu/fndrupal/framenets_in_other_languages.

Proceedings of the Workshop on Cognitive Aspects of the Lexicon,
pages 156–165, Osaka, Japan, December 11-17 2016.

2. Devise solutions in order to manage these differences and propose ways to link the content of a domain-specific resource and a general resource such as FrameNet. It should be pointed out that the two resources considered in this paper are under construction. Hence, the solutions proposed must take this fact into consideration.

It is assumed that the sets of lexical units (LUs) recorded in these resources (terms in the Framed DiCoEnviro and general LUs in FrameNet) share the same fundamental linguistic properties and that their relationship to human cognition is the same.[2] However, differences might occur at more superficial levels that should be managed inside Frame Semantics. This extension of Frame Semantics to specialized terms has theoretical implications and opens new perspectives for Natural Language Processing (NLP). From a theoretical viewpoint, this work implies that two different areas of the lexicon that were traditionally separated artificially – general and specialized – could be unified, thus revealing the general processes leading to the construction of meaning. From a more applied viewpoint, this new integration can lead to improving automated semantic processing systems by training them on texts annotated according to Frame Semantics.[3]

Previous studies have examined solutions to merge the contents of resources based on the same theoretical and/or methodological framework (e.g. Amaro and Mendes, 2012; L'Homme and Polguère, 2007; Magnini and Speranza, 2001). However, to our knowledge, no attempt has been made to devise methods to link general and domain-specific resources based on Frame Semantics. As will be seen below, Frame Semantics accounts for both a lexical level and a conceptual representation. While differences at the lexical level have already been studied, the conceptual level raises challenges that other resources (such as WordNet, for example) do not.

The paper is organized as follows. Section 2 is a brief overview of the structure and contents of FrameNet and the Framed DiCoEnviro and gives details about the subset of data analyzed. Section 3 lists the lexical and conceptual (frame) differences that were discovered in this data. Section 4 presents a series of solutions to deal with these differences and shows how they were implemented in the Framed DiCoEnviro.

2   Frame Semantics, FrameNet and a framed based domain-specific resource

2.1   Frame Semantics and FrameNet

Linguistic theories, including Frame Semantics, have been influenced by the seminal work on prototype theory, developed by Rosch in Berkeley in the 70s. Prototype theory highlighted the role played by cognitive processes of subjects in categorization. It soon became an alternative to the classic Aristotelian theory of categorization (based on necessary and sufficient conditions), a theory that constituted – albeit implicitly – the semantic basis of Western linguistic theories in the 80s. Research work carried out by Rosch (1973, 1975) provided experimental evidence that categorization is not achieved based on an abstract model, but rather is construed based on the comparison of objects or experience that better represent a category. Rosch's pioneering experiments showed that for a given semantic category, certain member concepts are consistently understood as more central to the category—the prototypes—than others.

Rosch's findings led linguistics to research on cognitive models, like semantic frames (Fillmore, 1985), image schemas (Lakoff, 1987), i.e. cognitive models which are created as a result of our interaction with our environment at a pre-conceptual level. It is these conceptual models that allow the speaker and the hearer to construct and understand the meanings that shape linguistic communication.

---

[2] This being said, it should be pointed out that in given fields of knowledge, efforts are made to standardize terminology and the way it is used and defined (e.g., animal and plant species, medical concepts). This might result in meanings assigned to lexical units that differ from those that appear in "general usage". Although these efforts usually concern a subset of the lexicon used in specialized texts, their impact on the lexicon need to be taken into account.

[3] Hence terms in domain-specific resources and lexical units in FrameNet could be unified, thus allowing the use of this "extended" lexicon in specialized language NLP using the same program (namely SEMAFOR http://www.cs.cmu.edu/~ark/SEMAFOR/) or other programs that combine statistically based systems such as SEMAFOR with the use of semantic frame hierarchies to extend the potential of lexical disambiguation and automatic semantic role labeling (Matos, 2014).

More specifically, Frame Semantics is based on the assumption that the meanings of lexical units are constructed in relation to background knowledge (experience, beliefs, conventions, etc.). Frame Semantics has devised a theoretical model and a methodology for structuring this background knowledge and make the connection between lexical units and the knowledge explicit. Prototypical situations are structured within "semantic frames" that are evoked by a certain number of lexical units.

In all the projects based on this theory, a large number of frames evoked by lexical units (LUs) were analyzed along with hierarchical semantic relations that hold between frames. The descriptions appear in FrameNets devoted to different languages.

FrameNet describes frames and lexical units in three different modules:

1. The description of the frame itself (in which a definition of the frame is given along with linguistic examples and a list of obligatory and optional participants (in Frame Semantics, participants are called *frame elements* (FEs)). For instance, a situation whereby "an organic substance undergoes the natural process of decaying from an initial state to a result" is structured in a frame called **Rotting** (FrameNet, 2016). This situation has a Patient (an obligatory participant, called a *core FE*, that undergoes the process of decaying) and a Degree, Circumstances, Duration, Frequency, etc. (optional participants, called *non-core FEs*).

2. Lexical entries: each LU that evokes a frame is described in a separate entry (that contains a short definition of the LU and lists of syntactic or valence patterns). For instance, the following LUs evoke the **Rotting** frame: *decay.n, decay.v, decompose.v, fester.v, moulder.v, perish.v, putrefy.v, rot.n, rot.v, spoil.v.* and each has its own entry.

3. Contextual annotations: a list of sentences – extracted from the British National Corpus – in which specific LUs appear are annotated in order to highlight their syntactic behaviour. The examples below show how sentences in which the verb *decay* appears are annotated:

   Were the corpses' hands honourably amputated during the funeral rites -- or later, after [Patientthe flesh] had DECAYED^Target ?

   [PatientTheir flesh] DECAYS^Target, their shells and their bones become scattered and turn to powder.

   -- Carnivorous animals -- which readily transmitted infection in a warm climate where [Patientflesh] DECAYED^Target [Speedrapidly].

4. Finally, frames are interconnected based on a number of relations (*Is Causative of, Inherits, Is Subframe of*, etc.) giving a more complete and precise picture of a general conceptual situation in which a frame is involved. Figure 1 shows the relationships held by the **Rotting** frame with other ones. Figure 2 shows how the **Run_risk** frame is connected to other frames defined in FrameNet (2016).

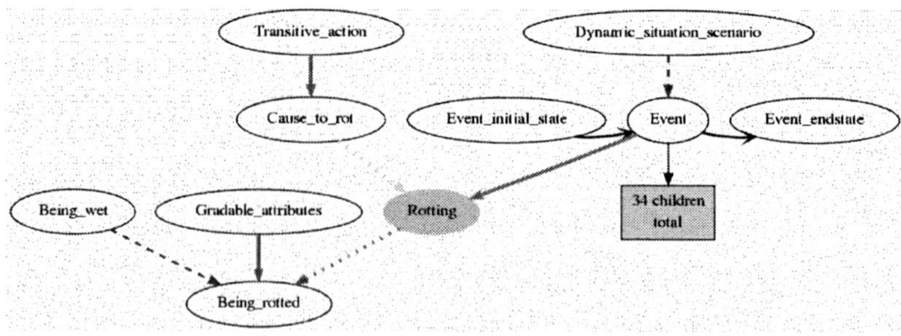

Figure 1. Relations between frames: **Rotting**

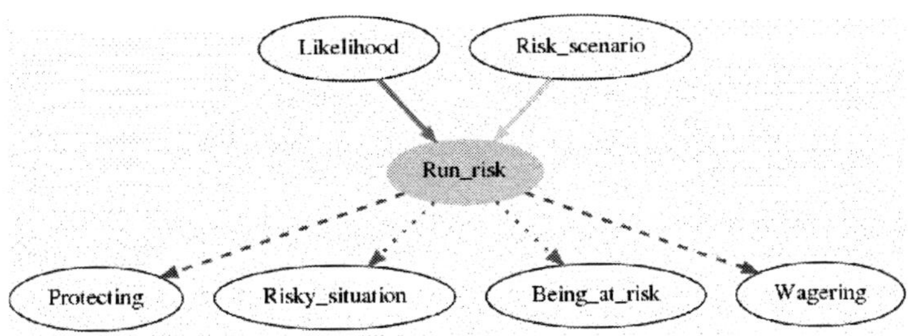

Figure 2: Relations between frames: **Run_risk**

The FrameNet data to which we refer in this paper is that contained in the 1.6 XML release (Baker and Hung, 2010).

2.2 A frame-based domain-specific resource

In previous work (L'Homme et al, 2014; L'Homme and Robichaud, 2014), we showed that the theory of Frame Semantics and the methodology devised within the FrameNet project (Fillmore et al., 2003; Ruppenhofer et al., 2010) provide useful means to account for the semantic and constructional aspects of terms (especially terms that denote events). It also provides for a connection between linguistic descriptions and a more abstract conceptual structure related to a terminological domain (in other words, relate the frame evoked by a term to a hierarchy of conceptual structures).

The specialized data considered in this work is extracted from a resource on the environment (called the *Framed DiCoEnviro*). In this resource, terms (e.g. *sustainable, contaminate, biodegradable, emission*) are grouped according to the frames they evoke. In addition, most frames are interconnected and these relations account for larger scenarios that inform about situations that occur in the field of the environment (e.g., Species activities, Risks, Contamination).

This first resource is linked to a terminological resource in which lexical descriptions of terms are given (called the *DiCoEnviro. Dictionnaire fondamental de l'environnement*). In addition, most lexical entries provide contextual annotations that show how terms combine with their participants (arguments and adjuncts). Figure 3 shows an example of the frame **Rotting** along with an entry and annotations that can be found in the DiCoEnviro. Figure 4 shows how relationships between the **Rotting** and the **Run_risk** frames were defined in the Framed DiCoEnviro.

This work takes into consideration the English data recorded in the Framed DiCoEnviro. This includes 363 terms that evoke 176 different frames.[4] Verbs, nouns, and adjectives have been dealt with at this point. All terms have up to 20 annotated sentences that are extracted from corpora that contain specialized texts on the environment. Annotated sentences for the terms analyzed amount to 7,189.

2.3 Basic differences between FrameNet and the environmental resource

Although the Framed DiCoEnviro was compiled according to the methodology devised in the FrameNet project (Ruppenhofer et al., 2010), some methodological choices were made that affect the way terms are described. We mention the most important ones below:

In the Framed DiCoEnviro (FD), participants are labelled *arguments* (for obligatory ones) and *adjuncts* (for optional ones). As was seen above, in FrameNet, participants are labelled *frame elements*, FEs (and these are divided into core and non-core).

---

[4] Note that the frames defined also include French and Spanish terms. However, for the purpose of the comparison with FrameNet, only the English data was considered.

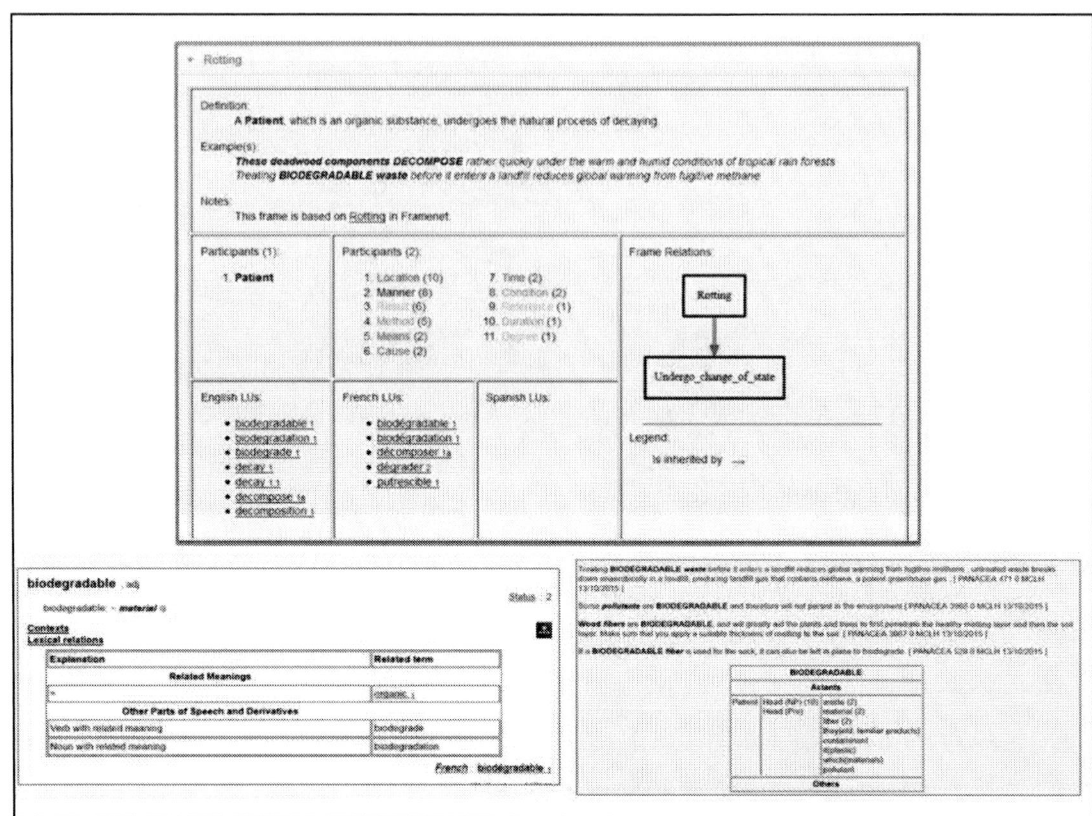

Figure 3: Rotting frame and lexical entry and annotations for the term *biodegradable*

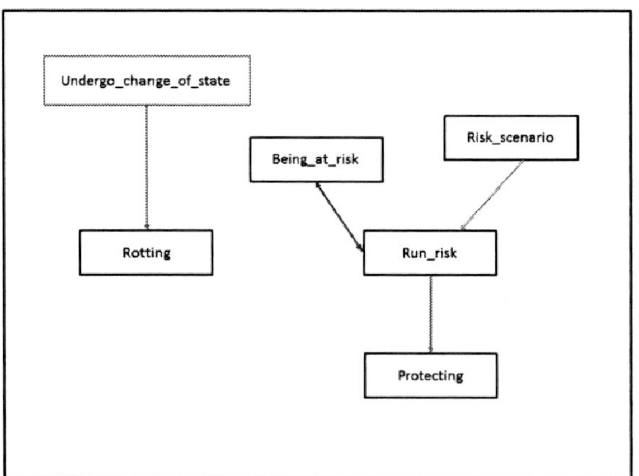

Figure 4: Relations between frames: **Rotting** and **Run_risk**

- In the FD, the methodology for discovering frames is bottom-up. According to this methodology, the definition of argument structures of terms precedes the description of frames. Once the terms and their argument structures have been described, we locate terms that have similar arguments structures and see if these terms can be associated to frames. The FrameNet methodology is slightly different. It consists of defining frames, their frame elements and then associate LUs to these defined frames. This methodological difference often results in different numbers of arguments vs. FEs between the two resources. For instance, in FrameNet the **Cause_change_of_temperature** frame has three core frame elements (Agent | Cause[5], Item, Hot_cold_source). The environmental terms that evoke this frame have only two arguments (Agent | Cause, Patient).

- In the FD, labels used for participants are more traditional (Agent, Patient, Destination) since they are defined for the entire set of terms in the resource. In FrameNet, FEs are defined according to a frame. This results in a much larger number of labels in FrameNet that may correspond to a single one in the FD (for instance, Patient, Theme, Undergoer, Item in FrameNet correspond to Patient in the FD).
- Alternations: Some distinctions were made in the lexical entries of the FD that are not always made in FrameNet. For instance, the FD contains two different entries for the verb *predict*: predict$_{1a}$ (*a model predicts a change*); predict$_{1b}$ (*an expert predicts a change with a model*). In many cases, the two terms are placed in the same frame, since they evoke the same situation.

We do not focus on these differences in this work since they are linked to methodological choices rather than relying on true semantic or conceptual differences between lexical units, terms or frames. However, we do account for them in the FD. First, we state if the number of arguments recorded in the FD differs with respect to the number of core FEs in FrameNet. We also mention cases of alternations. Finally, the FD lists (on demand) the different labels for participants used in each resource, as shown in Figure 5.

Cause_temperature_change
[…]
Notes:
This frame is based on <u>Cause_temperature_change</u> in FrameNet. The number of actants vs. core FEs differs.
[…]

Framed Di-CoEnviro	Participants(1) Agent | Cause Patient	Participants (2) Time (3), Degree (2), Value (2), Location (2), Duration (1), Result (1), Method (1)	
FrameNet	FrameNet Core FEs: Agent Cause Hot_Cold_Source Item	FrameNet Core-Unexpressed FEs	FrameNet Non-Core FEs: Container, Degree, Duration, Instrument, Manner, Means, Place, Temperature_change, Temperature_goal, Temperature_start, Time

Figure 5: Labels for participants in the FD and FrameNet

3   Specificities in specialized fields of knowledge

Many lexical items and lexical units (LUs) are similar in the Framed DiCoEnviro and FrameNet, and thus do not raise problems from the point of view of linking resources. However, several terms display some degree of difference with the lexical content of FrameNet. In this section, we make a list of the differences we observed keeping in mind the consequences these differences may have on the potential integration or specialized data in a general resource such as FrameNet.

3.1   Specificities at the lexical level

A.1 New lexical items: Many lexical items recorded in the FD do not appear in FrameNet. Some of these lexical items are highly specialized (*eutrophication, acidification, deforestation*); others have simply not been added yet to the general resource (*biodegradable, introduce, landfill*). These new lexical items are likely to evoke existing frames in FrameNet or lead to the creation of a new potentially domain-specific frame.

---

[5] We consider the "Agent | Cause" case as a split argument in the Framed DiCoEnviro. Hence we count it as one and apply to same principle when comparing this data to that contained in FrameNet.

A.2. New senses and *A.3* Specific "environmental" uses: In this case, the lexical item is recorded in FrameNet, but the meaning accounted for is not the one observed in the environment data. As with new lexical items, lexical units with different senses can evoke existing frames in FrameNet or require the creation of new ones.

We observed two different phenomena regarding meanings. First, there are new meanings per se (*A.2*). For instance, the adjectives *green* and *clean* do appear in FrameNet, but for the time being no frame accounts for their environmental meaning which can loosely read as follows: "that does not have a negative impact on the environment".

Specific "environmental" uses (*A.3*) apply to terms that cannot be said to convey a different meaning (such as *green* mentioned above). However, we noted a series of "sense modulations" caused by usage in a specialized field of knowledge, or a restriction imposed on arguments due again to the fact that the LU is used in a specialized field of knowledge (this latter case may be related to phenomena that Cruse (2011) labelled *microsenses or spectral subsenses*).

For instance, the verb *introduce* is used in the field of the environment to denote an activity whereby someone places a species in an area where it can live and reproduce (*Toad populations, predatory fish should not BE INTRODUCED into breeding ponds*). It is related to *reintroduce* and *introduction* and is opposed to *eliminate* and *extirpate*. In the general lexicon, *introduce* has a much broader meaning and includes activities in which someone places something in a given location. We also made meaning distinctions that appear relevant for the field of the environment but that might not be relevant in other contexts. For instance, two different meanings were identified for the verb *hunt*. One corresponds to the activity whereby an animal chases and captures other animals for food; the second corresponds to the activity carried out by human beings that consists in chasing animals for other kinds of reasons, this activity having a negative impact on the conservation of species. *Hunt$_1$* is linked to other terms, such as *predation*, and *predate*; while *hunt$_2$* is linked to *poach, capture,* and *fish.A.4* Different relationships between lexical units: This phenomenon is a consequence of the previous one (case *A.3*). Since lexical units such as *introduce* can be defined differently in the field of the environment, they are also likely to appear in different lexical networks. We already mentioned the relationship between *introduce* and *reintroduce* in the environment as well as the two sets of terms to which *hunt$_1$* and *hunt$_2$* are linked respectively. Given the broader use of *introduce* in general language, it is linked to a much larger set of different LUs (such as *imbed, implant, insert, place,* etc.).

3.2 Specificities at the level of frames

B.1 Different lexical contents: Many LUs we analyzed are compatible with the data that appear in FrameNet. We can thus consider that they evoke the same frames. However, in many of those frames, the LUs recorded in FrameNet and those that we could identify in our corpora differ as shown in Figure 6.

Rotting in FrameNet	**Rotting** in Framed DiCoEnviro
decay.n, decay.v, decompose.v, fester.v, moulder.v, perish.v, putrefy.v, rot.n, rot.v, spoil.v	*biodegradable 1, biodegradation 1, biodegrade 1, decay 1, decay 1.1, decompose 1a, decomposition 1*

Figure 6: Different lexical contents for the Rotting frame in FrameNet and the FD

B.2 "New" frames: new frames need to be created to account for environmental data. For the data considered in this work, 96 new frames were created (54,5% of frames necessary for the terms analyzed), Some of these frames include new lexical items and new senses (cases A.1 and A.2), some comprise LUs that are recorded in FrameNet but correspond to "environmental" uses (case A.3). For instance, a new frame called **Adding_species_in_location** was created for the LUs *introduce* (and contains terms such as *reintroduce,* and *introduction*). Similarly, a new frame called **Man_hunting** was created for the LUs *hunt$_2$*, (and will also contain verbs such as *capture, poach* and *fish* (a different frame – based on the one found in FrameNet – contains the term *hunt$_1$*).

B.3 Relationships between frames: Some relations between frames used in the FD are entirely compatible with relations frames hold in FrameNet. However, given that new frames were created (case *B.2*) and that some LUs lend themselves to "sense modulations", frames can appear in relations that differ from the ones described in FrameNet. Most of these appear to be domain specific. For instance, a whole set of new frames were created in the FD to account the different situations in which waste is managed: **Managing_waste**, **Collecting**, **Sorting**, etc. These frames are connected according to the order in which these different activities are carried out. The relations are certainly valid as far as the environment is concerned, but their generality might be questioned from the point of view of the general lexicon.

4   Dealing with differences

In this section, we present the solutions we devised and implemented to account for the similarities and highlight the differences between the two resources. For the time being, these solutions were implemented in the environmental resource.

4.1   Dealing with differences at the level of lexical units

Cases *A.1* and *A.2* can be solved quite easily. New LUs are added to an existing frame provided that there is one that accounts for their meaning (e.g. *biodegradable* is added to the **Rotting** frame). If no frame exists, then the solution consists in creating a new one (e.g. a frame **Judgment_of_impact_on_the_environment** was created for the LUs *green, clean,* and *environmental₂*).
Case *A3* may lend itself to different solutions. New frames may be created (case B.2) (for instance, an **Adding_species_in_location** frame is created to account for the use of *introduce* in the field since it evokes a situation that differs in the environment). For this reason, we did not add this term to the existing **Placing** frame.

It should be mentioned at this point that some "environmental uses" were not considered different enough from general usage to justify a separate description or the creation of a new frame in the FD. For instance, the transitive verb *warm* (as in *carbon dioxide warms the Earth*) is used in the field of the environment with a restricted set of arguments (Agents or Causes such as *gas, energy, increase*; and Patients such as *atmosphere, surface, Earth*). In general usage – at least based on the description given in FrameNet – the use of *warm* is much broader and includes but is not limited to the uses observed in the field of the environment. However, we did not create a new frame to account for *warm* in this case since the description given in FrameNet could be applied to it.
Case *A.4* is described in the next section (when dealing with case *B.3*).

4.2   Dealing with differences at the level of frames

B.1. Resources can provide views on the lexical content of frames that differ between general language and specific fields of knowledge if this lexical content is defined precisely. The lexical contents of FrameNet and the FD are highlighted as shown in Figure 7 for the frame **Rotting**.

Frame: **Rotting**
  […]
Notes:
This frame is based on Rotting in Framenet.

English LUs (in FD)	
<ul><li>biodegradable 1</li><li>biodegradation 1</li><li>biodegrade 1</li><li>decay 1</li><li>decay 1.1</li><li>decompose 1a</li><li>decomposition 1</li></ul>	[…]
FrameNet LUs in FD: decay.v, decompose.v	FrameNet LUs not in FD: decay.n, fester.v, moulder.v, perish.v, putrefy.v, rot.n

Figure 7: Lexical contents in the FD and FrameNet

B.2. New frames (96) are created on the basis of the environmental data. Frames created specifically for the environment are distinguished from others with a green color, as shown in Figure 8. They could also be added to the general resource and be connected to existing frames according to the solution devised for case *B.3.*

B.3. Cases in which frames appear in relations that would not necessarily be valid from the point of view of the general lexicon are much more difficult to handle since many appear to be domain-specific. For the time being, we provide access to the specific views on relations as they are recorded in each resource. Figure 8 shows the interconnections between the **Rotting** and **Run_risk** frames in the FD, on the one hand, and in FrameNet, on the other. As was mentioned earlier, domain-specific frames are those in the green rectangles. Frames that are common to both resources appear in the black rectangles. Finally, frames that were defined in FrameNet, but not used in the FD appear in ellipses.

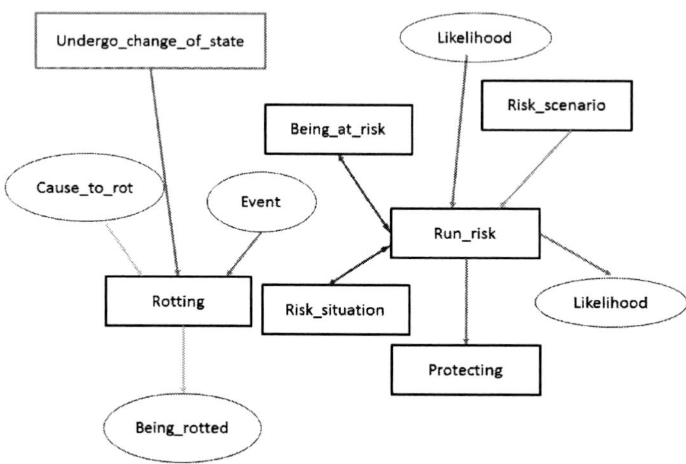

Figure 8: Relations in the FD and FrameNet for **Rotting** and **Run_risk**

5   Conclusion

In this paper, we made a list of lexical and conceptual differences observed between a terminological resource on the environment and FrameNet. The proposals made apply to the environmental terms (363) and frames (176) that we analyzed. At the lexical level, differences observed were: new lexical items, new meanings (or new lexical units) and sense modulations that can be explained by domain specific uses of units (sense distinctions that might appear irrelevant from the point of view of general language, more restricted used of LUs in the environment). Sense modulations can also lead to new relationships between LUs.

At the level of frames, differences can be summarized as: differences in lexical contents of similar frames, the need for new frames, and finally different relationships held between frames.

We devised various strategies to deal with these differences and implemented them in the Framed DiCoEnviro. The implementation allows users to view how the lexicon and frames differ when considered from the perspective of a specialized subject while still seeing how these connect to the way the general lexicon was defined and represented in a general resource such as FrameNet. In addition, if changes are introduced in either resources (since they are both under construction), there are immediately taken into account.

As future work, we plan to extend these strategies to Spanish (since we have started adding Spanish terms to the FD and that it could be compared to the content of Spanish FrameNet). We could also devise strategies to make the environmental lexical content and frames visible in the general resources themselves (FrameNet and Spanish FrameNet).

Acknowledgements

This work is supported by the Social Sciences and Humanities Research Council (SSHRC) of Canada and the Fonds de recherche Société et Culture du Québec.

References

Raquel Amaro, and Sara Mendes. 2012. Towards Merging Common and Technical Lexicon WordNets. In *Proceedings of the 3rd Workshop on Cognitive Aspects of the Lexicon (CogALex-III)*. Mumbai, India, 147-156.

Alan Cruse. 2011. *Meaning in Language*. Oxford: Oxford University Press.

Collin Baker, and J. Hung. 2010. *Release 1.6 of the FrameNet data*. International Computer Science Institute. Berkeley.

DiCoEnviro. Dictionnaire fondamental de l'environnement (http://olst.ling.umontreal.ca/cgi-bin/dicoenviro/search_enviro.cgi).

Charles J. Fillmore. 1985. Frames and the semantics of understanding. *Quaderni di Semantica*, 6(2): 222-254.

Charles J. Fillmore, and Collin Baker. 2010. A frames approach to semantic analysis. In *The Oxford Handbook of Linguistic Analysis*, Bernd Heine and Haiko Narrog (eds), 313-339. Oxford: OUP.

Charles Fillmore. C.R. Johnson, and Miriam Petruck. 2003. Background to FrameNet. *International Journal of Lexicography*, 16(3): 235-250.

Pamela Faber. (ed.). 2012. *A Cognitive Linguistics View of Terminology and Specialized Language*. Berlin/New York: Mouton de Gruyter.

A Framed version of the DiCoEnviro (http://olst.ling.umontreal.ca/dicoenviro/framed/index.php).

FrameNet. (https://framenet.icsi.berkeley.edu/fndrupal/)

Marie-Claude L'Homme, and Benoît Robichaud. 2014. Frames and terminology: representing predicative units in the field of the environment. In *Cognitive Aspects of the Lexicon (Cogalex 2014)*, *Coling 2014*, Dublin, Ireland.

Marie-Claude L'Homme, Benoît Robichaud, and Carlos Subirats. 2014. Discovering frames in specialized domains, In *Language Resources and Evaluation, LREC 2014*, Reykjavik, Iceland.

George Lakoff. 1987. *Women, Fire, and Dangerous Things: What Categories Reveal About the Mind* Chicago: University of Chicago Press.

Bernardo Magnini, and Manuela Speranza. 2001. Integrating Generic and Specialized Wordnets. In *Proceedings of Recent Advances in Natural Language Processing, RANLP 2001*, Tzigov Chark, Bulgaria, 149-153).

Ely Edison da Silva Matos. 2014. LUDI: *Um framework para desambiguação lexical com base no eriquecmento da Semântica de Frames*. Ph. D. Diss. Universidade Federal de Juiz de Fora.

Eleanor H. Rosch. 1973. Natural categories. *Cognitive Psychology*, 4.3: 328–350.

Eleanor H. Rosch, 1975. Cognitive representations of semantic categories. *Journal of Experimental Psychology*, 104(3): 192–233.

Josef Ruppenhofer, Michael Ellsworth, Miriam L. Petruck, Christopher R. Johnson, and Jan Scheffczyk. 2010. *FrameNet II: Extended Theory and Practice*. 2010. (http://framenet.icsi.berkeley.edu).

Thomas Schmidt. 2009. The Kicktionary – A Multilingual Lexical Resources of Football Language. In Boas, H.C. (ed). *Multilingual FrameNets in Computational Lexicography. Methods and Applications*, Berlin/NewYork: Mouton de Gruyter, 101-134.

Spanish FrameNet. An Online Lexical Resource and its Application to Spanish NLP (http://spanishfn.org/).

Carlos Subirats. 2013. Frames, constructions, and metaphors in Spanish FrameNet. In I. Verdaguer, N. J. Laso, and D. Salazar, eds. *Biomedical English: A corpus-based approach*. Amsterdam / Philadelphia: John Benjamins, pp. 185-210.

WordNet. A Lexical Database for English (https://wordnet.princeton.edu/).

Antonymy and Canonicity:
Experimental and Distributional Evidence

Andreana Pastena
University of Pisa

and.pastena@gmail.com

Alessandro Lenci
Computational Linguistics Laboratory
University of Pisa

alessandro.lenci@unipi.it

Abstract

The present paper investigates the phenomenon of antonym canonicity by providing new behavioural and distributional evidence on Italian adjectives. Previous studies have showed that some pairs of antonyms are perceived to be better examples of opposition than others, and are so considered representative of the whole category (e.g., Deese, 1964; Murphy, 2003; Paradis et al., 2009). Our goal is to further investigate why such *canonical pairs* (Murphy, 2003) exist and how they come to be associated. In the literature, two different approaches have dealt with this issue. The *lexical-categorical approach* (Charles and Miller, 1989; Justeson and Katz, 1991) finds the cause of canonicity in the high co-occurrence frequency of the two adjectives. The *cognitive-prototype approach* (Paradis et al., 2009; Jones et al., 2012) instead claims that two adjectives form a canonical pair because they are aligned along a simple and salient dimension. Our empirical evidence, while supporting the latter view, shows that the *paradigmatic* distributional properties of adjectives can also contribute to explain the phenomenon of canonicity, providing a corpus-based correlate of the cognitive notion of salience.

1 Introduction

Antonymy is one of the most important semantic relations between words and/or word-senses (Lyons, 1977; Cruse, 1986; Murphy, 2003; Jones et al., 2007; Jones et al., 2012; Paradis et al., 2009; Paradis et al., 2012; Van de Weijer et al., 2012) and a key organizational principle of the mental lexicon and of adjectives in particular. One important phenomenon about antonymy is that some adjectival pairs are perceived to be better examples of the relation than others, even when near-synonymic alternatives are available (Murphy, 2003; Paradis et al., 2009; Jones et al., 2012). For example, if we ask what the antonym of *hot* is, the majority of speakers will answer *cold*, even if *freezing* and *cool* are near-synonyms of *cold* and both express opposite concepts of *hot*. Thus, *hot – cold* is perceived as a better example of antonymy than *hot – freezing* or *hot – cool*. Antonymic pairs such as *hot – cold* are typically called *canonical antonyms* (Murphy, 2003) and the whole phenomenon – which is the central topic of the present paper – is known as *antonym canonicity*.

As first showed by Deese (1964) and later confirmed by others psycholinguistics studies (Gross et al., 1989; Charles and Miller, 1989; Paradis et al., 2009), members of canonical pairs are the ones eliciting one another in free word association tasks and whose responses are shared by the majority of speakers. Additionally, canonical pairs are perceived to be in opposition even when no context is available and they are stable across word senses (Lehrer, 2002; Murphy, 2003). Murphy (2003) and Paradis et al. (2009) claim that a canonical pair arises when two words that are semantically in opposition become "conventionalized" as a pair in language, that is they are strongly associated and learnt as a form-sense unit. Thus, cognitive evidence suggests that conceptual opposition is not a sufficient condition for an antonymic pair to be a canonical pair. At this point two questions arise: why do canonical pairs exist at all? What are the conditions that determine antonym canonicity?

Another question concerns the nature itself of canonicity. Gross et al. (1989) support a dichotomous

Proceedings of the Workshop on Cognitive Aspects of the Lexicon,
pages 166–175, Osaka, Japan, December 11-17 2016.

view, according to which a small group of canonical antonyms is strictly contrasted with a larger group of non-canonical ones. On the other hand, the fact that speakers are able to discriminate between "better" and "less good" instances of antonymy led some linguists to suggest that canonicity is a scalar phenomenon showing a prototypical structure, rather than a dichotomous one (Herrmann et al., 1986; Murphy, 2003; Paradis et al., 2009). In this sense, antonymic pairings would be aligned along a continuum of "goodness of opposition" with a few pairs – canonical ones – as representative members of the relation. As also confirmed by the data reported in the following sections, it is possible to individuate different degrees of canonicity, depending on reciprocal elicitation frequency of the adjectives, a fact that we also use as the main criterion to define canonicity.

The aim of this research is to bring new evidence on antonym canonicity and on its possible explanations. In particular, we show that pairs of adjectival antonyms with different degrees of canonicity exist in Italian as well, thereby complementing available data about English and Swedish and supporting the cross-linguistic validity of the phenomenon. In the next section, we discuss the two main models of canonicity. In the second part of the paper, we present the results of an elicitation experiment and distributional analysis of Italian canonical antonyms.

2   Models of canonicity

The existence of a group of antonymic pairs whose members elicit one another in free word association tasks was first reported by Deese (1964). He noticed that this kind of association seems to be consistent with most frequent English adjectives and proposed that two adjectives form a canonical pair because they share linguistic contexts (Deese, 1964; Deese, 1965). Two major models of canonicity have been proposed in the literature. Following the terminology used by Paradis et al. (2009), we refer to them as the *lexical-categorical approach* and the *cognitive-prototype approach*.

The former approach was developed within the structuralist framework, which is based on the assumption that the relations are the semantic primitives, meanings therefore derive from the relations words have among them in the lexical network (e.g., Lyons, 1977). In this sense, antonyms form a set of "stored lexical association", with an adjective having or not having a canonical antonym. This view is best exemplified by the way adjectives are organized in the Princeton WordNet model (Miller, 1995). Antonymy is treated here as a lexical relation and a group of canonical pairs – the *direct* antonyms – is strictly contrasted with a group of non-canonical ones – the *indirect* antonyms –, thereby creating a strict dichotomy. In order to explain canonicity within the lexical-categorical model, Charles and Miller (1989) claim that Deese's idea that direct (canonical) adjectives share linguistic contexts can be defined in two different ways: according to the *substitutability hypothesis*, two adjectives are learned as direct antonyms because they are interchangeable in most contexts, while according to the *co-occurrence hypothesis*, direct antonyms co-occur in sentences significantly more often than chance. Charles and Miller (1989) bring psychological evidence supporting the latter view, and Miller and Charles (1991) add that the substitutability hypothesis by itself would not allow to discriminate between antonyms and synonyms, since they both tend to co-occur in similar contexts. Additionally, Justeson and Katz (1991) individuate some syntactic patterns in which antonymic adjectives are often found to co-occur, such as *between X and Y* and *X or Y*. Moreover, Fellbaum (1995) argues that also nominal, verbal and cross-categorical antonyms (e.g., *to begin* (V) – *endless* (Adj)) co-occur in a sentence more often than chance, suggesting that antonyms do not have to be adjectives or to belong to the same syntactic category to express semantic opposition. Therefore, antonym canonicity would be explained by the syntagmatic nature of the relation, in accord with the co-occurrence hypothesis (Charles and Miller, 1989; Justeson and Katz, 1991).

On the other hand, the *cognitive-prototype approach* – developed in the Cognitive Linguistic framework – argues that producing antonyms is not a matter of automatic lexical association but a knowledge-driven process (Murphy and Andrews, 1993; Murphy, 2003; Paradis et al., 2009). Meanings are here considered to be conceptual in nature, therefore they do not form a stored network but are constantly negotiated by the speakers in the contexts where they occur, thanks to general cognitive processes (Paradis et al., 2009; Paradis et al., 2015). As suggested by Murphy and Andrews (1993) and later showed by Jones et al. (2007) and Van de Weijer et al. (2012), conceptual opposition turned out to be the cause of lexical relation, instead of the other way around. This evidence has led to treat antonymy as a context-sensitive semantic relation. In this respect, canonicity is a scalar phenomenon: Antonymic pairs are aligned along a continuum from "better" to "less good" examples of the relation – as first noted by Herrmann et al. (1986) –, but at the same time the category shows a prototype structure (Murphy, 2003; Paradis et al., 2009). Various studies have in fact pointed out the special status canonical antonyms enjoy, since the members of a canonical pair have both a relation of opposition and a strong lexical entrenchment in memory. The relation is therefore semantic *and* lexical (Jones et al., 2007; Paradis et al., 2009; Van de Weijer et al., 2012; Jones et al., 2012). In diagnosing an adjectival pair as canonical, Paradis et al. (2009) suggest that what is crucial is the dimension of *alignment*, which has to be cognitive salient. This means that the antonymic pairs perceived as the best examples of the relation by the speakers would be the ones describing simple (i.e., easily identifiable) properties, in which the two members occupy the opposite poles, with equal distance from the midpoint.

The behavioural data on Italian adjectives reported in the sections below confirm that antonym canonicity has indeed the gradient nature predicted by the cognitive-prototype model. Moreover, we show that canonicity has also an important distributional correlate, which however does not depend on their syntagmatic co-occurrence, as claimed by Miler & Charles (1989), but rather on their paradigmatic distributional similarity.

3   Elicitation Experiment

We have conducted an elicitation experiment to identify antonymic pairs with different degrees of canonicity in Italian. Each participant was asked to provide the best opposite for some Italian adjectives, divided in two different test sets. The antonymic pairs obtained in such way were classified accordingly to the frequency of reciprocal elicitation. Subject's production frequency has then been used to categorize the elicited data into canonical and non-canonical pairs: *Two adjectives A and B are canonical if and only if A elicited B as the most frequent response and vice versa.*

The elicited pairs were later analysed with respect to their frequency of co-occurrence (in terms of Pointwise Mutual Information, as a measure of association strength). The aim was to evaluate the lexical-categorical approach, in particular to test whether the co-occurrence hypothesis provides a good explanation of canonicity.

Even if the experiment was designed following the guidelines of Paradis et al. (2009), stimuli were selected on the basis of a different criterion, namely concreteness. Moreover, we also added adjectives that could generate morphologically derived antonyms. Furthermore, according to the view of canonicity as a scalar phenomenon (Herrmann et al., 1986; Murphy, 2003; Paradis et al., 2009), we expect that the number of response for each adjective will be extremely variable.

3.1   Stimuli

Two different datasets were used in the elicitation experiment and tested separately. The first set – Set_1 – was formed by 70 Italian adjectives selected manually on the basis of their concreteness: 35 were concrete adjectives – describing a concrete property (e.g., *aperto* "open") – while 35 were abstract ones (e.g., *felice* "happy"). Unmarked members of canonical pairs from Paradis et al. (2009) and Jones et al. (2007) were included in this test set, conveniently translated. The second test set – Set_2 – was formed by all the adjectives elicited by Set_1, removing duplicates and items already included in Set_1. Set_2 has therefore been used to investigate which adjectives mutually elicit each other. Set_2 consists of 132 stimulus words. Nonce words were included in both Set_1 and Set_2 and subjects were instructed to identify them. This was necessary in order to ensure that all participants were native Italian speakers.

3.2   Task

The task was performed on the online crowdsourcing platform *Crowdflower.com*[1]. Each participant was asked to provide the best opposite for 10 randomized adjectives from one of the two test sets. For each item a specific blank space was provided. Responses were automatically collected by the platform. Twenty answers were collected for each stimulus word. An example was given in the instructions, along with the recommendation to write one single word for each stimulus and mark nonce words. The participants were all Italian native speakers.

---

[1] *Crowdflower.com* allows users to access an online workforce of millions of people to clean, label and enrich data.

3.3   Results

As a pre-processing step, orthographic and typing errors were corrected and non-pertinent responses were cancelled (e.g., synonyms). Nouns, verbs and adverbs were eliminated or transformed into adjectives.

Data were then analysed taking into account the number of distinct responses provided from the participants for each stimulus adjective. As expected, the results confirm the previous findings stating the existence of a continuum of lexical association (Herrmann et al., 1986; Paradis et al., 2009). The mean value of distinct responses per adjective is 2.85, but the number varies from a minimum of 1 to a maximum of 10 distinct responses (see Table 1). The standard deviation value, 2.96, indicates that the majority of stimulus elicited just one or two antonyms. Moreover, Set_1 was more consistent than Set_2. Set_1 responses mean value is 2.14 (sd 1.54), while Set_2 responses mean value is 3.23 (sd 2.53).

Type-Token Ratio and Entropy were calculated in order to evaluate the amount of dispersion in responses. An entropy value equal to 0 was observed for 75 stimulus adjectives, suggesting they all elicited one and the same antonym (e.g., *veloce* "fast", *buono* "good", *vivo* "alive", *facile* "easy"). The highest entropy values were instead observed for abstract adjectives and for a group of Set_2 stimuli (e.g., *sciocco* "fool", 0.92; *austero* "austere", 0.9; *serio* "serious", 0.85; *libero* "free", 0.75).

Category	Response mean	Std. deviation	Entropy mean
All Stimuli	2.85	2.96	0.22
Set_1	2.14	1.54	0.15
Set_2	3.23	2.53	0.25

Table 1. Response and entropy mean for the two datasets.

We investigated to what extent adjective frequency estimated in a corpus[2] and concreteness influence the amount of dispersion in responses – in terms of entropy values. The first parameter does not seem to be correlated with entropy values (Pearson's correlation value, r= -0.211), indicating that the number of responses obtained is independent from the frequency the adjective is used in texts. On the other hand, there is a significant difference between entropy values of concrete and abstract adjectives, the abstract ones eliciting more different antonyms (Wilcoxon: p-value < 0.001, W=6670).

Stimuli were then paired with each antonym and we recorded the reciprocity of their elicitation, taking into account how many times the two members of each pair elicited one another (i.e., the frequency of reciprocal elicitation across participants). Among the 446 pairs emerged, 250 were not analysed because one of the members was not included in the stimuli. Remaining pairs were classified on the basis of their frequency of reciprocal elicitation into three groups: non-reciprocal, reciprocal and canonical. We observed 66 non-reciprocal pairs and 130 reciprocal ones. The canonical antonyms are a subset of the reciprocal pairs, for which the first member elicited as most frequent response the second one and vice versa. These consist of 65 pairs (see Appendix A).

Furthermore, different patterns of adjective reciprocity were individuated. Participants strongly agreed on 24 pairs, which were perceived as perfectly binary. Two different antonyms were provided for 16 adjectives in a one-to-two match. In the majority of these cases the two options were respectively an opaque and a morphologically derived antonym (e.g., *attivo – passivo/inattivo* "active – passive/inactive", *felice – triste/infelice* "happy – sad/unhappy", *vestito – nudo/svestito* "dressed – naked/undressed", *perfetto – difettoso/imperfetto* "perfect – defective/imperfect"). The other two reciprocity patterns were one-to-many and many-to-many. We observed the former in five cases (i.e., *concreto* "concrete", *comico* "comical", *fragile* "fragile", *libero* "free", *intelligente* "smart"), in which a single adjective elicited up to 8 possible antonyms and the relation held also in the opposite direction. Four instances of the many-to-many patterns were observed (i.e., *mobile* "movable", *improvviso* "sudden", *calmo/tranquillo* "calm/quiet", *sbagliato* "wrong"), where multiple and complex relations arose defining a highly complex semantic field of antonyms and synonyms.

---

[2]The adjectives frequencies were recorded on the Italian online corpus PAISÀ. It is a fully annotated corpus of authentic contemporary Italian texts from the web. It contains about 250M tokens. It is freely available at this website: http://www.corpusitaliano.it/.

In order to look more deeply into the canonicity phenomenon and its lexical or semantic nature, we recorded on the Italian online corpus PAISÀ the co-occurrence frequency of each pair[3] – and compared it with their expected frequency. The difference turned out to be always statistically significant (chi-squared test: p-value < 0.05), both for canonical and non-canonical pairs.

Pointwise Mutual Information (PMI) was also calculated and used as a measure of lexical association between the adjectives. We limited the analysis only to pairs with co-occurrence frequency $\geq$ 5. These were 217 pairs: 63 canonical – 27 abstract and 36 concrete – and 154 non-canonical – 91 abstract and 63 concrete. Moreover, pairs were marked according to frequency of production in both directions. Complete production data were observed for 138 pairs – all the 63 canonical pairs and 75 non-canonical, 36 concrete and 39 abstract.

There is a significant difference between the PMI of canonical and non-canonical pairs (t-test: p-value < 0.001, t = 6.7144). This confirms the statement that canonical antonyms have a strong lexical association. Actually, the correlation values between PMI and subjects production frequency reveal an interesting pattern. For canonical antonyms, no significant Pearson's correlation was observed (r = 0.107), suggesting that even the best examples of the relation could have a low PMI value. Conversely, the correlation between PMI and subject production frequency for non-canonical pairs is significantly higher (r = 0.419): The more the two members of a non-canonical pair are lexically associated the more they tend to elicit one another.

Concreteness does not influence these values. Even if abstract adjectives elicit more possible antonyms, abstract and concrete pairs are not significant different with respect to PMI values (t-test: p-value=0.1928, t=-1.3068). Both (non-)canonical abstract and (non-)canonical concrete pairs can be found and we can assume that concreteness is not a parameter of influence in canonicity. However, it is worth noting that the majority of abstract pairings – both canonical and non-canonical – are morphologically derived.

To sum up, both canonical and non-canonical pairs co-occur significantly more often than chance, against the prediction of the lexical-categorical approach. On the other hand, it is true that canonical adjectives have higher association strength as measured by PMI, even if this value does not correlate with subject production frequency. That is, there are frequently produced canonical pairs, which have low values of association strength. Conversely, PMI appear to correlate (albeit moderately) with the subject production frequency of non-canonical pairs. We can surmise that the fact they are strongly associated allow speakers to recognize them as antonyms, increasing their production frequency.

4   Distributional Analysis

The results of the elicitation experiment did not fully support the lexical-categorical model of antonym canonicity, and are instead consistent with the gradient interpretation of canonicity advocated by the cognitive-prototype approach. However, the notion of "salient dimension", which is central to the latter model, is not defined in a precise way. Moreover, when a pair such as *hot – cold* – whose dimension is clearly identifiable as TEMPERATURE in its basic literal interpretation – is used in a metaphorical sense, its dimension of alignment is not equally easy to identify.

With the aim of providing a more solid empirical grounding to this notion, we propose a distributional interpretation of the concept of "salient dimension" as similarity of the nominal contexts co-occurring with adjectives. Therefore, we argue that the salience of the dimension expressed by canonical adjectives depends on the fact that they share a high number of similar nominal co-occurrence contexts. As a matter of fact, if – as stated by Lehrer (2002) – a canonical pair can extend its opposition to a new semantic field when one of the members acquires a new sense, we would expect both members of the opposition to occur with the same nouns, thanks to the great amount of possible ontological domains they can apply in. Moreover, Paradis et al. (2015) demonstrate that members of canonical pairs are used in the same semantic contexts and structures not only when they co-occur but also when they are used individually. In the present case, we define nominal contexts of co-occurrence as the nouns each adjective modifies or is a predicate of. We have then represented adjectives with distributional vectors and used the cosine as a measure of context similarity. Since we assume that canonical pairs share a higher number of contexts than non-canonical ones, we predict that

---

[3]Co-occurrence frequencies were estimated using a text window from 0 to >3, specifying both words had to be tagged as adjective, and restricting search within sentence boundaries.

the cosine values of canonical pairs are significantly higher than those for non-canonical pairs.

4.1 Data

The distributional analysis was performed on the 138 pairs with co-occurrence frequency ≥ 5 and mutually produced by the subjects. Eight pairs were removed because one of the members was not included in the distributional model used for this analysis (cf. below) or were erroneously lemmatized (i.e., as past participle forms). Therefore, the distributional analysis was performed on 130 pairs, 62 canonical and 68 non-canonical.

4.2 Procedure

Noun-adjective co-occurrences were automatically extracted from *La Repubblica* corpus (Baroni et al., 2004) with *LexIt* (Lenci, 2014)[4]. All the nouns each adjective in the test pairs modifies or is a predicate of were collected. Co-occurrences were weighted with Positive PMI (PPMI) and represented as a multidimensional vector for each adjective. The cosine was used to measure the distributional similarity of each test pair (Turney and Pantel, 2010). Therefore, the higher the cosine of an antonymic pair, the more its members tend to co-occur with the same nouns.

4.3 Results

The overall mean cosine is 0.11 (sd 0.07) (see Table 2). Considering the two groups separately a relevant difference can be noted. The mean cosine value for the canonical pairs is 0.21 (sd 0.2), while for non-canonical ones is 0.12 (sd 0.17). Moreover, maximum cosine for canonical pairs (0.44) is much larger than the maximum one for non-canonical pairs (0.27).

Category	Mean	Std. Deviation	Max. Value
All Pairs	0.11	0.07	-
Canonical (62)	0.21	0.20	0.44
Non-canonical (68)	0.12	0.17	0.27

Table 2. Mean cosine and maximum values.

The difference between the cosines of canonical and non-canonical adjectives is highly significant (Wilcoxon test: *p*-value < 0.001, W=313). Once again, it turned out that concreteness is not a relevant factor. Nevertheless, it seems interesting to notice that canonical pairs with the lowest cosine values are the morphologically derived and abstract ones. What seems to be relevant is the correlation between cosine values and pair production frequency. The Pearson's correlation for canonical pairs ($r = 0.29$), though weak, is clearly larger than that for non-canonical ones ($r = 0.07$). In general, the distributional analysis shows that the goodness of opposition of a canonical pair of antonyms tends to be directly proportional to the distributional similarity of the adjectives with respect to the nominal contexts they co-occur with.

5 Summary and Discussion

The aim of the present paper was to identify antonymic pairs with different degrees of canonicity in Italian. We have defined as canonical those adjectives with the highest mutual production frequency in an elicitation task. We also intended to verify if – as suggested by Herrmann et al. (1986), Murphy (2003) and Paradis et al. (2009) – canonicity is a scalar phenomenon, that is if pairs are distributed on a scale – a continuum of "goodness of opposition" – from better to less good examples of the relation. The second goal of our research was to further investigate the canonicity phenomenon in order to explain the different behaviour of canonical and non-canonical antonyms. In particular, we tested the two previous approaches in the literature – *lexical-categorical* and *cognitive-prototype* – to determine

---

[4]*LexIt* is a platform to explore distributional profiles of Italian nouns, verbs and adjectives. *LexIt* distributional profiles contain a vast array of statistical information, automatically extracted from corpora with state-of-the-art computational linguistic methods. The contexts extracted are freely accessible at this website: http://lexit.fileli.unipi.it/.

which are the parameters that cause the strong association between the two members of a canonical pair. An elicitation experiment and a distributional analysis were carried out.

The elicitation experiment confirmed the existence of a continuum of "goodness of opposition", as already stated by the *cognitive-prototype approach* and contrary to the dichotomous view of the relation offered by the *lexical-categorical approach*. We observed pairs with strong agreement among the participants – only one or two distinct antonyms were elicited for a given stimulus – as well as adjectives that produced up to 10 distinct responses. Moreover, classifying pairs as canonical and non-canonical on the basis of the frequency of production allowed us to individuate different patterns of reciprocity, corresponding to different degrees of canonicity. Thus, as already stated by Jones et al. (2007), we can state that canonicity – and the whole antonymy relation in general – is not strictly binary in the sense that it does not require exclusivity. On the other hand, a small group of pairs obtained full agreement among the speakers, since members produced one another as unique response in the elicitation experiment. These pairs have a strong lexical association and entrenchment in memory, and confirm the prototypical internal structure of antonymy (Murphy, 2003; Paradis et al., 2009). Interestingly, these results also suggest the cross-linguistic validity not only of the scalar and prototypical structure of antonymy, but also of what adjectives are considered the best examples of the relation. Italian data, in fact, reveal a picture highly similar to the previous studies on Swedish and English and the best examples of the relation are the same in the three languages.

For what concern how canonical antonyms come to be associated, the elicitation experiment offered the possibility to evaluate the *lexical-categorical approach*. As noticed, observed co-occurrence frequency was always larger than expected both for canonical and non-canonical pairs. This means that both canonical and non-canonical pairs co-occur significantly more often than chance. Hence, the *co-occurrence hypothesis* alone is not sufficient to explain the existence of the canonicity phenomenon because it does not allow to discriminate between canonical and non-canonical antonyms. We found instead a correlation between PMI values and production frequency for the non-canonical pairs. This means that association strength, as measured by PMI, is a good indicator of the tendency of non-canonical antonyms to elicit one another, suggesting that the more they are observed and used together in text the more they are perceived as "good" antonyms.

Even if production statistics support the *cognitive-prototype approach*, the notion of "salience of dimension" used by such explanation lacks clear empirical criteria. As already mentioned, when a pair is used in a metaphorical sense the dimension of alignment is not so easy to identify. This seems to be confirmed by the behaviour of abstract and morphologically derived pairs, whose behaviour deserve further investigation. Therefore, we have proposed a distributional interpretation of the notion of salient dimension. We carried out a distributional analysis of the nouns co-occurring with the adjectives (in modification and predication contexts), assuming that the opposition between the two members of a canonical pair is stable across their senses. Thus, our hypothesis is the more the antonyms occur in the same nominal contexts, the more they are perceived as canonical. Vector cosine was used as a measure of the distributional similarity of adjectives in nominal contexts. As predicted, we found a significant difference between the cosine values of canonical and non-canonical pairs. This means that the members of a canonical pair tend to modify or be predicate of the same nouns.

In summary, our experimental evidence suggests that, *contra* Charles and Miller (1989, strong *paradigmatic distributional similarity*, rather than syntagmatic co-occurrence, is the distinctive feature of canonicity. Two adjectives form a canonical pair because they are used to describe the same things and the same situations, but from two opposite points of view. What can be *tall* can be also *short*, as what is *hot* can be also *cold*. This allows the opposition to be moved into a new semantic field when one of the members of a canonical pair acquires a new sense (Lehrer, 2002). Hence, high frequency of co-occurrence – in similar syntactic structures – has to be considered as an effect of this kind of relation. As correctly argued by Miller and Charles (1991), paradigmatic substitutability can not be used to characterize antonymy in general, since this feature is also shared by other semantic relations, most notably synonymy. However, paradigmatic substitutability can instead be used as an empirical criterion to define the subset of canonical adjectives. It is in fact likely that paradigmatic substitutability is also one of the factors determining the high cognitive salience of the property expressed by canonical adjectives.

References

Marco Baroni, Silvia Bernardini, Federica Comastri, Lorenzo Piccioni, Alessandra Volpi, Guy Aston, and Marco Mazzoleni. 2004. Introducing the 'la Repubblica' Corpus: A large, annotated, TEI(XML)-compliant corpus of newspaper Italian. *Proceedings of LREC 2004*, 1771–1774.

Walter G. Charles and George A. Miller. 1989. Contexts of Antonymous Adjectives. *Applied Psycholinguistics*, 10(3): 357-375.

Alan D. Cruse. 1986. *Lexical Semantics*. Cambridge University Press, Cambridge, UK.

James Deese. 1964. The Associative Structure of Some Common English Adjectives. *Journal of Verbal Learning and Verbal Behaviour*, 3(5): 347-357.

James Deese. 1965. *The structure of associations in language and thought*. Johns Hopkins University Press, Baltimore, MD.

Christiane Fellbaum. 1995. Co-occurrence and Antonymy. *International Journal of Lexicography*, 8(4): 281-303.

Derek Gross, Ute Fischer, and George A. Miller. 1989. The Organization of Adjectival Meanings. *Journal of Memory and Language*, 28(1): 92-106.

Douglas J. Herrmann, Roger Chaffin, M. P. Daniel, and R. S. Wool. 1986. The role of elements of relation definition in antonym and synonym comprehension. *Zeitschrift für Psychologie*, 194(2): 133–153.

Steven Jones, Carita Paradis, Lynne M. Murphy, and Caroline Willners. 2007. Googling for 'opposites': a web-based study of antonym canonicity. *Corpora*, 2(2): 129-154.

Steven Jones, Lynne M. Murphy, Carita Paradis, and Caroline Willners. 2012. *Antonyms in English: Construals, Constructions and Canonicity*. Cambridge University Press, Cambridge, UK.

John S. Justeson and Slava M. Katz. 1991. Co-occurrences of Antonymous Adjectives and Their Contexts. *Computational Linguistics*, 17(1): 1-19.

Adrienne Lehrer. 2002. Paradigmatic relations of exclusion and opposition I: gradable antonymy and complementarity. In D. A. Cruse, F. Hundsnurcher, M. Job, and P. R. Lutzeier (Eds.). *Handbook of Lexicology*, 498-508. Mouton de Gruyter, Berlin.

Alessandro Lenci. 2014. Carving Verb Classes from Corpora. In R. Simone, and F. Masini (Eds.). *Word Classes: Nature, Typology, and Representations*, 17-36. John Benjamins, Amsterdam.

John Lyons. 1977. *Semantics 1*. Cambridge University Press, Cambridge, UK.

George A. Miller. 1995. WordNet: A lexical database for English. *Communications of the Association for Computing Machinery*, 38: 39–41.

George A. Miller and Walter G. Charles. 1991. Contextual Correlates of Semantic Similarity. *Language and Cognitive Processes*, 6(1): 1-28.

Gregory L. Murphy and Jane M. Andrew. 1993. The Conceptual Basis of Antonymy and Synonymy in Adjectives. *Journal of Memory and Language,* 32(3): 301-319.

Lynne M. Murphy. 2003. *Semantic Relations and the Lexicon: Antonymy, Synonymy and other Paradigms*. Cambridge University Press, Cambridge, UK.

Carita Paradis, Caroline Willners, and Steven Jones. 2009. Good and bad opposites: Using textual and experimental techniques to measure antonym canonicity. *The Mental Lexicon*, 4(3): 380–429.

Carita Paradis, Joost van de Weijer, Caroline Willners, and Magnus Lindgren. 2012. Evaluative Polarity of

Antonyms. *Lingue e Linguaggio*, 11(2): 199-214.

Carita Paradis, Simone Löhndorf, Joost van de Weijer, and Caroline Willners. 2015. Semantic profiles of antonymic adjectives in discourse. *Linguistics*, 53(1): 153-191.

Peter D. Turney and Patrick Pantel. 2010. From frequency to meaning: Vector space models of semantics. *Journal of Artificial Intelligence Research*, 37(1): 141-188.

Joost van de Weijer, Carita Paradis, Caroline Willners, and Magnus Lindgren. 2012. As lexical as it gets: the role of co-occurrence of antonyms in a visual lexical decision experiment. In D. Divjak D. and S. T. Gries (Eds.). *Frequency effects in language representation*, 2: 255-279.

Appendix A. Canonical antonyms emerged from the elicitation experiment.

veloce	*lento*	"fast – slow"	*ordinato*	*disordinato*	"orderly – messy"
forte	*debole*	"strong – weak"	*rilevante*	*irrilevante*	"relevant – irrelevant"
grande	*piccolo*	"big/large – small/little"	*scuro*	*chiaro*	"dark – light"
largo	*stretto*	"wide – narrow"	*grasso*	*magro*	"fat – slim"
buono	*cattivo*	"good – bad"	*sicuro*	*insicuro*	"secure – insecure"
bello	*brutto*	"beautiful – ugly"	*mangiabile*	*immangiabile*	"eatable – uneatable"
aperto	*chiuso*	"open – close"	*mobile*	*immobile*	"movable – unmovable"
povero	*ricco*	"poor – rich"	*organico*	*inorganico*	"organic – inorganic"
alto	*basso*	"tall – short"	*calmo*	*agitato*	"calm – rough/upset"
lungo	*corto*	"long – short"	*piacevole*	*spiacevole*	"pleasant – unpleasant"
vivo	*morto*	"alive – dead"	*preciso*	*impreciso*	"precise – imprecise"
maschile	*femminile*	"male – female"	*duro*	*morbido*	"hard – soft"
pieno	*vuoto*	"full – empty"	*morale*	*immorale*	"moral – immoral"
pesante	*leggero*	"heavy – light"	*giusto*	*sbagliato*	"right – wrong"
sporco	*pulito*	"dirty – clean"	*uguale*	*diverso*	"identical – different"
stabile	*instabile*	"stable – unstable"	*credibile*	*incredibile*	"credible – incredible"
facile	*difficile*	"easy – hard"	*concreto*	*astratto*	"concrete – abstract"
pubblico	*privato*	"public – private"	*intelligente*	*stupido*	"smart – stupid"
positivo	*negativo*	"positive – negative"	*vestito*	*nudo*	"dressed – naked"
civile	*incivile*	"civilized – uncivilized"	*vecchio*	*giovane*	"old – young"
legale	*illegale*	"legal – illegal"	*attivo*	*inattivo*	"active – inactive"
onesto	*disonesto*	"honest – dishonest"	*attivo*	*passivo*	"active – passive"
fortunato	*sfortunato*	"lucky – unlucky"	*abbondante*	*scarso*	"abundant – scarce"
iniziale	*finale*	"initial – final"	*libero*	*prigioniero*	"free – prisoner"
bianco	*nero*	"white – black"	*luminoso*	*buio*	"bright – dark"
bagnato	*asciutto*	"wet – dry"	*felice*	*triste*	"happy – sad"
comodo	*scomodo*	"comfortable – uncomfortable"	*spesso*	*sottile*	"thick – thin"
completo	*incompleto*	"complete – incomplete"			
simmetrico	*asimmetrico*	"symmetrical – asymmetrical"			
vero	*falso*	"true – false"			
logico	*illogico*	"logical – illogical"			
limitato	*illimitato*	"limited – unlimited"			
possibile	*impossibile*	"possible – impossible"			
razionale	*irrazionale*	"rational – irrational"			
perfetto	*imperfetto*	"perfect – imperfect"			
pari	*dispari*	"even – odd"			
certo	*incerto*	"sure – unsure"			
dolce	*amaro*	"sweet – bitter"			

Categorization of Semantic Roles for Dictionary Definitions

Vivian S. Silva, Siegfried Handschuh and André Freitas
Department of Computer Science and Mathematics
University of Passau
Innstraße 43, 94032, Passau, Germany
{vivian.santossilva, siegfried.handschuh, andre.freitas}@uni-passau.de

Abstract

Understanding the semantic relationships between terms is a fundamental task in natural language processing applications. While structured resources that can express those relationships in a formal way, such as ontologies, are still scarce, a large number of linguistic resources gathering dictionary definitions is becoming available, but understanding the semantic structure of natural language definitions is fundamental to make them useful in semantic interpretation tasks. Based on an analysis of a subset of WordNet's glosses, we propose a set of semantic roles that compose the semantic structure of a dictionary definition, and show how they are related to the definition's syntactic configuration, identifying patterns that can be used in the development of information extraction frameworks and semantic models.

1   Introduction

Many natural language understanding tasks such as Text Entailment and Question Answering systems are dependent on the interpretation of the semantic relationships between terms. The challenge on the construction of robust semantic interpretation models is to provide a model which is both comprehensive (capture a large set of semantic relations) and fine-grained. While semantic relations (high-level binary predicates which express relationships between words) can serve as a semantic interpretation model, in many cases, the relationship between words cannot be fully articulated as a single semantic relation, depending on a contextualization that involves one or more target words, their corresponding semantic relationships and associated logical operators (e.g. modality, functional operators).

Natural language definitions of terms, such as dictionary definitions, are resources that are still under-utilized in the context of semantic interpretation tasks. The high availability of natural language definitions in different domains of discourse, in contrast to the scarcity of comprehensive structured resources such as ontologies, make them a candidate linguistic resource to provide a data source for fine-grained semantic models.

Under this context, understanding the syntactic and semantic "shape" of natural language definitions, i.e., how definitions are usually expressed, is fundamental for the extraction of structured representations and for the construction of semantic models from these data sources. This paper aims at filling this gap by providing a systematic analysis of the syntactic and semantic structure of natural language definitions and proposing a set of semantic roles for them. By *semantic role* here we mean entity-centered roles, that is, roles representing the part played by an expression in a definition, showing how it relates to the entity being defined. WordNet (Fellbaum, 1998), one of the most employed linguistic resources in semantic applications, was used as a corpus for this task. The analysis points out the syntactic and semantic regularity of definitions, making explicit an enumerable set of syntactic and semantic patterns which can be used to derive information extraction frameworks and semantic models.

The contributions of this paper are: (i) a systematic preliminary study of syntactic and semantic relationships expressed in a corpus of definitions, (ii) the derivation of semantic categories for the classification of semantic patterns within definitions, and (iii) the description of the main syntactic and semantic shapes present in definitions, along with the quantification of the distribution of these patterns.

Proceedings of the Workshop on Cognitive Aspects of the Lexicon,
pages 176–184, Osaka, Japan, December 11-17 2016.

The paper is organized as follows: Section 2 presents the basic structural aspects of definitions according to the classic theory of definitions. Section 3 introduces the proposed set of semantic roles for definitions. Section 4 outlines the relationship between semantic and syntactic patterns. Section 5 lists related work, followed by the conclusions and future work in Section 6.

2   Structural Aspects of Definitions

Swartz (1997) describe lexical, or dictionary definitions as reports of common usage (or usages) of a term, and argue that they allow the improvement and refinement of the use of language, because they can be used to increase vocabulary (introducing people to the meaning and use of words new to them), to eliminate certain kinds of ambiguity and to reduce vagueness. A clear and properly structured definition can also provide the necessary identity criteria to correctly allocate an entity in an ontologically well-defined taxonomy (Guarino and Welty, 2002).

Some linguistic resources, such as WordNet, organize concepts in a taxonomy, so the genus-differentia definition pattern would be a suitable way to represent the subsumption relationship among them. The genus and differentia concepts date back to Aristotle's writings concerning the theory of definition (Berg, 1982; Granger, 1984; Lloyd, 1962) and are most commonly used to describe entities in the biology domain, but they are general enough to define concepts in any field of knowledge. An example of a genus-differentia based definition is the Aristotelian definition of a human: "a human is a rational animal". *Animal* is the genus, and *rational* is the differentia distinguishing humans from other animals.

Another important aspect of the theory of definition is the distinction between essential and non-essential properties. As pointed by Burek (2004), stating that "a human is an animal" informs an essential property for a human (being an animal), but the sentence "human is civilized" does not communicate a fundamental property, but rather something that happens to be true for humans, that is, an incidental property.

Analyzing a subset of the WordNet definitions to investigate their structure, we noticed that most of them loosely adhere to the classical theory of definition: with the exception of some samples of what could be called ill-formed definitions, in general they are composed by a linguistic structure that resembles the genus-differentia pattern, plus optional and variable incidental properties. Based on this analysis, we derived a set of semantic roles representing the components of a lexical definition, which are described next.

3   Semantic Roles for Lexical Definitions

Definitions in WordNet don't follow a strict pattern: they can be constructed in terms of the entity's immediate superclass or rather using a more abstract ancestral class. For this reason, we opted for using the more general term **supertype** instead of the classical *genus*. A supertype is either the immediate entity's superclass, as in "footwear: *clothing* worn on a person's feet", being *footwear* immediately under *clothing* in the taxonomy; or an ancestral, as in "illiterate: a *person* unable to read", where *illiterate* is three levels below *person* in the hierarchy.

Two different types of distinguishing features stood out in the analyzed definitions, so the differentia component was split into two roles: **differentia quality** and **differentia event**. A differentia quality is an essential, inherent property that distinguishes the entity from the others under the same supertype, as in "baseball_coach: a coach *of baseball players*". A differentia event is an action, state or process in which the entity participates and that is mandatory to distinguish it from the others under the same supertype. It is also essential and is more common for (but not restricted to) entities denoting roles, as in "roadhog: a driver *who obstructs others*".

As any expression describing events, a differentia event can have several subcomponents, denoting time, location, mode, etc. Although many roles could be derived, we opted to specify only the ones that were more recurrent and seemed to be more relevant for the definitions' classification: **event time** and **event location**. Event time is the time in which a differentia event happens, as in "master_of_ceremonies: a person who acts as host *at formal occasions*"; and event location is the location of a differentia event, as in "frontiersman: a man who lives *on the frontier*".

A **quality modifier** can also be considered a subcomponent of a differentia quality: it is a degree, frequency or manner modifier that constrain a differentia quality, as in "dart: run or move *very* quickly or hastily", where *very* narrows down the differentia quality *quickly* associated to the supertypes *run* and *move*.

The **origin location** role can be seen as a particular type of differentia quality that determines the entity's location of origin, but in most of the cases it doesn't seem to be an essential property, that is, the entity only happens to occur or come from a given location, and this fact doesn't account to its essence, as in "Bartramian_sandpiper: large plover-like sandpiper *of North American fields and uplands*", where *large* and *plover-like* are essential properties to distinguish *Bartramian_sandpiper* from other sandpipers, but occurring in *North American fields and uplands* is only an incidental property.

The **purpose** role determines the main goal of the entity's existence or occurrence, as in "redundancy: repetition of messages *to reduce the probability of errors in transmission*". A purpose is different from a differentia event in the sense that it is not essential: in the mentioned example, a repetition of messages that fails to reduce the probability of errors in transmission is still a redundancy, but in "water_faucet: a faucet *for drawing water* from a pipe or cask", *for drawing water is* a differentia event, because a faucet that fails this condition is not a water faucet.

Another event that is also non-essential, but rather brings only additional information to the definition is the **associated fact**, a fact whose occurrence is/was linked to the entity's existence or occurrence, accounting as an incidental attribute, as in "Mohorovicic: Yugoslav geophysicist *for whom the Mohorovicic discontinuity was named*".

Other minor, non-essential roles identified in our analysis are: **accessory determiner**, a determiner expression that doesn't constrain the supertype-differentia scope, as in "camas: *any of several* plants of the genus Camassia", where the expression *any of several* could be removed without any loss in the definition meaning; **accessory quality**, a quality that is not essential to characterize the entity, as in "Allium: *large* genus of perennial and biennial pungent bulbous plants", where *large* is only an incidental property; and **[role] particle**, a particle, such as a phrasal verb complement, non-contiguous to the other role components, as in "unstaple: take the staples *off*", where the verb *take off* is split in the definition, being *take* the supertype and *off* a supertype particle.

The conceptual model in Figure 1 shows the relationship among roles, and between roles and the *definiendum*, that is, the entity being defined.

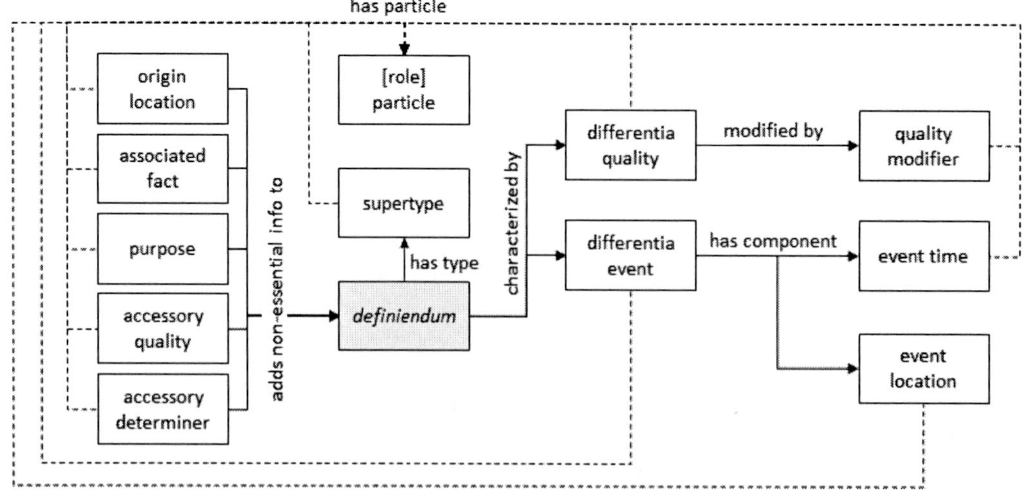

Figure 1: Conceptual model for the semantic roles for lexical definitions. Relationships between *[role] particle* and every other role in the model are expressed as dashed lines for readability.

4   Identifying Semantic Roles in Definitions

Once the relevant semantic roles were identified in the manual analysis, the following question emerged: is it possible to extend this classification to the whole definitions database through automated Semantic Role Labelling? Although most SRL systems rely on efficient machine learning techniques (Palmer et al., 2010), an initial, preferably large, amount of annotated data is necessary for the training phase.

Since manual annotation is expensive, an alternative would be a rule-based mechanism to automatically label the definitions, based on their syntactic structure, followed by a manual curation of the generated data. As shown in an experimental study by Punyakanok et al. (2005), syntactic parsing provides fundamental information for event-centered SRL, and, in fact, this is also true for entity-centered SRL.

To draw the relationship between syntactic and semantic structure (as well as defining the set of relevant roles described earlier), we randomly selected a sample of 100 glosses from the WordNet nouns+verbs database[1], being 84 nouns and 16 verbs (the verb database size is only approximately 17% of the noun database size). First, we manually annotated each of the glosses, assigning to each segment in the sentence the most suitable role. Example sentences and parentheses were not included in the classification. Figure 2 shows an example of annotated gloss. Then, using the Stanford parser (Manning et al., 2014), we generated the syntactic parse trees for all the 100 glosses and compared the semantic patterns with their syntactic counterparts.

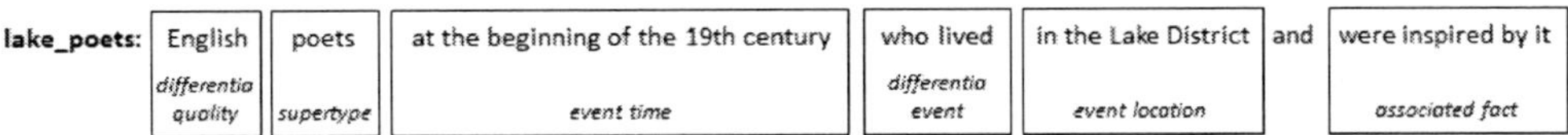

Figure 2: Example of role labeling for the definition of the "lake_poets" synset.

Table 1 shows the distribution of the semantic patterns for the analyzed sample. As can be seen, *(supertype) (differentia quality)* and *(supertype) (differentia event)* are the most frequent patterns, but many others are composed by a combination of three or more roles, usually the supertype, one or more differentia qualities and/or differentia events, and any of the other roles. Since most of them occurred only once (29 out of 42 identified patterns), it is easier to analyze the roles as independent components, regardless of the pattern where they appear. The context can always give some hint about what a role is, but we would expect the role's main characteristics not to change when their "companions" in the sentence varies. The conclusions are as follows[2], and are summarized in Table 2:

Supertype: it's mandatory in a well-formed definition, and indeed 99 out of the 100 sentences analyzed have a supertype (the gloss for *Tertiary_period* – "from 63 million to 2 million years ago" lacks a supertype and could, then, be considered an ill-formed definition). For verbs, it is the leftmost VB and, in some cases, subsequent VBs preceded by a CC ("or" or "and"). This is the case whenever the parser correctly classifies the gloss' head word as a verb (11 out of 16 sentences). For nouns, in most cases (70 out of 83) the supertype is contained in the innermost and leftmost NP containing at least one NN. It is the whole NP (discarding leading DTs) if it exists as an entry in WN, or the largest rightmost sequence that exists in WN otherwise. In the last case, the remaining leftmost words correspond to one or more differentia qualities. If the NP contains CCs, more than one supertype exist, and can be identified following the same rules just described. The 13 sentences that don't fit this scenario include some non-frequent grammatical variations, parser errors and the presence of accessory determiners, described later.

Differentia quality: for verbs, this is the most common identifying component in the definition. It occurs in 14 out of the 16 sentences. The other two ones are composed by a single supertype (that would better be seen as a synonym), and by a conjunction of two supertypes. The differentia quality is usually a PP (5 occurrences) or a NP (4 occurrences) coming immediately after the supertype. JJs inside ADJPs (3 occurrences) or RBs inside ADVPs (1 occurrence) are also possible patterns, where the presence of

---

[1] Adjectives and adverbs are not organized in a taxonomy in WordNet, so are less likely to follow a supertype-differentia pattern, probably requiring a different classification strategy

[2] POS tags and non-terminal symbols lists can be found at https://goo.gl/8ndYCw and https://goo.gl/kuJEc2, respectively

Pattern	Total
(supertype) (differentia quality)	27
(supertype) (differentia event)	13
(differentia quality) (supertype)	6
(supertype) (differentia event) (event location)	5
(supertype) (differentia quality) (purpose)	3
(accessory determiner) (supertype) (differentia event)	3
(accessory determiner) (supertype) (differentia quality)	2
(supertype) OR(differentia quality)+	2
(supertype) (origin location)	2
(differentia quality) (supertype) (differentia quality)	2
OR(supertype)+ (differentia event)	2
(differentia quality)+ (supertype)	2
(differentia quality)+ (supertype) (differentia event)	2
Other	29
Total	**100**

Table 1: Distribution of semantic patterns for the analyzed definitions. "Other" refers to patterns that ocurred only once. (*role*)+ indicated the occurrence of two or more consecutive instances of the role, and OR(*role*)+ indicates the same, but with the conjunction "or" connecting the instances.

CCs indicates the existence of more than one differentia quality. For nouns, two scenarios outstand: the differentia quality preceding the supertype, where it is composed by the leftmost words in the same NP that contains the supertype but are not part of the supertype itself, as described above; and the differentia quality coming after the supertype, predominantly composed by a PP, where the prevailing introductory preposition is "of". These two scenarios cover approximately 90% of all analyzed sentences where one or more differentia qualities occur.

Differentia event: differentia events occurs only for nouns, since verbs can't represent entities that can participate in an event (i.e., *endurants* in the ontological view). They are predominantly composed by either an SBAR or a VP (under a simple clause or not) coming after the supertype. This is the case in approximately 92% of the analyzed sentences where differentia events occur. In the remaining samples, the differentia event is also composed by a VP, but under a PP and immediately after the introductory preposition.

Event location: event locations only occur in conjunction with a differentia event, so they will usually be composed by a PP appearing inside a SBAR or a VP. Being attached to a differentia event helps to distinguish an event location from other roles also usually composed by a PP, but additional characteristics can also provide some clues, like, for example, the presence of named entities denoting locations, such as "Morocco" and "Lake District", which appear in some of the analyzed glosses.

Event time: the event time role has the same characteristics of event locations: only occurs in conjunction with a differentia event and is usually composed by a PP inside a SBAR or a VP. Again, additional information such as named entities denoting time intervals, for example, "the 19th century" in one of the analyzed glosses, is necessary to tell it apart from other roles.

Origin location: origin locations are similar to event locations, but occurring in the absence of an event, so it is usually a PP that does not appear inside a SBAR or a VP and that frequently contains named entities denoting locations, like "United States", "Balkan Peninsula" and "France" in our sample glosses. A special case is the definition of entities denoting instances, where the origin location usually comes before the supertype and is composed by a NP (also frequently containing some named entity), like the definitions for *Charlotte_Anna_Perkins_Gilman* – "United States feminist" – and *Joseph_Hooker* – "United States general [...]", for example.

Quality modifier: quality modifiers only occur in conjunction with a differentia quality. Though this role wasn't very frequent in our analysis, it is easily identifiable, as long as the differentia quality component has already been detected. A syntactic dependency parsing can show whether some modifier (usually an adjective or adverb) references, instead of the supertype, some of the differentia quality's elements, modifying it.

Purpose: the purpose component is usually composed by a VP beginning with a TO ("to") or a PP beginning with the preposition "for" and having a VP right after it. In a syntactic parse tree, a purpose can easily be mistaken by a differentia event, since the difference between them is semantic (the differentia event is essential to define the entity, and the purpose only provide additional, non-essential information). Since it provides complementary information, it should always occur in conjunction with an identifying role, that is, a differentia quality and/or event. Previously detecting these identifying roles in the definition, although not sufficient, is necessary to correctly assign the purpose role to a definition's segment.

Associated fact: an associated fact has characteristics similar to those of a purpose. It is usually composed by a SBAR or by a PP not beginning with "for" with a VP immediately after it (that is, not having the characteristics of a purpose PP). Again, the difference between an associated fact and a differentia event is semantic, and the same conditions and principles for identifying a purpose component also apply.

Accessory determiner: accessory determiners come before the supertype and are easily recognizable when they don't contain any noun, like "any of several", for example: it will usually be the whole expression before the supertype, which, in this case, is contained in the innermost and leftmost NP having at least one NN. If it contains a noun, like "a type of", "a form of", "any of a class of", etc., the recognition becomes more difficult, and it can be mistaken by the supertype, since it will be the leftmost NP in the sentence. In this case, a more extensive analysis in the WN database to collect the most common expressions used as accessory determiners is necessary in order to provide further information for the correct role assignment.

Accessory quality: the difference between accessory qualities and differentia qualities is purely semantic. It is usually a single adjective, but the syntactic structure can't help beyond that in the accessory quality identification. Again, the presence of an identifying element in the definition (preferably a differentia quality) associated with knowledge about most common words used as accessory qualities can provide important evidences for the correct role detection.

[Role] particle: although we believe that particles can occur for any role, in our analysis it was very infrequent, appearing only twice and only for supertypes. It is easily detectable for phrasal verbs, for example, *take off* in "take the staples off", since the particle tends to be classified as PRT in the syntactic tree. For other cases, it is necessary a larger number of samples such that some pattern can be identified and a suitable extraction rule can be defined.

Role	Most common syntactic patterns
Supertype	innermost and leftmost NP containing at least one NN
Differentia quality	leftovers[3] in the innermost and leftmost NP; PP beginning with "of"
Differentia event	SBAR; VP
Event location	PP inside a SBAR or VP, possibly having a location named entity
Event time	PP inside a SBAR or VP, possibly having a time interval named entity
Origin location	PP not inside a SBAR or VP, possibly having a location named entity
Quality modifier	NN, JJ or RB referring to an element inside a differentia quality
Purpose	VP beginning with TO; PP beginning with "for" with a VP right after
Associated fact	SBAR; PP not beginning with "for" with a VP right after
Accessory determiner	whole expression before supertype; common accessory expression
Accessory quality	JJ, presence of a differentia quality, common accessory word
[Role] particle	PRT

Table 2: Most common syntactic patterns for each semantic role.

---

[3]Words that are not part of the largest sequence in the NP found as an entry in WN

5   Related Work

The task described in this work is a form of Semantic Role Labeling (SRL), but centered on entities instead of events. Typically, SRL has as primary goal to identify what semantic relations hold among a predicate (the main verb in a clause) and its associated participants and properties (Màrquez et al., 2008). Focusing on determining "who" did "what" to "whom", "where", "when", and "how", the labels defined for this task include *agent*, *theme*, *force*, *result* and *instrument*, among others (Jurafsky and Martin, 2000).

Liu and Ng (2007) perform SRL focusing on nouns instead of verbs, but most noun predicates in NomBank, which were used in the task, are verb nominalizations. This leads to the same event-centered role labeling, and the same principles and labels used for verbs apply.

Kordjamshidi et al. (2010) describe a non-event-centered semantic role labeling task. They focus on spatial relations between objects, defining roles such as *trajectory*, *landmark*, *region*, *path*, *motion*, *direction* and *frame of reference*, and develop an approach to annotate sentences containing spatial descriptions, extracting topological, directional and distance relations from their content.

Regarding the structural aspects of lexical definitions, Bodenreider and Burgun (2002) present an analysis of the structure of biological concept definitions from different sources. They restricted the analysis to anatomical concepts to check to what extent they fit the genus-differentia pattern, the most common method used to classify living organisms, and what the other common structures employed are, in the cases where that pattern doesn't apply.

Burek (2004) also sticks to the Aristotelian classic theory of definition, but instead of analyzing existing, natural language definitions, he investigates a set of ontology modeling languages to examine their ability to adopt the genus-differentia pattern and other fundamental principles, such as the essential and non-essential property differentiation, when defining a new ontology concept by means of axioms, that is, in a structured way rather than in natural language. He concludes that Description Logic (DL), Unified Modeling Language (UML) and Object Role Modeling (ORM) present limitations to deal with some issues, and proposes a set of *definitional tags* to address those points.

The information extraction from definitions has also been widely explored with the aim of constructing structured knowledge bases from machine readable dictionaries (Vossen, 1992; Calzolari, 1991; Copestake, 1991; Vossen, 1991; Vossen and Copestake, 1994). The development of a Lexical Knowledge Base (LKB) also used to take into account both semantic and syntactic information from lexical definitions, which were processed to extract the definiendum's genus and differentiae. To populate the LKB, typed-feature structures were used to store the information from the differentiae, which were, in turn, transmitted by inheritance based on the genus information. A feature structure can be seen as a set of attributes for a given concept, such as "origin", "color", "smell", "taste" and "temperature" for the concept *drink* (or for a more general concept, such as *substance*, from which *drink* would inherit its features), for example, and the differentiae in a definition for a particular drink would be the values that those features assume for that drink, for example, "red", "white", "sweet", "warm", etc. As a result, concepts could be queried using the values of features as filters, and words defined in different languages could be related, since they were represented in the same structure. To build the feature structures, restricted domains covering subsets of the vocabulary were considered, since having every relevant attribute for every possible entity defined beforehand is not feasible, being more overall strategies required in order to process definitions in large scale.

6   Conclusion

We proposed a set of semantic roles that reflect the most common structures of dictionary definitions. Based on an analysis of a random sample composed by 100 WordNet noun and verb glosses, we identified and named the main semantic roles and their compositions present on dictionary definitions. Moreover, we compared the identified semantic patterns with the definitions' syntactic structure, pointing out the features that can serve as input for automatic role labeling. The proposed semantic roles list is by no means definitive or exhaustive, but a first step at highlighting and formalizing the most relevant aspects of widely used intensional level definitions.

As future work, we intend to implement a rule-based classifier, using the identified syntactic patterns to generate an initial annotated dataset, which can be manually curated and subsequently feed a machine learning model able to annotate definitions in large scale. We expect that, through a systematic classification of their elements, lexical definitions can bring even more valuable information to semantic tasks that require world knowledge.

Acknowledgements

Vivian S. Silva is a CNPq Fellow – Brazil.

References

Jan Berg. 1982. Aristotle's theory of definition. *ATTI del Convegno Internazionale di Storia della Logica*, pages 19–30.

Olivier Bodenreider and Anita Burgun. 2002. Characterizing the definitions of anatomical concepts in WordNet and specialized sources. In *Proceedings of the first global WordNet conference*, pages 223–230.

Patryk Burek. 2004. Adoption of the classical theory of definition to ontology modeling. In *International Conference on Artificial Intelligence: Methodology, Systems, and Applications*, pages 1–10. Springer.

Nicoletta Calzolari. 1991. Acquiring and representing semantic information in a lexical knowledge base. In *Workshop of SIGLEX (Special Interest Group within ACL on the Lexicon)*, pages 235–243. Springer.

Ann Copestake. 1991. The LKB: a system for representing lexical information extracted from machine-readable dictionaries. In *Proceedings of the ACQUILEX Workshop on Default Inheritance in the Lexicon, Cambridge*.

Christiane Fellbaum. 1998. *WordNet*. Wiley Online Library.

Edgar Herbert Granger. 1984. Aristotle on genus and differentia. *Journal of the History of Philosophy*, 22(1):1–23.

Nicola Guarino and Christopher Welty. 2002. Evaluating ontological decisions with OntoClean. *Communications of the ACM*, 45(2):61–65.

Daniel Jurafsky and James H Martin. 2000. *Speech and Language Processing: An Introduction to Natural Language Processing, Computational Linguistics and Speech Recognition*. Prentice-Hall.

Parisa Kordjamshidi, Marie-Francine Moens, and Martijn van Otterlo. 2010. Spatial role labeling: Task definition and annotation scheme. In *Proceedings of the Seventh conference on International Language Resources and Evaluation (LREC'10)*, pages 413–420. European Language Resources Association (ELRA).

Chang Liu and Hwee Tou Ng. 2007. Learning predictive structures for semantic role labeling of NomBank. In *Annual Meeting-Association for Computational Linguistics*, volume 45, pages 208–215.

Anthony C Lloyd. 1962. Genus, species and ordered series in Aristotle. *Phronesis*, pages 67–90.

Christopher D Manning, Mihai Surdeanu, John Bauer, Jenny Rose Finkel, Steven Bethard, and David McClosky. 2014. The Stanford CoreNLP natural language processing toolkit. In *ACL (System Demonstrations)*, pages 55–60.

Lluís Màrquez, Xavier Carreras, Kenneth C Litkowski, and Suzanne Stevenson. 2008. Semantic role labeling: an introduction to the special issue. *Computational linguistics*, 34(2):145–159.

Martha Palmer, Daniel Gildea, and Nianwen Xue. 2010. Semantic role labeling. *Synthesis Lectures on Human Language Technologies*, 3(1):1–103.

Vasin Punyakanok, Dan Roth, and Wen-tau Yih. 2005. The necessity of syntactic parsing for semantic role labeling. In *IJCAI*, volume 5, pages 1117–1123.

Norman Swartz. 1997. Definitions, dictionaries, and meanings. http://www.sfu.ca/~swartz/definitions.htm.

Piek Vossen and Ann Copestake. 1994. Untangling definition structure into knowledge representation. In *Inheritance, defaults and the lexicon*, pages 246–274. Cambridge University Press.

Piek Vossen. 1991. Converting data from a lexical database to a knowledge base. *Esprit BRA-3030 ACQUILEX Working Paper No 27*.

Piek Vossen. 1992. The automatic construction of a knowledge base from dictionaries: a combination of techniques. In *EURALEX*, volume 92, pages 311–326.

Corpus and dictionary development for classifiers/quantifiers towards French-Japanese machine translation

Mutsuko Tomokiyo
LIG-GETALP, IMAG-CAMPUS
700 avenue Centrale 38401 Grenoble
Mutsuko.Tomokiyo@imag.fr

Christian Boitet
UGA, LIG-GETALP, IMAG-CAMPUS
700 avenue Centrale 38401 Grenoble
Christian.Boitet@imag.fr

Abstract

Although quantifiers/classifiers expressions occur frequently in everyday communications or written documents, there is no description for them in classical bilingual paper dictionaries, nor in machine-readable dictionaries. The paper describes a corpus and dictionary development for quantifiers/classifiers, and their usage in the framework of French-Japanese machine translation (MT). They often cause problems of lexical ambiguity and of set phrase recognition during analysis, in particular for a long-distance language pair like French and Japanese. For the development of a dictionary aiming at ambiguity resolution for expressions including quantifiers and classifiers which may be ambiguous with common nouns, we have annotated our corpus with UWs (interlingual lexemes) of UNL (Universal Networking Language) found on the UNL-jp dictionary. The extraction of potential classifiers/quantifiers from corpus is made by UNLexplorer web service. Keywords : classifiers, quantifiers, phraseology study, corpus annotation, UNL (Universal Networking Language), UWs dictionary, Tori Bank, French-Japanese machine translation (MT).

1 Introduction

Recent Machine Translation (MT) evaluation tends to be conducted based on (1) Automatic evaluation metrics use reference translations for each segment such as BLEU, NIST, METEOR (Papineni et al., 2001; Banerjee and Lavie, 2005; Doddington, 2002).

This shows frequent efforts for MT, by measuring a similarity or a distance between a translation hypothesis and its post-editions. Basic operations used for post-editions are substitution, deletion, and insertion of words or phrases in a sentence, whatever the MT system is. (2) Subjective measures are based on human judgements of "intelligibility", "fidelity", "adequacy" and "fluency" of MT outputs.

These methods are really suitable for evaluating the progress of MT systems, but they do not contribute directly to improve the quality of MT outputs. Here we focus on lexical ambiguities, which are considered as a main cause of the degradation of the quality in MT for spoken or written sentences. Several types of ambiguity appear on each phase of MT for different types of documents.

We have categorized ambiguity problems according to the levels of MT analysis and to the MT contexts in which they are encountered, and we have proposed a formal ambiguity representation as well as guidelines for ambiguity labelling to build an ambiguity data base[1].

In fact, according to our studies of ambiguities, 14% of analysis errors[2] are due to polysemous words. Also, (G.Wisniewski and al., 2013) say the most frequent necessary post-edition in their French corpus translation into English is to correct articles like «les», «le», «du», etc., and the next one concerns lexical transfer errors of polysemous words. In addition, when polysemous words are used in their abstract or figurative meaning where they could be classifier or quantifier, translation results produced by current

---

[1]We have done research on ambiguity analysis from the lexical, semantic and contextual points of view since 1996. Ambiguities have been defined, categorized, and formalized as objects in an ambiguity database, and we have used this theoretical background to label ambiguities in Japanese-English interpreted dialogues, collected for the development of a speech translation system at ATR in Japan (1994). (Boitet and Tomokiyo, 1995; Boitet and Tomokiyo, 1996; ?)

[2]The ambiguity analysis includes assignment of speech acts, although generally speaking speech act ambiguity isn't taken account of, so the percentage is important.

Proceedings of the Workshop on Cognitive Aspects of the Lexicon,
pages 185–192, Osaka, Japan, December 11-17 2016.

MT systems are not at all good. Even measure words like cm, km, kg, etc. may be ambiguous with acronym (Anil K. et al., 2013).

Example: cm → centimètre, congrégation de la mission, coût marginal, etc.

The following example shows that «pincée (pinch, つまみ, tsumami) » in a quantifier phrase appears in form of «une pincée de», and is used in its figurative meaning. When one looks at the translation outputs produced by commercial MT systems, it's not hard to deduce there is a lack of phraseology studies and polysemy disambiguation method for the word «pincée»[3]. For the treatment of the classifier/quantifier expressions, at first, we must know whether a word or an expression in a document is the classifier/quantifier or not, and which kind of information is necessary to handle it in MT.

Example: Ajoutez une pincée de sel. (Add a pinch of salt.) →
塩のつねりを加えなさい/塩のピンチを加えなさい (Shio no tsuneri wo kuwaenasai/Shio no pinchi wo kuwaenasai)[4]

Sections 1 & 2 discuss the problems encountered in the processing of classifiers and quantifiers arising for meaning determination in the source language and from the structural differences between a language pair in the framework of MT. Section 3 describes morpho-syntactic problems between two languages for quantifier/classifier expressions. In Section 4, the difficulty of quantifiers/classifiers extraction is described. In Section 5, we propose a solution using a dictionary, edited from collected documents, themselves annotated with semantic UNL (hyper)graphs, presented as a parallel corpus, and give somme details about a small French-Japanese dictionary for quantifiers/classifiers, built for MT experimentation with an UNL system[5].

2   Lexical ambiguity for classifiers/quantifiers

We call here words or phrases which are used in some languages to indicate the class of nouns or nominal/adjectival phrases, depending on the type of these referent, classifiers/quantifiers, when they appear in quantitative expressions. They denote:

(a) temporal/spatial quantity of the referent and

(b) states of the referent in an idiomatic expression.

Type (a) classifiers/quantifiers express concrete measurement, and type (b) classifiers/quantifiers express quantitative states of the referent based on speaker's observation.

Examples:

Type (a): 2g de sel (2グラムの塩, 2-guramu-no shio, 2g of salt)

Type (b): une pièce de viande (一切れの肉, hitokire-no niku, a piece of meat) / un brin de causette (ちょっとしたおしゃべり, chottoshita osyaberi, a little chat)

Classifiers/quantifiers of type (a) are obligatory in quantitative expressions, and they often cause acronym ambiguities for MT as mentioned above, and also ambiguities due to the "floating quantifier" (Inoue, 1989) phenomenon in Japanese.

For classifiers/quantifiers of type (b), there are three different sorts of problems. The first one is the fact that classifiers/quantifiers have many to many meaning corespondences between source-target languages pairs. In the following example, the French word «pièce» is translated into «切れ, kire», «枚, mai», «点, ten», «頭, tou», etc. in Japanese, because, in many cases, Japanese classifiers depend upon the visual forms of referents.

The second problem arises in the case where classifiers/quantifiers don't appear explicitly in one language of a language pair, nevertheless they are mandatorily expressed in the other, like «冊», satsu in Japanese.

---

[3]"pincée" is used as quantifier/classifier for pulverized substances.

[4]These translations don't make sense. http://www.reverso.net/translationresults.aspx?langFR&directionfrancais-japonais. http://www.worldlingo.com/fr/products_services/worldlingo_translator.html.

[5]The UNL (Universal Networking Language) system denotes a language for computer, multilingual encoder-decoder system, UNL-UWs dictionary, parallel corpus, and linguistic ontology system. It has been developed under the aegis the Organization of United Nations University in form of international consortium for written languages processing since 1996. We are one of the pioneer members of the consortium. Bilingual dictionaries with UNL-UWs dictionary are edited by each "UNL language center". http://www.undl.org/unlsys/unl/unl2005/attribute.htm

Table 1: Translation of French word "pièce" into Japanese

French entries	Examples	Source	Japanese translations
pièce	une pièce de toile	Royal	一枚(mai)の布 (ichimai no nuno, a piece of cloth)
	une pièce de mobilier	Royal	一点(ten)の家具 (itten no kagu, a piece of furniture)
	dix pièces de bétail	Royal	１０頭(tou)の家畜 (jyuttou no kachiku, ten cattles)
	plusieurs pièces de bois	Royal	数枚(mai)の板 (suumai no ita, some boards)
	une pièce de vin est un tonneau de vin contenant environ 220 litres.	Wiki, pièce	一樽(hitotaru)のワインとは約２２０リットルを含むワイン樽である (hitoraru no wain toha yaku 220 littoru wo fukumu waindaru dearu, a barrel of wine includes 220 littles of wine)
	J'ai reçu une demi-pièce de ce vin.	Vinothèque	わたしは半樽(hantaru)のワインを受け取った。(watashiha hantaru no wain wo uketotta, I have received half barrel of this wine.)
	Dans une pièce de théâtre, il n'y a pas de narrateur pour raconter les faits.	http://www.etudes-litteraires.com/etudier-piece-de-theatre.php	ある作品(sakuhin)では事実を語るナレータがいない。(aru sakuhin deha jijitsuwo kataru nare)ta) ga inai, There is no narrator in a program.)
	Une pièce de viande	Royal	一切れ(kire)の肉 (hitokire no niku, a slice of meat)
	Une pièce de blé	Royal	一枚 (mai)の麦畑 (ichimai no mugibatake, a field of wheat)

Table 2: Translation of the French expression «pointe» into Japanese

French entries	Examples	Source	Jp translation	E.n translation
Pointe	une pointe d'ironie mal placée	J.L. Carré	場違いの皮肉をちくりと	the tip of , a hint of, a note of, a trace of
	relever la sauce avec une pointe d'ail	Livre de cuisine	ソースにニンニクをちょっときかせる	pick up the sauce with a hint of garlic
	avec une pointe d'agacement dans la voix	T. Jonquet	声にすこし苦しみをにじませて	with a hint of irritation in the voice
	mettre une pointe d'ironie dans sa question	Royal	質問にちくりと皮肉を込める	with a suggestion of sarcasm

Examples:
2 livres → 二冊の本 (ni-satsu no hon, two books)
un chat → 一匹の猫 (i-ppiki no neko, a cat) (see →Table 1)

The third problem occurs during the analysis/transfer phase as locutions problem like «un brin de»: «brin» signifies «茎, kuki, small stalk», and «un brin de» means «a little of». It's translated into «ちょっとした (chottosita, small)» in Japanese. This is due to the polysemy of «brin» and to the cognitive or metonymic differences between two languages.

Table 3: KWIC of "pointe" from Sketch Engine

doc#357	qui marque le déclin définitif de cette	pointe	de poussée et de sécrétions des hormones
doc#397	la sierra Pacaraima, qui constituent une	pointe	avancée du Sertao brésilien. </p><p> En janvier
doc#457	de nouveauté, un soupçon de douceur, une	pointe	d'exotisme : commence par te mettre dans
doc#517	Tafer ne sont capables d'évoluer seuls en	pointe	. </p><p> Arles - Marseille En concédant une

3 Morpho-syntactic differences between French-Japanese classifiers/quantifiers

As for the behaviour of floating quantifiers in Japanese (Inoue K.1989), the problem we encounter in building a Japanese-French MT lies in the fact that the Japanese quantifiers can be freely positioned between phrasal units in a sentence except after predicative verbs. They are morphosyntactically classified into two types of quantifier expressions: (1) noun phrases in form of "Number+Quantifier+の(no, of)+Noun («NQのN» type)", and (2) noun phrases in form of Noun+Number+Quantifier («NQN» type). The NQN type can syntactically be divided into «N» part and «QN» part and it's possible to use «QN» like an adverb before a predicative verb in a sentence.

Hence, three types of expressions are possible for the same meaning : (1) 二冊の本 (ni-satsu no hon, two books), (2) 本二冊 (hon ni-satsu, two books) and also (3) 本を二冊 (hon-wo ni-satsu, two books)[6]. The floating quantifier can produce meaningless translation result in some cases. For instance, "3kgの子豚がいました (3 kiloguramu no kobutaga imashita, There was a 3kg piglet.)" is acceptable as Japanese sentence, but "子豚が3kgいました(kobuta ga 3kiloguramu imashita)"[7] doesn't literally make sense, because, «子豚 (kobuta, piglet)» means only an alive pig and co-occurs with いました (there was), but "3kg" cannot do [12]. So, to avoid the translation output "子豚が3kgいました", we need to have supplementary information for "子豚 " and the verb "いる(iru, there is, or exist)" and implement method to use it. For that reason, we use the UWs dictionaries of the UNL system, which allows us to describe semantic constraints between words.

4 Recognition difficulty of quantifiers/classifiers

We extract type (a) quantifiers/classifiers from Tori Bank[8](See Annex), while referring to existing weights and measures dictionaries. For type (b) quantifiers/classifiers, it's laborious to pin down phrasemes[9] in row data.

Eg. "pointe" from Sketch Engine (Table 3).

However, French and English phrasemes are, in many cases, composed of "Number+Noun+de (Number+noun+of)+Noun without particle" like "une poignée de sable (a handful of sand)", "une pointe d'ironie (a touch of irony)", "un pouce de terre (a handful of)", so in order to collect data of type (b), we take note of the morphologic characteristic (Petit, 2004), and utilize a multilingual corpus management software, called Sketch Engine[10]. The software gives a list of tri-grams of keywords in context. The used documents are journals, magazines, novels, existing expression dictionaries, French, Japanese and English leaner's manuals. The assignment of the QC for obtained keywords is made by linguistic intuition, while watching output from MT experiences on UNL Explorer[11].

---

[6]In the full sentence, I bought 2 books (本を二冊 買いました, hon-wo nisatsu kaimashita)

[7]子豚が3kgいました, For the piglet, there was 3 kg*.

[8]Tori Bank is a phrase corpus which has been developed at Tottori Unversity in Japan in 2007. http://unicorn.ike.tottori-u.ac.jp/toribank/about_toribank.html

[9]The term "phraseme" means set phrase, idiomatic phrase, polylexical expression, etc.

[10]The Sketch Engine refers to a text corpus management and analysis software developed by Lexical Computing Limited since 2003. (http://en.wikipedia.org/wiki/Sketch_Engine)

[11]UNL Explorer is a web-based application, which combines all the components of the UNL system to be accessible online.

5 Specification of classifiers/quantifiers corpus

The corpus includes sentences which are manually or semi-automatically collected from novels, cooking articles, news papers, dictionaries, Tori Bank, etc. The description for "pointe" is given below as a typical example. The annotated keywords include, at the present time, about 1000 classifier/quantifier expressions for Japanese, French and English in PhraseBook II[12] (see Annex).

1. Identification number: XX
2. Keywords and class: pointe (n.)
3. English sentence: to season the sauce with a hint of garlic
4. French sentence: relever la sauce avec une pointe d'ail
5. Japanese sentence: ソースにニンニクをちょっときかせる
6. Source: Royal
7. UNL annotation (simplified):

{org:fr} Relever la sauce avec une pointe d'ail {/org}

{unl}

    agt(season(agt>person, obj>dish, icl>action>thing).@entry.@imperative, you)

    obj(season(agt>person, obj>dish, icl>action>thing).@entry.@imperative, sauce(icl>cooking).@def)

    met(season(agt>person, obj>dish, icl>action>thing).@entry.@imperative, garlic(icl>cooking))

    qua(garlic(icl>cooking), a hint of(icl>quantity))

{/unl}

{en} Season the sauce with a hint of garlic {/en}

{jp} ソースにニンニクをちょっときかせる {jp}

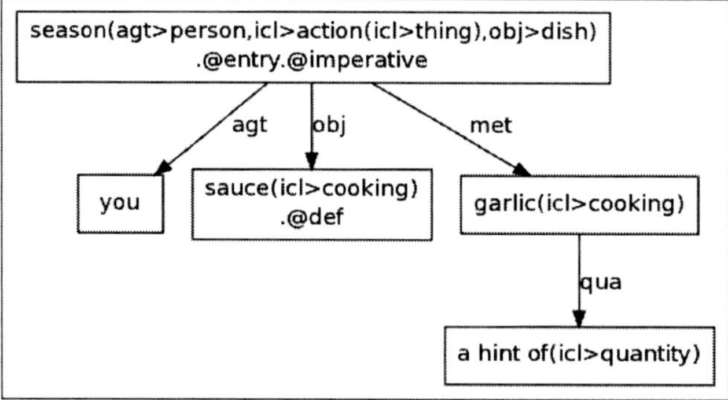

Figure 1: UNL graph for "Relever la sauce avec une pointe d'ail"

6 UNL-UWs dictionary for quantifiers/classifiers

The collected documents in Japanese, French, English are annotated by their UNL expressions[13], which are composed of interlingual lexemes called "universal words (UWs)[14], semantic boolean features, " and semantic relation tags[15]. In general, a UW is made of an English word or locution, its "headword", disambiguated by a list of restrictions. The set of UWs can be used as a lexical "pivot" between the

---

[12]The corpus is going to become larger by extracting classifiers/quantifiers expressions from Tori Bank

[13]UNL is a language for computer to represent the meaning of natural language expressions. The "Universal Words" (UWs) constitute its vocabulary. A UW is in effect an *interlingual lexeme*. Each node of a "UNL expression" (in effect, a semantic hypergraph) bears a UW and a possibly empty set of semantic attributes (Uchida et al.,2006).

[14]The UNL-UWs dictionary contains, at the moment 1269421 word senses (mapped to as many UWs) for Japanese, 520305 word senses for French, and 1458686 word senses for English.

[15]The semantic relations are represented by a fixed set of 42 relation 3-letter symbols, like agt, aoj, gol, etc., and the attributes are boolean, like .@def or .@soon-begin. There are about 200 attributes in the UNL specifications, and developers may introduce new attributes. These predefined attributes include syntactic, semantic or pragmatic information. The annotation labels are in fact, "icl", "equ", "quantity", etc. in description example.

"lexical spaces" of any set of natural languages, and the UNL graphs can similarly be used as an "anglo-semantic" abstract pivot language. The added information for classifier/quantifier expressions is merged into the UNL dictionaries. Here is an extract of our 3-lingual UNL dictionary. The first entry has 2 languages (jp, fr.). The second entry has 3 languages (jp, fr, en). The forth has again 2 languages (fr, en).

樽 (taru, pièce): cask(icl>wine,equ>2200 litres)

冊 (satsu, volume): volume(icl>quantity)

relever (to season): season(agt>person, obj>dish, icl>action>thing)

pointe (touch): touch(icl>amount) → une pointe de (a touch of)

"icl" and "equ" in our UW dictionary are semantic relation tags, and mean headword's sub-meaning and equivalent quantity, respectively. The semantic relation "agt" indicates that the volitional agent of "relever" is "person".

Perspectives and Conclusion

We are making French-Japanese MT experiments using the UNL system.

We have studied the methodology for phraseology treatment on MT systems while developing a French-Japanese-English parallel corpus and have concluded that a deeper linguistic analysis (Petit, 2004, Mari, 2011) is necessary for UW dictionary description. Our corpus will be useful for software developers, as well as for learners of languages, because it covers semantic information which cannot be yet found in any bilingual dictionary. We also plan to develop a language software by processing the corpus, where corresponding words between 2 languages are shown on demand by character blinking or where the meaning of nouns or verbs in a sentence is shown without any ambiguity by interpreting the UNL annotations. A prototype of the software has been already presented in a PhD thesis (Chenon, 2005).

References

S. Banerjee and A. Lavie. 2005. Meteor: An automatic metric for mt evaluation with improved correlation with human judgments. Association of Computational Linguistics (ACL), Association of Computational Linguistics (ACL).

Christian Boitet and Mutsuko Tomokiyo. 1995. Ambiguity and ambiguity labelling : towards ambiguity data bases. In Proc. of RANLP-95, Bulgaria. Recent Advances in Natural Language Processing, Recent Advances in Natural Language Processing.

Christian Boitet and Mutsuko Tomokiyo. 1996. On the formal definition of ambiguity and related concepts, leading to an ambiguity-labelling scheme. In Actes de MIDDIM-96. MIDDIM-96 Post-COLING Seminar, GETA.

Christophe Chenon. 2005. Vers une meilleure utilisabilité des mémoires de traductions, fondée sur un alignement sous-phrastique. Ph.D. thesis, Université Joseph Fourier, Grenoble.

George Doddington. 2002. Automatic evaluation of machine translation quality using n-gram co-occurrence statistics. In Proc. of HLT-2002, pages 128–132, San Diego. Human Language Technology, Human Language Technology.

Céline Gouverneur. 2005. The phraseological patterns of high-frequency verbs in advanced english for general purposes. TaLC 6.

Kazuko Inoue. pages 201–204. Taisyûkan-syoten.

Alda Mari. 2011. Quantificateurs polysémiques. Ph.D. thesis, Université Paris-Sorbonne.

Kishore Papineni, Salim Roukos, Todd Ward, and Wei-Jing Zhu. 2001. Bleu: a method for automatic evaluation of machine translation. Research report RC22176, IBM.

Gérard Petit. 2004. La polysémie des séquences polylexicales, syntaxe et sémantique. HAL, (Id-00648029).

Mutsuko Tomokiyo and Monique Axtmyer. 1996. Experiments in ambiguity labelling of dialogue transcriptions. MIDDIM-96 Post-COLING Seminar, MIDDIM-96.

Hiroshi Uchida, Meiyin Zhu, and Tarcisio G. Della Senta. 2006. Universal Networking Language. UNDL Foundation, Japan.

Guillaume Wisniewski, Anil Kumar Singhand Natalia Segala, and François Yvon. 2013. Un corpus d'erreurs de traduction. Les Sables d'Olonne, France. TALN-RÉCITAL, TALN-RÉCITAL.

Annex 「鳥バンク」(Tori Bank)

Examples: 「塁 (rui, base)」, 「寸 (sun, approx. 3.03 cm)」
AC00046100 P 11:二塁走者の生還を許し :VP@28:allowing the runner to score from second:VP
AC00046100 P 4:一塁へ悪投し、:VP@7:threw wild to first:VP
AC01599600 C6:一寸先も見え:CL@27:we could not see an inch ahead:CL
AC01599600 P6:一寸先も見え:VP@40:see an inch ahead:VP

Author Index

Association for Computational Linguistics
209 N. Eighth Street
Stroudsburg, Pennsylvania 18360